BARTHES AND UTOPIA

Barthes and Utopia

Space, Travel, Writing

DIANA KNIGHT

CLARENDON PRESS · OXFORD
1997

Oxford University Press, Great Clarendon Street, Oxford OX2 6DP
Oxford New York
Athens Auckland Bangkok Bombay
Calcutta Cape Town Dar es Salaam Delhi
Florence Hong Kong Istanbul Karachi
Kuala Lumpur Madras Madrid Melbourne
Mexico City Nairobi Paris Singapore
Taipei Tokyo Toronto
and associated companies in
Berlin Ibadan

Oxford is a trade mark of Oxford University Press

Published in the United States
by Oxford University Press Inc., New York

© Diana Knight 1997

All rights reserved. No part of this publication may be reproduced,
stored in a retrieval system, or transmitted, in any form or by any means,
without the prior permission in writing of Oxford University Press.
Within the UK, exceptions are allowed in respect of any fair dealing for the
purpose of research or private study, or criticism or review, as permitted
under the Copyright, Designs and Patents Act, 1988, or in the case of
reprographic reproduction in accordance with the terms of the licences
issued by the Copyright Licensing Agency. Enquiries concerning
reproduction outside these terms and in other countries should be
sent to the Rights Department, Oxford University Press,
at the address above.

British Library Cataloguing in Publication Data
Data available

Library of Congress Cataloging in Publication Data
Data available
ISBN 0–19–815889–0

1 3 5 7 9 10 8 6 4 2

Typeset by Cambrian Typesetters, Frimley, Surrey
Printed in Great Britain
on acid-free paper by
Biddles Ltd., Guildford and King's Lynn

For my Mother

In Memory of my Father

Cultural criticism is inherently impatient; it cannot proceed without desire.

(Roland Barthes, 'Writers, Intellectuals, Teachers')

Someone who had the paradoxical ability to understand things as they are yet invent them with unprecedented originality.

(Michel Foucault, Memorial Oration, Collège de France)

Acknowledgements

EARLIER versions of some sections of this book have appeared in the following places: *Paragraph*, *News from Nowhere*, *New Literary History*, *Modern and Contemporary France*, Michael Worton and Judith Still (eds.), *Intertextuality: Theories and Practices*, and Jean-Michel Rabaté (ed.), *Writing the Image after Roland Barthes*. I am grateful to the following for permission to reproduce this material: Addison Wesley Longman Ltd, Edinburgh University Press, The Johns Hopkins University Press, Manchester University Press, *News From Nowhere*, and the University of Pennsylvania Press.

Research grants from the following are gratefully acknowledged: the British Academy, the French Government, and the University of Nottingham; the latter has also been very generous in its provision of study leave.

I have been writing this book for a long time and have incurred many debts both professional and personal. For invitations to write or speak on Barthes, for sharing ideas, for support of a direct or indirect kind I warmly thank all of the following: Margaret Atack, Malcolm Bowie, Terence Cave, Rosemary Chapman, Margaret Davies, Elizabeth Fallaize, Jill Forbes, Johnnie Gratton, Ann Jefferson, Chris Johnson, Nicholas Hewitt, Leslie Hill, Marian Hobson-Jeanneret, Bob Knight, Annette Lavers, Toril Moi, Michael Moriarty, Michael O'Dea, John Parkin, Tony Pinkney, Chris Prendergast, Jean-Michel Rabaté, Michael Sheringham, Andy Stafford, Judith Still, Douglas Tallack, Margaret Whitford, Connie and Eric Williams, Michael Worton.

Contents

Note on Abbreviations, References, and Translations   x

Introduction   1

1. Making Space   20
2. Structuralism Utopian and Scientific   44
3. Charles Fourier: 'An Inventor not a Writer'   67
4. Colonial Mythologies   92
5. An Unhappy Sexuality: Morocco   115
6. 'A Reader not a Visitor': Barthes in 'Japan'   141
7. Turkey and China: 'But Where is the Orient?'   167
8. Tricks of the Text   194
9. Return Journey: The South-West   219
10. Maternal Space   244

Afterword   270

Bibliography   275
Index   283

Note on Abbreviations, References, and Translations

I HAVE made the difficult decision to quote from Barthes's writing in translation, and have used published translations (occasionally amended) where they exist. After quotations, titles of works by Barthes have been abbreviated as indicated below. Page references to French editions follow the English page references in every case. Since all books and collected essays by Barthes are in print in French, I have given page references for readily available French editions rather than for the three-volume *Œuvres complètes*. References for uncollected material are normally to the latter. Separate abbreviations of French titles are included only where relevant contents do not coincide; if there is only one page reference it can be assumed that no published translation exists and that translations are my own. For other material in French, translations are my own if no translator is listed in notes and bibliography. Full publication details of all works cited are included in the bibliography, as well as in a note following each first reference.

BR	*A Barthes Reader*
CE	*Critical Essays* / *Essais critiques*
CL	*Camera Lucida* / *La Chambre claire*
DZN	*Le Degré zéro de l'écriture* suivi de *Nouveaux Essais critiques*
ES	*Empire of Signs* / *L'Empire des signes*
ET	*The Eiffel Tower and Other Mythologies*
GV	*The Grain of the Voice* / *Le Grain de la voix*
I	*Incidents* / *Incidents*
L	*Leçon*
LD	*A Lover's Discourse: Fragments* / *Fragments d'un discours amoureux*
M	*Mythologies* (English translation)

Mi	Michelet / Michelet
My	Mythologies (French edition)
NCE	New Critical Essays
OC	Œuvres complètes
OR	On Racine / Sur Racine
PT	The Pleasure of the Text / Le Plaisir du texte
RB	Roland Barthes by Roland Barthes / Roland Barthes par Roland Barthes
RF	The Responsibility of Forms / L'Obvie et l'obtus
RL	The Rustle of Language / Le Bruissement de la langue
SC	The Semiotic Challenge / L'Aventure sémiologique
SFL	Sade, Fourier, Loyola / Sade, Fourier, Loyola
SZ	S/Z / S/Z
WDZ	Writing Degree Zero

Introduction

Confronting the present, my present, utopia is a second term that allows the sign to function: discourse about reality becomes possible, I emerge from the aphasia into which I am plunged by the turmoil of everything that upsets me, in this world that is mine.[1]

IT is the central argument of this book that utopias play a major role in Barthes's work. A surprising proportion of his ideas are formulated through an explicit vocabulary of utopia as adjective or proper noun, while implicit utopias often lie behind more negative evaluations: 'For me the ideal takes on a very precise form which is that of utopia. I have a utopian imagination and very often when I write, even if I'm not referring to a utopia, if, for example, I'm analysing particular notions in a critical way, I always do this through the inner image of a utopia: a social utopia or an affective utopia.'[2] This almost obsessive thought pattern—pinpointed by Philippe Lejeune in his very successful pastiche of Barthes: 'A utopia: I fantasize a pastiche . . .'[3]—is the impulse behind the semiological, sexual, and social utopias that pervade all of Barthes's writing, behind his admiration for Fourier (for him perhaps the greatest of utopian writers), behind the text that comes closest to being a generic utopia, his celebration of Japan in *Empire of Signs*.

As the meeting point of his lifelong concern with history, language, literature, sexuality, and the organization of everyday life, utopia is a concept (part theoretical, part ethical) that mediates the supposedly conflicting emphases of Barthes's

---

[1] Roland Barthes, *Roland Barthes by Roland Barthes* [1975], trans. Richard Howard (New York, Hill and Wang, 1977), 76 / 80.
[2] Barthes, 'Sur l'astrologie' [1976], in Roland Barthes, *Œuvres complètes*, ed. Eric Marty, 3 vols. (1993–5), iii. 443–9, first published in *Astrologiques* as 'L'Entretien du mois'.
[3] Philippe Lejeune, 'Le Roland Barthes sans peine', *Textuel 34/44*, 15 (1984), 11–19: 19.

various 'phases'. From Marxism to structuralism, from textuality and hedonism to his final preoccupation with love, pity, and death, Barthes never stopped hypothesizing and fantasizing how things might be otherwise—otherwise, that is, than in his own alienated and class-torn society. Barthes constantly worried about the extent to which an intellectual must, at the same time, take a stand on the contemporary terrain, about the extent to which utopia could never be more than a foil highlighting the shortcomings of present-day society, about the extent to which immersion in utopia might seem an escape from historical obligations. These remained ethical and political problems for him. Yet the liberation of an alienated culture, as Barthes himself said in 1972, is bound to take utopian forms, precisely because there are no known models.[4] Thinking otherwise, conceptualizing differently, means operating on the territory of the currently impossible, whether that impossibility is neurotically denied, whether it is defiantly affirmed in the face of an unacceptable present, or whether it is given self-consciously imaginary form in fictional representations. But all this, of course, is contained in the concept of utopia as its very meaning and scope.

To some extent Barthes's hesitations over the ethics of utopia have to do with the status of his own writing. The demystifying mythologist of 'Myth Today' defined his position (somewhat unhappily) as a purely critical one, excluding him from any compensatory reward, and above all from the very future of the history in the name of which he had written so negatively:

It is forbidden to him to imagine what the world will concretely be like, when the immediate object of his criticism has disappeared. Utopia is an impossible luxury for him: he greatly doubts that tomorrow's truths will be the exact reverse of today's lies. History never ensures the triumph pure and simple of something over its opposite: it unveils, while making itself, unimaginable solutions, unforeseeable syntheses. The mythologist is not even in a Moses-like situation: he cannot see the

---

[4] 'The Fatality of Culture, the Limits of Counterculture' [1972], in Roland Barthes, *The Grain of the Voice: Interviews 1962–1980*, trans. Linda Coverdale (London, Jonathan Cape, 1985), 150–6: 151 / 142–8: 143, first published in *Politique-Hebdo*.

Promised Land. For him, tomorrow's positivity is entirely hidden by today's negativity. . . . nothing protrudes.⁵ The mythologist's exclusion from the future world clearly worries Barthes. Is the exclusion really inevitable or simply self-imposed? A later Barthes, who has by now written an important essay on Charles Fourier, shows himself to be well aware of the traditional Marxist difficulty with so-called utopian socialism: 'Revolutionary writings have always scantily and poorly represented the daily finality of the revolution, the way it suggests *we shall live tomorrow*, either because this representation risks sweetening or trivializing the present struggle, or because, more precisely, political theory aims only at setting up the real freedom of the human question, without prefiguring any of its answers' (*RB* 77 / 81). Barthes understands this point of view, but is unwilling to be constrained by it. Or rather, by around 1970, he has ceased to be constrained by the role of mythologist or of political theorist, however impeccably revolutionary: 'Hence utopia would be the taboo of the revolution, and the writer would be responsible for transgressing it; he alone could risk that representation; like a priest, he would close the ethical circle, answering by a final vision of values to the initial revolutionary *choice* (the reason why one *becomes* a revolutionary).'

In other words, what is undoubtedly at stake here is Barthes's own status as a writer. Indeed, I should like to stress what I see as the particular interest of Barthes's personal investment in utopia—utopia links his desire to invent social values for the world with his own project of writing. For a long time this project was worked out through essays on other writers or on the contradictory aspirations of literature in general. But as Barthes gradually collapsed the distinction between meta-linguistic theorist or critic (*écrivant*) and creative writer (*écrivain*), his personal and psychological investment in the latter retained a broad social and ethical impulse. Utopia as a sort of writing will therefore emerge as the ultimate mediator between the literary and political dimensions of his work. Barthes's own writing plays out, in its way, the mission that he

⁵ Roland Barthes, 'Myth Today', in *Mythologies* [1957], trans. Annette Lavers (London, Granada, 1973), 109–59: 157 / *My* 191–247: 245–6.

attributed to literature at the very beginning of his career. For *Writing Degree Zero* ends with the following declaration of faith:

> Literary writing bears within it both the alienation of History and the dream of History; as Necessity, it testifies to the division of languages which is inseparable from the division of classes, as Freedom, it is consciousness of this division and the very effort which seeks to surmount it. Although it feels permanently guilty about its own solitude, it is none the less an imagination eagerly desiring the happiness of words; it hastens towards a dreamed of language whose freshness, by a kind of ideal anticipation, might portray the perfection of some new Adamic world where language would no longer be alienated. The proliferation of modes of writing brings a new literature into being in so far as the latter invents its language only in order to be a project: Literature becomes the Utopia of language.[6]

The language of literature bears witness to social alienation, yet it also inscribes the dream of social liberation. Barthes's lifelong fidelity to literature (perceived in this way) forms the baseline of his own utopian project.[7]

Thus the closing paragraph of *Writing Degree Zero*, strikingly imbued with the language of both Marxism and existentialism—history, alienation, need, freedom, project—establishes literature itself as Barthes's first politically grounded linguistic utopia. It is at the level of language that Barthes will always claim to experience the social divisions of the world: 'it is interlocution which is divided, alienated: thus he experiences the whole sphere of social relationships in terms of language' (*RB* 168 / 170). This equation of social divisiveness with a war of languages underlies his desire to conceive utopias either within or beyond language, for language is the 'contradictory condition of our alienation and our liberation, of our heaviness and our

---

[6] Roland Barthes, *Writing Degree Zero* [1953], trans. Annette Lavers and Colin Smith (London, Jonathan Cape, 1970), 93–4 / 126.

[7] Over twenty years later he will describe this tension between alienation and liberation in remarkably similar terms: 'I believe that literature will always be driven by a forward movement relative to the rest of society. It will always have an ambiguous role: to express unease and social hardship as long as they exist, but also to be utopian, to figure various utopias. As long as the world remains historically alienated, literature will have this dual function.' See 'Entretien avec Roland Barthes', *OC* iii. 424–9: 429, first published as a preface to *Littérature occidentale* (Éditions Grammont, Lausanne, 1976).

lightness'.[8] Barthes's utopias aspire to defeat or to bypass the sticky stereotypes of the *doxa* (especially familiar as the battleground of *Mythologies*); all strive towards an ideal social 'transparency' in the realm of speech: 'as if the consistency of social interlocution might one day be clarified, lightened, woven with interstices to the point of invisibility' (*RB* 138 / 141). And although the terminology shifts over the years, 'literature', 'writing' (*écriture*), and 'text'—practices of writing rather than bodies of works—continue to be aligned with 'the forces of freedom', and perhaps nowhere more confidently than in Barthes's inaugural lecture at the Collège de France in 1977. It is literature that works away at undermining language, 'not by the message of which it is the instrument, but by the play of words of which it is the theatre'—literature defined, that is, as 'this salutary trickery, this evasion, this grand imposture which allows us to understand speech *outside the bounds of power*, in the splendour of a permanent revolution of language'.[9] Since, for Barthes, the language and speech of our present society are unavoidably vehicles of power and aggression, and since there is no exit from language, the writer's dazzling utopian solution is to persuade literature to cheat speech of its meanings.

Barthes's evaluation of this human envelopment in meaning thus wavers quite dramatically between two poles. The early structuralist celebration of *homo significans* will stress humanity's infinite potential for creating its own meanings, and many of Barthes's proclamations on the utopian function of literature echo this euphoric tone. Following Saussure, Barthes views language as a sign system which obliges statements about the world to pass through a stage of mental conceptualization, that is through the relay of the signified with its proliferation of connotations. Moreover, if all apparently factual systems are really semiological ones, so that meaning is a function of difference rather than reference, then this is doubly so in the case

---

[8] Barthes, 'D'eux à nous' [1978], OC iii. 822–3: 823, first published in *Le Monde*. These are the final words of Barthes's contribution to a survey on current views of Voltaire and Rousseau, in which he suggests that their relative political serenity was due to a historical context in which language was still experienced as socially innocent.

[9] 'Inaugural Lecture, Collège de France', in *A Barthes Reader*, ed. Susan Sontag (London, Jonathan Cape, 1982), 457–78: 462 / *Leçon*, 16–17.

of literature, built out of words which already belong to a sign system in their own right:

> What am I to *say* about what I *see*? A bed? A window? A colour? Already I am busily cutting up this continuum which is before my eyes. What is more, these simple words are themselves values, they have a past, surroundings, their meaning is born perhaps less from their relation to the object they signify than from their relation to other words, at once adjacent and different: and it is precisely in this zone of surplus-signification, of secondary signification, that literature will be lodged and will develop.[10]

The structuralist development of a semiological approach to literature was enabling and exciting from many points of view, not least for the fascination of attempts to analyse representation as a function of conventions rather than as direct imitation of the real world. It was clearly a challenge for Barthes to turn the most realist of stories into festive adventures of language: 'the function of narrative is not to "represent", it is to constitute a spectacle which still remains very puzzling to us, but which cannot be of a mimetic order ... "what happens" in narrative is, from the referential (real) point of view, literally *nothing*, what "takes place" is language alone, the adventure of language, whose coming never ceases to be celebrated.'[11] At its best, a willing immersion in connotation is literature's joy and its strength, and Barthes both plays up and joins in the celebration.

Yet as social critic and fierce demystifier of ideological abuses Barthes will often present a pessimistic vision of humanity as *condemned* to meaning. In this context he emphasizes the negative and ubiquitous side of connotation, which cuts human beings off from each other. For it is at the stage of imposing, resisting, or choosing between competing connotations that people get caught up in the warring systems of meaning that

---

[10] 'Literature Today' [1961], answers to a questionnaire prepared by *Tel Quel*, in *Critical Essays* [1964], trans. Richard Howard (Evanston, Ill., Northwestern University Press, 1972), 151–61: 160 / 155–66: 164.

[11] 'Introduction to the Structural Analysis of Narratives' [1966], opening essay of a special issue of *Communications* on the structural analysis of narrative, in *The Semiotic Challenge*, trans. Richard Howard (Oxford, Basil Blackwell, 1988), 95–135: 134–5 / 167–206: 206.

alienate social relations. Barthes always accepted the necessity of political engagement with this war of meanings, a commitment which takes the well-known form in his early work of unmasking the ideological interests that masquerade as natural states of affairs. However, much of Barthes's writing testifies to his longing for a realm beyond such meanings, and this largely metaphorical space is invariably identified with utopia. Barthes often insisted on the beyondness of this utopian realm, somewhere on the far side rather than the near side of meaning, and therefore to be distinguished from any pre-semiological golden age: 'for him, it is not a case of recovering a pre-meaning, an origin of the world, of life, of facts, anterior to meaning, but rather of imagining a post-meaning: one must traverse, as in some initiation, the entirety of meaning, in order to be able to extenuate it, to exempt it' (*RB* 87 / 90). Hence Barthes's discussions of an outplaying of meaning in terms of its suspension or even of its theft. Hence his fascination with the uncertain status of Flaubert's writing, which manages to unsettle the *doxa* as if from the inside, or his idea of Robbe-Grillet as a writer who uses literature to drain the meaning from an overly significant world.[12] Hence, above all, Barthes's enthusiastic celebration of Zen Buddhism for its will to outstrip connotation, to get beyond 'the vicious infinity of language'.[13] Japanese haiku in particular will take on considerable importance for its refusal of 'Western' description and definition, for its ability to escape connotation through a perfectly readable discourse which remains both light and literal, like Barthes's ideal image of language.

In *Empire of Signs* Barthes seems to suggest that this exemption from meaning must remain a utopian aspiration, unavailable to Western discourse in general, and to Barthes in particular, except at the level of his self-conscious weaving of the text of Japan. Yet his fascination with haiku as an ideologically, aesthetically, and philosophically acceptable way

---

[12] See, for example, Roland Barthes, *S/Z* [1970], trans. Richard Miller (New York, Hill and Wang, 1974), 140 / 146, and 'The Last Word on Robbe-Grillet?' [1962], in *CE* 197–204: 203 / 198–205: 204.

[13] Roland Barthes, *Empire of Signs* [1970], trans. Richard Howard (London, Jonathan Cape, 1983), 75 / 100.

of writing the material world will lead him to a very important concept in his 1970s work. This is the novelistic (*le romanesque*), a way of relating to the politics of everyday life which Barthes will link quite specifically with the idea of utopian writing. At the same time the central gesture of haiku, the purely indicative 'so!' (*tel!*) will point Barthes himself in the direction of a reconciliation with the denotation which as structuralist he had treated as pure ideological trickery, as a particular sort of connotation.[14] For one of the problematic aspects of the structuralist orthodoxy which Barthes himself helped to fashion was precisely the gap it inserted between language and the world. This split between meaning and material reality left human beings not only cut off from each other (due to their power struggles over secondary meanings), but also cut off as individuals from direct access to the world.

By the time he writes *Camera Lucida* Barthes will be building an argument around unmediated denotation and the contingent reality of the photographic referent. That this late celebration of a direct contact with reality should be presented to the reader through a vocabulary of resurrection and madness suggests that Barthes, in his final period, has not only abandoned the semiological approach as method. More fundamentally, he seems to have moved into a different conceptualization of reality itself from that of an early text like *Mythologies*, and it is clear that alienation from material reality in the Marxist or the Saussurean sense has been joined by a psychoanalytic frame of reference. Barthes's passage through a series of theoretical contexts was bound, in line with this, to shift and complicate the terms of his conceptualization of utopia. For example, in his inaugural lecture, Barthes presents writers as people who quite simply refuse to accept the split between language and reality, even though, at another level, it is a split which they acknowledge:

> From ancient times to the efforts of our avant-garde, literature has been concerned to represent something. What? I will put it crudely: the real. The real is not representable, and it is because men ceaselessly try to represent it by words that there is a history of literature. . . . We can imagine a history of literature, or better, say, of productions of

---

[14] See especially *Empire of Signs*, 81–4 / 110–14.

language, which would be the history of certain (often aberrant) verbal *expedients* men have used to reduce, tame, deny, or, on the contrary, to assume what is *always* a delirium, i.e. the fundamental incommensurability of language and the real. (BR 465 / L 21–2)

This insistence on the impossible desire to represent reality in words (and even to testify to its ontological status?) is described by Barthes as both 'perverse' and 'perverted' (*pervers*), and as 'happy' for this very reason (466 / 23). Above all, what may seem a neurotic impulse (with no possibility of fulfilment) is presented as the 'utopian' function of literature.

This positive allusion to perversion, and a passing reference to Lacan's definition of the real as that which lies outside of discourse—not representable in words, but only demonstrable (*démontrable*)—suggests, however, that what is emerging is not only a new conceptualization of human alienation from reality. It also suggests a new set of strategies for overcoming this alienation, largely because of a different psychological attitude (perverse pleasure) towards the writer's still 'impossible' task. For example, fantasmatic formulation of the very detail of utopia will emerge as one of the missions of the utopian writer, in a clear transgression of the Marxist disapproval of retrograde representations of the as yet non-existent liberated society: 'It's not the outlines of a future society that we are afraid to draw. That society is already there, in politics itself; it's the *details* of this society, and it's from these that we deduce utopia, that we deduce desire. For utopia, and this is precisely its special feature, imagines times, places, and customs in minutest detail.'[15] Yet Barthes, in his reading of Fourier, will openly confront the difficult relationship between human need and human desire, and will explore, on the basis of that reading, a possible mode of writing that might respect both, in part through the newly defined category of 'the political' (*le politique*) that Barthes will formulate in the 1970s.[16] However, the embrace of desire as a fundamental dimension of utopia makes a tangible difference to

---

[15] See Barthes's brief piece, 'Utopia Today' [1974], OC iii. 44, first published in *Utopia rivisitato*, a special issue of *Almanacco Bompiani*.
[16] See, for example, the distinction drawn between *le politique* and *la politique* in 'Twenty Key Words for Roland Barthes' [1975], in GV 205–32 / 194–220.

its status and to the ethical questions surrounding the possible forms of its representation. From the late 1960s at least, desire will become increasingly central to Barthes's engagement with utopia, and will itself become increasingly interwoven with the Romantic affects that mark his very late writing: love, pity, and a preoccupation with death.

In general, then, I shall be tracing a progression in Barthes's work from a 1950s sense of alienation from history and from everyday reality, to a conception of utopian discourse which solves some of the theoretical and ethical dilemmas of his early writing, but which produces other problems in its turn. Barthes himself often pointed out that his basic concerns remained constant, whereas what changed were the theoretical languages through which he explored them. The point about Barthes, I believe, is that he does not necessarily have a consistent theoretical position on reality and representation. What he does have, as an increasingly self-conscious writer, is an unchanging concern with the relationship between language and the world, and with the role of literature and other creative forms of writing as mediator between the two. In this sense, for Barthes, utopia is very much a synonym for 'literature', 'writing', or 'text', just as these words often seem interchangeable with utopia. One could perhaps say that utopia is simply *the* word for a positive ethical, social, and affective solution to the difficult interrelationship of human beings, their desires, their needs, their language, and the world. It is as if Thomas More, in naming Utopia, had provided the languages of the world with a much needed metaphor. However, the metaphor of utopia is a deliberate catachresis, since there is, by definition, no such literal place.

Utopia, then, is not just my own organizing framework, a useful way of gathering all of Barthes's work into a coherent argument. I believe that utopia is an overlooked but crucial dimension of Barthes's writing, and that he consciously exploited it in a creative way. While it is true that utopia does not have a fixed content or even a fixed theory in Barthes's work, such slipperiness is intrinsic to a concept through which he brings together and addresses some of his most fundamental concerns as both thinker and writer. In embarking upon a detailed discussion of Barthes's utopias—in an analysis which will cover a wide range of his writing, both chronologically and thematically—I have two underlying and related aims. First, to open up a new internal reading of Barthes, of intrinsic interest and importance. Second, to argue a more general case for Barthes's continuing relevance as a utopian thinker for our age.

To begin with, Barthes belongs to a long and broad tradition of discursive and creative writing on utopia, of which we are inevitably reminded by the intertextual resonance of the term itself. There is a massive primary and secondary literature of and on utopia, both past and present, while utopia continues to flourish, especially in Marxist and feminist cultural theory.[17] Obviously, I have consulted many general studies of utopia (and read many fictional utopias) in the course of my research. However, in devising the shape of this book, I have made a conscious decision not to open with a historical or theoretical overview of utopia, which would then be 'applied' to the case of Barthes. I intend, rather, to read the letter and spirit of utopia within Barthes's texts, and to draw out any theoretical issues, as well as Barthes's place in the general context, as I proceed. It is because I personally started from Barthes, and because recent overviews of utopia have rarely seemed appropriate to his case, that I remain convinced that Barthes himself has a theoretical and political contribution to make to current thinking on utopia.[18]

It was whilst attending a seminar on Frankfurt School theories of utopia that I first sensed important connections with Barthes. Frankfurt School debates on the relationship between aesthetics and politics, and between realism and modernism, are

---

[17] In Fredric Jameson's happy formulation: 'One finds everywhere today—not least among artists and writers—something like an unacknowledged "party of utopia": an underground party, whose numbers are difficult to determine, whose program remains unannounced and even unformulated, whose existence is unknown to the citizenry at large and to the authorities, but whose members seem to recognize one another by means of secret masonic signals.' See *Postmodernism; or, The Cultural Logic of Late Capitalism* (London, Verso, 1991), 180.

[18] For recent scholarly overviews of writing on utopia see, for example, Barbara Goodwin and Keith Taylor, *The Politics of Utopia: A Study in Theory and Practice* (London, Hutchinson, 1982); Vincent Geoghegan, *Utopianism and Marxism* (London, Methuen, 1987); Krishan Kumar, *Utopia and Anti-Utopia in Modern Times* (Oxford, Blackwell, 1987); Ruth Levitas, *The Concept of Utopia* (Hemel Hempstead, Philip Allan, 1990); Angelika Bammer, *Partial Visions: Feminism and Utopianism in the 1970s* (New York, Routledge, 1991).

obviously relevant to Barthes's discussions of literature, art, and the role of the avant-garde. On the whole, however, this is not intended to be a study of Barthes's literary and aesthetic theory. Rather, it is largely a book about Barthes's more general writing on everyday life. But here too Barthes fits well into the tradition of Marxist critical theory that tends to construe utopia as gesture—the affirmation of a forward-looking human aspiration which cuts across ideological critique, and which can be read in some of the most alienated human activities of the past and present.[19] The relationship between this emphasis on utopia as gesture and the longer-standing tradition of utopia as genre is one of the issues which seems to dog critical attempts to circumscribe the general nature and function of utopian thought.[20] By generic utopias I mean fantasized, detailed representations of an ideal society located in a future place, a geographically other place, or a different place within. Through their reversal or inversion of the writer's contemporary society the traditional aim of such utopias has been to suggest a radical social critique. In Barthes's discussion of literature as utopia in his inaugural lecture, he himself seems suspicious of utopia as genre: 'Utopia, of course, does not save us from power. The utopia of language is recuperated as the language of utopia—a genre like the rest' (BR 467 / L 25). In many ways Barthes collapses the distinction between gesture and genre, just as, in his desire to escape the problems of metalanguage, he tends to dissolve the distinction between commentary on utopia and its inscription in fictional forms. Nevertheless, framing Barthes in

---

[19] For famous explorations of the intersection of ideology and utopia see Karl Mannheim, *Ideology and Utopia: An Introduction to the Sociology of Knowledge* [1936], trans. Louis Wirth and Edward Shils (New York, Harcourt Brace Jovanovich, 1985); Ernst Bloch, *The Principle of Hope* [1959], trans. Neville Plaice, Stephen Plaice, and Paul Knight, 3 vols. (Oxford, Basil Blackwell, 1986); Paul Ricœur, *Lectures on Ideology and Utopia*, ed. George H. Yaylor (New York, Columbia University Press, 1986); Fredric Jameson, *The Political Unconscious: Narrative as a Socially Symbolic Act* (London, Methuen, 1981).

[20] See, for example, Ruth Levitas, 'Utopian Literature and Literality: Nowhere and the Wanderground', *News from Nowhere*, 9, special issue on 'Utopias and Utopianism' (1991), 66–79. Levitas wants to resolve some of the 'interdisciplinary tensions' within thinking on utopia, and distinguishes 'literal' from 'metaphorical' utopias, the former considered political (blueprints of social structures), the latter literary (fantasy representations of alternative values). As will be seen, none of these oppositions works for Barthes.

the familiar tradition of detailed representations of ideal societies (Plato, More, Morris, Bellamy, Perkins Gilman, Le Guin, etc.) has alerted me to some relatively unexplored themes of his writing. Indeed, it is precisely this generic context which throws up important issues for Barthes's place within cultural theory and contemporary cultural politics.

The first of these is the politics of space. The familiar argument that structuralism is ahistorical—and hence apolitical—overlaps in interesting ways with some Marxist devaluations of utopia as static, devoid of temporal progression, and therefore reactionary. The new interest in space associated with postmodernism, and rendered respectable by the Marxist credentials of such theorists as Edward W. Soja, David Harvey, and Fredric Jameson, has shown up the naïvety of insisting on restricting history to its development through time.[21] Clearly space is historical through and through, it is human and cultural, and it is open to competing conceptualizations as well as to competing claims to ownership. Abstractions such as time and space *both* change through history. The fact that fictional representations of utopia, places that are 'good places' but also, by definition, 'no places', have to project themselves either into the future (through dreams or science fiction), or into some hidden geographical space (previously unknown, and stumbled upon through some chance adventure), suggests the intimate relationship of these two strategies. For both sorts of place (future or other) are profoundly implicated in the contemporary society which produces them: the impulse for both springs from history.[22]

When Barthes argued so vigorously that states of affairs which seemed natural were really historical, his arguments were

---

[21] Jameson, *Postmodernism*; David Harvey, *The Condition of Postmodernity: An Enquiry into the Conditions of Cultural Change* (Oxford, Blackwell, 1980); Edward W. Soja, *Postmodern Geographies: The Reassertion of Space in Critical Social Theory* (London, Verso, 1989). For a helpful overview see Tony Pinkney, 'Space: The Final Frontier', *News from Nowhere*, 8 (1990), 10–27.

[22] For a dogged ideological analysis of utopian spaces see Louis Marin, *Utopics: The Semiological Play of Textual Spaces* [1973], trans. Robert A. Vollrath (Atlantic Highlands, NJ, Humanities Press International, Inc., 1990). Most of Marin's book is devoted to a detailed reading of Thomas More's *Utopia*, though it also applies its findings to some contemporary spaces, notably in an inspired essay on Disneyland ('Utopic Degeneration: Disneyland', 239–57).

generally pitched in the domain of the spaces of his contemporary reality—colonial spaces, in particular, but many others as well.[23] Barthes could well be seen as a cultural geographer, on account of his interest in cities such as Paris, New York, and Tokyo as intelligible and rational human spaces, of his late and somewhat self-conscious promotion of the qualities of southwestern France,[24] and above all on account of his search for radically different, literally foreign spaces. This search marks a whole range of his writing, from commentaries on Stendhal's Italy and Loti's Turkey, to inscriptions of his own experience of Morocco, Japan, and China.[25] Clearly there is a dimension of utopian geography in Barthes's writing, which fits well with Fourier's flamboyant projections for interventions in the physical universe as well as with the latter's detailed invention of the smaller-scale space of the phalanstery.[26]

The second contemporary issue, arising squarely from the first, is that of Barthes's relationship to the ethical and political problem of Orientalism, defined by Edward Said as a set of discursive strategies which, whether consciously or unconsciously, construct the East as an object of Western knowledge and power.[27] As just indicated, Barthes's key utopias are projected into the 'Orient': Japan and China, and, perhaps most problematically, Morocco. I am thinking of the Morocco of the posthumously published 'Incidents', that of the supposedly autobiographical anecdote of eating rancid couscous, from which Barthes conjures up his essay on Fourier,[28] and even that which provides Barthes with the metaphors of a *wadi* or a *souk* when he wants to convey his utopian concept of text.[29] That such totally distinct parts of the world as Morocco and Japan should be subsumed under the label of the Orient is, of course,

---

[23] See, in particular, Chs. 1 and 4.
[24] See Ch. 9.
[25] See Chs. 5, 6, and 7.
[26] See Ch. 3.
[27] Edward Said, *Orientalism* [1978] (Harmondsworth, Penguin, 1985). Said's enormously influential book has given rise to a large (and still growing) body of work within the general field of colonial and postcolonial discourse, and there have, of course, been many critiques and refinements of his original argument (some by himself) in what is now nearly twenty years since its first publication. Yet the most general terms in which Said established the paradigm of Orientalism as a discourse do not seem to have been overturned, or even substantially modified. For further discussion see Ch. 4.   [28] See beginning of Ch. 5.   [29] See Ch. 8.

part of the problem to be discussed. Is Barthes writing in full awareness of the discourse of Orientalism, and experimenting with more liberated alternatives for writing about other cultures and their inhabitants?[30] Or does he, despite his best intentions and his awareness of the pitfalls, fall back into the exoticism and colonial complicity that he so vigorously denounces in *Mythologies*?[31]

If Orientalism arises from the politics of space, my third general issue for the politics of utopia arises in its turn from Orientalism. This is the question of Barthes's sexual politics. For a common Orientalist theme identified by Said is precisely the celebration—usually in the context of prostitution—of an easily available sexuality.[32] Traditional representations of utopian societies invariably pay attention to the social organization of sexual relationships, with new arrangements for reproduction and child-rearing resulting from the rethinking of sexual difference. Indeed the recasting of sexual morality, the liberation of sexuality from present-day social conventions and constraints, is a major preoccupation of many utopian writers, not least Barthes's favourite French examples, Fourier and Sade. Barthes states specifically that he finds in Japan a 'happy sexuality', so happy that it spills over into his writing on Japan.[33] If a happy sexuality means an easy, guiltless sexuality, this could reasonably be taken as a utopian ideal: the liberation of an alienated sexuality which is proposed by Fourier and Herbert Marcuse,[34] and which is surely thought desirable by Barthes. Later in this book I shall argue that Barthes gradually assumes, self-consciously if discreetly, the status of a homosexual writer, and that his own utopias implicitly embrace a very positively presented homosexual value system.[35] Moreover, in *Roland*

---

[30] See Said: 'Perhaps the most important task of all would be to undertake studies in contemporary alternatives to Orientalism, to ask how one can study other cultures and peoples from a libertarian, or a non-repressive and non-manipulative perspective. But then one would have to rethink the whole complex problem of knowledge and power' (*Orientalism*, 24).   [31] See Ch. 4.
[32] See Said's (relatively undeveloped) discussion of 'Oriental sex' (based especially on the case of Flaubert), *Orientalism*, 186–90.
[33] 'A happy sexuality found its corresponding discourse quite naturally in the continuous, effusive, jubilant quality of the writing' (*RB* 156 / 159).
[34] Herbert Marcuse, *Eros and Civilisation: A Philosophical Inquiry into Freud* [1955] (London, RKP, Ark Paperbacks, 1987).
[35] See, in particular, Ch. 8.

Barthes by Roland Barthes, prostitution will be proposed as an apparently ideal sexual contract, which shares with homosexuality in general the non-aggressive ethics of the 'no-will-to-grasp' (*le non-vouloir-saisir*), a notion borrowed (once again) from Eastern philosophy, and which permeates Barthes's writing from *Empire of Signs* onwards.[36] Yet what exactly was at stake in the projection of this sexual utopia on to an Eastern country? One disturbing aspect of what might be at stake is suggested by Barthes's own comparison of the power politics of the Sadeian castle with those of certain third-world countries of his own day:

Sadeian practices appear to us today to be totally improbable: however, we need only travel in any under-developed country (analogous, all in all, to eighteenth-century France) to understand that they are readily operable there: the same social division, the same opportunities for recruitment, the same availability of subjects, the same conditions for seclusion, and, so to speak, the same impunity.[37]

It is an observation that unavoidably affects evaluation of Barthes's own Moroccan text, 'Incidents'—written while he was teaching in Rabat from 1968 to 1969—for Barthes records many details arising from his own casual homosexual encounters with Moroccan adolescents.[38]

The posthumous publication of *Incidents* in 1987 was but the first of a series of controversies that continue to mark critical discussion of Barthes and his work. *Incidents* contained a further autobiographical text—'Paris Evenings'—a 'diary' written in the late summer of 1979 (just six months before Barthes's death) and explicitly concerned with homosexual prostitution and failed relationships with various young men.[39] François Wahl, Barthes's editor at the Éditions du Seuil, claims in his preface that Barthes was thinking of publishing both

---

[36] See *RB* 59 / 64, and Ch. 8 below.
[37] Roland Barthes, *Sade, Fourier, Loyola* [1971], trans. Richard Miller (New York, Hill and Wang, 1976), 131 / 135.
[38] Roland Barthes, 'Incidents', in *Incidents* [1987], trans. Richard Howard (Berkeley and Los Angeles, University of California Press, 1992), 11–41 / 21–61.
[39] 'Paris Evenings' is my own translation, used throughout this book in preference to Richard Howard's retention of the original French title. See 'Soirées de Paris', ibid. 49–73 / 71–116.

INTRODUCTION 17

texts.⁴⁰ While it seems unlikely that Barthes would have done so without considerable revision (notably the removal of recognizable proper names in 'Paris Evenings'), it is difficult now not to accept them as part of Barthes's *œuvre*. Indeed both texts will be important to the argument of this book, and will be discussed in some detail in due course.⁴¹

The second controversy was the publication in 1990 of the first biography of Barthes by Louis-Jean Calvet.⁴² Here it became clear from reviews and replies to reviews that Wahl, acting as Barthes's literary executor, had been hostile to the very idea of a biography (supposedly on the grounds that Barthes himself would have been similarly disapproving) and that Calvet had been refused permission to quote from two important collections of private correspondence. The reception of Calvet's biography has revealed a bizarre lack of interest in its actual contents, despite the fact that it contains important new material for anyone interested in the contexts of Barthes's work. Calvet's sections on Barthes's employment and lifestyle abroad (notably in Romania, Egypt, and Morocco), as well as information on his family, have been especially useful to me, and will feed into my study at various points.⁴³

The third and most fraught dispute has been over Wahl's refusal to permit publication in any form of the four lecture courses given by Barthes at the Collège de France between 1977 and his death in 1980. From the point of view of this study this is especially frustrating, in that the lectures deal with explicitly utopian themes, the first course bearing the general title 'How to Live Together' (*Comment vivre ensemble*). The fact that *le Tout-Paris* seems to have been at the lectures in person accounts perhaps for the initial lack of concern over their non-appearance in the wider academic domain. However, the publication of *Incidents* and of Calvet's biography provoked considerable discussion of the fate and control of Barthes's *inédits*, in

---

⁴⁰ See the French edition of Roland Barthes, *Incidents* (Paris, Seuil, 1987), 7–10, especially 8 and 9. Wahl's preface was not included in Richard Howard's English translation.   ⁴¹ See Chs. 5 and 10.
⁴² Louis-Jean Calvet, *Roland Barthes* [1990], trans. Sarah Wykes (Cambridge, Polity, 1994).
⁴³ On Calvet's biography and its reception see my review article 'Vie de Barthes', *Modern and Contemporary France*, NS 3 (1995), 463–8.

particular of the Collège de France teaching which was so obviously a major part of his very productive final period. In 1991 the whole issue was deliberately brought into the open by the publication in *La Règle du jeu* of a transcribed tape recording of Barthes's introductory lecture to the second course on *Le Neutre* (the neuter/the neutral/neutrality).⁴⁴ This resulted in Grasset, publishers of *La Règle du jeu*, being taken to court by Barthes's half-brother, the holder of his estate. The court awarded damages against Grasset, banned further publication, and reconfirmed the French law of 1957 which rules that pedagogical lectures as well as broadcasts are copyright, and therefore belong to the author's estate. One of the major arguments put forward against publication of the lectures was Barthes's supposed theoretical distinction between oral communication and writing. 'Writing is the loss of every origin, of every voice', declared one of the judges in November 1991, quoting a passage from Barthes's essay 'The Death of the Author', by way of proving the author's intentions.⁴⁵ This legal argument was both comical and ironically inappropriate, in that the Barthes of the 'death of the author' years so obviously wanted to undermine the property rights over intended meanings of both authors and their spokespersons.⁴⁶ What is more, while it is true that Barthes saw writing and speech as very different activities, it is simply not true that he promoted one at the expense of the other. In fact, as will be seen, several of Barthes's most important texts on utopia were originally oral in form.⁴⁷

⁴⁴ 'Le Désir de neutre', *La Règle du jeu*, 5 (1991), 36–60.
⁴⁵ For details of the lawsuit see: 'A qui appartient la parole des maîtres disparus?', *Le Monde* (18 Oct. 1991), 26, and Maurice Peyrot, 'L'Écriture "contrefaçon" de la parole', *Le Monde* (22 Nov. 1991), 46. In pointing out that the aim of the law was to prevent the holders of an estate from substituting their own preferences for those of the author, the judges presumably failed to see that, here too, this was a possibility. The court ruled against withdrawal of copies already in circulation. For an interesting (if inevitably one-sided) collection of reactions, see 'L'Affaire Barthes', *La Règle du jeu*, 6 (1992), 130–98.
⁴⁶ For Barthes's infamous (and often misrepresented) essay, first published in 1968, see 'The Death of the Author', in *The Rustle of Language*, trans. Richard Howard (Oxford, Basil Blackwell, 1986), 49–55 / 61–7. See too his comments in a 1970 interview, to the effect that 'textual' criticism (of the sort outlined in *S/Z*) 'tries to subvert and destroy the idea of an author's ownership of their text' ('Critique et autocritique' [1970], OC ii. 987–8: 992).
⁴⁷ In addition to Barthes's inaugural lecture at the Collège de France [1977] see, for example: 'Music, Voice, Language' [1977], in *The Responsibility of Forms*:

The crucial issue underlying all these controversies is the status of Barthes the man relative to his body of work. This undoubtedly affects critical readings of that work as well as the outcome of disputes over publication. If the later Barthes increasingly collapsed the distinction between his own life and his writing it is apparent, at least retrospectively, that Barthes's *œuvre* was never a series of disembodied texts. Yet this 'amicable return of the author' (*SFL* 8 / 13), which Barthes himself so obviously desired, is bound to affect the way all of his work is read. For a start, the acknowledgement of a biographical dimension brings into sharper focus the sometimes difficult evaluation of Barthes's politics and values, whether of class, race, or sexuality. However, I wish to argue that the very possibility of placing him in these political contexts is a sure sign of the continued importance of his work. What makes Barthes's case so interesting is the fact that his utopian quests for radically other symbolic systems—increasingly pursued through an explicit celebration of cultural difference and an implicit assumption of homosexuality—should be so openly tied to the material complexity of human relations. Not the least complex of these relations are those between Barthes himself and his subject matter.

Critical Essays on Music, Art, and Representation, trans. Richard Howard (Oxford, Basil Blackwell, 1986), 278–85 / 246–52; 'The Romantic Song' [1976], in *RF* 286–92 / 253–58; ' "Longtemps, je me suis couché de bonne heure" ' [1978], in *RL* 277–90 / 313–25; 'One Always Fails in Speaking of What One Loves' [1980], in *RL* 296–305 / 333–42.

I
Making Space

Only empty space can really hold the future in store.[1]

It is ironic that Barthes's structuralism, even as it harnessed semiology to the cause of ideological mystification, should have come under attack on the grounds that spatial structures are static, that they set aside time, and that those who analyse them therefore turn their backs upon history and change.[2] If space—along with language and sexuality—is one of the crucial dimensions of Barthes's engagement with utopia, it is precisely because space is as socially and historically marked as everything else. Of course it can be conceptualized in different ways, with markedly different effects. Many spatial framings do indeed seek to naturalize stasis and political inertia, and Barthes fought an uphill struggle, through polemical critiques, to demystify all spaces which he perceived as alienated. Less prominent in his early texts, but nevertheless still to be found there, is a complementary strategy of approaching these alienated spaces indirectly, through the postulation of utopian alternatives. Throughout this book this double approach will be seen to apply to places and spaces that were both literal and metaphorical.

---

[1] Roland Barthes, 'Le Prince de Hombourg au TNP', OC iii. 203–9: 205, first published in Lettres nouvelles (Mar. 1953).

[2] Fredric Jameson, for example, in 1972, spoke of his desire to free structural analysis 'from the myth of structure itself, of some permanent and spatial-like organization of the object', proposing his own Marxist hermeneutic as the only possible reconciliation of the 'apparently incommensurable demands of synchronic analysis and historical awareness, of structure and self-consciousness, language and history' (The Prison-House of Language: A Critical Account of Structuralism and Russian Formalism (Princeton, Princeton University Press, 1972), 216). For a recent denunciation of French structuralism as a deliberate denial of history and politics (with Barthes as one of the chief culprits) see Kristin Ross, Fast Cars, Clean Bodies: Decolonization and the Reordering of French Culture (Cambridge, Mass., MIT Press, 1995), especially Ch. 4, 'New Men', 157–96.

An example of the way in which the early Barthes focuses upon space to make his points is provided by the conclusion to an essay on classical Dutch painting, first published in 1953. Barthes has pursued a lengthy analysis of the way gender and class values can be read in the iconography of the faces of this somewhat self-satisfied society, especially those faces depicted in the almost obsessive portrayals of corporations of merchants. Yet he allows himself finally to be struck by the way the *Doelen* gaze out of the picture at the viewer, for it is this gaze which 'disturbs, intimidates, and turns man into the ultimate term of a problem'.[3] Above all, it institutes a final suspension of history: 'In this perfectly contented patrician world, absolute master of matter and evidently rid of God', the gaze provokes a strictly human interrogation and promises that history will always keep something back for the future. Even at the pinnacle of a materially determined sense of well-being, Dutch painting is not satiated by its class-bound nature, for the something that is left over belongs to the rest of humanity as well. According to Barthes, this inscription of human potential is a direct result of the spatial relations created by the aesthetic device of an outward gaze. This, then, is a utopian inflection of a largely ideological reading of these past paintings. Paradoxically, the negative foil is provided by *The Artist's Studio*, Gustave Courbet's manifesto painting for a revolutionary realist art: 'shut up in a room, the artist is painting a landscape he does not see, turning his back on his (naked) model, who for her part watches him painting. In other words the artist represents himself installed in a space carefully emptied of any gaze but his own.' Courbet's crime is to have promoted a two-dimensional closure, in that this 'shop-window spectacle captured by a painter-voyeur' can only create in its turn the mundane flatness suggested by the apt term *une platitude*. For 'depth is born only when the spectacle itself slowly turns its shadow towards man and begins to look at him'.

Throughout the early 1950s, Barthes reflected upon a space which could be seen as mediating the literal and the metaphorical, namely theatrical space and the literal space of the

[3] 'The World as Object', in *CE* 3–12:11 / 19–28: 27; quotations that follow are from 12 / 28.

stage. Indeed he seemed to view the theatre as a microcosm, a sort of laboratory for constructing the liberated social space of utopia. Meanwhile, however, he had to contend with the omnipresence of another microcosm, in that French commercial theatre of the day seemed to act as a focus for many of the features of contemporary France that Barthes most despised. One of his fiercest critiques of this theatre is also one of the earliest, an essay on the Folies-Bergère published in *Esprit* in 1953. In fact so negative is Barthes's account that he turns the Folies-Bergère into an exemplary anti-theatre: 'Thus, no other theatre could ever negate the very being of theatre to this degree, and it is in this sense that the Folies-Bergère is an exemplary place.'[4] The text is intriguing for its relatively clumsy narrative device of speaking through the voice of a fictitious bourgeois—a Normandy horse-dealer, a Belgian merchant, or an American hat salesman—newly arrived in Paris, entering the Folies-Bergère at eight in the evening and expecting good value from his thousand-franc ticket. For what is basically wanted from three hours at the Folies-Bergère is the experience of a closed and self-sufficient world which will project a reassuring image of one's own money and of one's own complacent self. This theatre offers an enclosed space where *nothing* opens out on to anything but itself. Like some cosy cocoon, 'it absorbs me into its self-assurance, rids me of my ignorance, and lays out for me all the elements of my make-up in a condensed and digestible form: wealth as a fabricated heaven, people reified by my money, objects which cannot threaten since they all have a name, the whole world in the form of a catalogue' (280).

Space is the crucial factor which divides the Folies-Bergère—an archetypal petty bourgeois theatre, like the Châtelet and the Paris Opera—from the 'great popular theatres'. Whereas Greek theatres were always circular, just as circuses and sports arenas still are, the stage of the Folies-Bergère, like Courbet's painting, is simply a two-dimensional 'shop-window theatre'. Here nothing more ambiguous will happen than the passage before the spectator's eyes of an elaborate decor, whereby historical events, for example, are reduced to expensive *tableaux vivants*.

[4] 'Folies-Bergère', *Esprit* (Fed. 1953), in OC i. 195–202: 196; quotations that follow are from 195–6 and 202.

Indeed the abolition of time and forward movement is the ultimate sin of a theatre which is simply 'frontal and decorative': 'Any argument, speech or seed of movement is sucked back into the immobile expanse of objects, the whole theatre solidifies into gold, pink, and feathers: everything is simply placed before you, theatrical action is emptied of its anguish, all that remains is a decor raised to the status of a spectacle'. The time that passes gives birth to nothing, it simply renews a static fascination with the eternal power of money. In short, if the Folies-Bergère constitutes an anti-theatre for Barthes, it is because it has totally lost what he considers to be theatre's very *raison d'être*. Since the golden age of Greek tragedy, theatre has gradually shed its 'power of advent' (*vertu d'avènement*), it has lost all sense of an opening on to a future which will contain other human beings: 'I no longer fear the existence of other things or of other people who might understand me.'

A very similar analysis appears in the editorial of the fifth issue of *Théâtre populaire*, published in 1954. This was unsigned, but is known to have been written by Barthes.[5] Bourgeois theatre, alienated above all by the money which infiltrates it at every level, is repeatedly likened to an enclosed space, of which the standard box-like stage (with its missing fourth wall) acts as a perfect emblem. This enclosed space is seen as cynically fostering a closing down of human potential for development, in the same ploy which Barthes was soon to identify as the aim of many a bourgeois myth. The audience comes in search of reassurance and excuses, to be painlessly rid of its minor anxieties or its bad conscience, and will find, thanks to its money, 'a closed, deadened, stifled place' which is exactly what it wants in order to keep itself in its chosen state of complacent inertia. The task of *Théâtre populaire*, for the foreseeable future, is presented as an entirely negative and critical one. The route to an ideal theatre is bound to be indirect, and must pass through exposure of the errors and mystifications of the bourgeois theatre of the day: 'For the time being our task can only be to destroy. We cannot claim to define Popular Theatre as anything other than a theatre purified of bourgeois structures, freed from the alienation of money and its masks. . . .

[5] *Théâtre populaire* (Jan.–Feb. 1954), in *OC* i. 381–3, quotations from 382–3.

Concerted demystification is the only possible reply to the current sway of myths.'

In this negative atmosphere, the best hope for the establishment of a genuinely popular theatre seemed to be the Théâtre National Populaire (TNP) under the directorship of Jean Vilar. A month after this editorial, in a review of a production of *Richard II*, Barthes introduced a change of tone by producing a markedly utopian image for the TNP: 'Like all the famous vessels of history, fragile but dogged conveyors of future races and continents, the ark of the TNP is the sole bearer of the future of popular theatre (theatre that is rid, that is, of its bourgeois structures).'[6] While much of the support that *Théâtre populaire* gave to the TNP was tied up with its explicit attempts to undermine commercial theatre and to alter the social composition of audiences, Barthes's more utopian essays and reviews are built around analyses of Vilar's overturning of a mystified theatrical space. The two levels of analysis are linked of course, in that the relationship between the performance and the audience lay at the centre of Barthes's reflection on the function of the stage. Moreover, the latter may well be a reflection that was Barthes's own as much as Vilar's, inflected as it was at that time with Barthes's acute interest in Greek tragedy.[7]

Barthes seems to me to have written his most creative pieces on the theatre for journals other than *Théâtre populaire*. A good example is his review of Vilar's production of Kleist's *The Prince of Hamburg*, which had been published in *Lettres nouvelles* just one month after the text on the Folies-Bergère. Barthes's negative points are made in contrast to the very positive conception of space that he attributes to this production, and which has led him to rediscover a representation of *avènement*, for him the lost essence of tragedy. While this utopian dimension allows Barthes to formulate more forcefully its negative ideological counterpart, it is important in its own right as a developed insight into a significant theatrical

---

[6] 'Fin de *Richard II*', *Lettres nouvelles* (Mar. 1954), in OC i. 389–92: 389.
[7] As an undergraduate Barthes was a founding member of the Sorbonne Ancient Theatre Group; for his *Diplôme d'études supérieures* he worked on the role of ritual speeches (*incantations* and *évocations*) in Greek tragic theatre.

alternative. Like the Folies-Bergère piece, the review opens in semi-narrative mode. However, the mystified, narrow-minded horse-dealer from Normandy (or his moneyed peer from abroad) has now been transformed into an intelligent theatre-goer perched high up in the gods. This is the Barthes who is able to reflect on the theatrical experience with which he is confronted: 'Contemplating the stage of the *Prince of Hamburg*, enormous and open to the elements like some dark ship interspersed with lights, faces or flags, I reflected upon our other bourgeois theatres, enclosed and shut in like provincial brothels, half bijou apartment, half prison, where the stage and the audience stare straight at each other, trapped in this intimate and private family confab.'[8] The vantage point in the gods creates the high-angle vision of the sports stadiums, rings and arenas of 'great popular spectacles', a theatrical experience of *avènement* is conjured up by the sensed proximity of night-time and the open air: 'this profound night, made up out of a space which is truly three-dimensional, and which no longer dangles in the usual fashion from painted backcloths.'

The motivation for the more familiar enclosed bourgeois space is assumed to be a deliberate desire to reverse this sense of *avènement*, to uncover a secret cut off 'from the shadows, from mystery, from possibility', to protect an essential image of humanity by shutting it up in a finite place. Tragedies, on the other hand, have always been written for open spaces, 'where what lies behind and to the side of the stage possesses a sort of basic undecidability, without which neither terror nor generosity is possible'. Whereas bourgeois theatre presents the audience with a puzzle to solve concerning past events—'something has happened, now you must try to find out what'—the tragic stage must always present a threat: 'something is going to happen, and you already know this to be the case.' Space itself, therefore, must be empty and available: 'Only empty space can really hold the future in store; it is because stage scenery has been cast aside that night-time, war, the city, and the elector's palace gradually invade the *Prince of Hamburg*, just as the sudden blast of air from an open door reveals Nature, season, atmosphere and time of day more surely than any verbal description.' Hence Barthes's

---

[8] '*Le Prince de Hombourg* au TNP', quotations from *OC* i. 203, 205, and 208.

admiration for Vilar's rejection of the flat, figurative backcloth, or of other stage sets attached to the play as if as an afterthought. Vilar's achievement is to have produced a genuine link between the action and language of the play and the material space of its *mise en scène*, for the dynamism of this relationship is essential to creating the sense of *avènement*. The essence of tragedy lies neither in the tragic mask, the iambic pentameter, nor the *cothurne*, but in 'space generously facing an anticipated Calamity, which may come from the gods, from Nature, or from History, but never from other human beings'.

This conceptualization of theatrical utopia as an empty space, pregnant with some extreme situation, is central to another interesting essay of the period, a short piece on Vilar's annual festival of the TNP. 'Avignon in the Winter' was published in *France-Observateur* in April 1954.[9] The familiar analysis of alienated and liberated theatrical spaces recurs, but here in an explicitly utopian and self-conscious frame, indeed with an underlying metaphorical structure worthy of Zola's *Germinal*. In yet another narrativized opening ('A few days ago . . .') Barthes describes himself, one grey and chilly afternoon in late winter, glancing into the courtyard of the Palais des Papes at Avignon, which later that year would become the site of the TNP's summer festival. The courtyard is bleak and empty, yet it is precisely from this 'neutral and available place' (rather than from an actual production in its summer setting) that Barthes chooses to draw out his claim that Popular Theatre is a theatre which 'places its trust in man'. Once again Barthes is reminded, by contrast, of the packaged sets, props, and costumes of 'our theatres for the wealthy', which leave the minds of the audience in a state of enforced (if willingly assumed) idleness, in front of a theatrical space which they have no responsibility for choosing, constructing, or bringing into being: 'this prudently enclosed space, sealed off on all sides, without a chink for the slightest shadow that might provoke escape, fear, or dreams.' Reduced to passive objects, tied to their seats in the stalls by their money—or to the gods by their lack of it—the audience is trapped in the shadow of a brightly lit stage.

---

[9] 'Avignon, l'hiver', *France-Observateur* (15 Apr. 1954), in OC i. 393–5, quotations easily locatable.

But Vilar's open stages restore to theatre-goers their freedom to participate in the creation of a dramatic meaning, to divide off for themselves day from night, tragic clarity from the everyday shadows, nature from human speech, the theatre from the non-theatre ('the world from its proscenium arch'). It is important that the space thus created should be a precarious one:

But the two spaces should struggle as well, give way to each other reluctantly, take time to disentangle themselves, they should tear each other apart; dark edges should ceaselessly bite into the central clarity, should gnaw away at it, consume it; and all through the performance one should feel that the fragile space of the actor is threatened, fascinated and almost reconquered by this fearsome elsewhere against which a single human gaze steadfastly struggles.

The vital role of the audience is summed up in Barthes's earliest recourse to a favourite image. The open stage differs from the closed bourgeois box in that it is 'the field of the auspex', so that (as Barthes informs a hypothetical member of the audience): 'it is you who are the priest, seer, controller of destinies, it is you who, across all this potential space, must trace out the field of your questioning.' From winter courtyard to summer spectacle, the changing seasons have ushered in the growth of an adult audience, and hence, too, of an adult theatre: 'Thus it is from Avignon-in-the-Winter that everything has germinated: from nothing, from stone, from silence, from a tree—it is adult theatre that has been founded.' In short, Barthes has conjured up a utopia from the courtyard of the Palais des Papes, a space that might have been thought to be as ideologically marked as any. Yet far from being a privileged site which 'oozes spirituality', the courtyard is perceived as a simple, cold, and natural place, 'so available that man could finally install there the work of men'. It is a place without hypocrisy, where the responsibility for everything is put back into human hands. This utopian proposition is summed up with a final flourish: 'You only have to poke your head, one winter's day, through the huge closed wooden door of the Festival courtyard, to understand that in the theatre too men are alone and that they can do anything.'

When Barthes looks back over his involvement with *Théâtre populaire*, in an interview filmed in 1970, his interest in Vilar is very much played down in favour of his subsequent enthusiasm for Brecht.¹⁰ The Berliner Ensemble's performance of *Mother Courage*, which Barthes attended in Paris in the summer of 1954, dazzled him and acted as a revelation. Clearly, it also took him by surprise. There is a comical aspect to this sudden discovery of a fully realized theatrical utopia, just one year after the setting up of *Théâtre populaire*, and so soon after Barthes's editorial committing the journal to a long uphill struggle of entirely negative critique. As he himself put it in a review published just a few months after the Avignon piece: 'this performance has perhaps saved us years of critical reflection.'¹¹ For Brecht had given material form to that socially liberated theatre that *Théâtre populaire* had simply postulated as an ideal, but which it now discovered 'in its adult and already perfect form'. Barthes found in Brecht a subtle Marxist aesthetic entirely to his taste: a reflection on the theatrical sign which he could never praise too highly and which he would seek to emulate in his own thinking on other systems of meaning. To a large extent Barthes's encounter with the Berliner Ensemble's productions of Brecht deflected his own attempts to define a popular theatre. As we have seen, these moved between reflections on Greek tragedy and defence of the activities of the TNP, with largely positive reviews of Vilar's productions. In the 1970 interview Barthes suggests that Vilar lacked a theoretical foundation for his theatrical practice (as if the search for a theory was a particular gap which Brecht had filled), and insists that *Théâtre populaire*'s interest in the TNP had been focused on its practical attempts to de-commercialize the theatre. Yet this is a very distorted account of what Barthes himself was writing in 1953 and 1954, in that it entirely omits his obvious interest at that time in Vilar's exploitation of theatrical space.¹²

¹⁰ This was one of two interviews, filmed in 1970 and 1971 for the 'Archives du XXᵉ siècle', broadcast on French television (*Océaniques*, FR3) in 1988. They were partially published in *Tel Quel* as 'Réponses' [1971], *OC* ii. 1307–24 (see 1312–13).
¹¹ '*Mutter Courage* au Festival international de Paris', *Théâtre populaire* (July–Aug. 1954), reprinted in *CE* as 'Mother Courage Blind', 33–6: 35–6 / 48–50: 50, wrongly dated as 1955 (this mistake has been carried over into the *Œuvres complètes*). The first phrase quoted has been accidentally omitted from the English translation.
¹² For a more spectacular distortion, see Barthes's extraordinary claim—during the conference on his work at Cerisy in 1977—that he never really liked open-air

It is true that Barthes's interest in the theatre changes in kind after the discovery of Brecht. Fascination with the alienation technique of Brecht's epic theatre replaces interest in the emotional and social catharsis of Greek tragedy, just as reflection on Brecht's use of the sign tends to replace that on Vilar's use of space. But this is not to say that these early obsessions disappear from Barthes's writing. His infamous essay on Racine, for instance, opens with a structural reading of the tragic *spaces* of the Racinian universe—the seraglio in *Bajazet* as a microcosm of this universe, a geographical separation into 'three Mediterraneans', a tripartite division of tragic space into chamber, antechamber, and the world outside.[13] Moreover, extreme emotions will resurface in Barthes's very late work, where *Camera Lucida* has interesting links with his early writing on theatrical tragedy. Apart from recurrent metaphors of darkness and light, I am thinking too of the neurotic intersection of space and time whereby, looking at a photograph, Barthes is filled with terror by the thought of a future death that he nevertheless knows has already taken place.[14] This is close indeed to the audience's participation in the creation of a tragic experience, as outlined in Barthes's review of *The Prince of Hamburg*. For the audience must know and yet fear that something irremediable is about to happen. Tragic time, once consumed, will leave a bare place 'where something has happened *for ever*' (OC i. 204).

The irreversibility of these temporal structures may seem to undermine the connection between tragedy and utopia which I have claimed to find in Barthes's pre-Brechtian theatre writings. How could a theatrical experience of this sort prefigure changed human relations? First, we should remember that Barthes is

theatre, even during the period of Vilar's festival at Avignon (discussion of Jean-Loup Rivière, 'La Déception théâtrale', in *Prétexte: Roland Barthes*, colloque de Cerisy sous la direction d'Antoine Compagnon (Paris, UGE, 1978), 110–28: 125–6).

[13] 'Racinean Man' [1960], in Roland Barthes, *On Racine*, trans. Richard Howard (New York, Performing Arts Journal Publications, 1983), 1–137: 3–8 / 13–132: 15–20.

[14] 'In front of the photograph of my mother as a child, I tell myself: she is going to die. I shudder, like Winnicott's psychotic patient, *over a catastrophe which has already occurred*' (Roland Barthes, *Camera Lucida: Reflections on Photography* [1980], trans. Richard Howard (London, Fontana, 1984), 96 / 150).

trying to find in Greek theatre ways of elaborating a genuinely *popular* theatre. Second, he claims that the tragic misfortune may come from nature or the gods, but never from other human beings. Barthes's stress on the audience's mental restructuring of the space of the stage foregrounds a *human* control, both of their own world and of the metaphysical forces of tragic terror. Such control may be merely mental and aesthetic, but it acts as an important imaginary rehearsal, not least for dealing with those social structures which remain eminently historical and therefore open to change in the real world. Third, he plainly views tragedy as something positive from an existential point of view, and this in itself has social implications for him, bearing in mind the complacent, inward-looking mentality attributed to the moneyed theatre-goer of the day. Indeed, it cannot be overstressed that Barthes's utopias, even in his later and most pleasure-conscious period, have nothing whatsoever to do with a mindless, happy-go-lucky sort of space of the kind already denounced—as 'soothing mythologizing'—in both his Folies-Bergère essay and his editorial to the fifth issue of *Théâtre populaire*. The point is made even more forcefully in 'Matisse or the Joys of Life', an uncollected mythology published in *Les Lettres nouvelles* in January 1955.[15] If Matisse's obituaries are marked by a relentless celebration of the *cheerful* qualities of his paintings, Barthes ferociously denounces this as the 'soothing myth' of an entirely bogus utopia. The 'decorative aspect' attributed to Matisse's work is derided by Barthes for fostering a mythical *bonheur de vivre*, and an ethos which is 'more sunny than solar'. Given that 'solar' (*solaire*) is one of Barthes's favourite words for the stark existential world of Greek tragedy, it is clear that 'sunny' (*ensoleillé*) is being set up here as its very negative counterpart. This sunny ethos is likened by Barthes to the aesthetics of a *congé payé* on the French Riviera, and to a Taylorist 'whistle while you work' mentality. Both, he claims, are purified of any social context or sense of a personal destiny: 'To celebrate the "joys of life" without ever considering the conditions, limits, and sacrifices of these joys, can only be done

---

[15] 'Matisse ou le bonheur de vivre', OC iii. 1308–9 (accidentally omitted from OC i.), quotations easily locatable.

by turning one's back, in one way or another, on the history of their struggle.'

If 1954 was the year in which Barthes turned from Vilar to Brecht in his theatre writings, it was also that in which he began (in November) to produce his monthly mythologies for *Les Lettres nouvelles*. Many (but not all) of these would later be collected and published with Barthes's theoretical afterword ('Myth Today') as *Mythologies*.[16] Barthes continues to reflect upon ideological and utopian spaces, both literal and metaphorical, and the very arguments made in response to bourgeois commercial theatre are now a response to the real world of 1950s France. If a broadly existentialist vocabulary of consciousness, choice, destiny, and responsibility reveals Barthes's commitment to an ethos of human fulfilment, it is clear that he associates this closing down of human potential with a parallel refusal of historical movement. Past determinations and future change are cynically collapsed into an unchanging present which blocks out the notion of human choice. Thus, in many of the examples upon which Barthes focuses in the visual and verbal representations of a right-wing press, a 'miraculous evacuation of history' and the 'irresponsibility of man' endlessly reaffirm each other (*M* 151 / *My* 239). The link between the two often operates through a denial of social class and economic differentiation, whereby advertisements and press features seek to establish bourgeois rituals as the 'norm as dreamed'—though not, of course, actually lived—for their petty bourgeois and working-class readership. 'Immobilization and an impoverishment of consciousness' are the inevitable result of this alienated dream life; for example, 'it is from the moment that a typist earning twenty pounds a month *recognizes herself* in the high society wedding that bourgeois ex-nomination achieves its full effect' (141 / 228–9).[17]

In 'Nuptials' (*Conjugales*), one of the earliest mythologies

---

[16] In addition to the selection of mythologies translated by Annette Lavers, see Roland Barthes, *The Eiffel Tower and Other Mythologies*, trans. Richard Howard (New York, Hill and Wang, 1979).
[17] 'The bourgeoisie is constantly absorbing into its ideology a whole section of humanity which does not have its basic status and cannot pretend to it except in imagination' (*M* 141 / *My* 228).

which was first published in December 1954, Barthes finds that the mythological value of three different categories of marriage is linked to the specific temporal and spatial focus of their press coverage.[18] First, the high society wedding is typically represented just after the ceremony itself, with the public space outside the church as the theatre of a spectacular *potlatch* between two aristocratic or bourgeois families. The ritual consumption of wealth and social values—the burning of money, the highest roles of the establishment (army, government, Legion of Honour) thrown into the flames for good measure—must be seen to take place before the emotionally aroused audience of the Parisian crowd. In a very different example, the fiction of a remote future wedding between Marlon Brando and a fisherman's daughter is an obvious concession to conventional morality. But Barthes is more interested in the setting ('the little French town, the beach, the market, the cafés and grocery shops of Bandol') in which Brando is placed by the magazine *Une semaine du monde*: ' "Marlon, accompanied by his (future) mother-in-law and his (future) wife, takes a peaceful stroll before dinner, like any French petty bourgeois" ' (*ET* 26 / *My* 49). Whereas one might have expected articles that represented the small town of Bandol bathing in the reflected glory of such a famous film star, in fact the connotations work in the opposite direction. Petty bourgeois reality stamps its scenery and its status on the dream situation (a Hollywood star falls in love with a local girl), and it is Marlon Brando who is enriched and consecrated by Bandol rather than the reverse.[19]

Barthes's third and best example is the decision by Miss Europe 1953 to give up the chance of fame and fortune and to marry her childhood sweetheart, an electrician from working-class Palaiseau. The stress here is on the deliberate choice of a humble petty bourgeois existence—when something far grander had supposedly been possible—and for this reason the press reports focus on the early period of the couple's married life. The setting is their tiny flat and its everyday surroundings, as

---

[18] Translated by Richard Howard as 'Conjugations', *ET* 23–6 / *My* 47–50.
[19] 'Reality imposes upon the dream its decor and its status, for the French petty bourgeoisie is clearly passing, at the moment, through a phase of mythical imperialism' (*ET* 26 / *My* 49–50).

they are photographed as a very happy couple having breakfast together, or returning from the market and cinema. This idealized representation of poverty ('love spiritualizes the little home, and the little home masks the slum' (25 / 48–9)) is torn apart as Barthes demystifies the closed horizons of this lifestyle. It is a lifestyle typical of petty bourgeois women, which is cynically glorified and promoted through the fortuitous example of Sylviane Carpentier, Miss Europe 1953:

> Here love-stronger-than-glory gives a boost to the moral code of the social status quo: it is not sensible to leave your position in society, it is glorious to return to it. In exchange for which the position itself can develop its advantages, which are essentially those of escapism. Happiness, in this universe, is to play at a kind of domestic retreat: 'psychological' questionnaires, gadgets, do-it-yourself, household appliances, schedules for this and that, this veritable paradise of utensils of *Elle* or *L'Express* exists to glorify the confinement of the couple, their cosy introversion (*introversion pantouflarde*), everything which keeps them busy, infantilizes them, renders them innocent and cuts them off from a broader social responsibility. (24–5 / 48)

The social irresponsibility is that denounced in the Matisse mythology, while the mode of denunciation is similar too: something represented in the popular press as an idyll is overturned by Barthes and revealed as an ideological trap, a hell with minor compensations and distractions.

The alienation of this claustrophobic lifestyle is masked by the illusory contentment summed up in Barthes's favourite negative adjective of this period. This is the *pantouflard* (derived from *la pantoufle*, the French for a carpet slipper), an ideology of domestic cosiness indicating the extent to which class confinement is mediated by the home, and partly explaining why non-working women are such a crucial target for media myths of the time.[20] Even apparently liberated female spaces follow the logic of the gynaeceum: 'a self-contained freedom watched over by the external gaze of men.'[21] This is Barthes's description of the equally illusory spirit of choice fostered by the problem pages of

---

[20] See Claire Duchen, *Women's Rights and Women's Lives in France 1944–1968* (London, Routledge, 1994), especially Chs. 3 and 4 ('House and Home', 64–95, and 'Marriage and Motherhood', 96–127), and Kristin Ross, 'Hygiene and Modernization', Ch. 2 of *Fast Cars, Clean Bodies*, 71–122.
[21] 'Agony Columns', in *ET* 91–4: 97 / *My* 125–8: 127.

women's magazines, while in 'Novels and Children', Barthes's mythology on the representation of women writers in an article in *Elle*, the gynaeceum is defined as the very world of this particular post-war magazine.[22] Clearly, the gynaeceum of *Elle* lacks the slightest utopian potential. Its cookery pages are a good example of the alienating fantasy world that masks economic inequalities, in that its 'dream cookery' is based upon pictures of elaborate dishes for which its readers could never afford the ingredients.[23]

This *introversion pantouflarde* is even foisted upon children through the elaborate nature of modern French toys. In a mythology of February 1955 these are described by Barthes as a microcosm of the modern adult world, a catalogue of all those things—like war and bureaucracy—that adults take for granted. The effect is to turn children into possessive consumers of the world rather than its inventors. Indeed their world is closed off before they have even had a chance to discover it: 'faced with this world of realistic and complicated objects, children can only identify themselves as owners, as users, never as creators; they do not invent the world, they use it: they are offered ready-prepared actions without adventure, without wonder, without joy. They are turned into little stop-at-home householders (*propriétaires pantouflards*) who do not even have to invent the mainsprings of adult causality; these are supplied to them ready-made' (M 53–4 / My 59).

Not surprisingly, even the stars column in *Elle* is completely devoid of an oneiric dimension. Predictions are restricted to a few banal ups and downs in such spheres as 'At Home' and 'Outside the Home', so that the stars actually provide a narrow and realistic description of the routine activities and social environment (family and work colleagues) of the office workers and shop assistants who make up its readership. However, Barthes seems to prefer this to the phoney dream world of the cookery page or to an invitation to identify with an upper-class wedding. Rather than denouncing it as the usual closing down of human potential, he makes the interesting suggestion that this

---

[22] 'The feminine world of *Elle*, a world without men, but entirely constituted by the gaze of man, is very exactly that of the gynaeceum' (M 50–2: 51 / My 56–8: 58).
[23] See 'Ornamental Cookery', in M 78–80 / My 128–30.

dull mirror image has a semi-positive function, which is to 'exorcize reality by naming it'. As such it takes its place amongst 'all those semi-alienating (or semi-liberating) activities, which take it upon themselves to objectify reality, without however going as far as to demystify it'.[24]

Barthes's relentless denunciations of attempts to naturalize the social status quo, though scintillating in their irony and acuity, leave depressingly little space for utopia. In this generally negative context, the rare attribution of a utopian dimension (however ambiguous) becomes doubly interesting. In trying to inject a utopian dimension into material that is, in many ways, imbued with ideology, Barthes strikes me as hesitating, during the period in question, between stressing the metaphysical or the social. In the case of Greek tragedy, he felt able to link these dimensions, and to subsume individual commitments on both terrains into the category of ethics. But in the real world of postwar France, abstractions like 'humanity' and 'the community' break down in the face of economic division and social class, and leftovers of the tragic ethos subsist, at best, in degraded form. Barthes's fascinating mythology 'The Tour de France as Epic' attempts to hold these various terms together, in that the literary epic is the framework for Barthes's analysis of a communal struggle with the natural world.[25] On one level the Tour is a national phenomenon, projected, what is more, on to the literal, physical space of France. At the same time, the physical and moral ordeals of the competitors suggest rather a 'Homeric geography' which touches the very ends of the earth (Mont Ventoux as 'hell') in an encyclopedic survey of human space: 'if we were to refer to some Viconian scheme of History, the Tour would represent in it that ambiguous moment when

---

[24] 'Astrologie', in *My* 165–8: 168, my translation (omitted from both selections in English translation). Barthes makes a similar point in '*The Lady of the Camellias*' (M 103–5 / *My* 179–82), where the heroine's sentimentalized love is described as 'a very particular state of myth, defined by a semi-awareness, or to be more precise, a parasitic awareness. Marguerite is *aware* of her alienation, that is to say she sees reality as an alienation. But she follows up this awareness by a purely servile behaviour: either she plays the part which the masters expect from her, or she tries to reach a *value* which is in fact a part of this same world of the masters. . . . In spite of the grotesqueness of the plot, such a character is not without a certain dramatic richness . . . she would need very little to achieve the status of a Brechtian character, that is an alienated character but a source of criticism' (105 / 181–2).

[25] ET 79–90 / *My* 110–21.

man strongly personifies Nature in order to confront it more readily and to free himself from it more completely' (*ET* 82–3 / *My* 114).

Yet—and here ideology returns—the Tour is saved from too much discomforting freedom by the stable (essential) characters of its epic heroes and villains. It is simply an unpredictable conflict of predictable essences (like characters from the *commedia dell'arte*) transposed into an episodic form built around the successive stages of the Tour. The clarity which emerges from the myth is not the clarity of tragedy since it is purely psychological. This superficial grasp on the world is achieved above all by the gradual merging of the character traits of the leading cyclists with their names and nicknames: 'as if man were, above all, a name which enables him to master events' (79 / 111). Indeed it is this public consumption of their names which elevates a set of private individuals to the 'heroes' proscenium' (80 / 111). With this theatrical metaphor a particular conception of space is once more shown to have negative effects on human relations, for Barthes claims that the true epic site is not the actual battle but the tent, the public threshold where the warrior elaborates his intentions, from which he hurls his insults and challenges or reveals his secrets: 'The Tour de France is thoroughly familiar with this glory of a false private life in which insults and embraces constitute the most important instances of human interaction. . . . Here the accolade is the expression of a magnificent euphoria provoked by the closure and the perfection of the heroic world' (80 / 111–12).

The series of crises that constitute the epic timescale is therefore far removed from the dialectical progression of a single conflict in tragic drama. Yet what intrigues Barthes in the myth of the Tour de France is its bizarre mixture of capitalist competitiveness (the realistic recognition that the point is to win), and the leftovers of an ancient feudal chivalry and a tragic ethos—the sacrifice of a cyclist to his team mates, for instance, or, better still, of Jean Bobet to his brother 'Louison' (the Louis Bobet who, in 1955, was to win the Tour for the third year running).[26] Indeed, the obvious tactical intelligence of Louis

---

[26] For interesting information on the history, economics, and ideology of the Tour de France see Serge Laget, *La Saga du Tour de France* (Paris, Gallimard, 1990).

Bobet produced a monstrous combination of roles which are normally kept separate. An ambiguous mix of the sacrificial ethos and 'the harsh law of success' (86 / 118) made of him a perfect incarnation of the basic ambiguity of the Tour (idealism versus realism), in all an admirable mask for the economic determinations which underlie the whole event. Yet Barthes is less concerned to attack the latter (though he is of course perfectly aware of them) than to celebrate the 'best example ever encountered' of a 'total, hence an ambiguous myth':

> The Tour is at once a myth which expresses something and a myth which projects something; it's realistic and utopian all at the same time. The Tour expresses and liberates the French people through a unique fable in which the traditional impostures (psychology of essences, ethics of combat, supernatural power of the elements, hierarchy of supermen and servants) mingle with forms of a positive interest, with the utopian image of a world which stubbornly seeks reconciliation through the spectacle of a total clarity of relations between man, men, and Nature. (87 / 118–19)[27]

Despite the disguised commercial interests, the Tour remains a fascinating national phenomenon, whereby the epic dimension expresses 'that fragile moment of history in which Man, however clumsy and deceived, nonetheless contemplates through his impure fables a perfect commensurability between himself, the community, and the universe' (88 / 119).

If 'Paris Not Flooded' seems a wholly positive mythology it is perhaps because it is set entirely in the open air.[28] Analysing the media coverage of the floods that affected the suburbs of Paris in January 1955, Barthes finds that, despite all the practical problems for those whose homes were flooded, and despite the threat to the city itself, the press photographs choose to maintain a communal and festive viewpoint on a potential disaster. What is especially striking is Barthes's lack of interest in demystifying this as some piece of ideological trickery. A

---

[27] Barthes is doubtless alluding to Marx's description of communism as 'the *genuine* resolution of the conflict between man and nature and between man and man'. See Karl Marx, *Economic and Philosophic Manuscripts of 1844*, trans. Martin Milligan and Dirk J. Struik, in Karl Marx and Frederick Engels, *Collected Works*, xxxi (London, Lawrence and Wishart, 1975), 229–346: 296.

[28] *ET* 31–4 / *My* 61–4.

sense of euphoria is provoked by the way pictures produce defamiliarizing effects of cars reduced to their roofs, tops of streetlamps sticking out of the water like water lilies, and houses cut up like children's building blocks. Such strange sights renew human perception without threatening it, since they remain basically rational—it is as if viewers were responding to a successful optical illusion rather than a disquieting piece of magic. Thus Barthes claims that pictures of the floods instigate a renewal of the very synaesthesia of the landscape, which crucially overturns the proprietorial world-view of the *pantouflard*:

> Standard points of reference of the land registry, curtains of trees, rows of houses, roads, the riverbed itself, those straight lines and right angles which are so good at constructing the forms of ownership, all this has been wiped out, the angles have been flattened: no more streets, no more riverbanks, no more right directions; a flat substance which is not going anywhere, and which thereby suspends the becoming of man, detaches him from motivations, from the usefulness of places. (*ET* 31–2 / *My* 61–2)

Without the familiar line of the river to orient geographical perception, the contingencies of space lose both their context and their hierarchy (river, road, fields, mounds, bits of wasteland), and the panoramic view loses its major role of organizing space according to its various functions. Human potential is released by this suspension of the traditional appropriations of space: what humanity will become hangs in the balance.

But pictures of the floods also provoke the euphoric pleasure of restructuring space in the imagination: rearranging a village or a part of town, giving it new roads, as if one were literally sorting out a stage set. Paradoxically, the floods have created a more accessible world, which can be manipulated with all the pleasure of children arranging, exploring, or enjoying their toys: 'the houses have become mere cubes, the rails isolated lines, the herds of cattle transported masses, and it is the little boat, the superlative toy of the childhood universe, which has become the possessive mode of this arranged, outspread, and no longer rooted space' (33 / 63). For pictures of families going shopping by rowing boat or—in Barthes's most engaging example—of a priest gliding through the door of his church in a canoe, belong to the most eagerly consumed series of press photos: those of boats going along streets. Finally and crucially, the press coverage fostered a myth of human solidarity. Since the worst flood levels were predictable in advance, people united to struggle against time and nature through strategic dam building (the grand myth of the insurrectionary barricades), and through dramatic evacuations, of which the rescue of 'children, the elderly and the sick' emerged as a special press favourite. If the myth of Noah's Ark is here described by Barthes as an innocent, happy, and positive one, it is because 'humanity takes its distance with regard to the elements, concentrates itself and elaborates the necessary consciousness of its powers, making disaster itself provide evidence that the world can be reordered' (34 / 64).

In 'Paris Not Flooded' Barthes seems to empathize with the mental reorganization of geography which, if only in the imagination, can be exploited to undermine an ethos of ownership. Yet the value of this human control of the natural world remains ambiguous in Barthes's writing, in that—despite its utopian dimension—it is often linked to the progressive and appropriative world-view of a rising bourgeoisie. As such, it simply extends and confirms the ethos it had seemed to undermine. Barthes's 1953 essay on Dutch painting, to which I have already referred, opens in a rather similar fashion to 'Avignon in the Winter', in that it sets its stage by alluding to the completely empty church interiors of the paintings of Saenredam. However, these turn out to be a foil for the 'object-world' of the title of the essay. Barthes's argument is that classical Dutch painting has washed away religion to replace it with man and his empire of things. This inevitable human presence does seem utopian if a threatening physical nature provides the setting. Thus, even bleak and wild winter landscapes bear the human inscription of a bridge, a house, or a man walking along a road, conjuring up as he goes (and thereby maintaining the parallel with the Avignon imagery) the image of a seed in the earth. Crucially, human control of the natural world gives way to the creation of a dwelling: 'Here, then, men inscribe themselves upon space, immediately covering it with familiar gestures, memories, customs, intentions. They establish themselves by means of a path, a mill, a frozen canal, and as soon as they can they arrange their objects in space as in a room, everything in them tends toward *habitation* pure and simple: it is their heaven.' In short, Dutch painting recognizes no authority other than its own stamp on an inert world of matter. It is above all the 'sturdy egg-shaped fullness' of the Dutch canal boat—combining the virtues of the boat and the home—that acts as an emblem of this blissful state of 'an absence of emptiness' (*CE* 4 / 20). But this complacent world-view is problematic in that it is class-bound and, for the time being at least (and despite the *Doelen* gazing out of the picture), leaves a considerable proportion of humanity out in the cold.

In short, the myth of Noah's Ark is not always straightforward. In a later essay, 'The Plates of the Encyclopedia' (1964), Barthes refers to the classifying and proprietorial gesture whereby the Ark, for the eighteenth-century Encyclopedists, is more like a floating goods locker than a ship with an oneiric dimension.[29] It is a similar point to the one that Barthes has already made in the closing lines of 'The *Nautilus* and the Drunken Boat', a mythology on a novel which he describes as 'almost perfect': Jules Verne's *The Mysterious Island*.[30] It is the ending of Barthes's essay that explains its title, for the eponymous Drunken Boat of Rimbaud's poem is introduced as a foil for the self-contained universe of the *Nautilus*, Captain Nemo's famous submarine. Because the Drunken Boat is a ship without a crew, Barthes describes it as no longer a 'possessed and possessive' object, but a 'travelling eye, which comes close to the infinite, it constantly begets departures' (*M* 67 / *My* 82). Only the boat that says 'I', liberated from its concavity, can allow man to pass from a 'psychoanalysis of the cave' to a 'genuine poetics of exploration'.

If the opposition between the two boats was as obvious as this particular contrast suggests, it would be hard to understand the near perfection that Barthes attributes to Verne's novel. His analysis is all the more important in that *The Mysterious Island* is an archetypal utopia: 'Verne has built a kind of self-sufficient cosmogony which has its own categories, its own time, space, fulfilment and even existential principle' (65 / 80). It is on this

---

[29] Roland Barthes, *New Critical Essays* [1972], trans. Richard Howard (Berkeley and Los Angeles, University of California Press, 1990), 23–39: 27 / 89–105: 93.
[30] *M* 65–7: 65 / *My* 80–2: 80.

account that Verne will later be listed with Barthes's other favourite creators of cosmogonies (Balzac, Zola, and Proust), for these fictional spatio-temporal universes constitute a successful utopian form.[31] The ambivalence of Verne's fictional spaces lies in the fact that he is a travel writer, but one whose imagination is based upon an 'exploration of enclosure'. The childlike dimension of Verne does not come from the fact that his novels are adventure stories, but from a shared passion for seclusion in huts, tents, and other refuges: 'to enclose oneself and to settle in, such is the existential dream of childhood and of Verne.' The heroes of *The Mysterious Island* thus come to figure an archetypal man-child who 're-invents the world, fills it, closes it, shuts himself up in it, and crowns this encyclopedic effort with the bourgeois posture of appropriation: slippers, pipe, and fireside, while outside the storm, that is the infinite, rages in vain' (65 / 80). Even the ship (here Captain Nemo's submarine) loses its status as a means of transport and symbol of departure as it, too, comes to figure a dwelling and an emblem of enclosure:

> An inclination for ships always means the joy of perfectly enclosing oneself, of having at hand the greatest possible number of objects, and having at one's disposal an absolutely finite space. To like ships is first and foremost to like a house which is absolutely perfect on account of its unremitting enclosure, and not at all to like vague voyages into the unknown: a ship is something you live in rather than travel in. Sure enough, all of Jules Verne's ships are perfect 'firesides', and the vast distances they cover further increase the bliss of their closure, the perfection of their inner humanity. (66 / 81–2)

An obsession with plenitude fills every last corner of Verne's world with a human presence: 'his work proclaims that nothing can escape man, that the world, even in its most distant part, is like an object in his hand, and that, all told, property is but a dialectical moment in the general enslavement of Nature' (65 / 80). Nor is there any desire to extend the scope of the world, or to acknowledge an infinite dimension. Rather, the world is reduced to a known and enclosed space, in which a

---

[31] See, for example, 'The Ethnological Temptation' (*RB* 84–5 / 87), where Barthes likens the cosmogonies of Racine, Sade, and Michelet, as well as Balzac, Zola, and Proust, to little societies, but above all to an encyclopedia which notes and classifies even the most trivial aspects of the world.

totally self-sufficient humanity could live in comfort, with no other concern than 'to adapt as perfectly as possible to situations whose complexity, in no way metaphysical or even ethical, quite simply springs from some provocative whim of geography' (66 / 81).

Barthes's nostalgia for ethical and metaphysical complexity recalls his positive investment in the stark existential universe of Greek tragedy. Could it be that Barthes shares the contradictory dreams which (just one month later) he will attribute to the myth of Einstein's brain? For the discourse and representations surrounding Einstein's supposed genius—derived by Barthes from the obituary articles which followed Einstein's death in 1955—mythically reconcile 'the infinite power of man over nature with the "inevitablity" (*fatalité*) of a sacred order that man cannot yet do without'.[32] In 'The *Nautilus* and the Drunken Boat' the final allusion to Rimbaud (placed in the same position as the reference, in the Einstein mythology, to a human need for the sacred) seems to be Barthes's own attempt to reinject a metaphysical element into a fictional cosmogony where human self-sufficiency has actually gone too far.

Barthes is clearly being pulled in different directions in the mid-1950s, so that here he seems to resist the appeal of the 'existential principle' (65 / 80) exemplified in Verne's novel by Granite House and the *Nautilus*. However, just two years later, a very similar psychology and set of values is given a completely positive reading in 'The Cathedral of Novels', a wonderful essay on Victor Hugo's *Notre-Dame of Paris*.[33] Barthes describes Hugo's novel as a 'voluptuous book' precisely because it is, in every sense, 'the book of enclosure'. What is more, the cathedral seems like a whole world not because of its size but because it is so self-enclosed:

Frolo and Quasimodo reign over a place which is finite, complete, hermetic (this word has a happy ambiguity), which is entirely self-sufficient, materially and spiritually. It is a place which incarnates that oh so ancient privilege of every autarchy, a supernatural state of independence and warmth, which is the ultimate object of all great imaginations: the childish, the poetic, the neurotic.

[32] 'The Brain of Einstein', in *M* 68–70: 70 / *My* 91–3: 93.
[33] 'La Cathédrale des romans', *Bulletin de la Guilde du Livre* (Mar. 1957), in *OC* i. 725–7, quotations from 725–6.

safe in the storm

But if the 'happy nature' of a poetic refuge is to be fully experienced, Barthes claims that it must be juxtaposed with an open space, and defined in relation to it: 'the ship with the ocean, the cabin with the forest, Notre Dame with Paris'. Moreover, Hugo has not simply brought together two spaces (one enclosed, one open) but rather a height and an expanse. In the same way (Barthes now suddenly announces) Jules Verne made many a grown-up dream 'by conjugating depth and height in the retreat in which Cyrus Smith and his companions shut themselves away'. This intersection of the enclosed space with height—retrospectively noticed in *The Mysterious Island*—is the 'stroke of genius' which alters the value of the microcosmic fictional world: 'substituting for the secular reverie of the lair and the cave, in a word of depth, the image of the aerial terrace, of the hanging garden (*jardin suspendu*)'. But what exactly is suspended or left hanging in *Notre-Dame of Paris*, in that 'outside, far from the profound meaning of this place, lies the agitated, grotesque and inessential civil world: the king, the law, thieves'? Clearly, Barthes cannot intend to identify here a dismissal of the outside world of the sort he might elsewhere describe as socially irresponsible. The imagery is familiar (egg-like plenitude etc.) but the evaluation seems to be quite different: 'As refuge, Notre-Dame incarnates all the happiness of a world which is finally complete, full in the manner of an egg, and with an interior life which, entirely self-sufficient, suspends and denies everything that surrounds it: time, space, hatred, political becoming (*devenir*) of the world.' This, surely, is a utopian overturning of a world of negative social and cosmic relationships—an overturning which is imaginary and certainly neurotic, but whose goal is a cosmogony free of alienation.

sc

2
Structuralism Utopian and Scientific

> Scholasticism, brought down from its ancient theological heaven and applied to reality, becomes progressive once again.[1]

BARTHES'S model of myth as a two-tier sign system offers a powerful and self-confident analysis of the way in which alienating mystifications achieve their purpose. 'Myth Today', therefore, might be considered an optimistic declaration of the political potential of Saussurean semiology: 'whatever its mistakes, mythology is certain to participate in the making of the world.' Indeed the ethical impulse is explicitly utopian: 'founded on a responsible idea of language, mythology thereby postulates the freedom of the latter. It is certain that in this sense mythology *harmonizes* with the world, not as it is, but as it wants to create itself.' To convey this notion of a critical accord with the world Barthes quotes one of his favourite Brechtian concepts, the *Einverstandnis* which embraces the two senses of 'intelligence': 'at once an understanding of reality and a complicity with it' (M 156 / My 244).

Yet the remainder of the concluding section of 'Myth Today' ('Necessity and limits of mythology') is a strangely pessimistic confession of the contradictions—'a few difficulties in feeling, if not in method'—in which Barthes, as mythologist, finds himself caught up. First, he is excluded from political action on the world by the fact that he merely speaks about it, a metalinguistic participation which is at best vicarious. Second, Barthes worries about cutting himself off from the community of myth-consumers, which may well be quite simply *the* community: 'Any myth with some degree of generality is in fact ambiguous,

---

[1] Roland Barthes, 'The Two Salons', first published in *Les Lettres nouvelles* (Nov. 1959), ET 137–40: 140 / OC i. 828–9: 829.

because it represents the very humanity of those who, having nothing, have borrowed it. To decipher the Tour de France or "good French wine" is to cut oneself off from those who, having nothing, have borrowed it' (157 / 245). Thus the mythologist's honesty is his only authentic link with the human beings on whose behalf he writes—his 'sociality' is merely theoretical, and his connection with the world is of a 'sarcastic order'. If this relationship is openly assumed at the end of the brief preface to *Mythologies* (as unavoidable at that moment of history), it is, presumably, an uncomfortable position to occupy: 'what I claim is to live to the full the contradiction of my time, which may well make of sarcasm the condition of truth' (12 / 10).[2]

Worse, Barthes is personally excluded from the very future in the name of which he pursues his Sisyphean task of demystifying the present. In the passage which I have already quoted in my introduction, he suggests that utopia is an impossible luxury for the mythologist who, less privileged even than Moses, cannot see the Promised Land: 'tomorrow's positivity is entirely hidden by today's negativity ... nothing protrudes' (157 / 246). Indeed concrete formulations cannot be part of his task since 'tomorrow's truths' will hardly be the exact opposite of 'today's lies', and since history 'unveils, while making itself, unimaginable solutions, unforeseeable syntheses'. Mythological destruction is basically an act of blind faith in a radically different future: 'this subjective grasp of history in which the potent seed of the future *is nothing but* the most profound apocalypse of the present.' For some people there is, then, 'a subjective, dark night of history where the future becomes an essence, the essential destruction of the past' (158 / 246).

Despite the extravagant and apocalyptic tone here, we should bear in mind the frequency with which Barthes links history

---

[2] In an early, uncollected mythology on the myth of Rimbaud that has been omitted from the *Œuvres complètes*, Barthes conceptualizes this relationship in a different but equally interesting way: 'When I learn of some new Martian mystification, or of the (future) marriage of Marlon Brando, I can see perfectly well that I must denounce it; but such denunciation is basically explanation, and I find myself tied to my period more closely than ever, committed to it in a dialectical relationship that is truly amorous. For in so far as all myth-making is the palpable surface of human alienation, it is humanity that I find in all myths: I hate this alienation, and yet I can see that for the time being this is the only place to find my fellow human beings.' See 'Phénomène ou mythe', *Lettres Nouvelles* (Dec. 1954), 951–3: 952–3.

with the present moment in time. It is logical, then, that the mythologist's fourth exclusion should be from contemporary everyday reality, and I believe that this worries Barthes far more than his exclusion from the entirely unpredictable *future* of humanity. If utopia is to find itself a place in Barthes's thinking, it must negotiate with ideology on the terrain of the present. Hence the crucial importance of his relationship with reality. Barthes seems to believe himself to be condemned to deal with 'the goodness of wine' (for example) as myth, to be unable to transcend this sober role in order to communicate the goodness of wine as subjectively and communally experienced. If he has slipped into the latter role it is somewhat deceitfully, as he apologetically suggests in a footnote: 'finding it painful constantly to work on the evaporation of reality, I have started to make it excessively dense, and to discover in it a surprising compactness that I have savoured with delight, and I have given a few examples of a "psychoanalysis of substances" applied to some mythical objects' (158 / 247). If the mythologist performs his appointed role and restricts himself to myths, 'he constantly runs the risk of causing the reality which he purports to protect, to disappear':

> There is as yet only one possible choice, and this choice can bear only on two equally extreme methods: either to posit a reality which is entirely permeable to history, and ideologize; or, conversely, to posit a reality which is *ultimately* impenetrable, irreducible, and in this case, poeticize. In a word, I do not yet see a synthesis between ideology and poetry (by poetry I understand, in a very general way, the search for the inalienable meaning of things). (158–9 / 246–7)

Forced to a choice, Barthes would appear to opt for 'ideologizing', with an element of 'poeticizing' (a guilty source of delight) smuggled in by stealth. When Barthes transgresses his self-imposed exclusions in this way, thickening the myth by a degree of recreation instead of merely taking it apart, a sort of synthesis is achieved at the level of his writing. But the result is in large measure a repetition of the turnstile effect that Barthes identifies so acutely as crucial to the general consumption of myths.[3] The reality which is grasped by this ambivalent

---

[3] See 'Myth Today', (*M* 123 / *My* 209).

mythologist—torn as he is between liberating the object but destroying it, or respecting its mystified density—is necessarily unstable. Our inability to get beyond this is presented by Barthes as the very measure of our present alienation, 'blinded and fascinated' as we are by the split in the social world: 'and yet, this is what we must seek: a reconciliation between reality and men, between description and explanation, between object and knowledge' (159 / 247).[4]

No theorist of utopia can bypass the relationship between ideology and utopia, or the intersection of both with reality. Of the difficulties listed by Barthes, this, I believe, is the one which grounds the others. In the next chapter, I shall explore the important theoretical solutions that Barthes will find in the writing practices of Charles Fourier, archetypal utopian socialist. However, I shall suggest that aspects of Barthes's analysis of Fourier, first published in 1970, are simply rationalizations and clarifications of his own engagement with reality in his structuralist years. Would-be radical commentators variously deplore Barthes's desertion of the Marxist rhetoric of *Mythologies* for the formal flights of High Structuralism.[5] Yet Barthes's particular conception of structuralism is far removed from some inhuman scientificity, so much so, I shall argue, that it steers him towards—rather than away from—the reconciliation between knowledge and the world to which he pessimistically aspires at the end of 'Myth Today'. Misrepresentations of Barthes's structuralism make the mistake of assuming that scientificity and abstraction are necessarily inhuman.

---

[4] Barthes writes of this problem in similar terms when discussing the 'ethical ambiguity of fashion'. If a sign system is to 'open itself to the world', it will necessarily enter the realm of alienation, if it is to understand the world it must take its distance from it—to act on the world and to reflect upon it seem to be activities profoundly opposed to each other. See Roland Barthes, *The Fashion System* [1967], trans. Matthew Ward and Richard Howard (London, Jonathan Cape, 1985), 290 / 289.

[5] 'The turn to the New Novel and Structuralism is a retreat from vulgarity, a situating of the activity of critique under the auspices of scientific rigor rather than those of history, an identification with the engineer rather than the novelist or historian' (Kristin Ross, *Fast Cars, Clean Bodies*, 183–4). In *The Poverty of Structuralism: Literature and Structuralist Theory* (London, Longman, 1991), Leonard Jackson describes structuralism as a science marked by two 'negative movements', the first the 'drive towards systematicity', the second the 'withdrawal from politics' (142–3).

Two late mythologies, both dating from 1959, seek to demonstrate the utopian potential of an abstract, structuralist perception of space. 'Buffet Finishes off New York' is a review of an exhibition of Bernard Buffet's paintings of New York.[6] In fact it is Barthes himself who 'finishes off Buffet' in a vigorous counter-attack upon what he persuasively analyses as a visual dystopia. His method is completely to reverse Buffet's conception of the spatial relations pertaining between New York and its inhabitants. Buffet, according to Barthes, has created a 'petrified infantile necropolis looming up out of an "abstract" age (but not, alas! out of an abstract art)'. Indeed Buffet has 'figured' New York the better to get rid of it, and has then 'geometrized' it the better to depopulate it: 'a city of geometric heights, a petrified desert of grids and lattices, an inferno of greenish abstraction under a flat sky, a real Metropolis from which man is absent by his very accumulation.' Yet for Barthes, newly returned to Paris from an invigorating encounter with New York, 'one of the lessons of this marvellous city is that abstraction is alive', so that only a supposedly 'sterile' abstract painter could do justice to the living meaning of the planes and the lines. One of the strategies attributed to Buffet for removing the life from New York is shared with the bourgeois theatre producers so derided by Barthes. It is to 'flatten the landscape', to foreground the skyscraper as individual object by painting the city face-on. Even where this represents an attempt to convey the width of this 'splendidly *set*' city, it is always height which wins out, so that a wide-angled view simply emphasizes the succession of jagged skyscrapers, while a bridge in the foreground sets off their aggressive power: 'Instead of altitude being absorbed in the foreground mass (for New York is in fact a deep city, not a high one), Buffet bestows on this altitude an absurd solitude: he paints the skyscrapers as if they were empty cathedrals.' Worst of all (the *coup de grâce* of the title), he even empties the streets of their people. This indeed is the worst thing he could do, since for Barthes the peopled streets are basic to the meaning of New York: 'it is not up, towards the sky, that you

---

[6] Roland Barthes, 'Buffet Finishes off New York', first published in *Arts* (11–17 Feb. 1959) as 'New York, Buffet et la hauteur', *ET* 149–52 / *OC* i. 781–3, quotations easily locatable.

STRUCTURALISM 49

must look at New York, rather you should look down, towards men and merchandise: by an admirable static paradox, the skyscraper establishes the block, the block creates the street, the street offers itself to man.'

Buffet's emphasis on the height of New York therefore gives credence to an old myth that geometry kills man. Yet in Barthes's counter-reading the whole point of New York's geometry is that 'each individual should be *poetically* the owner of the capital of the world':

> Urbanism itself, this checkerboard of nameless streets, is the price that has to be paid in order that the streets be useful and no longer picturesque, in order that men and objects circulate, adapt themselves to the distances, rule effectively over this enormous urban nature: the biggest city in the world (with Tokyo) is also the one we possess in an afternoon, by the most exciting of operations, since here *to possess* is *to understand*: New York exposes itself to intellection, and our familiarity with it comes very quickly.

This, according to Barthes, is the purpose of the regularly distanced and numbered streets, not to make the city into a vast machine and human beings into automata, 'as we are repeatedly and stupidly told by those for whom tortuosity and dirt are the gauges of spirituality'. Buffet is accused, finally, of diverting history into metaphysics, of blaming technology rather than the profit motive for the ills of America, for Buffet's 'anti-city' would have us believe that the modern is sinister, that we are bored when we have a good standard of living, that money does not buy happiness, and that we are distinctly happier in Belleville than Manhattan. The sheer euphoria of Barthes's engagement with such a vast and exuberant space—'this fabulous metropolis', the 'most prodigious city in the world'—seems to have removed Barthes's nostalgia for a metaphysical dimension, with metaphysics written off, in this case, as an alibi for capitalism. Since material space (with its distances and directions) can be mastered by the mind, then this vast space of twelve million people becomes available for a purely human manipulation: 'this fabulous reservoir, this world emporium in which all goods exist except the metaphysical variety.'

---

⁷ Barthes derides 'an exoticism which confirms the French in the excellence of their own habitat'. For more detailed discussion of this theme see Ch. 4.

My second example, 'The Two Salons', is an extraordinary celebration of the interplay between space, structure, and a utopian building of the world. The first *salon* of the title is the Paris Motor Show, which in 1955 had provided the setting for a spectacular dream object, the new Citroën DS 19.[8] It now pales into insignificance beside the enthralling spectacle of the Office Equipment Show. The Ancient Egyptians, Barthes reminds us, used to inscribe their temples within a symbolic space corresponding to the figure of the human body. The Office Equipment Show inscribes itself rather upon the space of the human brain. This observation will take Barthes far beyond a simple reversal of the familiar proposition that machines mechanize human beings. For Barthes gradually builds up an over-the-top justification of a structuralism of the manically classificatory variety.

If the reader is carried along this is doubtless on account of the panache with which Barthes conjures up his parallel between the layout of the exhibition and the different tasks carried out by the different parts of the brain: 'here the functions of memory (filing systems), there those of written language (typewriters) or of spoken language (dictaphones), and over there the motor functions (classification and transfer of orders)' (*ET* 137 / *OC* i. 828).[9] While the cars at the Grand Palais are simply competitive variations of the same object, the office items both differ from and complement each other: 'they participate in an economy of the mind.' The Office Equipment Show should therefore be seen as 'a little cosmography, the representation of a structure', as 'a whole topological ensemble of gestures and information, of which the Show itself, in its material enclosure, from the dictaphone department to that of the retrieval systems, represents the giant memory'. The myth of this structured world is *organization*: 'articles are sold, but what we look at is a complex substance, consisting of objects, gestures, and time, and this substance is manipulated, distributed in a rational way.' The Office Equipment Show is therefore deemed far more avant-garde than the Motor Show with its technological feats and surprise gadgets, for it represents 'that *elegant* effort (in the mathematical sense of the adjective) of human intelligence *to*

---

[8] See Barthes's mythology 'The New Citroën', in *M* 88–90 / *My* 150–2.
[9] *ET* 137–40: 137 / *OC* i. 828–9: 828, other quotations are easily locatable.

begin reality over again according to the order of men and not according to the order of things'. So that whereas Western science (from alchemy to atomic physics) has traditionally been obsessed with the transmutation of matter from one substance to another, Barthes detects here the emergence of a new myth—a radical shift to the notion that to classify the universe is to appropriate it through an entirely material, human activity: 'to distinguish, to compare, to cite, to reject, these are today *universal* operations, no longer destined, as they were for centuries, to tranquilize the mind, to feed it reassuring alibis, but to modify reality in terms of technology.' Of course society, with its anti-intellectual prejudices, still regards all forms of analysis with suspicion, yet it is precisely 'the intellectual act *par excellence*, the *distinguo*', which marks out an entirely new conception of research, from computers to the planning of the technocrats. I doubt if anyone has ever produced a more flamboyant justification for structuralism than Barthes's climactic final flourish: 'scholasticism, brought down from its ancient theological heaven and applied to reality, becomes progressive once again.'

Thus, this little-known but extremely engaging mythology captures the euphoric spirit of an excited espousal of structuralism and, albeit ironically, goes some way to explaining its significance. In a well-known interview with *Tel Quel* published in 1971, Barthes summed up his structuralist years with an infamous phrase which has often been read as a repudiation: 'I indulged in a (euphoric) dream of scientificity.'[10] Barthes is asked whether his failure to produce a book between 1957 and 1963 was linked to a methodological difficulty. He replies by reminding his interviewer that he published no less than seventy articles in that period, and that the motivation was, more accurately, a methodological intoxication. His discovery of Saussure in 1956 acted as the touchstone of a 'sense of *wonder* when faced with the almost magical potential of a semiological analysis which could be applied to objects of very different sorts. . . . In other words, I lived with the exhilaration of having in front of me an enormous programme of work of which the method was new and positively inspiring.' The point could not

---

[10] Roland Barthes, 'Réponses' [1971], OC ii. 1307–24: 1314.

be more forcefully made: the period in question had represented 'years of methodological enchantment, of enchantment with my work'.[11]

In another well-known formulation, Barthes had earlier declared that the object of structuralism was *homo significans*, not 'man endowed with meanings but man as maker of meanings' (how meaning is possible, at what cost and by what means).[12] The 'structuralist activity' which he defends in 1963 is 'responsible' because historical, and historical because the forms which it analyses are themselves part of the world: 'Structuralism does not withdraw history from the world: it seeks to link to history not only certain contents (this has been done a thousand times) but also certain forms, not only what is material but also what is intelligible' (CE 219 / 219). Although the title of the essay might lead one to expect some step-by-step account of the structuralist method, Barthes seems more interested in explaining its point. The aim of model building is not just to create a copy of something but, in explaining how that something works, to make it intelligible:

Structural man takes the real, decomposes it, then recomposes it; this appears to be little enough (which makes some say that the structuralist enterprise is 'meaningless', 'uninteresting', 'useless', etc.). Yet, from another point of view, this 'little enough' is decisive. For between the two objects, or between the two stages of structuralist activity, there occurs something *new*, and what is new is nothing less than the generally intelligible: the simulacrum is intellect added to the object, and this addition has an anthropological value, in that it is made up of man himself, his history, his situation, his freedom, and the very resistance which nature offers to his mind. (215 / 214–15)

Structuralism thus conceived does not, as Barthes seemed to fear at the end of 'Myth Today', destroy its object by speaking of it analytically. Rather, it puts the object together again, having inserted into it a new dimension of intelligibility. What is now

---

[11] Barthes's 'replies' to Thibaudeau are extracts from the 'Archives du XXᵉ siècle' interviews filmed in 1970 and 1971, and broadcast on French television in 1988 (*Océaniques*, FR3). These last comments are not included in the published text.
[12] See Roland Barthes, 'The Structuralist Activity' [1963], CE 213–20: 218 / 213–20: 218 (page numbers coincidentally identical).

visible in the object may well be social alienation, but it is also human history and its aspiration to freedom.

This injection of intelligibility into the real world is discussed in Barthes's 1964 preface, briefly mentioned in the last chapter, to an edition of Diderot and d'Alembert's eighteenth-century *Encyclopedia*.[13] Barthes's analysis focuses upon the relationship between the two halves of the two-tier illustrative plates. Typically, the top half of the plate depicts a scene (say a bakery, or an upholsterer's workshop) in a representational mode, while the bottom half is a technical diagram breaking down into figures the tools and machines which can be seen in operation in the picture: 'first of all the illustration analyses and enumerates the scattered elements of the object or the operation in question, throwing them as it were on to a table under the reader's eyes; then it recomposes them, even attaching to them finally the density of the scene, that is of life' (NCE 33 / DZN 99). What Barthes likes is the way these divided plates invite a double reading, depending on whether one moves from the scene to its analysis (the intelligible), or from the explanation of parts to their conjunction in the picture (the lived experience of the *vécu*):

We see the ambiguity of the didacticism of the *Encyclopedia*: very strong in the lower (paradigmatic) part of the plate, it is diluted at its syntagmatic level, when it is merged again (though without really being lost) with what can only be called the novelistic truth of all human action. At its demonstrative level, the encyclopedic plate constitutes a *radical language*, consisting of pure concepts, with neither word-tools nor syntax; at the upper level, this radical language becomes a human language, it willingly loses in intelligibility what it gains in lived experience. (31 / 97–8)

But this movement will, of course, be repeated in both directions, so that lived experience will be constantly renourished by intelligibility. In fact most of the objects from the lower half of the plate are scattered in the upper picture like signs demanding to be deciphered, so that the picture is a representation of real life which at the same time has the density of a rebus.

A related example can be found in Barthes's analysis of the

---

[13] Roland Barthes, 'The Plates of the Encyclopedia' [1964], in NCE 23–39 / DZN 89–105.

experience of looking at the view of Paris from the Eiffel Tower.[14] Here, reality is no longer mediated by printed diagrams and mimetic illustrations. Rather, structuralism goes straight into action on the material reality of Paris, so that sensation is transcended by the bird's-eye view and the city is transformed into a structure. In an engaging comparison with Molière's Monsieur Jourdain (who discovers to his delight that he speaks in prose), Barthes explains that every visitor to the Eiffel Tower is an unknowing structuralist who transforms the city lying below into a rebus:

> What, in fact, is a panorama? An image we attempt to decipher, in which we try to recognize known sites, to identify landmarks. Take some view of Paris seen from the Eiffel Tower; here you make out the hill sloping down from the Chaillot, there the Bois de Boulogne; but where is the Arc de Triomphe? You can't see it, and this absence compels you to inspect the view once again, to look for this point which is missing in your structure; your knowledge (the knowledge you may have of Parisian topography) struggles with your perception, and, in a sense, that is what intelligence is: to *reconstitute*, to make memory and sensation cooperate so as to produce a simulacrum of Paris, of which the elements are in front of you, real, ancestral, but nonetheless disoriented by the total space in which they are given to you, for this space was unknown to you. (*ET* 10 / *OC* i. 1387)

Barthes makes his point about this active panoramic vision with reference to two works in which 'the (perhaps very old) fantasy of a panoramic vision received the guarantee of a major poetic writing'. These are the chapter of Hugo's *Notre-Dame of Paris* entitled 'A Bird's-Eye View of Paris', and Michelet's historical *Tableau of France*. What Barthes admires about 'these two great inclusive visions' is the way they promote intellectual understanding, 'for the bird's-eye view, which each visitor to the Tower can assume in an instant as their own, gives us the world to *read* and not only to perceive' (9 / 1386–7). Barthes suggests that a new visual sensibility is at stake here. Rather than thrusting the reader into the midst of sensation (his example is

---

[14] Roland Barthes, 'The Eiffel Tower' [1964], in *ET* 3–17. This translated extract (also included in *A Barthes Reader*, ed. Susan Sontag) is the first half of Barthes's essay only. For the full text see *OC* i. 1379–400, originally published as *La Tour Eiffel*, text by Roland Barthes, photographs by André Martin (Paris, Delpire, 1964).

Rousseau's 'promenades'), these Romantic writers seem to have anticipated both 'the construction of the Tower and the birth of aviation', so that their bird's-eye views allow the reader to 'transcend sensation and see things *in their structure*'. Yet, crucially, this does not entail an inhuman, ahistorical abstraction, since the two perceptions merge, and 'intelligible' objects keep their materiality. Barthes is dealing with a category which he calls 'concrete abstraction'; indeed he claims that the very meaning of the word structure is 'a corpus of intelligible forms'.

The earliest example of the panorama as a vehicle of historical knowledge occurs in Barthes's essay 'Michelet, History, and Death', published in *Esprit* in 1951 and largely subsumed into the 1954 *Michelet*.[15] These essays long pre-date Barthes's first official foray into Saussurean semiology, which would normally be considered the beginning of his structuralist period.[16] As such, they reveal the extent to which, ever eager to conceptualize space, Barthes was always sensitive to what he would later call (in 'The Structuralist Activity') both a structuralist imagination and a structuralist imaginary:

> We can in fact suppose that there exist certain writers, painters, and musicians in whose eyes a certain *practice* of structure (and no longer merely its conceptualization (*sa pensée*)) represents a distinctive experience, and that both analysts and creators should be placed under the common sign of what we might call *structural man*, defined not by his ideas or his languages, but by his imagination, or, better still, by his *imaginary*—by the way, that is to say, in which he mentally experiences structure. (CE 214 / 214)

If the panoramic view from Notre-Dame or the Eiffel Tower becomes a metaphor of structure, Michelet's panoramas are in themselves metaphorical. In the section of *Michelet* entitled 'Michelet the walker', Barthes focuses upon two alternating modes of history writing: 'either the discomfort of plodding

---

[15] Roland Barthes, 'Michelet, l'Histoire et la Mort', *Esprit* (Apr. 1951) (*OC* i. 91–102); Roland Barthes, *Michelet* [1954], trans. Richard Howard (Oxford, Blackwell, 1987).

[16] See Barthes's preface to the 1970 (Points) edition of *Mythologies*, in which he refers to his discovery of Saussure and to having produced his first attempt at semiological analysis in 'Myth Today' (*M* 9 / *My* 7). The year 1956 is similarly given as the date of Barthes's first reading of Saussure in 'The Semiological Adventure' [1974] (*SC* 3–8: 4–5 / 9–14: 10–11).

along, or the euphoria of the panoramic view' (*Mi* 22 / 20). In both history is conceived as a geographical space, held together by the *body* of the historian who journeys through it or pauses to contemplate it. The greater proportion of Michelet's texts are taken up with the negative, uphill struggle of 'Michelet the walker' or 'Michelet the swimmer': periods of discomfort, lethargy, and incomprehension. The historian flounders in a thankless historical substance with its petty and colourless motivations, suffocating in a history which is basically too close to him. But if narrative is a 'calvary' of 'impatience and anguish', the *tableau* is both celebration and a well-earned rest: 'Narrative history is a Passion, Michelet suffers, toils, hopes, he makes his way towards a station where everything will at last be comprehensible from a static vantage point' (OC i. 92). The moment of overview (*survol*) leaves him in possession of History rather than merely travelling through it. History is transformed from movement to meaningful spectacle ('objects refind that state of simultaneous existence which only an operation related to visual contemplation can restore to them'), and the historian passes into an active, creative mode: 'Michelet's *tableaux* thus more or less fulfil the role of the ancient cosmogonies: in both cases, the earth and the past are perceived as a creation; provided with a spatial order, they become objects under the gaze or in the hands of an operator.'

Whereas the attempt to 'recount Louis XI' is an alienating experience (passive, mutilating, and uncomprehending), the *tableau* (fifteenth-century Flanders, for example), like many a structuralist experience of space in Barthes's writing, equals a liberation: 'a reconciliation which reveals to the historian the profound ubiquity of causes and effects, of bodies, ideas and actions.' In this 'spatialized time' historical events lose their solitude by being fitted into a pattern that links them with their past and with their *future*, which in Michelet's conceptualization of French history is the French Revolution. This human mastery of time, space, and human events is euphoric, especially when the panoramic view is sudden and revelatory. Michelet and his reader pass, for a while at least, from labour to festive repose. It is because he has filled out the material past ('introduced into the past the living order of matter' (93)) that Michelet as historian recovers his serenity—liberation, like alienation, passes through his body, as tiredness and ignorance are replaced with 'rest, new strength, and vision' (*Mi* 22 / 21).

This physically liberating alliance of the mind and the body will be recreated in 'The Eiffel Tower', as Barthes himself retrospectively suggests in 1975: 'Even in his structuralist phase, when the essential task was to describe human *intelligibility*, he always associated intellectual activity with a physical delight: the panoramic view, for example—what one sees from the Eiffel Tower—is an object both analytical and happy (*intellectif et heureux*): it liberates the body even as it gives it the illusion of "comprehending" the field of its vision' (*RB* 103 / 107). This is a very different subjective experience from the overdetermined loneliness of the mythologist at the end of 'Myth Today'. Taking the Eiffel Tower itself as the subject and creator of the panoramic view, it is clear that the Tower projects knowledge into its object (Paris) without destroying it, and thereby figures the reconciliation between human understanding and reality to which Barthes aspires. He describes the Tower as a friendly presence, a discreet witness watching over Paris, a link for all those bound together by the sight of it. Nothing, then, could be less like the repressive, all-seeing panopticon.[17] As a benevolent mediator of the human space of Paris, Barthes's Eiffel Tower is undoubtedly a metaphorical structuralist and a vehicle of utopia.

Barthes's reading of Paris as a material, historical, and socially significant spatial structure to some extent imitates that of Hugo's chapter on the bird's-eye view of Paris. The specific allusion suggests that this is done self-consciously. In the 1957 essay on Hugo's novel, to which I have already referred in my first chapter, Barthes called the description of Paris a 'model of intelligent geography'.[18] In 1964 Barthes stresses too the temporal dimension whereby to perceive Paris from above is unavoidably 'to imagine a history' (*ET* 11 / *OC* i. 1388). Through his sustained, detailed, and lively meditation on the

---

[17] For Michel Foucault's influential discussion of Jeremy Bentham's *Panopticon*, see *Discipline and Punish: The Birth of the Prison* [1975], trans. Alan Sheridan (Harmondsworth, Penguin, 1982), especially 200–9. For a discussion of the ideology and aesthetics of some nineteenth-century panoramic views of Paris, see Christopher Prendergast, 'The High View: Three Cityscapes', Ch. 3 of *Paris and the Nineteenth Century* (Oxford, Blackwell, 1992), 46–73.

[18] Roland Barthes, 'La Cathédrale des romans' [1957], *OC* i. 725–7.

view from one of the towers of Notre-Dame, Hugo creates a palimpsest from the architecture and history of Paris, moving to and fro through the centuries from the Roman foundation of Paris to the nineteenth-century city. Barthes's Eiffel Tower, transformed into a living vehicle of vision, conceptualizes a social geography—three major zones of pleasure, commerce, and learning, two zones of habitation, a gradual development towards the west—just as duration (four extensive historical periods) becomes panoramic.

But a significant difference emerges. Hugo is nostalgic for the original, unadulterated architecture and decoration of the medieval cathedral, and much of the contemporary nineteenth-century view he describes is subjected to fiercely ironic aesthetic criticism. There is little doubt what he would have thought of the Eiffel Tower, had he lived the three or four extra years that would have been necessary for him to see it. In that Barthes centres his reading of Paris on the view from the Eiffel Tower rather than from Notre-Dame, he crucially reverses the critical and backward-looking thrust of Hugo's long meditation. For it turns out to be a part of the utopian function of the Tower to negate Notre-Dame, just as the Tower also negates the mythical view of Paris—'from the Cluny Baths to the Sacré Cœur'—as symbol of the past:

> In contrast to this forest of old-fashioned symbols (steeples, domes, arches) the Tower rises up like a deliberate rupture which aims to undo the sacred weight of past time, to set against the fascinating stickiness of history (no matter how rich) the freedom of a new age; everything about the Tower marked it out for this symbolically subversive role: the boldness of the conception, the novelty of the material from which it was built, the unaesthetic form, the functional gratuitousness. One could say that it has conquered its position as symbol of Paris against the city of Paris itself (its old stones, the density of its history); it has tamed the ancient symbols, just as physically it has risen above their domes and their pointed spires. In a word, it could only accede fully to its status as symbol of Paris once it was able to remove the obstacle of its past, thereby making itself into the symbol of modernity. (OC i. 1396–7)

Thus, if Notre-Dame is a symbol of a historical past, the Eiffel Tower is a beacon of a historical future which Barthes wishes, as always, to read in the present.

The Eiffel Tower inspires the most important and sustained utopian essay of Barthes's structuralist period, both in content and in tone. Barthes deals quickly enough with the possible dystopian perception of the Eiffel Tower expressed by Maupassant and other artists in an angry petition of 1887—a monstrous and useless eyesore straight from the baroque and commercial imagination of an engineer, bound to dishonour and disfigure Paris for ever more. For Barthes, its very uselessness is essential to its utopian potential. Despite Eiffel's best functional alibis (aerodynamic measurements, physiology of the climber, etc.), men return the Tower to him 'in the form of a great baroque dream which quite naturally touches on the borders of the irrational' (ET 6 / I 1385). The Eiffel Tower is basically a degree zero monument, an empty signifier which attracts secondary meanings like a lightning conductor—meanings extracted by human beings 'from their knowledge, their dreams, their history' (5 / 1384).

Like Hugo's Notre-Dame and the other cosmogonies so often referred to by Barthes, the Eiffel Tower 'takes on finally the essential function of all the great human places: autarchy; the Tower can live on itself ... one can feel cut off from the world and yet the owner of a world' (17 / 1391). Barthes's favourite example of the ship is quoted once again. In these self-sufficient worlds, one can dream, eat, observe, understand, experience amazement, and even buy things. Indeed Barthes is surprisingly sympathetic to the everyday life of postcard stalls and so on which has sprung up around the pillars and on the platforms of the Tower. Commerce, he claims, has a space-taming function, and since the Eiffel Tower is not a sacred monument, there is no taboo on the establishment of these reassuring activities.

If the values of comfort and ownership seem to revert here to the ideology of the *pantouflard* discussed in the last chapter, the metaphorical sequence that follows subsumes it into a higher purpose. The iron from which the Tower is constructed connotes all the Balzacian and Faustian passion of the nineteenth century (fire, energy, lightness, and work), its victory over weight prefigures twentieth-century aviation, and it is once more the human domination of physical geography that is suggested by the association of iron with bridges, aqueducts, and canals. Moreover the Eiffel Tower, exemplary as a feat of successful planning and safe execution, is consumed by its visitors and admirers at the level of its construction. At this point, having already justified the gift shops which one might have expected him to demolish with sarcasm, Barthes enters into a somewhat delirious celebration of the ubiquitous souvenir ornaments and models. The endless simulation of the Eiffel Tower is a properly 'structuralist' notion which conjures up the idea of the designer's working model (*OC* i. 1395). This is the *maquette* which will be favourably compared, in *Roland Barthes by Roland Barthes*, with the 'plan', presumably for its utopian dimension.[19] Each purchaser of knick-knacks relives by procuration 'the creative adventure of the Tower', since the miniature Tower becomes the model of the *future* Tower, still to be built. The lucky owner becomes a creative engineer, a conqueror of matter, who can vary at will the material out of which the Tower is to be made—copper, matchsticks, seashells—in short, an 'all-embracing fantasy of creation' (*une fantaisie panique*),[20] since there is no end to what can be conceived and accomplished on the basis of this very simple notion: the Eiffel Tower. Indeed a court case having established that there is no copyright on reproductions, even the law has consecrated this mad proliferation of Eiffel Towers—the Tower belongs to everyone and to all imaginations. Barthes then concentrates on the great archetypes of sensation which endlessly reinvent the Eiffel Tower as a poetic object, from the liberating euphoria of height and lightness, to a series of metaphorical transformations based on the Tower's shape and appearance: plant, animal, standing human being, sitting human being, genitalia. All this means that the Tower is mythically established as a baroque being, whose metaphoric instability carries it off in the direction of unknown and never entirely achieved states. It is a pure sign, open to all ages, images, and meanings, an unstoppable

---

[19] See *RB* 129 / 131.
[20] Barthes appears to use the French adjective *panique* in the way suggested here. He later comments that his usage is incorrect but justified by etymology: ' "Panic" relates to the god Pan; but we can play on etymologies as on words (as has always been done) and pretend to believe that "panic" comes from the Greek adjective that means "every" or "all" (*tout*)'. See *A Lover's Discourse: Fragments* [1977], trans. Richard Howard (New York, Hill and Wang, 1978), 49 / 60.

metaphor: 'through the Tower men exercise that great imaginary function which is their freedom, since no history, no matter how dreadful, has ever been able to take it away from them' (OC i. 1400).

At the level of content, this *tour de force* commentary on the infinite human meanings attracted to the Eiffel Tower represents a celebration of the *homo significans* who, for Barthes, constitutes the proper subject of structuralism. At the level of writing, it is the best possible introduction to the projective, utopian side of this structuralism, in that Barthes's own abuse of metaphors turns the essay itself into an example of the 'all-embracing fantasy of creation' experienced by the vicarious inventor of Eiffel Towers. However, this creative euphoria is taken so far that it is difficult, given the inclusion of serious and quite major utopian themes in the essay, to gauge the status of the discourse. Is such self-consciously ridiculous writing (the office equipment mythology poses the same problem) to be taken seriously? The earlier sarcasm which cut Barthes off from the community of myth consumers, and which represented his only authentic relationship with the world, was far simpler to identify and—as an ideologically motivated, demystifying strategy—far simpler to place. Does the generalized euphoria of Barthes's positive mythologies indicate a reconciliation with the community and its viewpoint on the world, in that Barthes seems far more willing to write from within the experience of a 'we'? What is certain is that Barthes's writing has little to do with the strait-laced and indifferent discipline characterized in the following quotation from *Roland Barthes by Roland Barthes*: 'Thus, he thought, it was because it refused to let itself get *carried away* that the science of semiology didn't turn out too well: often it was no more than a murmur of indifferent labours, each of which thereby rendered indifferent object, text, and body. Yet how could it be forgotten that semiology is tied up with the passion of meaning: its apocalypse and/or its utopia?' (*RB* 160–1 / 163). Barthes's own essay on the Eiffel Tower is a shining example of a semiology which has quite deliberately let itself get carried away. This, Barthes implies, is a utopian prerequisite, in that 'the passion of meaning' clearly belongs on the problematic but apocalyptic terrain of the end of 'Myth Today'.

When Barthes, as often happens, is positioned as a spokesperson for structuralism, he generally manages to distance himself from the '(often very grim) science of semiologists' (*RB* 71 / 75) which he will later describe as a cumbersome imaginary (*imaginaire*) displacing the 'semiological science' for which he had originally wished.[21] An instructive example is a conference paper, 'Semiology and Urbanism', which was delivered in 1967 to an audience of urban specialists in Naples and later published in an architectural journal.[22] Barthes sets out to address what might be meant by a semiology of the city. Although he engages, somewhat half-heartedly, with a language of strong elements and neutral elements, marked elements and unmarked elements, he soon announces that it is not, after all, his intention 'to evoke here the procedures for discovering an urban semiology', which would *probably* consist in 'disassociating the urban text into units, then in distributing these units into formal classes, and, thirdly, in finding the rules of combination and of transformation for these units and for these models' (*SC* 196 / 265). If one shudders at the thought of how the Eiffel Tower essay might have turned out if Barthes had applied this sort of approach, it is soon clear that the lecture is in fact an apology for Barthes's own sort of semiology. For the 'scientific' approach ('investigations or functional studies of the city') is gradually displaced in favour of a plea for 'a certain ingenuity', an accumulation of personal readings of the city, 'of which, unfortunately, till now, only writers have given us some examples' (201 / 270). No one, of course, could be fooled by Barthes's 'unfortunately'. By the end of a short lecture he has moved from an opening statement of his modest credentials as speaker on the topic—both lover (*amateur*) of signs and lover of the city—to an unambiguous statement of his own creative investment in writing the city. Followed to their logical conclusion, the ideas thrown out by Barthes in this lecture (to be explored in more detail at a later stage) will lead to the creation of the imaginary and eroticized Tokyo of *Empire of Signs*, rather than to some 'functional

---

[21] On Barthes's relationship to semiology, see his lecture, 'The Semiological Adventure' [1974], *SC* 3–8 / 9–14.
[22] *L'Architecture d'aujourd'hui*, 53 (Dec. 1970–Jan. 1971). See *SC* 191–201 / 261–71.

study of the city' which was clearly never on Barthes's agenda.

When asked, in a 1972 interview, to clarify his relationship to 'science', Barthes suggests that the ambivalence of his position derives from external perceptions of the nature of his discourse. On the one hand, as one of the first semiologists, he is assumed to project an aura of scientificity. On the other, he is sometimes judged to be 'insufficiently rigorous and scientific, too subjective and impressionistic'.[23] However, he personally rejects the notion of a specifically scientific discourse which would act as the vehicle for, say, a science of literature. For either would-be objective discourse is caught up in the same bad faith that marks every other form of discourse, or this scientific imaginary (in the Lacanian sense) is dissolved by a practice of writing which renders irrelevant or uninteresting the traditional relationship between subject and object, 'between subjectivity as an attribute of impressionistic discourse and objectivity as an attribute of scientific criticism' (*GV* 165 / 156). Nevertheless, Barthes suggests that a purely formal language of algorithms, a language of pure relations which would be entirely free of signifieds, might escape both ideological connotations and the bad faith of the Lacanian subject. Yet this, of course, is to assume that this language of purely formal relations exists in a void, which is not the sort of assumption one associates with the Barthes of this period, let alone the Barthes who had perceived how easily a formula like '$e = mc^2$' could acquire a mythical value.[24] Although his own inability to exploit 'proper algorithms' is blamed on a lack of mathematical and logical ability—as if some better-equipped literary scientist might one day produce an appropriate scientific language—we encounter a full-scale debunking of 'the fondness for algorithms' in *Roland Barthes by Roland Barthes*.

Recalling his passing enthusiasm for 'apparently simple equations, outline plans, tables, tree diagrams', Barthes states in cavalier fashion that all these diagrams, 'truth to tell, are of no use whatsoever' (*RB* 100 / 104). They are so many simple toys

---

[23] 'Pleasure/Writing/Reading' [1972], interview with Jean Ristat originally published in *Les Lettres françaises*, see *GV* 157–71: 164 / 149–64: 155.
[24] See 'The Brain of Einstein', in *M* 68–70 / *My* 91–3, especially 69 / 92–3.

with which one plays for one's own amusement, just like—in yet another revealing literary comparison—Zola making a plan of Plassans purely for his own benefit. Nor do they even really attempt to provide a scientific grounding for his discourse; after all, 'whom could they fool?' Just as Fourier will be seen to pepper his writing with intricate but entirely fantasmatic numerical calculations, Barthes plays at being scientific, pasting in bits of science here and there.[25] In short, 'there are fantasies of discourse'. And although this may appear a purely retrospective attempt on Barthes's part to give psychoanalytic dignity to past naïvety (by lending it the status of a fantasy), it is worth recalling that it is the period when Barthes is moving beyond so-called scientific structuralism that reveals the greatest abuse of tables, tree diagrams, maps, and sketches of every kind. I am thinking of *Empire of Signs*, of *Sade, Fourier, Loyola*, and perhaps above all of *S/Z*. Indeed the latter contains what must qualify as the most carefully worked out yet most ridiculous of all the diagrams in Barthes's work: the intricate and accurate transfer of all the semes identified in the first thirteen lexias of *Sarrasine* on to an orchestral score (*SZ* 29 / 36). This is a classical structuralist model, of the sort described in 'The Structuralist Activity', a simulacrum whereby 'intellect is added to the object' (*CE* 215 / 215), for the carefully drawn-up score does, once deciphered, assist understanding of the text that precedes it. Yet in its recourse to a flamboyantly metaphorical model this is also a self-consciously ironic structuralism, and the irony cannot but contaminate the status of those diagrams that might at first sight appear more scientific.[26]

When Barthes speaks, in *Roland Barthes by Roland Barthes*, of the 'minor scientific delirium' (145 / 148) that marked his structuralist period, he should not, then, be seen as devaluing 'scientific semiology' in favour of a theoretically more sophisticated textuality. He is certainly alluding to the words I have

---

[25] Ironically, a good foil for Barthes's playful approach to 'scientific structuralism' would be Louis Marin's *Utopics: The Semiological Play of Textual Spaces*, first published in French in 1973, and riddled with diagrammatic representations of its semiological argument.

[26] For examples, see *SZ* 27–8 / 34–5, 85 / 91, 129 / 135, and *SFL* 43 / 49, 57 / 62, 113 / 117, 142 / 146, 147 / 151. Of the four essays in *SFL*, only the earlier essay on Sade, first published in 1967, contains no diagrams. The sketch plans included in *Empire of Signs* will be discussed in Ch. 6.

already quoted from his 1971 interview with *Tel Quel*: 'I indulged in a (euphoric) dream of scentificity.' This interview, as I have already mentioned, has often been seen as marking Barthes's 'break' with structuralism.²⁷ However, the immediate context in which Barthes's euphoric dream is further reduced to a minor delirium is crucial to an evaluation of both formulations. The later remark is part of Barthes's commentary on a schematic diagram representing his own intellectual development in terms of a series of phases. Clearly, the diagram itself has an ironic status as an example of the sort of structuralism in question: 'the cutting up of a period, of a work, into phases of development—although a purely imaginary operation—lets you into the game of intellectual communication: you make yourself intelligible' (*RB* 145 / 148). Indeed, even as Barthes stresses the imaginary status of structuralist models, he multiplies the layers of irony by reproducing on the following page the well-known cartoon 'Structuralist Fashions' (*La Mode structuraliste*), in which Barthes, Lacan, Lévi-Strauss, and Foucault sit in a group on the ground in grass skirts (146 / 149).

On the whole, then, Barthes's assumption of 'scientificity' as a passing mania aptly undermines any distinction between 'objective' and 'creative' structuralisms, both of which are caught up in their own public and private imaginaries. To maintain the distinction between a scientific and a utopian structuralism one would need to separate off the '(often very grim) science of semiologists'—with its cumbersome imaginary values of objectivity, authority, universality, and self-importance—from a self-conscious and delirious semiology. Barthes's preferred solution, however, ironically reconciles the ideal science of semiology with its worthy but dull practitioners. Whoever, as he asks in *Roland Barthes by Roland Barthes* (117 / 121), would still claim to be 'a structuralist'? (*Structuraliste, qui l'est encore?*)

---

[27] For example, it is a significant turning point in the account of Barthes's intellectual trajectories to be found in Stephen Heath, *Vertige du déplacement* (Paris, Fayard, 1974). Annette Lavers takes issue with what she calls this *Bildungsroman* of Barthes's progressive shedding of semiological naïvety, and pinpoints the *Tel Quel* interview as a source of misleading 'admissions' on Barthes's part which should be read symptomatically. See Lavers, *Roland Barthes: Structuralism and After* (London, Macmillan, 1982), especially 180.

Thus, in what will be seen in the next chapter to constitute a manœuvre typical of Fourier's discourse, scientific 'structuralism' is *subsumed* as utopian semiology's pompous and somewhat outdated *alter ego*.[28]

---

[28] Compare, too, what Barthes will later write in a preface to Brillat-Savarin's *Physiology of Taste* (Paris, Hermann, 1975), in a section to which he gives the title 'Science': 'B.-S. tries his hand at science, or at least at scientific discourse; . . . his audacity is stylistic: the use of a learned tone in order to speak of a sense reputed to be trivial. . . . Science is the great Superego of *The Physiology of Taste*. . . . B.-S. strews his discourse with scientific solemnities. . . . B.-S. took science in a fashion at once serious and ironical; his project of establishing a science of taste, of stripping culinary pleasure of its habitual signs of triviality, was certainly close to his heart; but he performs it rhetorically, i. e. with irony.' See 'Reading Brillat-Savarin', in *RL* 250–70: 265–6 / 285–306: 301–2.

3
Charles Fourier: 'An Inventor not a Writer'

> Utopia is the state of a society where Marx would no longer criticize Fourier.[1]

THE crux of Barthes's inspired and very important reading of Fourier is his recognition that a set of idiosyncratic writing strategies could be the central ingredient of a political and ethical vision.[2] That it is difficult to spell out a full description of Fourier's self-consciously mad cosmogony may explain why non-French commentators on utopia do not always recognize his importance, even if censorship, the relatively recent publication of *New Amorous World*, and the unavailability of translations may also have played a part here.[3] For Barthes is right that there is not really a summarizable 'content' to be found in Fourier's texts, and that the experience of reading him is above all a bizarre engagement with the experience of writing a utopia. That Barthes's own modes of analysis (his way of writing reality) should share with Fourier so many rhetorical

---

[1] Barthes, 'Pleasure/Writing/Reading' [1972], in *GV* 157–71: 171 / 149–64: 164.
[2] Barthes, 'Fourier', in *SFL* 76–120 / 81–124, first published as 'Vivre avec Fourier' in *Critique*, 281 (1970).
[3] For a detailed intellectual biography of Fourier, with useful primary and secondary bibliographical information, see Jonathan Beecher, *Charles Fourier: The Visionary and his World* (Berkeley and Los Angeles, University of California Press, 1986). The most complete edition of Fourier's writings is still the *Œuvres complètes*, 12 vols. (Paris, Anthropos, 1966–8). Volume vii, *Le Nouveau Monde amoureux* [1967], ed. Simone Debout-Oleszkiewicz, was previously unpublished. For translated extracts from Fourier see Jonathan Beecher and Richard Bienvenu (eds.), *The Utopian Vision of Charles Fourier: Selected Texts on Work, Love, and Passionate Attraction* (Boston, Beacon Press, 1971). For important discussions of Fourier in the general context of utopian thought see Bloch, *The Principle of Hope*, 558–61, Frank E. Manuel, 'Toward a Psychological History of Utopias', in Frank E. Manuel (ed.), *Utopias and Utopian Thought* (London, Souvenir Press, 1973), 69–98, and Ricœur, *Lectures on Ideology and Utopia*, 301–14.

strategies may explain why he, too, is hard to summarize, and is no longer considered an important 'theorist'. In a crucial fragment, Barthes quotes the distinction drawn by Marx and Engels in *The German Ideology* between the 'real content' of utopian socialist systems and the pathetic attempts of various disciples to try them out in literal incarnations of their 'systematic form'. Thus orthodox Fourierists, for all their apparent orthodoxy, are simply 'doctrinaire bourgeois', the very opposite of Fourier himself (*SFL* 109–10 / 114).[4] For Barthes, it is precisely this orthodoxy that betrays a fundamental misunderstanding of the scope and point of Fourier's utopian vision, a misunderstanding of which Marx and Engels, whose response to Fourier was far more positive than some commentaries suggest, were well aware.[5] This may serve as a useful parallel for the relationship, discussed in the previous chapter, between Barthes's own vision of the potential of semiology and the '(often very grim) science of semiologists'. For what might be called the 'real content' of Barthes's work is neither a methodology nor an occasionally precious style, both of which have attracted disciples of sorts over the years. It is, rather—like Fourier's—a project of taking apart and reinventing the real world.

What is more, Barthes uses the distinction made by Marx and Engels to establish an important new binary of 'system' (their 'systematic form') and 'systematics' (their 'real content'). This binary is particularly suggestive in relation to my wish to account for the relative *status* of structuralist methodology within Barthes's retrospective discussions of his semiology. At first it may seem that 'system' is a totally negative concept based on a naïve perception of the relationship between language and reality:

The system being a closed (or monosemic) one, it is always theological, dogmatic; it is nourished by illusions: an illusion of transparency (the language employed to express it is purportedly purely instrumental, it

---

[4] For the passage quoted by Barthes, see Karl Marx and Frederick Engels, *The German Ideology* [1845–7], trans. Clemens Dutt, W. Lough, and C. P. Magill, in Marx and Engels, *Collected Works*, v (London, Lawrence and Wishart, 1976), 19–539: 462.
[5] For a very clear account of the attitude of Marx and Engels towards French utopian socialism, see Geoghegan, 'Marx, Engels and Utopianism', Ch. 2 of *Utopianism and Marxism*, 22–34.

is not a writing) and an illusion of reality (the goal of the system is to be *applied*, i.e. that it leave language in order to found a reality that is incorrectly defined as the exteriority of language); it is a strictly paranoid insanity (*délire*) whose path of transmission is insistence, repetition, catechism, orthodoxy. (109 / 114)

Fourier's body of writing, never intended to constitute a system, only became one retrospectively, when people tried to create real phalansteries (which inevitably turned out to be disastrous failures). 'Systematics', on the other hand, is the positive term of the binary. As in other pairs of concepts to be found in Barthes's work at around this time—dissertation and essay, product and production, structure and structuration—the apparently privileged term represents the 'play' of the system. It involves language which is open, infinite, tolerant of ambiguities and contradictions, and, above all, which is free of any pretensions to application in reality.

This may sound like a classic distinction between a structuralist and poststructuralist view of language, with a clearly emerging allegiance to the latter (even Marx and Engels are allowed to read Fourier 'non-referentially'). What is interesting, however, is less the theoretical downgrading of system than its indispensability within the binary in question. For when Barthes tells us that systematics has no aspirations to application, he adds a vital parenthesis: 'except at the level of a pure imaginary, of a theatre of discourse' (110 / 115). The imaginary referred to here is clearly the Lacanian one discussed at the end of the last chapter, at which point 'system' acquires the relative dignity of a structural role. Inscribed in the 'systematics' as 'ambivalent parody, shadow, game', system is now described as that part of Fourier's systematics that 'plays with the system in an imaginary way'. Thus systematics is not just the play *of* the system, but play *with* its illusory but persistent claim to be taken seriously and tried out in the real world.

Barthes identifies an important rhetorical strategy whereby Fourier maintains the systematic content of his utopia as a parodic shadow of its idiosyncratic discourse. This is his incessant habit of providing glimpses and brief summaries of the future wonders of Harmony, all the while deferring the definitive exposition of the full workings of the system until a later stage. Since the promised global account—'perfectly clear, perfectly persuasive, perfectly complex' (RB 173 / 176)—is (of course) infinitely deferred, Barthes very acutely describes Fourier's doctrine as 'simultaneously arrogant and dilatory' (SFL 110 / 115). This dilatory manœuvre is passed off by Fourier as necessary protection of his readers from the mortal physical shock that might result from too abrupt a revelation of excessive pleasure (' "fearing to allow you to glimpse the vastness of these pleasures, I have only discoursed upon..." ' (84 / 89–90), and so on). The real point, however, is the creation of a strategy of writing with which Barthes will immodestly but convincingly associate his own 'foible of providing "introductions", "sketches", "elements" ' (RB 173 / 175), thereby postponing the 'real' book until a later stage: 'these dilatory manœuvres, these endlessly receding projects may be writing itself. First of all, the work is never anything but the meta-book (the anticipatory commentary) of a future work which, *not actually getting written*, becomes this work itself: Proust, Fourier only ever wrote "Prospectuses" of this sort' (174–5 / 177).

On the one hand Fourier fantasizes scenes connected with the future reception of his works, such as a dialogue between bookseller and customer, a court trial with a full cast of judge, jury, and lawyers, or a rich reader who sends for the author to clarify some minor points. At the same time the texts themselves develop all sorts of rhetorical sub-categories aimed at different sorts of reader (the curious, the critical, etc.), as Fourier shifts between expositions, descriptions, confirmations, bits of theory, insights, summaries, and fragments of elaborate dissertations. The books become mobile works with wildly varying pace and intermittent concretization of their content. But whereas one might expect an overall effect of redundant repetitiveness, Barthes claims that 'the duplicity of the discourse produces a gap through which the subject leaks away' (SFL 90 / 95). Fourier's message is simply the announcement of a forthcoming message: 'his book is *subjectless*: its signified is dilatory, incessantly withdrawn to a greater distance: only the signifier remains, stretching out of sight, *into the book's future*' (90 / 96). Thus Barthes establishes a relationship between system-building and system-writing which might save even his own most conventionally structuralist texts—say *Elements of Semiology* or 'Introduction to the Structural Analysis of Narratives'[6]—from a poststructuralist critique. For instead of the writing transparently representing some pre-existing system, by offering a mere foretaste it in effect projects that imaginary system into an ever-receding future.

Barthes's analysis of Fourier's meta-book (this dilatory discourse) is directly followed by a powerful account of Fourier's irony. It is an analysis which illuminates the deliberately uncertain status of Barthes's own more manic texts, from the structuralist mythologies of 'The Two Salons' and 'The Eiffel Tower' to S/Z and Empire of Signs, the last two both published in 1970, the very year of the Fourier essay. Barthes begins with the 'grain of madness' which marks Fourier's description of the 'nocturnal furnishings' of Harmony, with its development of a string of insulting metaphors for Civilization's somewhat pathetic moon: 'Nocturnal furnishings will be considerably assorted and composed of our vivid and variously coloured moons, next to which Phoebe will appear as what she is, a pale ghost, a sepulchral lamp, a Swiss cheese. One would have to have as bad taste as the Civilized to admire this pallid mummy' (SFL 91 / 96–7). Further, Fourier enjoys concocting ridiculous and slightly transgressive phrases in which futile objects are associated with highly abstract terms—'the 44 systems of tiny pastries', 'the tiny pastries adopted by the Council of Babylon' (93 / 98), and so on—and is particularly fond of elevating to prestigious status those objects (such as forms of rubbish) that are especially despised in Civilization. Thus Barthes quotes the fictional episode of New Amorous World in which a mock crusade made up of cobblers (dealers in old shoes and boot cleaners) arrives on the territory of the Empire of the Euphrates to be greeted by a magnificent firework display. The display ends with a spectacular representation of 'an old shoe ablaze' (Barthes's title for this section of his essay) beneath which blazes the legend: 'Long live pious cobblers!' (94 / 99).[7]

---

[6] Both were first published in the semiological journal *Communications*. See Roland Barthes, *Elements of Semiology* [1964], trans. Annette Lavers and Colin Smith (London, Jonathan Cape, 1967), and 'Introduction to the Structural Analysis of Narrative' [1966], in *SC* 95–135.

[7] For the episode of the crusade of the pious cobblers, see Fourier, *Le Nouveau Monde amoureux*, 361–78.

Fourier is of course aware that his examples are objectively ridiculous, and that his conjunctions of abstract concepts with base material objects sin against the normal proprieties of the linguistic hierarchy. Fourier's solution is to exaggerate the incongruity with the air of a martyr: 'Bah! glory in old shoes, our Civilized will say; exactly the stupid response I expected from them.' Where is Fourier in all this, asks Barthes: in the invention of the absurd example, in the indignant response to the imagined ridiculing of his example, or in the reading that encompasses all of these layers? Barthes sees this typical strategy as promoting the loss of the subject of the discourse, with the result that it is impossible for any reading ever to pin down what exactly is supposed to be going on. His final example is a suggestive emblem of the ironic status of the utopian order of Harmony in its entirety. This is Fourier's discussion of the ironic quality of the melon, a quality apparently bestowed by God who has deliberately made it difficult for the inhabitants of Civilization reliably to detect a good melon:

> God, says Fourier, displays a subtle and judicious irony in creating certain products that are enigmatic in quality, like the melon, made for the innocent mystification of banquets ill-suited to divine methods, without in any way deceiving the gastronomes who keep to the divine or societary diet. I do not mean to say that God created the melon solely for the sake of this jest, but it is part of the fruit's many uses. Irony is never overlooked in the calculations of nature.... The melon has amongst its properties that of *ironic harmony*. (95 / 100)[8]

In short, says Barthes, Fourier's ironic melon is an element in a *writing*. Moreover, no reader could ever claim to get on top of such a statement, to position it as an object of laughter or criticism: 'in the name of *what other language?*' The example captures the way in which irony is perhaps intrinsic to the production of utopian discourse.[9]

---

[8] See Fourier, *Œuvres complètes*, iv. 49. Fourier is perhaps alluding ironically to Bernardin de Saint-Pierre's claim that melons, since divisible into slices, seem 'destined' for family meals; indeed, even larger fruits like the pumpkin can be shared with the neighbours. Flaubert, too, planned to mock this promotion of Providence by quoting it alongside other stupidities in the second volume of *Bouvard et Pécuchet*. See Roger Huss, 'Nature, Final Causality and Anthropocentrism in Flaubert', *French Studies*, 33 (1979), 288–304: 288 and 301 n. 2.

[9] This is a point also made by Ricœur in *Lectures on Ideology and Utopia*, 303. Ricœur, who does not mention Barthes's essay on Fourier, suggests that 'because the concept of utopia is a polemical tool, it belongs to the field of rhetoric' (310).

It is very much Barthes's general point that Fourier's utopianism (his systematics) is a writing, and one which—unlike mythological demystification—is able to protect the integrity of reality: 'Is it not the characteristic of reality to be *unmasterable*? And is it not the characteristic of any system to *master* it? What, then, can one do if one rejects mastery? Get rid of the system as apparatus, accept *systematics* as writing (as Fourier did)' (*RB* 172 / 174–5). Irony is intrinsic to systematics in that it unsettles mastery. On the one hand, it renders uncertain the authority of the speaking voice, on the other, irony is built into the very reality that is its object. In the case of Fourier, at least, the crux of utopian discourse seems to lie in its *modal* relationship (in the grammatical sense) with reality. This utopian mood seems to lie somewhere between the indicative of positive affirmation and the subjunctive of uncertain status. The precise status of the reality which is the object of this discourse is explored more explicitly in the section of the Fourier essay which directly follows the sequence on irony. Indeed, 'Hieroglyphics' is a very powerful analysis of the basic principles underlying Fourier's reinvention of the world, and of the relationship between that fantasized world and the real one.

Fourier, says Barthes, wants to decipher the world in order to remake it, and one might well suppose that the former is a prerequisite for the latter. However, the two activities are quite different in scope and kind, in that deciphering implies the notion of hidden depths in the object being deciphered, whereas cutting up implies a spatial distribution of a set of relationships. According to Barthes, deciphering the world is actually a rather minor aspect of Fourier's total endeavour, which comes down to denouncing the lies and hypocrisy of the commercial ethos of the bourgeoisie. The essential aspect of his utopian reading of the world is based elsewhere: in the cutting up operation by which Fourier takes apart and reorders the world into a new system. This, then, is no longer a 'denunciatory, reductive' reading (limited to unmasking the lies of the bourgeoisie), but is, on the contrary, an 'exalting, integrating, restorative' reading, extended to the plethora of universal forms (*SFL* 96 / 101). Since Harmony is a complex and total space linking 'societies, sentiments, forms, natural kingdoms', Fourier's men and women are incorporated into the universe, including the stars and planets. Bearing in mind the ambivalent nostalgia for metaphysics detected in Barthes's 1950s writing, it may well be that Barthes found in the ironized cosmic dimension of Fourier's Harmony a utopia entirely to his taste.

Barthes now raises the central question of the place of reality in this affirmative and expansive reading of the world:

> We are accustomed to regarding the 'real' and the residue as identical: the 'unreal', fantasmatic, ideological, verbal, proliferating, in short the 'marvellous', is supposed to conceal from us the 'real', rational, infrastructural, schematic; from the real to the unreal there would be the (self-interested) production of a screen of arabesques, whereas from the unreal to the real there would be critical reduction, an alethic, scientific movement, as if the real were at once more meagre and more essential than the superstructions (*surstructions*) with which it has been covered over. (96/101)

This view of ideology and utopia as parallel *distortions* of reality—as variant forms of false consciousness despite their operating from opposed power bases—is a relative constant of Marxist thought, albeit one that is particularly associated with Karl Mannheim.[10] In using it as a foil for Fourier's very different conceptualization of the relationship between utopia and reality, Barthes intervenes both constructively and very significantly in twentieth-century debates around utopia, marked as they inevitably are by the spectre of 'utopian socialism' as mere fantasy writing, to be negatively opposed to a 'scientific socialism' which is somehow more basic and real, and more in tune with the materiality of history.[11]

---

[10] See Mannheim, *Ideology and Utopia: An Introduction to the Sociology of Knowledge*. For useful secondary accounts see Ricœur, *Lectures on Ideology and Utopia*, 159–80 and 269–84, and Levitas, *The Concept of Utopia*, 67–82.

[11] Geoghegan points out that Engels's famous essay 'Socialism Utopian and Scientific' [1882] was a translated extract from his work *Anti-Dühring*, which had, as its original title, *Die Entwicklung des Sozialismus von der Utopie zur Wissenschaft* (the development of socialism from utopia to science). This, suggests Geoghegan, actually implies a historical contextualization and a materialist analysis of utopian socialism, rather than a sharp division of world-views between two sorts of socialism, 'one true, one false' (*Utopianism and Marxism*, 30). Indeed, Engels writes of Fourier and Owen as follows: 'The utopians, we saw, were utopians because they could be nothing else at a time when capitalist production was as yet so little developed. They necessarily had to construct the elements of a new society out

Obviously, Fourier is working on a conceptual material whose make-up belies this contrast and which is that of the *marvellous real*. This marvellous real is contrasted with the marvellous ideal of novels; it corresponds to what we might call, contrasting it directly with the novel, the novelistic. The marvellous real very precisely is the signifier, or, if one prefers, 'reality', characterized, relative to the scientific real, by its fantasmatic train. (96–7 / 101)

This highly suggestive gloss, the starting point of which is one of Fourier's imagined dialogues between bookseller and purchaser of his works,[12] takes us to the theoretical heart of Fourier's utopian practice and explains its importance to Barthes. This is true in terms of both the status of the latter's earlier structuralist analyses of a real world (of which the Eiffel Tower mythology remains my best example), and the experimentation with the *novelistic* which will be central to *Empire of Signs*, as well as to much of his writing in the 1970s.[13] From the 'concrete abstraction' of the bird's-eye view of Paris to Fourier's 'marvellous real' is not a large step, and on the whole a reading of material reality which establishes it as the marvellous real depends only upon an affirmative *intention*, on a positive complicity that contrasts with the demystifying sarcasm described in 1957 as the mythologist's only authentic relationship with the world.[14]

It is important to note the sense in which Barthes uses the word 'signifier' to describe the fantasmatic dimension of reality, for it explains why his logothetes are also cosmogonists—the new languages that they invent are new conceptualizations of reality. Reality is already the raw material of their languages, and in Fourier's case it is reality with individual, social, and cosmic dimensions all intertwined. Barthes's explanation of

---

of their own heads, because within the old society the elements of the new were not as yet generally apparent; for the base plan of the new edifice they could only appeal to reason, just because they could not as yet appeal to contemporary history.' See Engels, *Anti-Dühring*, trans. Emile Burns, in Marx and Engels, *Collected Works*, xxv (London, Lawrence and Wishart, 1987), 1–309: 253.

[12] 'Bookseller: "Now here is a quite extraordinary discovery: a mathematical proof of Association. People go looking for the marvellous ideal in novels, but what we have here is the marvellous real". Customer: "Pooh! another fraud! There's such a lot of it about!" ' (Fourier, *Œuvres complètes*, ii, p. iii)

[13] See Chs. 2, 6, and 7.

[14] See M 12 / My 10 and 157 / 245.

Fourier's hieroglyphics sets out to explain the idiosyncratic but entirely logical principles on which that language is built. It was Marx and Engels who commented that in order to criticize Fourier's 'series' you need first to understand how to construct them,[15] and Frank Paul Bowman, a Fourier specialist, suggests that Barthes has provided the clearest explanation of Fourier's hieroglyphics available in the critical literature.[16] These postulate a formal and entirely arbitrary correspondence between the various realms of the universe, 'for example between forms (circle, ellipse, parabola, hyperbola), colours, musical notes, passions (friendship, love, paternity, ambition), the races of animals, the stars, and the periods of societal phylogenesis' (97 / 102). Whereas we have tended to naturalize substitutional, analogical thinking, by which we might wonder why a particular animal should stand for a particular quality, Fourier has a serial imagination based on association and homology. Thus his hieroglyphics work by contrasts and alliances, but above all by *progressive series* ('branches: giraffe, stag, buck, roebuck, reindeer, etc.' (98 / 103)). The series, which is a kind of extended paradigm made up of subtle differences and proximities—the distinction between white-rose growers and yellow-rose growers is my favourite example[17]—is the basic principle of social organization in Harmony, in that the phalansteries bring together contrasting groups of individuals linked by an affinity. These syntagmatized paradigms are not only actualizable but liveable and even felicitous, 'whereas the semantic paradigm is subject to the law of rival, inexpiable opposites, which cannot cohabit' (98 / 103). Barthes's extended example of the 'baroque semantics' which grounds Fourier's systematics—'open to the proliferation of the signifier, infinite and yet structured' (99 / 103)—gives the flavour of his enjoyment of Fourier's idiosyncratic logic and style. Barthes asserts that progression (the series) is both what Fourier has added to meaning as linguists

---

[15] See Marx and Engels, *The German Ideology*, 511.
[16] Frank Paul Bowman, '*Roland Barthes par Roland Barthes* et Charles Fourier', *Romanic Review*, 3 (1978), 236–41: 236.
[17] Quoted in Raymond Trousson, *Voyage au pays de nulle part: Histoire littéraire de la pensée utopique* (Brussels, Editions de l'Université de Bruxelles, 1975), 191.

would normally conceive it, and what, as a result, frustrates its arbitrariness. Why, he asks, in Association, is the giraffe the hieroglyph for Truth?

A farfetched notion and assuredly unjustifiable if we try, desperately, to discover some affinitive or even contrasting trait shared by truth and this huge mammiferous ungulant. The explanation is that the giraffe is caught up in a system of homologies: Association having the beaver as its practical hieroglyph (because of its associative and constructive abilities) and the peacock as its visual hieroglyph (because of the spread of its nuances), we need, across from but yet in the same series, that of animals, a properly unfunctional element, a kind of neuter, a zero degree of zoological symbolism: this is the giraffe, as useless as the truth is in Civilization; whence a counter-giraffe (complex term of contrast): this is the Reindeer, from which we derive every imaginable service (in the societary order there will even be a new animal created, more ecumenical even than the Reindeer: the Anti-Giraffe). (98–9 / 103)

But the real key to Harmony is Fourier's elaboration of the *passionate series*, the formal principle of social combination of 1,620 character types into the phalanstery, the latter being both part of Harmony and its microcosm. For the passion ('character, taste, mania') is the basic unit with which Fourier the logothete works: 'the irreducible unity of the Fourierist *combinatoire*, the absolute grapheme of the utopian text' (100 / 105). It is derived from the subdivision and permutation of twelve more broadly defined passions, of which five are sensual (the five senses), four affective (friendship, love, kinship, ambition), and the last three, crucially, distributive: the Cabalistic (love of intrigue), the Composite (love of sensual excess), and the Variating, Alternating, or Butterfly (*la Papillonne*) (obsessive changing of occupation or love-object). What Barthes most values about Fourier's passions is that they are themselves entirely free of connotations or social values, for normality and abnormality are meaningless concepts in Harmony. What we might call a mania, whim, foible, or perversion is the very being of a passion, which is 'neither deformable, nor transformable, nor reducible, nor measurable, nor substitutable: it is not a force, it is a number'. It is not a case of bringing people together to share their unusual tastes in comfortable, narcissistic fashion, nor of a liberal understanding or tolerance for those different from ourselves. The point is to exploit the passions, to find a way of combining them for the greater pleasure and happiness of all:

The combination of differences implies the respecting of the individuation of each term: there is no attempt to redress, to correct, to annul taste, whatever it may be (however 'bizarre' it may be); quite the contrary, it is affirmed, it is emphasized, it is recognized, it is legalized, it is reinforced by associating everyone who wishes to indulge it: taste being thus incorporated, it is allowed to act in opposition to other tastes at once affinitive and different: a game of rivalry (indeed of intrigue, but *coded*) is initiated between the lovers of bergamot pears and the lovers of butter pears: to the satisfaction of a simple taste (a fondness for pears) is then added the exercise of other, formal, combinatory passions: for example, *cabilistics*, or the passion for intrigue, and *butterfly*, should there be unstable Harmonians who take pleasure in switching from the bergamot pear to the butter pear. (99 / 104)

Every preference is of use for Fourier's 'semantic construction' of the world, as long as it can be classified, counted, and built into a calculation for a more rational and pleasurable reordering. Fourier's systematics is above all 'that unique space which embraces both the individual fantasy and the social *combinatoire*' (80 / 86)—the slightest inflexion of desire is linked to the most broadly conceived organization of a materially liberated society.

It is in this sense that Barthes can claim that to reject or to be ironic about Fourier is to censor the signifier, for the signifier is simply the raw material with which Fourier invents his new world: 'Perhaps, following Fourier, we should henceforth call *inventor*, and not *writer* or *philosopher*, someone who brings into being new modes of expression and thereby takes over, by means of fragments, *immensely and in detail*, the space of the signifier' (88 / 94). As usual, Barthes is elaborating a key theoretical point on the basis of Fourier's own words: 'As for me, I am an inventor and not an orator', and 'I am not a writer but an inventor' (88 / 93–4).[18] He interprets these claims in the sense of a repudiation of the writer as a 'certified manager of good writing, of literature, someone who guarantees decorative

---

[18] 'We should never forget that I am an inventor, not an orator. My task is not to be flowery but to be new' (*Le Nouveau Monde amoureux*, 112).

literature and thus the fundamental separation of content and form'. Fourier, on the other hand, 'places himself at the limit of meaning, what we today call Text' (88 / 94), for what he aspires to invent is 'the absolutely new, that about which nothing has yet been said' (88 / 93). When, in the final section of his essay, Barthes sums up the *impossibilia* or *adunata* of Harmony—spectacular changes in the climate and geography, modifications to the height, physiology, and life-span of humankind—he saves until last 'the most insane (and most resistant)' of these impossibilities, which is 'not the one that upsets the laws of "nature" but the one which upsets the laws of language':

Fourier's *impossibilia* are his neologisms. It is easier to predict the subversion of 'the weather' than to imagine, as does Fourier, a masculine form of the word '*Fées*' and to quite simply write it as '*Fés*': the coming into being of a strange graphic configuration from which the feminine gender has dropped out is an example of a veritable *impossibility* : an impossibility gleaned from sex and language: in '*matrones* and *matrons*' it is truly a new *object*, both monstrous and transgressive, that has come to humanity. (119–20 / 124)[19]

Here, Fourier's linguistic fantasy breaks down the binaries of gender in a way to which Barthes himself (from *S/Z* to the lecture course on the *neutre*) constantly but pessimistically aspires.[20] At the same time, the semantic logic of his series works against the paradigmatic oppositions that enforce divisive choices within human meaning, just as the endless withdrawal of the signified, and the purely denotative value of the passions, dissolve the ideological struggles that are mediated by connotations. Crucially, for Barthes, Fourier's utopia of human relations builds in the liberation of language as mediator of social and sexual oppression. Of Barthes's three logothetes (Sade, Fourier, and Loyola) it is Fourier's language which is described in the

---

[19] *Une fée* means a fairy and is gendered feminine; *une matrone* which originally meant a matronly woman of serious character, was later used to refer to an *entremetteuse* (female pimp) and thereby acquired a pejorative connotation. In Fourier this second meaning was no doubt ironically reabsorbed back into the first. The main linguistic point, however, is that Fourier's male counterpart of *un matron* is a fanciful invention (the French morphological equivalent would be *un patron*).

[20] On this theme in Barthes's work see Serge Doubrovsky, 'Une écriture tragique', *Poétique*, 47 (1981), 329–54.

preface as the 'least centred', in that the passions and the stars are ceaselessly 'dispersed' and 'ventilated' (6 / 11). Here then, is a utopian projection of the 'freshness' of a liberated language evoked in *Writing Degree Zero*, the desired social transparency in the realm of speech whereby 'the consistency of social interlocution might one day be clarified, lightened, woven with interstices to the point of invisibility' (*RB* 138 / 141). The phalanstery is an enclosed space but it is also a 'well-aired' one; indeed it is the unfettered *circulation* of passions, pleasures, and words that best defines this social and linguistic microcosm and its appeal for Barthes.

Harmony, then, is not just some fictional microcosm placed in another time or space: the world as we know it is subsumed and subjected to a radical reorganization. Indeed, Fourier's texts represent a very dramatic instance of the utopian reshaping of human space explored in Chapter 1. In an exaggerated version of the mental reworking of geography invoked in Barthes's 1955 floods mythology, Fourier changes the physical features of the world, turning the seas into lemonade, swapping around the sites of cities (St Petersburg and Turin), moving the climate of Andalusia to the North Pole, displacing and replacing the stars and the planets. Just as the Barthes of the Tour de France mythology aspired to a reconciliation of individuals, society, and the natural world, so Fourier claims to have discovered the creative principles for the interaction of human beings both with each other and with this radically improved universe. For human concerns and meanings are at the very centre of cosmic ones, so that cosmic change lies in human hands, and anyone who has the means to found a phalanstery 'can bring about changes in the temperament of the planet, correct its aromas, change its temperature and atmosphere, cleanse the seas, stock them with magnificent new species, make changes in the aromas of the sun and the various stars, move five of them so that they orbit around our globe, and adorn the globe with two rings like Saturn'.[21] If the phalanstery itself represents systematics incarnated in the material form of human interchange—a structural model providing for infinite but regulated permutations of real human relationships based in work, convivial

[21] Fourier, *Œuvres complètes*, xii. 5.

company, and sexual and sensual pleasure—this basic materialism seems to be the anchor point of even the wildest of Fourier's cosmic fantasies.

Although Engels is responsible for the infamous binary of utopian and scientific socialism, both he and Marx stressed the materialism of Fourier and Saint-Simon, contrasting French 'Utopian Socialism' very positively with the idealism and essentializing humanism of German 'True Socialism'.[22] However, the response of Marx and Engels to Fourier acts as a useful foil to that of Barthes. While they claim to have admired the 'vein of true poetry' in Fourier's writing—whereas Owen and Cabet, according to Engels, had 'not a shred of imagination'[23]—Fourier's materialism is largely associated with his radical attack on bourgeois institutions (his brilliant satires of commerce, the stock exchange, the army, the Church, and marriage), his historical understanding of the past and present, and his generally dialectical mode of argument.[24] But they are far less attuned to the positive dimension of Fourier's utopia. Marx, for instance, completely failed to recognize the seriousness and central importance of Fourier's theory of 'attractive labour', whereby work and sexuality were perceived as two major spheres of human alienation which might be jointly liberated by the establishment of phalansteries based on the passionate series. When Marx affirms that labour has not yet created the subjective and objective conditions in which work itself (as opposed to 'not-work') might entail freedom, happiness, and self-realization, he condescendingly adds: 'which in no way implies that it might become mere fun, mere amusement, as in

---

[22] Marx and Engels, *The German Ideology*, see especially 462, where a fiercely ironic attack is mounted on True Socialism's belief in 'eternity', in 'what is "natural" ', and in 'the essence of Man'. It seems likely that Barthes's general critique of such values in *Mythologies* was a result of his reading of *The German Ideology*, which is quoted three times in footnotes to 'Myth Today' (M 141 / 229, 144 / 231, 151 / 239).
[23] Marx and Engels, *The German Ideology*, 461.
[24] 'Fourier is not only a critic; his imperturbably serene nature makes him a satirist, and assuredly one of the greatest satirists of all time.... But Fourier is at his greatest in his conception of the history of society.... Fourier, as we see, uses the dialectic method in the same masterly way as his contemporary, Hegel.' See Engels, *Anti-Dühring*, 247–8.

Fourier's shop-girlishly naïve conception.'[25] Engels, for his part, wished to see Fourier translated into English, 'omitting, of course, the cosmogonic nonsense', in that 'the information contained in Fourier's posthumous work is confined entirely to the *mouvement aromal* and the mating of the planets which would appear to take place *plus ou moins* from behind'.[26]

The first point to be made here concerns the response of Marx and Engels to the sexual dimension of Fourier's utopia. It is true that Engels comments favourably on Fourier's insistence that the general level of liberation of society should be measured against the relative freedom of women at any given point in time.[27] Yet his ironic allusion to the sexual preferences of Fourier's planets is typical of a lack of interest in—or refusal to take seriously—Fourier's central project of liberating sexuality from all forms of social and psychic repression. He and Marx fail to recognize that this project is integral to all aspects of Fourier's system. Barthes, of course, does see this, doubtless appreciating in Fourier the same interconnectedness of the themes of social organization, language, pleasure, and the body that underlie his own general concerns. This is certainly why Fourier forms a recurrent point of reference in *Roland Barthes by Roland Barthes* where Barthes is largely attempting to trace the underlying logic of his own writing. Bowman, who has very acutely traced these Fourierist references in *Roland Barthes*, argues that in Fourier, as in Barthes, 'the analysis of sexuality is an integral and harmonious (more than parallel) part of society, history, economics, language'. For the musical metaphor of Harmony should be taken literally in that 'sexual, social and semantic scales' are all 'in tune' with each other. Moreover, he describes the brief but famous sequence in *Roland Barthes* concerning 'Goddess H' (Goddess Homosexuality) as an extremely rich meditation on the relationship between politics, sexuality, and freedom, 'in short, the very project of *New Amorous World*'.[28] Yet, as Barthes notes in his section of the

[25] Marx, *Outlines of the Critique of Political Economy (Rough Draft of 1857–58)* [First Instalment], trans. Ernst Wangermann, in Marx and Engels, *Collected Works*, xxviii. 49–537: 530, translation amended.
[26] Letters from Engels to Marx (17 Mar. 1845 and 19 Aug. 1846), in Marx and Engels, *Collected Works*, xxxviii. 26 and 55.
[27] Engels, *Anti-Dühring*, 248.
[28] Bowman, 'Roland Barthes par Roland Barthes et Charles Fourier', 239–40.

Fourier essay devoted to the positive structural role of 'transitions' (of which 'sapphïsm' and 'pederasty' are merely examples, along with nectarines, amphibians, bats, and so on), 'everything rejected in Civilization, from pederasty to Death, has in Harmony a value that is eminent (but not pre-eminent: nothing dominates anything else, everything combines, meshes, alternates, revolves)' (*SFL* 108 / 113).

The second point is that Barthes obviously understands the function of Fourier's 'cosmogonic nonsense' within an overall utopian systematics which links social, sexual, linguistic, and planetary relations and which can be entered at any point. Unlike Engels, Barthes plays down (or takes for granted) Fourier's fiercely sarcastic, radical critique of contemporary society. This is partly because he is using an analysis of Fourier's writing strategies to move beyond (theoretically as well as in practice) his own negative, demystifying period, which had brought with it the ethical problems outlined at the end of 'Myth Today'.[29] But above all, as we have seen, it is Fourier's concept of the 'marvellous real' that really interests Barthes. For the marvellous real is the key to a utopian discourse that subsumes a fantasmatic perception of material reality—fantasy and materiality are simply not in opposition.

By taking the signifier (this fantasmatic reality) as his raw material, Fourier *chooses* to leave out the signified, the generalized realm of nameable 'science' and 'politics'. If this is the source of his importance for Barthes it is also, of course, a source of political ambivalence for others. It is an ambivalence about which Barthes himself intermittently worries, and it is one that he directly confronts in his discussion of Fourier as 'An Inventor, not a Writer'. The mutual 'forgetting' of each other's importance on the part of both pleasure and politics is described as an aporia in the grip of which 'we are still floundering':

Politics and Domestics (the name of Fourier's system), science and utopia, Marxism and Fourierism, are like two nets whose meshes are of different sizes. On the one hand, Fourier allows to pass through all the science that Marx collects and develops; from the political point of view (and above all ever since Marxism managed to give an indelible name to its shortcomings), Fourier is completely *off to one side*,

[29] See Ch. 2.

unrealistic and immoral. However, the other, facing, net allows pleasure, which Fourier collects, to pass through. Desire and Need pass through, as though the two nets were alternatively superimposed, playing at topping hands. However, the relationship of Desire and Need is not *complementary* (were they fitted one into the other, everything would be perfect), but *supplementary*: each is the *excess* of the other. The *excess*: what does not pass through. (SFL 87–8 / 92–3)

Barthes hesitates, I think, in his evaluation of this supplementary structure, not entirely daring to be seen to choose Fourier *over* Marx. Thus, in a 1972 interview on *Sade, Fourier, Loyola*, the tone of his defence of Fourier is apologetic: 'We must not forget Marx's critique, which Fourier cannot be defended against, but neither should we forget that Fourier says some things that Marx left out' (GV 171 / 163).

Nevertheless, the implication of many of Barthes's remarks is that politics has more to learn from pleasure than vice versa: 'It has been said, with me in mind, I believe, that *these residues of hedonism should be liquidated*. Well I don't agree, it's not that they should be liquidated, it's that a way should be found whereby they cease to be residues' (GV 163 / 154). The personal reference is pertinent here, for it reminds us that the Fourier essay, with its negative comments on a purely political discourse, was written in the wake of Barthes's equally negative reaction to May '68: 'isn't politics *every language less one*, that of Desire?' (SFL 85 / 90). This comment, made in the second section of the Fourier essay, is illustrated by a significant anecdote. During the May events, a proposal had been put to one of the study groups that had spontaneously formed at the Sorbonne. The idea (in an obvious allusion to Fourier) was to study 'Domestic Utopia': 'to which the reply was made that the expression was too "studied", hence "bourgeois"; politics is what forecloses desire, except when they come together in the form of neurosis: political neurosis or, more exactly: the neurosis of politicizing.' Louis-Jean Calvet is obviously right to assume that Barthes is describing the rejection of his own suggestion.[30] Similarly, the somewhat defiant definition of 'writing' as excess—basically as a *displacement* of social responsibility—with which Barthes ends his preface to *Sade, Fourier, Loyola* is surely a defence of

[30] Calvet, *Roland Barthes*, 164–5.

Barthes himself as well as of his subject matter: 'The social intervention of a text (not necessarily achieved at the time the text appears) is measured neither by the working-class make-up (*popularité*) of its audience nor by the fidelity of the socio-economic reflection it contains or projects to a few eager sociologists, but rather by the violence that enables it to *exceed* the laws that a society, an ideology, a philosophy set up in order to agree amongst themselves in a fine surge of historical intelligibility' (10 / 16). I assume that this 'fine surge of historical intelligibility' is a further sarcastic reference to the self-righteous political discourse of May '68 that Barthes so disliked.[31] Barthes's true view seems to be that utopia (including Fourier's Harmony) in fact embraces the claims of both Need and Desire. After all, Fourier's supernumerary (thirteenth) passion of 'Unity-ness' or 'Harmony-ism', contrasting with the negative 'Simplism' which marks Civilization ('the use of the mind without the marvellous, or of the marvellous without the mind'), is defined by Barthes as Fourier's own. If for Fourier it was Simplism that 'made Newton miss out on the discovery of the system of nature and Bonaparte on the conquest of the world', for Barthes 'Simplism (or totalitarianism, or mono-logism) would today be either the censoring of Need or the censoring of Desire, which in Harmony (in Utopia?) would be resolved by conjugating the two together' (102 / 107). Barthes quotes these lines on Simplism in the same 1972 interview, and concludes with a definition of utopia as 'the state of a society where Marx would no longer criticize Fourier' (GV 171 / 164). This is a useful formulation for Barthes—whilst suggesting that the Marxist critique of utopia is motivated by the historical *conjoncture*, it nevertheless implies a lacuna (a Newtonian or Napoleonic Simplism) in Marxist analysis as such.[32]

---

[31] For some comments made shortly after the May events, see 'Structuralisme et sémiologie', interview with Pierre Daix, *Lettres françaises*, 31 July 1968 (*OC* ii. 523–7). Barthes obviously resents the fact that the students believe their ideological critiques to be original: 'Ever since Marx, Nietzsche, and Freud, the great task of the century has been to *critique*, to tear away the ideological envelopes with which our society covers over knowledge, feelings, behaviour, and values. You really shouldn't keep starting from scratch' (13). He also detects in May '68 student discourse an element of Poujadist anti-intellectualism beneath the veneer of Marxist vocabulary.

[32] Herbert Marcuse, of course, did dare to suggest this. If Barthes and Marcuse could be seen to have much in common this is probably because of their shared

A short piece on 'Utopia Today', published in an Italian journal in 1974, is a clear overview of Barthes's analysis of the paradoxical relations between politics and utopia, and of the now familiar failure of each to understand the other: 'need disapproves of the irresponsibility and futility of desire; desire disapproves of the censorship operated by need and of its reductive drive.'[33] It is explicitly stated that Barthes wants to collapse this distinction between politics and utopia, for he believes that the fantasmatic, desiring dimension of utopia has an importance that is precisely political: 'Desire should be reinjected into Politics, which is to say that Utopias are not only justifiable, they are also necessary.' The ability to imagine the concrete details of a future society is described as requiring more courage than the elaboration of its general shape and values: 'it's not the outlines of a future society that we are afraid to draw. That society is already there, in politics itself.' But utopia possesses 'the rarest sort of courage, that of pleasure'—its defining characteristic is to imagine 'times, places, and customs in minutest detail' and it is from details alone that desire can be deduced. Whilst stressing relentlessly the wrongs of the present world, utopia simultaneously invents pictures of happiness, and

---

interest in Fourier. The early Marcuse is strangely reticent about the influence of Fourier on *Eros and Civilization*, though many aspects of his own rereading of Freud towards a utopia of integrated libidinal and social liberation could well have been derived from Fourier. Yet the latter is mentioned only briefly, and though praised for 'elucidating the dependence of freedom on non-repressive sublimation', is then dismissed on account of the 'repressive elements' of 'a giant organization and administration' (218). However, in the late 1960s, he claims that Fourier is the essential complement to Marx, that scientific socialism must give way to utopian socialism rather than vice versa. (See 'The End of Utopia' [1967], in *Five Lectures: Psychoanalysis, Politics and Utopia* (Boston, Beacon Press, 1970), 62–82, and *An Essay in Liberation* (London, Allen Lane, 1969).) Marcuse alludes several times to *Writing Degree Zero* in *One Dimensional Man: Studies in the Ideology of Advanced Industrial Society* (London, RKP, 1964), and it is possible that he and Barthes met at the École Pratique des Hautes Études, where Marcuse was a visiting Director of Studies in the Sixth Section in 1958 and again in 1960. To my knowledge, although *Eros and Civilization* was translated into French in 1963, Barthes never mentions Marcuse. One major difference between them is, of course, Marcuse's famously enthusiastic reaction to May '68. For discussions of Marcuse in a French context see Barry Katz, *Herbert Marcuse and the Art of Liberation: An Intellectual Biography* (London, Verso, 1992) and Jean-Michel Palmier, *Herbert Marcuse et la nouvelle gauche* (Paris, Minuit, 1973).

[33] OC iii. 44, first published in *Almanacco Bompiani* (special issue on utopia).

it invents them 'in their special colours, with their own precision and variations, with their own absurdity'. The mark of utopia as the 'political form of fantasy' is therefore the everyday—it is less a matter of theoretical proclamations than of a minutely detailed conjuring up of the organization and quality of everyday life, which is why the greatest utopian thinkers are bound also to be writers.[34] Fourier's phalanstery—and Sade's castle—may be literally impossible, 'but the detailed inflections of the Utopian system return to our world like lamps of desire, of possible exultation. If we could be more alert to them, they would prevent politics from solidifying into a totalitarian, bureaucratic, moralizing system.'

The bringing together of Fourier and Sade as 'two of our greatest utopian writers' may seem strange in the context of discussions of Fourier in which Barthes appears to address the possible shortcomings of Marxism. Of course Barthes had already juxtaposed them as logothetes in *Sade, Fourier, Loyola*, stressing (in his preface) the delight in classification which they shared with Loyola, the obsession with cutting up and counting, the fantasmatic quality of their imaginations, the ordering of a logical but infinitely permutatable *combinatoire*. But in foregrounding their parallel writing strategies Barthes deliberately played down the content and motivation of their particular language systems, as if they had not believed 'in God, in the Future, in Nature', and as if their 'Sadeian, contestatory, and mystic' practices were recuperated neither by 'sadism, revolution, or religion'. Thus it appears to be presented as a fact of little importance that 'from Sade to Fourier, sadism is lost; from Loyola to Sade, divine interlocution' (3 / 7).

In *Sade, Fourier, Loyola*, the presence of Loyola as the third logothete, and Barthes's determination to distance the content

---

[34] See Barthes's comment in *Roland Barthes by Roland Barthes*, partially quoted in my introduction: 'Revolutionary writings have always scantily and poorly represented the daily finality of the revolution, the way it suggests *we shall live tomorrow*, either because this representation risks sweetening or trivializing the present struggle, or because, more precisely, political theory aims only at setting up the real freedom of the human question, without prefiguring any of its answers. Hence utopia would be the taboo of the revolution, and the writer would be responsible for transgressing it; he alone could risk this representation' (77 / 81).

of these systems, prevents him from exploring the more specific relationship between Fourier and Sade to which he elsewhere draws attention. For the loss of sadism in the passage from Sade to Fourier is hardly equivalent to the disappearance of divine interlocution in the passage from Loyola to Sade. As Barthes comments in the *biographeme* that closes his book, 'Fourier had read Sade'. If many French commentators explore the connections between these two near contemporary figures, it is in recognition of the fact that Sade is an important (and conscious) intertext for Fourier. As Simone Debout-Oleszkiewicz puts it in her introduction to *New Amorous World*, Fourier claimed both to have understood and to have gone beyond Sade. He had understood him in the sense of appreciating the atheism and radical existential solitude that had led Sade to centre his sexual, social, and cosmic system around evil, and had shared his insight into the 'new regions of being' uncovered by Sade's 'criminal' fantasies, his creation of a new moral system in which his own socially proscribed desires would find their place.[35] Fourier turns Sade's system on its head by recentring it on universal human happiness, yet by accepting and addressing the element of excess he remains very much on Sade's territory. For Fourier, 'vices' are the result of a faulty ordering of society which does not know how to use and transform them; it is only in Civilization that the passions, because constricted, have been turned into harmful perversions. As Barthes explains:

Fourierist pleasure is free from evil: it does not include persecution, in the Sadeian manner, but on the contrary dissipates it.... But what if someone's mania is persecuting people? Should this be allowed? The pleasure of persecution is due to a congestion; Harmony will decongest the passions, sadism will be reabsorbed: Dame Strogonoff had the unpleasant habit of persecuting her beautiful slave by piercing her breast with pins; in fact, it was a counter-passion: Dame Strogonoff was in love with her victim without knowing it: Harmony, by

---

[35] Debout-Oleszkiewicz, introduction to Fourier, *Le Nouveau Monde amoureux*, see pp. lxxvii–cxii. For a well-known discussion placing Sade and Fourier within a common frame, see Pierre Klossowski, 'Sade et Fourier' [1970], in *Derniers Travaux de Gulliver, suivi de Sade et Fourier* (Montpellier, Fata Morgana, 1974), 33–70. For a discussion of Sade as a utopian writer, published in the wake of Barthes's essays, see Gilles Lapouge, *Utopie et civilisations* (Geneva, Weber, 1973), 210–21.

authorizing and favouring Sapphic loves, would have relieved her of her sadism. (*SFL* 82 / 87–8).

Sadism has 'dropped out' of Fourier to the extent that it has been consciously defused and transformed—Fourier has not only read Sade but offers a reading of him.

Barthes is clearly aware of this, yet never offers an overview of the relationship between Fourier and Sade which might help us to fit his general enthusiasm for Sade into the framework of his overall thinking on utopia. Although he attempts to distinguish between a 'Sadeian text' or signifier and a signified 'sadism',[36] this is hardly the same productive relationship that he establishes between Fourier's utopian discourse and its parodic shadow in the dilatory actuality of Harmony: the nature of the subsumed value system (however ironic its status) and the subsumed sexual politics must surely matter. The relationship between the Sadeian castle and a general utopian liberation of human relations is indirect to say the least, but it is a relationship that Barthes tries intermittently to establish, and which will be seen to underpin, if only negatively, the relationship between society, sexuality, and language that is at the heart of all of Barthes's thinking on utopia.

The way in which Sade shares Fourier's specifically utopian investment in the details of everyday life is elaborated early in the first Sade essay where the Sadeian city is specifically likened to the Fourierist phalanstery. The hermetic isolation from the outside world of the Sadeian retreat (of which the castle of Silling is the archetype) serves not only as practical protection from the eyes of the world and its laws. Above all, it establishes the self-sufficient social autarchy that Barthes invariably associates with utopian cosmogonies: 'Once shut in, the libertines, their assistants, and their subjects form a total society, endowed with an economy, a value system, a discourse, and a timescale which is divided up into schedules, jobs, and festivities' (*SFL* 17 / 23). It is isolation which creates a system and facilitates the pleasurable and detailed fantasy of life in a finite and organized space: 'timetables, menus, plans for what to wear, interior design, rules for conversation or communication, all this can be found in Sade: the Sadeian city is based not solely on its

---

[36] See the fragment 'Sadism', *SFL* 170 / 174.

"pleasures", but also on its needs: it is thus possible to outline an ethnography of the Sadeian village.'[37]

Has Barthes stressed the fantasmatic signifier of Sade's novels in order to suppress the graphic social and sexual alienations of this fictional microcosm? In a section of the second Sade essay entitled 'Social', Barthes points out that the plots of Sade's novels are given a perfectly real historical context in the eighteenth-century France of Sade's youth, and that the power structures and social oppression of this world are 'brutally underlined' (130 / 134). The libertines are drawn from the aristocracy and the exploitative class of financiers, slave traders, and *prévaricateurs* (who have made their fortunes from the wars of Louis XV and from all forms of corruption and despotism); the victims of debauchery are recruited from the urban subproletariat or from amongst the feudal serfs of the landed aristocracy.[38] But unlike the realist novelist of the nineteenth century, who would invent individual biographies with a direct link to the real world of French society (Coupeau the roofer for Zola, César Birotteau the shopkeeper for Balzac), Sade transports social relations into an artificial model of society. Class division is indirectly but brutally present in this miniature cosmogony: on the one hand 'exploiters, possessors, governors, and tyrants', on the other the 'lower orders' (*le petit peuple*), even if it is profit of a specifically sadistic kind which motivates such division (' "Every imaginable vexation and injustice was visited upon the lower orders, in the certain knowledge that the greater the tyranny, the greater the sum of pleasures to be gained" ' (131 / 135)). From this Barthes concludes that the Sadeian novel is actually more real than the realist 'social novel' ('Balzac as read by Marx'), and produces in support of this claim the now infamous parallel between fictional Sadeian society and the socio-economic structures of today's 'underdeveloped' countries:

---

[37] This idea of a founding isolation from the world is very suggestively developed in Pierre Macherey's essay on *The 120 Days of Sodom*: 'Sade and the Order of Disorder', Ch. 8 of *The Object of Literature* [1990], trans. David Macey (Cambridge, Cambridge University Press, 1995), 147–77: 148–50.

[38] With the exception of those subjects of debauchery whose noble origins increase the transgressive pleasure (see SFL 130 / 134).

Sadeian practices appear to us today to be totally improbable: however, we need only travel in any under-developed country (analogous, all in all, to eighteenth-century France), to understand that they are readily operable there: the same social division, the same opportunities for recruitment, the same availability of subjects, the same conditions for seclusion, and, so to speak, the same impunity. (131 / 135)

Barthes may well have sharpened his 'social' reading of Sade in the four years that separate his second essay on Sade from the original publication of the first, and it is of course significant that the year spent in Morocco fell within this period.³⁹ Inevitably, one way of reading Barthes's possible allusion to Morocco is to take it as an alarming comment on his own behaviour there, and it is indeed difficult to discuss 'Incidents' without some reference to this quotation. However, it is important to remember that its original context is in fact Barthes's analysis of Sade's own analysis of social oppression. If Barthes's first-hand experience of Moroccan society adds a new dimension to his reading of Sade, we shall see that Sade is present in his turn in some of Barthes's reflections on the 'Orient'.⁴⁰ Barthes had already argued that the sexual relationships of Racine's tragic universe were laid in place by its power structures rather than vice versa.⁴¹ In his attempt to think through in his own terms the interrelationship between social division and sexual alienation, Barthes—like Fourier—perceives the relevance of Sade at the same time as trying to go beyond him.

---

³⁹ 'Sade I' was first published as 'L'Arbre du crime' in *Tel Quel*, 28 (1967), and as a preface to vol. xvi of Sade's *Œuvres complètes* (Paris, Cercle du Livre précieux, 1967), 509–32. 'Sade II' and Barthes's 'Life of Sade' (173–82 / 177–86) were published for the first time in *Sade, Fourier, Loyola*.
⁴⁰ See Chs, 5 and 8.
⁴¹ 'It is not the sexes that create the conflict, it is the conflict that defines the sexes', OR 1–137: 14 / 13–132: 26.

4
Colonial Mythologies

> The Orient and the Occident, cardinal points of an entirely historical star.[1]

THE collection of photographs that opens *Roland Barthes by Roland Barthes* contains a distant photo of Barthes performing in a play put on by the Sorbonne theatre group of which he was a founding member (*RB* 33 / 37). The play is *The Persians* by Aeschylus, and the hooded and masked figure of Barthes represents the Persian King Darius, returned from the grave to lament the victory of the Greeks over his son King Xerxes. This Greek tragedy performed in the open air courtyard of the Sorbonne provides a fine link with Barthes's early reflections on the utopian potential of theatrical space;[2] moreover, the date of the performance is 4 May 1936, the very day of the euphoric electoral victory in France of the left-wing Popular Front.[3] In all, this photo may seem to represent an overdetermined utopian moment in which, what is more, the author himself plays a part.

However, and by a precious coincidence, *The Persians* is Edward Said's earliest example of Orientalism—it is a Greek representation that speaks for and explains the 'Orient' to the West.[4] Said defines Orientalism as a style of thought based on an epistemological and ontological distinction between the 'Orient' and the 'Occident', commonly encountered, he claims, from Aeschylus to Karl Marx. The underlying aim of the discourse of Orientalism is to restructure conceptualizations of the East in the interests of Western domination. In periods of Western colonial ascendency and supremacy celebrations

---

[1] Abdelkebir Khatibi, *Figures de l'étranger dans la littérature française* (Paris, Denoël, 1987), 85.   [2] See Ch. 1.
[3] On this electoral context, see Calvet, *Roland Barthes*, 36–7.
[4] Said, *Orientalism*, 21, 56.

of Oriental difference and exoticism act as naturalizations of Eastern lack of power. In short, in the body of texts analysed by Said, Orientalism has always operated as an ideological prop for European and American colonialism. I want to use this chance encounter of Barthes and Said—in which Barthes is curiously positioned acting out the role of the represented Persian—to set up the general problem to be explored in many of the chapters to follow. This is the relationship of Barthes's largely utopian writing on foreign lifestyles to the ethical, political, and aesthetic problems of Orientalism as defined by Said. The latter quotes the ironic definition of an Orientalist included by Flaubert in his *Dictionary of Received Ideas*: 'a man who has travelled widely'.[6] Barthes travelled famously to Japan and China, and held teaching posts in Romania, Egypt, and Morocco—in short, he not only travelled, but travelled to some archetypal 'Oriental' destinations. However, before attempting to situate his own writing on Morocco, Japan, and China, I want in this chapter to demonstrate that the early Barthes was a quite exemplary demystifier of Orientalist discourse and of the ideological connotations attaching to various instances of travel writing. Above all, he was especially alert to the ways in which an Orientalist rhetoric mediated the pro-colonial ideology of 1950s France, as can be seen in a series of powerful analyses to be found in *Mythologies*.

When, in 1955, two right-wing journalists from the *Figaro* report on their holiday cruise to the Soviet Union, their aim is clearly to project a dystopia which would indirectly reflect the greater perfection of France. This is not, of course, what they

---

[5] For introductory definitions of Orientalism in his sense of a discourse, see Said, *Orientalism*, 1–4. For his own development of his ideas, see *Culture and Imperialism* (London, Chatto and Windus, 1993). For a very useful selection of work on colonial and postcolonial discourse, which contains various critiques of Said's work as well as examples of the main developments in the field (and an extensive bibliography), see Patrick Williams and Laura Chrisman (eds.), *Colonial Discourse and Post-Colonial Theory: A Reader* (Hemel Hempstead, Harvester Wheatsheaf, 1993). Of the wealth of important work that has been produced over the last ten years or so, I have found Robert Young's books especially useful: *White Mythologies: Writing History and the West* (London, Routledge, 1990), and *Colonial Desire: Hybridity in Theory, Culture and Race* (London, Routledge, 1995).

[6] *Dictionary of Received Ideas*, trans. Robert Baldick, in Gustave Flaubert, *Bouvard and Pécuchet*, trans. A. J. Krailsheimer (Penguin, Harmondsworth, 1976), 320, quoted by Said, *Orientalism*, 185.

pretend to be doing. But, as Barthes points out in 'The *Batory* Cruise', it is disingenuous for a newspaper which regularly engages in anti-Soviet propaganda to assume a cloak of touristic ignorance, of inability to judge so important a country in so short a space of time, and this 'at the very moment when its envoys can at last approach what they used to speak of so readily and so decisively from a distance'.[7] Tourism, then, is identified as a wonderful alibi for looking without understanding, for travelling without taking any interest in political realities. The only reality granted to the tourist is the neutral territory of the street, a space for observation rather than judgement. If a few exotic details serve as a timely reminder of the inherent backwardness of the Soviet Union (trains that moan rather than whistle, Chinese writing on the carriages, wooden station platforms, no cafés, nothing to drink but pear juice), the main purpose of the myth of the street is to establish a sharp distinction between the people and the political regime. This is in order to introduce possibilities of nostalgic envy for all things French, so that an old woman's tears, or the flowers given by a dock worker, can be represented as if they were being offered up to a symbol of French freedom and happiness—its bourgeoisie *en voyage*.

Illuminated by the 'sun of capitalist civilization' (96 / 132), the spontaneity and generosity of the Russian people signify a deficiency in their own regime, the image of which remains, moreover, faithful to its traditional caricature. When the waiter of a sleeping car asks one of the journalists for the spoon that belongs with his glass of tea, they infer a 'gigantic paperwork bureaucracy whose sole concern is to maintain a precise inventory of teaspoons' (97 / 133). This fantasy of Soviet order for its own sake leads the *Figaro* to what Barthes calls a 'new pasture for national vanity': the disorderly individualism of the French visitors who amaze the Russians by chatting during museum visits or 'fooling around' in the metro (97–8 / 133). In Barthes's carefully structured mythology this is his final point of attack, in

---

[7] *ET* 95–8: 95 / *My* 130–3: 131. *Paris-Match* seems to have sent two of its journalists (Jean Roy and Michel Simon) on the same trip and in exactly the same spirit: 'They endeavoured to look at Russia with tourists' eyes rather than as professionals' (*Paris-Match*, 338 (17–24 Sept. 1955), 30–1).

that it is juxtaposed with the *Figaro*'s contrasting coverage of the episode of 400 members of the French Air Force who refused to be recalled for service in Algeria. Here 'disorder' was far from symbolizing the 'glorious Gallic virtues' of endearing anarchy and enviable individualism. Rather, it was the 'lamentable' artificial product of a few 'ringleaders', in brief a shameful act of treason. French individualism, in the pages of the *Figaro* at least, is described by Barthes as a luxury product, and one strictly for export: 'freedom in the shop window', but 'Order at home' (98 / 133). Soviet communism serves as a foil for Western freedom, celebration of which is a useful mask, in this period, for Western colonial oppression.

While nearly all the myths that Barthes analyses, whatever their subject matter, are vehicles for imposing a particular world-view, those that attach themselves to travel and to other cultures arguably hold the key to the rest. It is not for nothing that the so-called human interest stories of the popular press range nervously, in this period, around the colonial outposts of France and her European neighbours, for the Poujadism that marks French internal politics in the mid-1950s is symbiotically linked to the accelerating decolonization of France's overseas territories. If the spatial range of French proto-fascist myths extends from Parisian interiors to the deserts and forests of France's most distant colonies, the temporal span contracts in proportion—the past and future of historical determinations and change are cynically collapsed into an unchanging and unchangeable present. Barthes has not always received the political credit he deserves for establishing this connection—both for tracking down many examples of pro-colonial myths and for relating them to other forms of mystification.[8]

---

[8] Kristin Ross, in *Fast Cars, Clean Bodies: Decolonization and the Reordering of French Culture*, is on the precise territory of *Mythologies* in her very interesting attempt to bring French domestic and colonial ideology into a single interpretative frame. But whereas she mobilizes Barthes for her discussions of cars and of ideals of hygiene, she completely overlooks his frequent demystification of pro-colonial propaganda. This is even to the extent of twice using the phrase 'greasy French fries' (presumably an allusion to 'Steak and Chips', M 62–4 / *My* 77–9) without mentioning that Barthes is analysing a fine example of French media propaganda after the humiliating defeat at Dien Bien Phu in May 1954. When *Paris-Match* celebrated General de Castries's patriotic and nationalistic gesture on his release from captivity—the request that his first meal should be a plate of chips—the chips

In 'A Few Words from Monsieur Poujade', Barthes focuses upon the endless celebrations of 'common sense' that mark the rhetoric of Poujade's political speeches, a common sense that 'blocks all dialectical solutions, defines a homogeneous world in which we are at home, sheltered from the disturbances and evasions of "dreaming" '.[9] The mythology was published in May 1955, the very year of Barthes's repeated unmasking of attempts to keep women, and the petty bourgeoisie in general, enclosed in the home. In this period at least Barthes was finely attuned, not only to the imbrication of gender and class oppression in the propaganda saturating the popular press, but to the complicity of the latter with more overtly right-wing discourse.[10] A curiously appropriate photograph, which I discovered in *Paris-Match*'s coverage of the 1956 legislative elections, portrays a newly elected Poujadist *député* at home *in his carpet slippers*. This is none other than the 27-year-old Jean-Marie le Pen, of whom the caption tells us: 'Former parachute officer in Indochina, he represents the avant-garde of Poujadism.'[11] The route from the petty bourgeois *pantouflard* to the colonies passes—in both directions—through the euphoria of the same:

> Monsieur Poujade's language shows, once more, that all of petty bourgeois mythology implies the refusal of otherness, the negation of difference, the euphoria of identity, and the exaltation of the same. In general, this equational reduction of the world prepares an expansionist phase in which the 'identity' of human phenomena quickly establishes a 'nature' and thereupon a 'universality'. (*ET* 53 / *My* 87)[12]

If difference really cannot be avoided, myths have all sorts of strategies at their disposal for reducing otherness to a negative mirror image of the same. In short, the French will always and

---

are clearly established as racially superior to the daily portion of *rice* that had been the general's unfortunate lot during his four months in Indo-Chinese captivity. See the photograph of General de Castries, captioned 'First Wish: Some Chips', in *Paris-Match*, 285 (11–18 Sept. 1954).

[9] *ET* 51–3: 53 / *My* 85–7: 87.
[10] For a second mythology on Pierre Poujade, see 'Poujade and the Intellectuals', *ET* 127–35 / *My* 182–90.
[11] *Paris-Match*, 353 (7–14 Jan. 1956), 66.
[12] Robert Young writes that it took Aimé Césaire and Frantz Fanon to point out that fascism was simply colonialism brought home to Europe (*White Mythologies*, 8). Clearly, Barthes is also aware of a connection.

everywhere find confirmation of the excellence of their own habitat, for indirect pointers to the superiority of French culture can be discovered in settings as arbitrary and as geographically distinct as a tropical jungle or a Soviet city.

Barthes's preface to Voltaire's *Novels and Tales*, 'The Last Happy Writer', is a good example of his awareness that the relationship between travel writing, Orientalism, and the colonial context has a specific history. The essay was first published in 1958, when Barthes's main point had been that the bourgeoisie was historically so close to taking power that it could afford to immobilize the world. Voltaire was a 'happy' writer in the sense that his ease with his own position in the world was reflected in his writing. In expanding this preface in *Critical Essays* in 1964 Barthes added a section on travel and cultural difference.[13] Both are basically linked to the territorial expansion that accompanied the rise to economic power of the eighteenth-century bourgeoisie, to 'the definitive organization by modern capitalism of its world market from China to South America' (*CE* 87 / 98). The superficial relativization of space in Voltaire's stories makes use of a familiar set of exotic stereotypes (the Egyptian sage, the Muslim Arab, the Turk, the Chinaman, the Siamese, the Persian). The result is not the exploration of space that one might have expected, but rather a shallow survey of space, as Voltaire takes his readers on a landlord's tour of the new dwellings (from the River Seine to the River Ganges) in which essential humanity is currently flourishing: 'these Oriental countries, which today have so heavy a weight, so pronounced an individual role in world politics, are for Voltaire simply so many empty squares, mobile signs without any content of their own, zero degrees of humanity, deftly appropriated in an act of self-signification' (88 / 98–9). The movement of travel is illusory, for it is, in this case, an immobilizing operation which aims to confirm rather than to transform the self. For if travel reveals the existence of other customs, laws, and moral standards, such diversity rapidly returns to its point of equilibrium in an underlying human essence. Indeed acknowledging a superficial cultural difference is the best way to conjure it

---

[13] Barthes, 'The Last Happy Writer', in *CE* 83–9 / 94–100, first published as a preface to Voltaire, *Romans et contes* (Paris, Club des librairies de France, 1958).

away: 'let man (Occidental man, that is) multiply himself a little, let the European philosopher be doubled by the Chinese Sage, the ingenuous Huron, and universal man will be created' (88 / 99).[14]

In the myths of the 1950s, Barthes finds that Voltaire's optimistic ideology of a universal human nature has been inherited pretty much in its original form. *The Family of Man*, a famous (and still mythical) American photography exhibition ('503 photos from 68 countries') aimed to prove that by scratching the superficial diversity of skins and cultural institutions, one rapidly reaches the solid rock of a universal human nature.[15] Barthes suggests that its aura of sentimental humanism may be partly due to the decision to put on the show in Paris with its title translated as the *great* family of man (*La Grande Famille des hommes*).[16] However, the brief prologue and introduction to the original catalogue reveal that the American packaging of the exhibition was just as moralizing and sentimental as the French version. This is especially apparent in the exuberant prologue by Carl Sandburg: 'People! flung wide and far, born into toil, struggle, blood and dreams. . . . Here are ironworkers, bridgemen, musicians, sandhogs, miners, builders of huts and skyscrapers, jungle hunters, landlords and the

---

[14] Barthes's attack on Voltaire, who after all denounced the abuses of slavery if not the developing economic system of which they were a part, is obviously related to his contemporary obsessions and targets. It is interesting to note Barthes's nostalgic allusion to Voltaire's attacks on religious intolerance in a diary extract [1977] included in the essay 'Deliberation' (*RL* 359–73 / 399–413): 'Idea of compiling a *contemporary* dictionary of examples of intolerance (literature, in this case Voltaire, cannot be abandoned, as long as the evils to which it bears witness still exist)' (364 / 404).

[15] Barthes makes a similar point in the opening paragraph of a 1961 review of Foucault's *Madness and Civilization*, 'De part et d'autre', translated by Richard Howard as 'Taking Sides', though the French implies that both sides are taken into consideration (*CE* 163–70 / 167–74): 'Human mores are variable: this is the consensus of classical humanism, from Herodotus to Montaigne and Voltaire. But precisely: mores were then carefully detached from human nature, as the episodic attributes of an eternal substance: on the one hand timelessness, on the other, historical or geographical relativity; to describe the different ways of being cruel or generous was to acknowledge a certain essence of cruelty or generosity, and in consequence to diminish its variations; on classical terrain, relativity is never bewildering because it is not infinite; it stops very soon at the inalterable heart of things: it is reassuring, not disturbing' (163 / 167).

[16] 'The Great Family of Man', *M* 100–2 / *My* 173–6.

landless, the loved and the unloved, the lonely and abandoned, the brutal and the compassionate—one big family hugging close to the ball of Earth for its life and being.'[17] This is the myth of a human 'community' which Barthes describes as the baseline of this sort of humanism, and which does indeed allow the exhibition organizers to project the *Family of Man* as a utopian microcosm of a world of shared hopes and dreams. However, Barthes's point is that the myth functions in two stages, and to reach this underlying unity it first celebrates the infinite minor variations in human morphologies and behaviour: 'exoticism is insistently stressed, . . . the diversity in skins, skulls and customs is made manifest, the image of Babel is complacently projected over that of the world. Then, from this pluralism, a type of unity is magically produced: man is born, works and dies everywhere in the same way . . . diversity is only formal and does not belie the existence of a common mould' (*M* 100 / *My* 174). In exactly the way Barthes describes, Sandburg conflates the two sides of the myth without comment, continuing his image of one big family hugging the earth as follows: 'Alike and ever alike we are on all continents in the need of love, food, clothing, work, speech, worship, sleep, games, dancing, fun. From tropics to arctics humanity lives with these needs so alike, so inexorably alike.'[18]

Edward Steichen's introduction to the catalogue is explicit about the aims of the exhibition in a way that clearly confirms Barthes's analysis. For a start, he explains that his 273 photos represent a distillation of over *two million* photos sought out over three years 'from every corner of the earth'. Moreover, this infinite human variety was conceived 'as a mirror of the universal elements and emotions in the everydayness of life—as a mirror of the essential oneness of mankind throughout the world'. The passionate mission attributed here to photography is that of 'explaining man to man', while the vehicle of that lesson will be: 'Photographs concerned with the religious rather than religions. With basic human consciousness rather than social consciousness.'[19] I do not know whether Barthes had

---

[17] Carl Sandburg, prologue to *The Family of Man* (New York, Maco Magazine Corporation for the New York Museum of Modern Art, 1955), 2–3: 2.
[18] Ibid. 2.
[19] Edward Steichen, introduction to *The Family of Man*, 4–5.

access to these revealing texts which certainly back up his claim that 'the content and appeal of the pictures, the discourse which justifies them, aims to suppress the determining weight of History: we are held back at the surface of an identity, prevented precisely by sentimentality from penetrating into this ulterior zone of human behaviour where historical alienation introduces some "differences" which we shall here quite simply call "injustices" ' (M 101 / My 174). Thus Barthes cuts through the bogus humanism of the exhibition, both on its home territory of the United States ('but why not ask the parents of Emmet Till, the young black assassinated by the Whites, what *they* think of *the great family of man?*'), and on his own French doorstep: 'let us also ask the North African workers of the Goutte d'Or district in Paris what they think of *the great family of man*' (102 / 176).[20] False humanism is replaced with what Barthes calls the 'progressive humanism' of the mythologist: upending the ancient 'imposture' which naturalizes history, so as to present human natures as materially determined and Human Nature as a historical concept.[21]

Barthes's mythology on the Hachette *Blue Guide* to Spain contains one of his clearest exposures of 'the denial of history' as the grounding rhetorical strategy of French myths of the 1950s.[22] It also spells out very clearly the concept of history

---

[20] However, I suspect that Nigerian novelist Wole Soyinka would find fault with Barthes here, just as he does with the ending of the mythology 'Wine and Milk' (*M* 58–61 / *My* 74–7). Barthes reminds his reader that wine is a product of alienated labour and colonial expropriation ('the big settlers in Algeria who impose on the Muslims, on the very land of which they have been dispossessed, a crop of which they have no need, they who lack even bread' (*M* 61 / *My* 77)). According to Soyinka: 'This is the radical conscience saved—by a double appropriation of the labour of the Algerian worker: first converting his labour into the language exchange of the intellectual class, then crediting this act with a basic political consciousness. Neither achieves anything concrete for the expropriated Algerian worker.' See Wole Soyinka, 'The Critic and Society: Barthes, Leftocracy and Other Mythologies', in Henry Louis Gates, Jr. (ed.), *Black Literature and Literary Theory* (New York, Methuen, 1984), 27–57.
[21] Barthes's attacks on a dehistoricized Human Nature are presumably strongly influenced by the formulations of Marx and Engels in *The German Ideology*, especially their discussion of the German 'True Socialists' (see Ch. 3). Barthes very acutely demonstrates that the concept of Human Nature can be exploited in a colonial as well as a class context. See Robert Young's brief discussion of 'The Great Family of Man' in *White Mythologies*, 122–3.
[22] 'The *Blue Guide*', M 74–7 / My 121–5.

with which he is working: history intersects with geography in that it is concerned with the social and political determinants of present-day reality. The *Blue Guide* dismisses the material reality of Franco's Spain by acknowledging 'only one type of space, that which weaves, across a few nondescript lacunae, a close web of churches, vestries, reredoses, crosses, altar curtains' (*M* 75 / *My* 123), so that the sole purpose of travel seems to be to visit churches. 'By reducing geography to the description of an uninhabited world of monuments' the *Blue Guide* is wilfully blind to a countryside 'which is real *and which exists in time*'; it dissolves the reality of the land and that of its people, 'it accounts for nothing of its present, that is, nothing historical' (76 / 123). Thus, appropriately, it is an actual travel guide that betrays the mythological value of tourism.

Another example of disingenuous geography is directly related to France's last major struggle in this period to stem the tide of decolonization. This is a linguistic example: the use of the verb 'to be' in the phrase 'Algeria *is* French'. Barthes is writing in 1959, five years into the Algerian War. His mythology (one of the brief but important series published that year in *Les Lettres nouvelles*) brings together the history and politics of space in an excellent example of what he means by a language war.[23] To employ the present tense in such a context is to transform a mere wish into the illusion of a permanent state of affairs: 'History here is simply something that happened at an earlier stage, it can only be conjugated in the past tense; the world has changed but is not going to change any more' (*OC* i. 811). Thus, in what Barthes calls 'far-right grammar', the function of the verb 'to be' changes when the tense changes: the past tense deals with facts, the present tense with essences. The original French conquest of Algeria is openly granted its historical status, while the current Algerian 'rebellion', in as far as its existence is acknowledged at all, is a mere chance event with little relevance to '*the nature of things*'. However, declares Barthes, with one of his finest of fierce flourishes (and with an unusual pretence of a direct address to the enemy): 'All the far-right grammar in the world will never prevail against the reality of an endless war, nor that

---

[23] 'Sur un emploi du verbe "être" ' (on a use of the verb 'to be'), first published in *Lettres nouvelles* (Apr. 1959), *OC* i. 811–13.

of a social disparity which you have created in the course of this Past, and to which you owe both your essence and your condemnation' (*i.* 812).[24]

The extent to which Barthes's mythologies have been isolated from their original context is in itself an interesting fact of the history of their reception. For instance, despite the plethora of critical commentaries on Barthes's famous semiological analysis of the cover picture of a saluting black soldier,[25] no one, to my knowledge, has thought to investigate the contents of this 1955 issue of *Paris-Match* (25 June–2 July 1955).[26] The subject of the photograph, surprisingly, turns out to be a saluting black child, a fact that enhances the assumed innocence behind the pro-colonial connotation. The immediate context of the photo is publicity for a military tattoo which was actually sponsored by *Paris-Match*. This is the 'prestigious' and 'fantastic spectacle' of the 'Nuits de l'Armée' (Army Nights), whose 4,000 participants are drawn from the Paratroop Regiment, the Foreign Legion, the Republican Guard, the Black Guard of Dakar, and so on. The saluting boy ('Little Diouf') has come from Ouagadougou (then Upper Volta, now Burkina Faso) 'with his friends, children of A-O.F. soldiers', to take part in the opening ceremony.[27] The

---

[24] Another North African example of the intersection of language and colonial politics is to be found in the paired mythologies 'Moroccan Lexicon' and 'Moroccan Grammar' (*Lettres nouvelles*, Nov. 1955), which Barthes renamed 'African Grammar' when they were collected in *Mythologies* (*ET* 103–9 / *My* 137–44). Barthes analyses official French discourse on the independence struggles in Morocco and Algeria, focusing especially on the intimidatory connotations imposed upon such words as 'destiny', 'politics', 'population', 'war', before reaching some general conclusions on the predominance of noun forms (related to the high consumption of concepts required to cover over reality), on particular uses of plural nouns, the ambiguous function of adjectives, etc. In the 1959 mythology, Barthes demonstrates that the Algerians even change their national status depending on the context, at one moment subsumed as '10 million French', at another returned to non-Frenchness along with 'a Muslim (Ali Khodja), whose representative role has been granted by the French authorities' (this 'Muslim' had offended the political sensibilities of the newspaper *Carrefour*). As Barthes puts it in a favourite image of the bat, the Algerians constitute 'a body which is half-mouse, half bird: French when it keeps quiet, Muslim when it dares to speak' (*OC* i. 812).

[25] See Michael Moriarty's ironic apology for producing the '297th' account, in his *Roland Barthes* (Cambridge, Polity, 1991), 1.

[26] *Paris-Match*, 326 (25 June–2 July 1955).

[27] Afrique-Occidentale française (A.-O.F.) was the name of the federation of French colonies centrally administered from Dakar between 1910 and 1958. These countries gained independence between 1958 and 1960.

magazine's celebration of this event (which spills into the following issues) takes the form of enthusiastic captions of the sort: '*Paris-Match* is proud of the 1955 Army Nights.'[28] However, in the stories contained inside Little Diouf's cover, *Paris-Match* enhances patriotism with crude pro-colonial propaganda. Here are three examples. First, coverage of King Baudouin's visit to his adoring subjects in the Belgian Congo, which includes a photograph of a row of black schoolchildren with 'Long live the King!' spelled out in large letters (one letter each) across their chests.[29] Second, an article on cannibalism in Papua New Guinea implies through its title, 'In the Land of the Last Survivors of Prehistory', that history has not yet got started in such distant parts. Moreover, it is 'only men killed in battle' who are eaten by these natives who—until the arrival of their intrepid visitors—had 'never seen a white man', and who are compared to circus clowns on account of their colourful headdresses and their painted faces.[30] Finally, 'Slave Dealers Still Exist' is a piece on slavery in the Sudan ('such are African customs today') which draws an unequivocal connection between slavery and Islam, to end as follows: 'None of all this is new under the African sun, neither slavery, nor human sacrifices, nor cannibal practices. Nothing, that is, except the French presence. We might do well to dwell on the words of Albert Schweizer: "An enormous debt weighs upon us and our civilization. We are not free to choose whether or not we wish to do good to black men, it is our duty." '[31]

The racist rhetoric so happily embraced by *Paris-Match* is astutely analysed by Barthes in his mythology 'Bichon and the Blacks' (*chez les Nègres*).[32] This is the illustrated tale of a French couple who set off on a 'dangerous' painting-cum-filming trip to an ill-defined and vaguely situated African land. The title is Barthes's own, but anything else that the reader might take as ironic exaggeration is directly drawn from his source.[33] Close

---

[28] *Paris-Match*, 328 (9–16 July 1955), 16–17.
[29] Ibid. 326, 16–17.
[30] Ibid. 56–7 and 67–70.
[31] Ibid. 94–8: 98.
[32] *ET* 35–8 / *My* 64–7.
[33] 'The Wonderful Adventure of a Child Explorer', *Paris-Match*, 305 (29 Jan.–5 Feb. 1955), photos 34–42, text 43 and 68. The racist author of the piece is Georges de Caunes, the very same civilizing white journalist who (with the help of a black Christian priest) had gone to the rescue of a cruelly treated Islamic slave and drawn his conclusions in 'Slave Dealers Still Exist' (see above).

examination of the latter reveals that the country in question is Nigeria, but Barthes is undoubtedly right that *Paris-Match* refers to it to begin with as the 'Country of the Red Negroes' so as to conflate 'the colour of their painted skins with the human blood they supposedly drink there' (*ET* 36 / *My* 65).[34] In a series of photographs, and above all through the overtly racist captions, the curly blond baby Bichon ('Darling') is seen to tame the threatening black cannibals with his superior white charms: 'Right in front of Bichon, a cannibal from the tribe of the "Red Negroes". He was nearly eaten. The eaters of men were won over by his childish smile. He became their idol.'[35] The basic trick of what Barthes calls the 'Bichon-operation' is to create illusory images of potentially dangerous situations (the small child alone, confronting a circle of towering black men) in order to make the reader fear that the child is really about to be eaten, and above all to present these images from the child's own point of view, so that scenes of Nigerian life take on the appearance of a *guignol* or Punch-and-Judy show. Indeed one of the captions actually refers to a tribal ritual as Bichon's 'first Punch-and-Judy show', and to a funeral dance as 'his first ring-a-ring-a-roses'.[36] Since this wilful reductiveness coincides with stereotypical views of supposedly exotic customs, readers of *Paris-Match* are confirmed in their ignorant inability to imagine anything that differs from their own experience: 'the Black has no complete and autonomous life: he is a bizarre object, reduced to a parasitical function, that of diverting the white man by his vaguely threatening outlandishness: Africa is a somewhat dangerous Punch-and-Judy Show' (*ET* 37 / *My* 66). It is here that Barthes points out the enormous gulf between contemporary ethnology and these reactionary media representations of other

---

[34] 'The *Kaleris* are cannibals who refuse to have any contact with White Men; they go about naked and owe the name "red negroes" to the mixture of ground laterite and palm oil with which they daub their bodies.' And, after a tale of turn-of-the-century butchery: 'The *Kaleris* have not evolved since these events, they have never evolved' (ibid. 43).

[35] Ibid. 38–9. 'Clearly, White Men are destined to become gods', says Barthes (*ET* 36 / *My* 65), who could have added the detail that when Bichon is born (appropriately, if mysteriously, during the temporary absence of his father) curious natives turn up bearing gifts of milk, cream, and butter, 'like the three kings visiting the Infant Jesus' (*Paris-Match*, 305, 68).

[36] *Paris-Match*, 305, 40 and 41.

cultures (the 'distressing divide between knowledge and mythology'), to stress that 'we are still living in a *pre*-Voltairean mentality'. For in the days of Voltaire and Montesquieu, the astonishment provoked by Persians and Hurons was at least tied up with the ingenuousness attributed to them: 'Today Voltaire would not write up Bichon's adventures the way *Match* has done: instead, he would imagine some cannibal (or Korean) Bichon contending with the napalmized Punch-and-Judy show of the West' (38 / 67).

The allusion to Korea is well placed here. In fact Barthes's best example of an archetypal Orientalism is the filmed travelogue *Lost Continent*, which portrays a vaguely defined ethnographic expedition to some equally vague corner of South-East Asia:

Our explorers are good fellows, who fill up their time with child-like amusements . . . Which means that these good people, anthropologists though they are, don't bother much with historical or sociological problems. To penetrate the Orient never means more for them than a little trip on a boat, on an azure sea, in an essentially sunny country. And this same Orient which has today become the political centre of the world we see here all flattened, made smooth and gaudily coloured like an old-fashioned postcard.[37]

Barthes identifies the complementary rhetorical strategies at work here for dealing with anything foreign. The first is identification, which in *Lost Continent* takes the form of presenting Buddhism as a mere variant of Christianity. Thus forms of otherness are defused by their projection as reflections of Western phenomena.[38] The second (as in 'Bichon and the Blacks') is recourse to exoticism, reducing the other to the status of object, clown, or Punch-and-Judy show. Two versions, for

---

[37] '*Lost Continent*', M 94–6: 94 / *My* 163–5: 163.

[38] Barthes's mythology 'Martians' (based on press articles inspired by a spate of sightings of flying saucers) analyses an extreme version of identification in the service of petty bourgeois mythical imperialism: 'Otherness is the concept most antipathetic of all to "common sense". Every myth tends ineluctably to a narrow anthropomorphism and, worse still, to what we might call a class anthropomorphism. Mars is not only Earth, it is petty bourgeois Earth, it is the little *canton* of mentality cultivated (or expressed) by the popular illustrated press. No sooner has it taken form in the sky than Mars is thus *aligned* by the most powerful of appropriations, that of identity.' See ET 27–9: 29 / *My* 42–4: 44.

Barthes, of the familiar denial of history which is ironically captured by his comment on a procession of unidentified refugees: 'eternal essences of refugees, which it is in the *nature* of the Orient to produce.' The mythology ends with a splendid line: 'We therefore see that the "beautiful images" of *Lost Continent* cannot be innocent: it cannot be innocent to *lose* the continent that has found itself again at Bandoeng' (M 96 / My 165). To appreciate the force of Barthes's point, the specific context of the Bandung Conference is indeed crucial. For *Lost Continent* was first shown at the Cannes film festival in May 1955, a month after the conference opened on 19 April.[39] Some weeks earlier, *Paris-Match* had reported this forthcoming meeting in Indonesia of non-aligned countries (eighteen independent Asian countries, seven African—the United States, England, France, and the Soviet Union excluded) and had voiced its fears of 'demands' from French North African and British colonies.[40] Four issues later, it had found the appropriate mode for defusing this threat, captioning its photo-reportage as follows: 'From India to the Philippines, exoticism on parade! . . . The Javanese Aix-les-Bains has been transformed into a gigantic, real-life costume museum.'[41] It would be hard to find a more convincing example of Barthes's figure of exoticism as a basic rhetorical prop for French pro-colonial discourse.

Still in the Orient, if closer to home, Barthes sets up a related demystification of the media's representation of Algerian women. In 'Cottage Industry' ('Tricots à domicile'), an important 1959 mythology, he analyses a report about the campaign to provide income and occupation for Muslim women.[42] Appropriately, this was spearheaded by the wife of General Massu. Along with an amusing analysis of the mythical connotations of Madame Massu's stark headquarters in Algiers, and a more serious attack on the spiritual and charitable values which prop up this regressive form of labour, Barthes touches

---

[39] There is a reference to *Lost Continent* in *Paris-Match*, 321 (14–21 May 1955), 64.
[40] Ibid. 314 (2–9 Apr. 1955), 27.
[41] Ibid. 318 (30 Apr.–7 May 1955), 30–1.
[42] *ET* 145–8 / *OC* i. 805–7. Originally published in *Lettres nouvelles* (Apr. 1959).

on a theme of major importance in much Orientalist discourse—the representation of women. Barthes suggests that images of Algerian women have been especially prominent since the events of 13 May 1958 because women act as a convenient and harmless substitute for the Algerian proletariat.[43] Against the demands for real material improvement that acknowledgement of a proletariat would entail, this spotlight on women permits a touching marriage between local colour and political integration: 'still veiled but voting with determination' (*ET* 148 / *OC* i. 806). For this is the gentle rhythm of civilized evolution, so preferable to revolution or even real reform. Behind this, of course, lies an attempt to change perceptions of the historical cause of the Algerian 'problem', for 'to claim, in a Muslim country, to liberate its women is surreptitiously to transform the colonial responsibility into an Islamic one', to offload all of colonialism onto the 'rotten ship of religious obscurantism'. Not that criticism of the latter will lead the French to abandon the handy alibi that such colonies are part of a 'different civilization', one whose 'substantial exoticism (native in a *gandourah* standing in front of an oil well, black man in a loincloth harvesting "the wealth of the tropics") is necessary to the ecumenicism of Greater France'. Islam therefore provides both an excuse for favourable French comparisons and a 'distracting decor'. In short, the twin strategies of identification and exoticism combine in this instance to 'integrate these women without unveiling them' (148 / 807).

By delving into Barthes's source material, the same strategy can be found at work in *Paris-Match*'s worthy insistence on the backwardness of women's rights in cannibal society. To begin with (in Papua New Guinea at least) 'women are never eaten, obviously'. Further, there is an intriguing reversal of French gender roles, in that it is men who have 'the right of coquettishness'. Of one photograph we are told: 'It is the men who make themselves up, using a leaf filled with water to reflect

---

[43] 13 May 1958 was one of the most significant dates in the Algerian War. An insurrection of soldiers and French settlers in Algiers, and fears of a coup in France itself, led to the return to political power of Charles de Gaulle and the end of the Fourth Republic.

their faces. An amazed witch doctor (on the left) discovers the existence of the mirror.' It is in front of these seated men that the woman ('a slave in the house') cooks sweet potatoes between hot stones.[44] Meanwhile, over in Bichon's Africa, 'the women spend their time working in the fields and the forest, the men delicately tend the heavy red locks of their hair attire or freshen up their make-up'. Moreover, when the chief's daughters watch the funeral dance along with Bichon, naturally they are 'veiled'.[45] Barthes is, of course, acutely aware of the reality of women's position in France in this period, and the 'Cottage Industry' mythology should certainly be read alongside 'Choosing a Job', which was published just one week later.[46] Based on the advice dispensed in specialist features of women's magazines, it is one of Barthes's most forceful denunciations of their unequivocal recommendation to French women—'stay where you are!' (OC i. 810).

If the values of the *pantouflard* and of colonialism are linked in the ideological subtexts of French myths of the 1950s, there is, however, one mythology in which Barthes seems curiously uninterested in making this specific connection. This is his reading of Jules Verne's utopian novel *The Mysterious Island*. Although Barthes is preoccupied, as we saw in Chapter 1, with the 'slippers, pipe, and fireside' that emblematize a bourgeois appropriation of nature, he does not seem unduly concerned that the heroes of *The Mysterious Island* are hardly struggling to master an empty space.[47] Given the many denunciations of colonialism in mythologies written in the same period, a politically motivated colonization is surprisingly absent as a frame of reference. What is more, Rimbaud's 'Drunken Boat' is celebrated as somehow 'more utopian' than Verne's island, without any allusion to its own colonial context (nevertheless specific at the beginning of the poem), or to Rimbaud's more

---

[44] *Paris-Match*, 326, 56–7 and 67–70.
[45] Ibid. 305, 43 and 41.
[46] 'Le Choix d'un métier', OC i. 808–10, originally published in *Les Lettres nouvelles* (Apr. 1959). In particular, Barthes is analysing the advice dispensed by Berthe Bernage in her column in *L'Écho de la mode*.
[47] 'The *Nautilus* and the Drunken Boat', M 65–7 / *My*, 80–2.

than dubious later career in East Africa.[48] However, in the more detailed reading of *The Mysterious Island* which Barthes published in 1970, the utopian colonization of the world emerges as precisely that—an archetypal colonial episode despite its idealization. 'Where to Begin?', published in the same year as *S/Z*, Barthes's essay on Fourier, and *Empire of Signs*, is a text that brings together Barthes the structuralist and Barthes the anti-colonial mythologist.[49] At the same time it is a text that raises important questions about the complicity of utopia and colonialism, and as such will serve as a transition to a discussion of Barthes's ideological blind spots where his own travel writing is concerned.

Originally written for the very first issue of the journal *Poétique*, 'Where to Begin?' sets out in pedagogical mode, with methodological advice for would-be structuralists decked out in the language of linguistics and cybernetics. This demonstration rapidly dissolves into an inspired reading of the utopian themes of the novel, of which the 'structural imagination' shared by Verne and Barthes is a key component. *The Mysterious Island* emerges as an archetypal utopian cosmogony and its hero, Cyrus Smith—like Sade, Fourier, and so many others whom Barthes analysed at this time—as an archetypal logothete. Cyrus Smith is a demiurge, not least in the etymological sense of the term: a craftsman. For Barthes describes the novel as the very opposite of science fiction: not at all a projection into the future but a novel 'of the extreme past' which euphorically recreates the conquest of the tool.[50] Barthes's sparkling analysis of the 'code of the tool' combines insights from both *S/Z* and the

---

[48] Rimbaud's poem (1871) is close in time to Verne's novel, set in the 1860s and published in 1874. The crew of Rimbaud's boat (Verne's heroes *en route* for Iowa perhaps?) have been killed by American Indians. While its escape from a colonial function might seem to back up Barthes's claim that the crewless, wandering boat, 'freed from its concavity', can lead humanity to a 'genuine poetics of exploration' (67 / 82), Rimbaud himself not only explored parts of East Africa, but traded in gold, ivory, and arms. For details, see Enid Starkie, *Rimbaud in Abyssinia* (Oxford, Clarendon Press, 1937).

[49] 'Where to Begin?', NCE 79–89 / DZN 145–55.

[50] Barthes's comparison of Michelet's *tableaux* with ancient cosmogonies (see Ch. 2) is appropriate for his perception of *The Mysterious Island*: 'the earth and the past are perceived as a creation; provided with a spatial order, they become objects under the gaze or in the hands of an operator' (*OC* i. 92).

Fourier essay in that it is equivalent to the theme of *transformation*, 'which is at once technological (the transmutation of matter), magical (metamorphosis), and linguistic (the generation of signs)' (NCE 87 / DZN 153). While the novel's transformations are legitimized through reference to appropriate scientific codes (physics, chemistry, etc.), the results invariably build in an element of surprise—the island's seals, it turns out, can be transformed into forge bellows and candles, the canvas from their wrecked balloon into underwear and windmill sails:

> We sense the proximity of this code—which is a perpetual introduction of new, unexpected classifications—to linguistic operations: the Engineer's transforming power is a verbal power, for both consist in combining elements (words, materials) in order to produce new systems (sentences, objects) and both draw for this upon very sure codes (language, knowledge), whose stereotypical elements do not preclude a poetic (and poietic) yield. (87–8 / 153)

Barthes then identifies *naming* as the subcode which is an essential prerequisite for this transformation of the world. No sooner have the castaways reached the top of the mountain which gives them a panoramic view of the island—confirming that it is indeed an island as the genre demands—than they proceed to make a map out of it by both drawing and naming its features, in what Barthes describes as a linguistic appropriation: 'as if all the island's chaotic substance, object of future transformations, acceded to the status of functional reality only through the net of language.' In mapping the reality of their island the colonists simply 'fulfil the very definition of language as a "mapping" of reality' (88 / 154).

In many ways this analysis picks up the theme to which I gave a positive utopian interpretation in Chapter 2: the panoramic view as a privileged locus of a structuralist comprehension, classification, and remaking of the world. What is interesting about Barthes's reworking of this notion in 'Where to Begin?' is the degree to which his discussion problematizes this euphoric intellectual mastery of the world. The mapping and naming of the island is indeed a key scene, for this is hardly some arbitrary naming as in a Saussurean linguistic model. These supporters of the North in the American Civil War, who had escaped by balloon from the enemy stronghold of Richmond, Virginia, decide that the key features of their island should remind them of America, so that the newly named 'Lincoln Island' will be home to Union Bay, Washington Bay, Mount Franklin, and Lake Grant. As Pencroff the sailor enthusiastically puts it, whilst begging his companions to consider themselves 'colonists' rather than 'castaways': 'we'll turn this island into a little America! We'll build towns and railways, install a telegraph system, and then one day, once it's completely transformed, properly equipped, and fully civilized, we'll go back and give it to the government of the Union!'[51] Barthes unravels the various codes of the novel within a squarely colonial framework that is explicit in the novel itself—from the precise historical references to the American Civil War and the assassination of Abraham Lincoln, to the closing scene whereby the colonists, their island destroyed by a volcanic eruption, are whisked back to America to establish a flourishing colony in Iowa, 'a Western territory whose natural inhabitants, the Sioux, are as magically "absented" as any native of the Mysterious Island' (NCE 85 / DZN 151).

Barthes does not add, but might well have done so, that when Granite House is attacked and occupied by the local monkeys, the eventually victorious colonists capture, spare, and tame one of the invaders, naming him Jup, training him as a discreet servant to wait on them at table, dressing him in human clothes, and in an ultimate act of acculturation which Barthes unbelievably overlooks, converting him to the *pantouflard* pleasures of fireside and pipe.[52] So successful is this particular civilizing mission that the colonists marvel at Jup's inability to communicate in their own language. Moreover, it is the only black member of the party, the ex-slave Nab, freed but bound in gratitude to his humane master, Cyrus Smith, who undertakes Jup's training. As Barthes puts it, referring in passing to *Robinson Crusoe*, an acute problem underlies the colonial myth of the desert island: 'how to cultivate without slaves' (85 / 151). Not only are the legitimate inhabitants of the two colonized territories—Lincoln Island and Iowa—simply conjured away,

---

[51] Jules Verne, *L'Île mystérieuse* [1874] (Paris, Librairie générale française, 1989), 139–40.   [52] See, for example, 382, 406–7, 457.

but the euphorically utopian discourse seeks to purify colonial labour of its alienations. Since a bounteous Nature magically provides the basic raw materials for Cyrus Smith's transformations, wherever and whenever he needs them, labour is reduced to a question of intellectual problem-solving, its only constraints the limits of the engineer's ingenuity: 'So they need fishing lines to catch birds? *Right there, on the spot*, are creepers for lines, thorns for hooks, worms for bait' (84 / 149). In *Robinson Crusoe*, by contrast, Defoe insists upon the length of time and the degree of physical labour involved in Crusoe's slow transformation of his island (such as the days and weeks required to move a heavy canoe), so that the discourse depicts work in slow motion, and thereby restores to it the 'time value' which is the very measure of its alienation. In *The Mysterious Island*, on the other hand, time and fatigue are completely ignored when the cutting down of an enormous tree, almost without tools, 'is "liquidated" in a sentence'. Of course, one way of 'liquidating' labour is to pass it on to someone else. Hence, despite the willingness of all the colonists to lend a hand to the communal cause, the hierarchical division of tasks that Barthes astutely identifies: boss and technocrat (Cyrus Smith), hunter (Spilett), heir (Herbert), unskilled worker (Pencroff), servant (Nab). Nevertheless, this social division of labour is disguised by the grace and facility with which work is expedited in Verne's text:

> We see clearly the omnipotence, at once diegetic and ideological, of this insistent discourse: Verne's euphemisms allow the discourse to advance rapidly, in the appropriation of Nature, from problem to problem and not from effort to effort: it transcribes at once a promotion of knowledge and a censorship of work: this is truly the idiolect of the 'engineer' (represented by Cyrus Smith), of the technocrat, master of science, poet of the transforming power of work at the very point when, entrusting it to others, he conjures it away; Verne's discourse, through its ellipses and euphoric flights, dismisses time and effort, that is to say, labour, to the nothingness of the unnamed: work leaks, flows out, and gets lost in the interstices of the sentence. (84 / 150)

Verne's spiriting away of alienated labour is a fascinating variant on the bogus bourgeois *consecration* of work—'an eternal aesthetics of laborious gestures' (*M* 102 / *My* 176)— denounced as colonial ideology in 'The Great Family of Man'

COLONIAL MYTHOLOGIES   113

and '*Lost Continent*'[53] or attributed to 'rural folklore' in Barthes's brilliantly suggestive 1956 mythology 'At the Music Hall'.[54] The latter is in fact a rare and precious example of a happy myth inscribing the utopian liberation of work. Describing the music hall as a genuinely popular theatrical form, a product of Anglo-Saxon urban industrialization, Barthes suggests that the juggling, conjuring, and acrobatic acts create their own artificial myth of work. Thus each act appears either as the product or the literal performance of labour, the climax of long hours of practice or its complete recreation in front of the audience. Moreover, the effort behind it is figured by the precarious moment 'when it is about to be engulfed in the perfection of its achievement, without having altogether put behind it the risk of its failure':

What we have here is a way of making possible a contradictory state of human history: that the artist's gesture should set forth at one and the same time the rough musculature of arduous physical labour—belonging to the past—and the aerial smoothness of an easy action issuing from a magical heaven: the music hall is human work memorialized and sublimated; danger and effort are signified at the very moment they are sublimated through laughter and through grace. (*ET* 124–5 / *My* 178)

The history of artefacts is restored to them (the hard and alienating work which produced them), while at the same time labour is magically effaced by the connotations of facility conjured up by the airy substances and shiny metallic balls. Thus the music hall act combines in its way the contrasting inscriptions of work of both *Robinson Crusoe* and *The Mysterious Island*. It is the *proletarian* provenance of the myth that allows it to project a genuinely joyful sublimation of labour, whereas the 'grace' bestowed by Verne on the fulfilment of all tasks takes on a different meaning—its appeal derives ultimately from a particular bourgeois perspective, one that

---

[53] 'If we are concerned with fishermen, it is not at all the type of fishing which is shown; but rather, drowned in a garish sunset and eternalized, a romantic essence of the fisherman, presented not as a worker depending for his skills and his income on a particular society, but rather as the theme of an eternal condition, in which man is far away and exposed to the perils of the sea, while woman remains weeping and praying at home' ('*Lost Continent*', *M* 95 / *My* 165).
[54] 'At the Music Hall', *ET* 123–6: 125 / *My* 176–9: 179.

conveniently forgets about labour as exhausting physical work rather than inscribing labour and sublimating it.

In all, *The Mysterious Island* is an excellent example of a utopia that is predicated upon colonization. Michel Foucault, in his essay 'Des espaces autres' (other spaces), makes the point that the first American colonies must have seemed, to their idealistic founders, absolutely perfect places. For Foucault, the colony is an example of a heterotopia, a place or space that is different in kind from, but contained within, a real space, as opposed to the absolute 'no place' of a true utopia.[55] However, despite the interest of Foucault's essay, I do not find his distinction between utopias and heterotopias especially useful. Utopias are generically and etymologically 'no places', but they are always in some sense places within, so that the distinction between an imaginary place and the fantasized celebration or transformation of an existing place loses its significance. Verne's 'mysterious island' (both heterotopia and utopia) fulfils all the requirements of the genre. Cut off from the social world by Nature—the violent hurricane which takes the federalists there in the first place, the volcano that finally engulfs the island and sets in train their return to America—this utopia, the narrative of which is very specifically dated in the 1860s, is both outside and inside history. Its geographical status is similarly ambiguous. Cyrus Smith, having used his astronomical knowledge to calculate the exact latitude and longitude of the island, remains puzzled by the result—if such an island existed with those coordinates, he, the all-knowing Cyrus Smith, would certainly have heard of it![56] On the one hand, then, this is a 'no place' with no location in this world; on the other, not only does the detailed narrative of the colonization of the island foreshadow the establishment of a 'real' colony in Iowa, but the island itself is provided with precise spatial coordinates which locate it in the South Pacific Ocean. Though Barthes does not comment on this South-East Asian setting, it cannot be mere chance that Verne's hurricane should have blown the patriotic federalists all the way to the Orient. And the Orient, as we know, is at once a Western invention and a very real part of the world.

[55] Foucault, 'Des espaces autres', *Architecture, Mouvement, Continuïté* (1984), 46–9: 49, lecture delivered 14 Mar. 1967.
[56] Verne, *L'Île mystérieuse*, 189.

5
An Unhappy Sexuality: Morocco

Nothing so excites a semanticist, even on a stroll through the *souk*, as a silent dawning of meaning observed in someone's eyes.[1]

'FOURIERIST pleasure is the end of the tablecloth: pull the slightest futile incident, as long as it concerns your happiness, and all the rest of the world will follow' (*SFL* 80 / 85). In his own engaging and skilfully developed example, Barthes imitates Fourier's practice of elaborating an entire social system on the basis of a trivial personal preference. This is an anecdote concerning a Moroccan dinner party, whereby, in order not to offend his host, Barthes has both to eat and to appear to enjoy something he finds distasteful: a couscous cooked with rancid butter. How, he asks, would Fourier have helped him in this delicate situation? First, by persuading him that the rancidity of couscous is a subject worthy of serious philosophical debate; next, by pointing out that this need to hide his distaste is an example of the faulty gearing of a hypocritical society (which will not be at ease with itself until Barthes's apparently idiosyncratic preference for couscous cooked in fresh butter can be accommodated); finally, by taking him away from this lengthy and boring dinner party and sending him off to the group of Anti-Rancists, from which base he would maintain excellent relations of friendly rivalry with the Rancist sect.[2]

Is it significant that Barthes has chosen an anecdote set in Morocco as the end of his utopian tablecloth? The title of this opening section—*Départs*—is an obvious allusion to the departures of travel as well as to the more straightforward

---

[1] Barthes, 'Right in the Eyes' [1977], published for the first time in *RF* 237–42: 242 / 279–83: 282.   [2] See *SFL* 77–8 / 83–4.

'beginnings' of Richard Miller's English translation. Wherever we travel, suggests Barthes, it is possible to wonder what Fourier would have made of 'this place, this adventure': 'Here I am one evening in a southern Moroccan motel: some hundred metres outside the populous, ragged, dusty town, a park filled with rare scents, a blue pool, flowers, quiet bungalows, hordes of discreet servants' (79 / 85). In Harmony, Barthes proposes, the motel would be frequented by all those with 'this strange taste, this idiosyncratic liking for lanterns in the bushes, candlelit dinners, a fairy-tale staff of native servants, nocturnal frogs, and a camel in a meadow under your window'. Not that French Harmonians would really need to travel to such an exotic place, since its pleasant climatic conditions would be available in Jouy-en-Josas and Gif-sur-Yvette. However, the roaming Fourierist hordes, driven by that taste for travel and amorous adventures which seems to keep them permanently on the move, would sometimes descend upon this idyllic motel for their councils of love and gastronomy.[3] Here Barthes moves on to a point which explains his choice of a motel as the setting for his Fourierist reflections:

> In Fourier's day none of the Fourierist system had been achieved, but what about today? Foreigners converging in one location, crowds, the collective search for desirable climates, pleasure trips—all these exist, in the derisory and fairly dreadful form of the package tour, the transplantation of a holiday club (with its classified population and planned pleasures) into some fairy-tale site; the Fourierist utopia projects a real replica of itself which has been realized in the mode of farce by mass society: this is *tourism*. (80 / 86)

Barthes describes tourism as the price that has to be paid when a fantasmatic system manages to 'forget' politics (for all that, in Barthes's now familiar argument, politics is well able to take its

---

[3] Frank E. Manuel points out that the utopias of Saint-Simon and Fourier are far from static. The Saint-Simonians 'are continually building roads, railways and canals, the great arteries for the unification of mankind, and they are constantly moving over them, making occasional overnight stops at well-furnished motels'. The Fourierists, for their part, 'may have a home base in a small phalanstery; but there are armies of bayadera and their male counterparts who are always touring, vast programs of cultural interchange, and great itinerant battalions of young workers for public projects'. See 'Toward a Psychological History of Utopias', in Manuel (ed.), *Utopias and Utopian Thought*, 69–98: 81.

revenge by forgetting to calculate for pleasure). In the demystifying days of 'The *Batory* Cruise' and '*The Blue Guide*', Barthes denounced tourism (as we saw in the last chapter) as a fine alibi for travelling without taking any interest in political realities. That is to say, politics had not really been forgotten at all. What happens when Barthes himself goes travelling in search of utopia, and what sorts of politics are relevant there? Barthes, after all, describes himself as a guest at the idyllic motel with its unassuming servants and rare scents. The scents reappear in the first *biographeme* of Fourier's 'Life' at the end of *Sade, Fourier, Loyola*: 'at the court of the King of Morocco, there is said to be a Director of Royal Scents: apart from the fact of the monarchy, and that of the director, Fourier would have been enchanted by this title' (183 / 187). Barthes knows that monarchs and directors have no place in Harmony. Would Fourier have been equally ambivalent (the rare scents and the nocturnal frogs notwithstanding) about the Moroccan motel, whose luxurious lifestyle conjures up the pleasurable existence of a wealthy European in some congenial colony?

A significant link between utopia and the Orient underpins all those intersections of Harmony and Morocco that Barthes invents on Fourier's behalf. This is Fourier's own choice of Constantinople (that most 'Oriental' of cities) as the capital city of Harmony. What is more, the major narrative episode of *New Amorous World* is set in the Orient, a geographical location of which Fourier ironically points out that it is 'vaguely named'.[4] *New Amorous World* is a sexual utopia, and sexual liberation is achieved partly by the lifting of repression of every kind. For a start, prostitution plays an especially interesting role there, as Barthes did not fail to notice: 'pleasure itself becomes an exchange value, since Harmony recognizes and honours collective prostitution under the name of the Angelicate: it is in a way like the monad of energy whose bounce and scope ensure societary movement' (84 / 89). In Harmony it is pleasure that changes hands, not money. In a spectacular parody of 'Civilized' prostitution, an enlightened, selfless, and non-exploitative system of prostitution (spearheaded by the Angelicate, made up of both sexes) is one of the major vehicles of universal sexual

---

[4] Fourier, *Le Nouveau Monde amoureux*, 362.

satisfaction. Moreover, it is a crucial feature of Harmony that pleasure should be shared by the old and the ugly, both male and female, as well as by the recently disappointed in love or the possessors of unusual erotic preferences. Does the fact that Fourier provides an Oriental context for this sexual utopia mean that he is caught up in a negative Orientalism? His ironic equation of the 'Orient' with a 'vague name'—or the fact that Fakma, the most famous and beautiful woman in the Orient, offers intelligent friendship[5]—tends to suggest the opposite. Even more telling, perhaps, is the episode of a mock crusade by a gigantic army of pious cobblers. For these *sabatiers pieux* replace the *chevaliers preux* (bold knights) of old, in that their crusade is basically a very humble and philanthropic one, a joint undertaking by five European empires seeking redemption for past wrongs committed in the name of religion and greed.[6] *New Amorous World* seems to underline the Orientalist link between an alienated sexuality and colonialism—on the one hand Fourier parodies it, on the other he fantasizes a way beyond it. Was Barthes as aware as Fourier of this particular imbrication of oppressions? In what follows I shall attempt to situate Barthes's often problematic representations of Oriental sexuality, in particular those with a colonial context. If Barthes is right to suggest that mass tourism is a farcical replica of Fourier's utopia, is so-called sexual tourism the ultimate way in which the new amorous world of Harmony has replicated itself as a very dubious farce?

One of the photographs reproduced in *Camera Lucida* is an 1882 portrait by Nadar of Savorgnan de Brazza (52 / 85). Brazza acquired for France that portion of Africa which became known as *le Congo-Brazzaville* or the French Congo, the capital of which is still Brazzaville. That Barthes's own maternal grandfather was a military 'explorer' turned colonial administrator—'his' town was Bingerville in the Ivory Coast that he governed for three years from 1893 to 1896—might seem reason alone for dwelling on the significance to Barthes of the Nadar photo.[7] The reason Barthes gives, however, is that the

---

[5] Fourier, *Le Nouveau Monde amoureux*, 174. [6] Ibid. 361–78.
[7] On Barthes's own references to his maternal grandfather, see the captioned photograph in *Roland Barthes by Roland Barthes* (12 / 14), and the entry from the

portrait contains a typical example of his notion of the photographic *punctum*. He describes the placing of the young black sailor's hand on Savorgnan de Brazza's knee as an eccentric gesture which is both coded and banal; his own interest is caught rather by the folded arms of the other sailor (51 / 84). Given that we learn in the very next sentence that Barthes is attracted to Bob Wilson in the Mapplethorpe photo that follows, I think we may nevertheless take Barthes's comments on the Nadar photograph as an indirect allusion to homosexuality. The portrait of Savorgnan de Brazza is in fact a fine example of Orientalism: an aesthetic and very staged representation of the sexual availability of the black colonial subject. As such, and given the many examples of Barthes's sexual relations with young Moroccans recorded in 'Incidents', I was intrigued by Barthes's use of this beautiful but ideologically problematic photograph. My initial reaction was to read it as a perfect emblem of white–black and intergenerational sexual relations, both rendered exploitative by the relative positions of the participants in the colonial power structure.

It was Jonathan Dollimore's important book *Sexual Dissidence* which first made me think more carefully about these issues. For in Dollimore's well-chosen words, 'homosexuals have been among those who have literally (rather than metaphorically or theoretically) embraced the cultural and racial difference of the "other" '.[8] This is indeed an ambiguous alternative to a politically correct but merely verbal promotion of 'cultural difference', and if it is arguably more sincere, it is

---

Larousse dictionary that Barthes quotes (but also hides) in the list of sources of illustrations at the end of the book: 'Binger (Louis-Gustave), French officer and administrator, born in Strasbourg, died at L'Isle-Adam (1856–1936). He explored the territory from the loop of the Niger to the Gulf of Guinea and the Ivory Coast' (185 / 190). Calvet's biography contains a fascinating section drawing attention to the nature of the grandfather's career, to the existence of racist overtones in his published accounts of his travels, and to Barthes's strange claim in the photo caption that his grandfather 'had no part in language' (*il ne tenait aucun discours*) (Calvet, *Roland Barthes*, pp. xi–xiv, 2–7). Of several works by Louis-Gustave Binger held in the Bibliothèque Nationale in Paris, I found *Esclavage, islamisme et christianisme* (Paris, Société d'éditions scientifiques, 1891) the most suitably racist and pro-colonial candidate for a Barthesian demystification.

[8] Jonathan Dollimore, *Sexual Dissidence: Augustine to Wilde, Freud to Foucault* (Oxford, Clarendon Press, 1991), 332.

perhaps also more interesting. Dollimore discusses the fact that many homosexual men have felt sexually exiled from their home cultures, stressing that the finding of fulfilment outside of this culture should not be seen as a second best:

> Over and again in the culture of homosexuality, differences of race and class are intensely cathected. That this has also occurred in exploitative, sentimental, and/or racist forms does not diminish its significance; if anything it increases it. Those who move too hastily to denounce homosexuality across race and class as essentially or only exploitative, sentimental, or racist betray their own homophobic ignorance. This crossing constitutes a complex, difficult history, one from which we can learn.[9]

Dollimore's basic point is that the politics of consensual homosexual relations across ethnic, class, and age boundaries are not straightforward. Barthes offers an interesting and ambiguous example, not least because—in texts that he published as well as in those that he may have intended to keep private—he appears to offer himself up as an example.

Dollimore opens his book with a detailed reading of the episode in André Gide's autobiography in which he records meeting Oscar Wilde in Algeria, having first tried to avoid him.[10] Gide, of course, offers an interesting point of comparison for Barthes, in that—quite apart from the references to Gide in Barthes's later writing[11]—homosexuality and French North Africa come together in the writing of both. Dollimore refuses to make 'personal culpability' an issue in his discussion of Gide's relationships with young Algerian boys: 'In his personal relationships with Athman, and his political stance on colonial oppression, Gide could claim to have said and done more than most at that time.' Nevertheless, he stresses Gide's status as a sexual tourist of private means, able to come and go at will, seeking out the exotic other in order 'to lose everything,

---

[9] Dollimore, *Sexual Dissidence*, 250.   [10] Ibid. 3–18.
[11] For the context of Barthes's self-conscious references to Gide see my essay 'Roland Barthes: An Intertextual Figure', in Michael Worton and Judith Still (eds.), *Intertextuality: Theories and Practices* (Manchester, Manchester University Press, 1990), 92–107, especially 95.

including ourselves—everything that is but the privilege which enabled us to go in the first place'.[12]

Although Barthes's inscriptions of prostitution tend to give the impression that he belongs within this familiar tradition, he does not entirely fit the model of the nineteenth- and early twentieth-century traveller of private means. For a start, he certainly never travelled as a *rentier*. For many years he remained outside of any secure career structure, so that during the years he spent in Romania and Egypt (from 1947 to 1950), though in his early thirties, he was employed in low-paid and short-term teaching jobs. At the time of writing the Moroccan 'Incidents' he was teaching at the University of Rabat, and in Japan he was a guest of the French Institute in Tokyo. In China he had the bizarre status of a member of the *Tel Quel* visiting delegation. Nor is Barthes's involvement in a homosexual lifestyle whilst abroad some stereotypical new development which accompanied middle age and relative wealth. In the filmed television interviews about his life which were made in 1970 and 1971, partially published at the time in *Tel Quel*, but only shown in full on television long after his death, Barthes alludes euphemistically but explicitly to an unrepresssed enjoyment of his homosexuality whilst living in Romania. All of his talent, he tells us, was put into his life—an allusion to Oscar Wilde's famous claim (which was precisely made to Gide, and recorded in the latter's autobiography) to have put his talent into his work, but to have reserved his genius for his life.[13] Similarly, Barthes tried to spend this time abroad in a manner 'as novelistic (*romanesque*) and as hedonistic as possible'. The period in Romania is recalled as one of the points in his life when he was very happy and at ease with himself and his surroundings, so that he did not really 'need or want to write'.[14]

---

[12] Dollimore, *Sexual Dissidence*, 337, 342. For an important recent essay on the general theme of sexual tourism and Orientalism, see Joseph Boone, 'Vacation Cruises; or, The Homoerotics of Orientalism', *PMLA* 110 (Jan. 1995), 89–107, especially the final section, 'The Tourist Trade in Boys' (99–104). Barthes is not discussed but is listed with other 'literary-artistic vacationers and sojourners' in North Africa (104).

[13] See André Gide, *Si le grain ne meurt* [1920] (Paris, Gallimard, 1928), 340–1.

[14] 'Archives du XXe siècle' interviews, filmed in 1970 and 1971, broadcast on French television in 1988 (*Océaniques*, FR3). This allusion to Barthes's homosexuality was not included in the extracts published as 'Réponses' [1971], OC ii. 1307–24.

Although Barthes had not anyway started regular 'writing' at this stage, the comment provides an interesting contrast with the way in which the 'happy sexuality' found in Japan supposedly spilled over into writing.[15] In 'Incidents', written in Morocco in 1969, Barthes was clearly trying to combine his life and his writing, and to give homosexuality its due place in the latter.[16] However, unlike the more or less contemporary *Empire of Signs*—which is also, in its way, marked by homosexuality[17]— Barthes decided against publication. Although there may have been many reasons for this, I would personally suggest that what is missing from 'Incidents' (and therefore what Barthes, too, may have felt the absence of) is this 'happiness' of sexuality and writing. In other words language and sexuality are still intertwined, but both emerge in a negative light.[18]

Barthes had often visited Morocco and was very much in love with it as a country. In the autumn of 1968 he accepted a three-year post at the University of Rabat; in the event he only stayed one year. Working in Morocco on a long-term basis, as he explains in his posthumously published paper on Stendhal's relationship with Italy, was an entirely different matter from the fantasy of living there that had overcome the tourist: 'the magic vanished; confronted by administrative and professional problems, I plunged into the thankless world of motivations and decisions. I surrendered the holiday atmosphere of Festivity for Duty.'[19] Reading 'Incidents', it seems to me that Barthes was above all unhappily caught up in the social and political divisions of Morocco at that time—both as he observed them around him and as he experienced them on account of his own position as a teacher of French literature in what had been until recently (from 1912 to 1956) a French protectorate. In short he found himself caught up in an exacerbated form of the 'war of

---

[15] 'A happy sexuality found its corresponding discourse quite naturally in the continuous, effusive, jubilant happiness of the writing' (*RB* 156 / 159).
[16] 'Incidents', in *I* 11–41 / 21–61.
[17] For further discussion, see Ch. 6.
[18] For an interesting overview of the relationship between language, meaning, and sexuality in Barthes's work, see Doubrovsky, 'Une écriture tragique'.
[19] 'One Always Fails in Speaking of What One Loves' [1980], in *RL* 296–305: 299 / 333–42: 337.

languages' that he had probably hoped—along with the events and discourse of May '68—to leave behind him in France.[20]

I have already stressed the extent to which Barthes considers alienation within language to be the lived form of social alienation, since the power struggle between competing systems of meaning is entirely imbricated in social divisions. Though one might aspire, like Barthes, to an ideal social transparency in the realm of speech, in a divided society the struggle for liberation, unless utopian, can only take place within the context of meaning. From his first formulation of the concept of 'writing degree zero' (in one of the very early articles subsumed into the book of that name), through to his many discussions of the notion of 'text' around 1970, Barthes worries about the politics of attempts to liberate language while social relations in general remained alienated.[21] In the case of language utopias, then, Barthes underlines the problems of jumping ahead of history. However, in what follows I shall argue that Barthes ignores the parallel problem entailed in trying to liberate sexuality (here homosexuality) in advance of the liberation of other human relations. This blind spot goes some way, I think, to explaining the ambiguities of Barthes's sexual politics. And it is surely sexual politics which tie Barthes to an Orientalism that he seeks, in other ways, to go beyond.

Barthes does not treat linguistic and sexual alienation as separate or even parallel phenomena. Rather, as we shall see, he specifically analyses the alienation of sexuality as a by-product of the war of meanings that follows from the social alienation of language. This may seem an exceedingly depressing account of the human situation. Yet it follows from this interlinking of alienations that a linguistic or literary utopia can logically subsume the liberation of sexuality—as long, that is, as it acknowledges its utopian status. This, as I hope to have shown, is what Barthes finds so perfectly exemplified in Fourier. When Barthes speaks of finding a 'happy sexuality' in Japan, I assume that one of the senses of 'happy' is 'socially innocent'—I do not

---

[20] See Ch. 3.
[21] 'Is it possible to liberate speech (*la parole*) before history?' are the last words of 'Le Degré zéro de l'écriture', *Combat* (1 Aug. 1947), 2. Barthes's concept of 'text' will be discussed in Ch. 8.

think that he is referring to a temporary shedding of inhibitions or to finding a sexuality to his taste.[22] Whether the fact of not speaking Japanese literally conjured away social divisions, or whether it simply blinded Barthes to them, is a point not really worth pursuing.[23] For as far as I know, there is no information in the public domain about what Barthes actually did in Japan, or about how he lived the sexual experiences to which he alludes. The value system of the textual Japan, *Empire of Signs*, is another matter, for this is self-consciously and explicitly presented as a utopia, based on Japan but at the same time not quite Japan. I was very interested to discover that although Barthes made his most extensive visit to Japan in 1966, he was finishing *Empire of Signs* while he was living in Morocco from 1968 to 1969.[24] If sexual relations—between Moroccans, as well as between Moroccans and French—were bound to be alienated in a postcolonial Morocco where the French language retained its social and cultural hegemony, it was inevitable that the text of 'Incidents' would in some manner inscribe this alienation. However, at the same time, Barthes was weaving a fantasized utopian civilization which he called 'Japan', where what had perhaps been an illusory impression of a 'happy sexuality' was transformed into a general principle of happy liberation for a whole society or textual system. It is amusing to think of Barthes actually living in one part of the 'Orient' and using it as the negative basis on which to refantasize a better one called 'Japan'—further off still, and where, crucially, they do not speak French.

My sense of an important link between 'Incidents' and *Empire of Signs* is backed up by an interview ('Digressions') that Barthes gave to the journal *Promesse* in 1971.[25] Guy Scarpetta's questions are basically about the theoretical and political implications of *Empire of Signs*, and the interview is more or

---

[22] Just as Voltaire was the 'last of the happy writers' (see Ch. 4).
[23] See, however, Barthes's comments that the fragments of *Empire of Signs* were 'happy' mythologies because of his situation as a tourist and outsider, which had allowed him to ignore the influence on Japanese culture of its own version of petty bourgeois ideology: 'I was spared from mythological nausea' ('Réponses' [1971], OC ii. 1307–24: 1319). On the relationship between Barthes's written Japan and the real country, see Ch. 6.
[24] See Calvet, *Roland Barthes*, 176.
[25] GV 113–27 / 109–21.

less framed by allusions to Orientalism. In two important sections, to explain what he was trying to explore through his utopian reading of Japan, Barthes reverts to talking about his experience in Morocco. This is in answer to questions about language and sexuality respectively. He explains that political issues in postcolonial 'Arab' countries actually cathect language, and suggests that linguistics needs some equivalent of Marxism's *Capital* in order to theorize the appropriation and ownership of the resource of language. Its main task would be to decide where language stops, or rather, since Barthes already knows what he thinks on this issue, to show that it never stops: 'In certain countries still encumbered by the former colonial language (French), there currently prevails the *reactionary* idea that one can separate language from "literature", that one can teach French (as a foreign language) and repudiate French literature (as "bourgeois")' (GV 121–2 / 116). But for Barthes, as we know, language has no threshold. At the very most, he claims, one could isolate grammar for prescriptive teaching, but as soon as one gets to vocabulary and the connotative life of language one is back with the war of meanings, a war of which literature is the extended ideological field.[26]

Calvet detects a bitterness on Barthes's part here which, no doubt rightly, he relates to a perceived hostility on the part of Barthes's Moroccan students. This hostility was partly focused on the inclusion on their literature syllabuses of supposedly imperialist (French and Spanish) literature. It is Calvet's view that French literature and native French lecturers were a misplaced target relative to the internal repression of the regime of King Hassan II. In the context of a general ban on political and intellectual opposition, it was easier to attack a symbolic target.[27] Nevertheless, Barthes's students would have been born under the Protectorate, and the University, for all its recent expansion and relative democratization, was situated in the European, formerly administrative, half of Rabat.[28] Meanwhile

---

[26] See Ch. 4 for discussion of two mythologies dealing with specifically Moroccan and Algerian 'language wars': 'African Grammar' (*ET* 103–9 / *My* 137–44), and 'Sur un emploi du verbe "etre" ' (*OC* i. 811–13).
[27] See Calvet, *Roland Barthes*, 170–5.
[28] For a useful account of the development of the education system in Morocco, both during the period of the Protectorate and since independence, see Abdelâli

Barthes, offended at being positioned as politically on the right by his students, went on teaching Proust and Verne's *Mysterious Island*.[29]

When asked, in the *Promesse* interview, about the status and place of sexuality in Japan, Barthes picks up Morocco more or less where he left it with his comments on the politics of language. In the following passage, which I quote at some length on account of its importance to Barthes's argument, Morocco seems to be aligned with the meaning regime of the West (and as such opposed to Japan). This is clearly because of its relationship to the French language:

In the Occident sexuality lends itself at best to a somewhat pathetic language of transgression. But to make of sexuality a field of transgression is still to keep it imprisoned in a binary logic (*for/against*), a paradigm, a meaning. To think of sexuality as a dark continent is still to submit it to meaning (*white/black*). The alienation of sexuality is inseparable from the alienation of meaning, of alienation through meaning. What is difficult is not to liberate sexuality according to a more or less libertarian project, but to disengage it from meaning, including transgression as meaning. Take the Arab countries again. Certain rules of a 'correct' sexuality are readily transgressed there by a relatively unproblematic homosexuality . . . ; but this transgression remains implacably subject to a regime of strict meaning: homosexuality, a transgressive practice, immediately reproduces within itself (through a sort of defensive plugging of a gap, a panic reflex) the purest paradigm imaginable, that of *active/passive, possessor/possessed, niqueur/niqué, tapeur/tapé* (these *pieds-noirs* words are opportune here: a good example of the ideological value of language). (GV 123 / 117–18)[30]

Bentahila, *Language Attitudes among Arabic-French Bilinguals in Morocco* (Clevedon, Multilingual Matters Ltd., 1983). The general context of Bentahila's account is the politics of language choice in Morocco.

[29] Barthes's rather unthinking faith in the exportability of French culture perhaps dates back to his early career, not least his time as librarian at the French Institute in Bucharest (which culminated in a brief period as *de facto* cultural attaché). Calvet's account of this includes a summary of Barthes's valedictory lecture—a defence of the invulnerability of French culture—prior to his expulsion from Romania when the Institute was finally closed down in 1949. (See Calvet, *Roland Barthes*, 83–9, especially 88.) Moreover, on his return from Alexandria in 1950, Barthes worked for two years for the French overseas cultural services within the Ministry of Foreign Affairs.

[30] Since I am unsure of the precise register and connotations of *niqueur/niqué* and *tapeur/tapé*, I have followed the practice of the translator (Richard Howard), and

By attributing this vocabulary of sexual binaries to the *pieds-noirs* (the French colonial population), Barthes is presumably suggesting the following. First, that the French language with its obsessive paradigms is to blame for what he sees as restricted and restricting homosexual practices, second, that the French language is to blame for the perception of homosexuality as transgressive in the first place. Thus oppressive sexuality is underwritten by oppressive colonialism. Any sexual practice that tries to get out of this structure of alternatives by confusing it or simply delaying it—what some Moroccans, Barthes intriguingly tells us, scornfully refer to as 'making love'—will not only be banned. More fundamentally, it will not be understood. So that when Barthes proposes an ideal of sexual 'delicacy', he is advocating subtlety at the level of language protocols, rather than a simple lifting of the taboos on homosexuality in the name of some mythically spontaneous freedom (123–4 / 118).

A long extract from this same passage is quoted in *Roland Barthes by Roland Barthes* in a fragment which is entitled 'Active/Passive', and which adds *virile/non-virile* to the paradigm. It is glossed with yet another allusion to Barthes's experience in Morocco. Again, socio-economic structures and sexuality are mediated in a negative way by language: 'this structure of alternatives marks the language above all of bourgeois or petty-bourgeois adolescents (*garçons*) who, since they are caught up in the sphere of social advancement, need a discourse which is both *sadistic* (anal) and *clear* (buttressed by meaning); they want a pure paradigm of meaning and sex, without leaks, flaws, or any spillage towards the margins.' Once again, this negative picture goes hand in hand in Barthes's text with its utopian alternative: 'Nonetheless, once the structure of alternatives is rejected (once the paradigm is blurred) utopia

---

left Barthes's sexual vocabulary (here and elsewhere) in euphemistic French. An active form is followed by a passive in each binary. As far as I can tell from consulting dictionaries, *niquer* is a vulgar term for sexual intercourse which originated in a French North African pidgin. It has a possible connotation of prostitution but is not restricted to homosexuality. While the noun *tapette* can allude pejoratively to a 'passive' homosexual (normally a prostitute), *taper* and *se taper* can be used for heterosexual or homosexual intercourse. I have not found any information linking *taper* to the *pied-noir* context as Barthes suggests.

begins; meaning and sex become the object of a free play, at the heart of which the forms (polysemic) and the practices (sensual), liberated from the binary prison, will achieve a state of infinite expansion. Thus may be born a Gongorian text and a happy sexuality.' (*RB* 133 / 137)

But what of a happy society? Has Barthes simply conjured away any equivalent of the Westernized Moroccans whose discourse and sexual behaviour he obviously finds oppressive—without, it seems, dwelling for too long on the causes? Barthes appears to me to have fallen into the problematic area to which I have already alluded: proposing a dubious liberation of language and sexuality *in advance* of the liberation of other social relations. At the end of the *Promesse* interview, Barthes is asked a question which is very specifically about the political implications of his utopian Japan, both at the level of a supposed cultural fetishism (ignoring the basically economic implications of advanced capitalism), and at the level of what is happening in the real world not so far south of Japan. Guy Scarpetta suggests bluntly that the confrontation of signs has given way to the confrontation of weapons, and invites Barthes to situate *Empire of Signs* relative to this paradigm. Barthes's response is by now predictable—he wants to say that signs and weapons are one and the same thing: 'For my part, the paradigm that I try to take as an example (that's to say, beyond any personally preferred political position) isn't *imperialism/ socialism*, but *imperialism/something else*. ... I must resign myself to the fact that this raising of the slash mark at the moment the paradigm is about to be formed, ... this gaping utopia, is the only place for me at the moment. Imperialism is fullness, on the other side is what is left over, unsigned: a titleless text' (*GV* 127 / 121). Barthes is clearly making the point that he will elaborate in a fragment on *Le Neutre* in *Roland Barthes by Roland Barthes* (and which precedes the 'Active/ Passive' section discussed above): 'The Neutral is therefore not the third term—the zero degree—of an opposition which is both semantic and conflictual'; rather it is the second term of a new paradigm, 'of which violence (combat, victory, theatre, arrogance) is the full term' (*RB* 132–3 / 136). Nevertheless, to relegate 'socialism' to the status of a warrior signified, subsumed moreover into imperialism, is to take a big leap out of politics, to say the least. Was socialism not then Barthes's utopia after all, but merely a passing personal preference? What could such a statement mean in the context of a postcolonial Morocco which is such an obvious microcosm of Barthes's ubiquitous and politically grounded war of languages?

'Incidents' is in fact a fascinating tapestry of a divided and contrasting society. Though there is only one specific reference to the Protectorate, the postcolonial scene is set on the first page by the neurotically angry young boy who screams 'Go home!' (in English) to a European man (13 / 23). Its characters include the 'king's cousin' and various repressive policemen, as well as the more culturally hegemonic French teachers and lecturers, of whom Barthes himself—variously portrayed reading Proust and Lacan[31]—is not the least interesting example. Islam coexists with Judaism and Catholicism, as we discover when Mohammed, 'a textile worker', insists that the church of the Spanish *Capucins* is the 'Jewish mosque' (16 / 27). If Ramadan restricts love-making and smoking until after dusk, Barthes's cigarette is further curtailed, one Friday evening, as Ramadan gives way directly to the Jewish sabbath. The towns are full of all sorts of European and American tourists, not to mention the ubiquitous hippies whose choice of lifestyle Barthes criticizes (in an interesting article written in Morocco during the same period) as an ideologically dubious parody of Moroccan poverty and all that it entails—from rags, bare feet, and undernourishment, to communal housing and dirt.[32] Gentle adolescent peasants and poor working-class town dwellers are constantly contrasted by Barthes with aggressive petty bourgeois students and teachers (both indigenous and *pieds-noirs*):

All on the same day:
 on the one hand, the petty bourgeois student, who, inanely, to show off in front of the others, to embarrass the lecturer (*pour 'coller' le prof*), challenges me so stupidly, so idiotically, that the only message that comes over at all is the spiteful intention;
 on the other hand, the *peuple*, Mustafa, known as Musta: almost

---

[31] See *I* 39 / 57–8.
[32] Barthes, 'Un cas de critique culturelle' [1969], OC ii. 544–6, first published in *Communications*.

shaven head, beautiful almond shaped eyes, an almost Roman face, if it weren't so gentle; he's eighteen years old, comes from Fez, had to give up his studies because he's too poor, came to Rabat to look for work, has found himself a place at the Akkari as a carpenter; he earns 3,500 francs a month. His father doesn't do anything, his mother has a job processing wool. He lives with one of his sisters. He's a person quite devoid of hostility. (31–2 / 48)

The pages of 'Incidents' are in fact filled with cultural contrasts—Western versus Moroccan, Westernized Moroccan petty bourgeois versus Moroccan peasant—and Barthes invariably sets up the Western pole as the negative one. The Day and Night café in Rabat is a notable source of examples, such as that of the shoe cleaner Driouch—'a glance and a smile before applying himself to the job.... As he leaves, already some distance away, he gives me a friendly wave' (25 / 39)—who is followed in the text by a young *pied-noir*: 'reconstructed petty bourgeois with his sweater draped over his shoulders, the sleeves knotted in front; puts his car keys down on the table of the Day and Night café; he speaks in a peremptory and curt manner' (26 / 40).

A negative example of the ethos of hitchhiking is presented through two pretentious and impolite European hippies—on their way to Marrakesh to buy up calico tunics which they will sell for a vast profit in Holland—who settle into the back of Barthes's car as if this were their right (34–5 / 52). On the other hand Abdellatif, a gentle, 12-year-old peasant boy ('sensible, serious, reserved'), carefully clutches his purchases of oranges and groceries in the lap of his djellaba, before asking Barthes to stop in the middle of nowhere, pointing out the distant plain for which he is heading, kissing Barthes's hand, and offering him the two *dirhams* of his unspent bus fare (35 / 52). In a similar example Barthes gives a lift of just a few hundred metres to Abdelkhaïm, a poor adolescent who is carrying a 'round rustic basket' and who does not speak any French. Hardly has Abdelkhaïm got into the car than he pulls a teapot out of his basket and offers Barthes a glass of mysteriously hot tea, before melting away like his predecessor (36 / 54).

These episodes are reminiscent in their way of the ecstatic smiles and hand-holding with which the local natives supposedly respond to Gide's generosity as he travels down the Congo with

Marc Allégret.[33] Barthes, however, seems oblivious to the alienated colonial gratitude that his accounts suggest, not thinking to place such 'incidents' alongside the few specific examples of colonial alienation that he does point out, such as a ticket collector who laughs with good-natured servility when a young Frenchwoman describes all station porters as dishonest (32 / 49). Barthes presumably wishes, with his hitchhiking anecdotes, to draw attention to an alternative economy. In another example, 'Little I' turns up with a bunch of wild flowers because Barthes had previously given him a piece of paper with his name typed on it in several different ways: 'flowers for writing', concludes Barthes (40 / 59–60).[34] More often, Barthes simply records examples of his own generosity towards the poor Moroccans with whom he constantly mixes: trivial gifts—of which the most extraordinary is a souvenir Eiffel Tower (24 / 37)—as well as lifts, cigarettes, and money. Cynically, one might think back to Barthes's famous mythology about the Abbé Pierre, in which the signs of charity were denounced as a poor substitute for 'the reality of justice', and one might wonder what exactly is at stake in this particular manner of attenuating economic need.[35]

Beggars of all ages and kinds are inevitably a central feature of Barthes's attentive, detailed, and sympathetic portrayal of Moroccan poverty, yet the text makes no reference to political determinations and remedies.[36] Nevertheless, Barthes's reflections on begging are interesting, and develop as the text

---

[33] See André Gide, *Voyage au Congo: Carnets de route* (Paris, Gallimard, 1927), for example 129 and 142–3. Barthes obviously knew this text, given that the mythology 'The Writer on Holiday' opens with a reference to Gide reading Bossuet while going down the River Congo. See M 29–31: 29 / *My* 30–3: 30.

[34] For a discussion of such episodes and of other Orientalist aspects of 'Incidents', see Ross Chambers, 'Pointless Stories, Storyless Points: Roland Barthes between "Soirées de Paris" and "Incidents" ', *L'Esprit créateur* (Summer 1994), 12–30: 25–9. Chambers pursues the very interesting strategy of reading 'Incidents' and 'Soirées de Paris' ('Paris Evenings') together by placing them within a single postcolonial frame.

[35] Barthes, 'The Iconography of the Abbé Pierre', in M 47–9: 49 / *My* 54–6: 56 ('I get worried about a society which consumes the display of charity with such avidity that it forgets to ask itself questions about its consequences, its uses and its limits' (48 / 55–6)).

[36] Rana Kabbani discusses dehumanizing representations of beggars as an Orientalist commonplace in *Europe's Myths of Orient: Devise and Rule* (London,

progresses. When two elderly American women grab hold of an equally elderly blind man and march him across the street, Barthes comments that this 'Oedipus' would certainly have preferred money to their helping hand (14 / 24). Another blind man forms a tragic cameo with the adolescent who begs on his behalf—while the statuesque old man ('ancient, Sophoclean, theatrical') stands imposingly and impassively in his djellaba and white beard, the face of the boy 'assumes in its entirety the expressive burden required by such a situation: agonized features, contorted by a disdainful pout, display acute suffering, poverty, injustice, fatality: Look! look! says the child's face, look at this man who can no longer see' (16 / 27). When a girl approaches Barthes for money (' "My father's dead. It's to buy an exercise book, etc." ') he reflects that 'the ugly part of begging is the tedium of the stereotypes' (37 / 55). However, a further example—that of Farid—shows Barthes going back on a first reaction, and learning to decipher the apparent clichés of the Moroccan discourse of begging:

Farid, whom I met at the Day and Night café, got angry with a beggar who first of all asked me for a cigarette, then, when I'd given him one, asked for some money 'to buy something to eat'. This blueprint for progressive exploitation (though very banal) seemed to make him indignant: 'You see how he rewards you for giving in!' But then, saying goodbye to Farid and giving him my whole packet of cigarettes (which he pocketed without a word of thanks), I realized that he was asking for five thousand francs 'to buy something to eat'. Seeing me burst out laughing he claimed there was a 'difference'. Everyone, here, asserts themself as different. It's because they think of themself not as a person but as a need. (22–3 / 36)

It is not always possible to detect where the examples of Barthes's generosity merge with those 'incidents' which involve instances of prostitution. The only specific allusions to prostitution in the text are to an old woman who 'initiates' the village boys for the sum of 50 francs each (39 / 58), and to the 'whore' whom a group of boys club together to pay for, one of them

---

Macmillan, 1986), where her chief culprit is Elias Canetti's *The Voices of Marrakesh*. Another topos identified by Kabbani is wanton cruelty, to people but especially to animals (122–9). See 'Incidents', 37–8 / 56, for Barthes's description of the cruel treatment of a camel.

fetching her from 30 kilometres away on his bicycle (40 / 60). Where Barthes's own activities are concerned, he refrains from mentioning the handing over of money, so that we do not know whether the initial exchange with 'Little I' was writing for sex as much as writing for flowers. Often the sexual context is explicit but is not the main point of the fragment. Mustafa, for example, is in love with his cap (' "I love my cap" '), and refuses to remove it to make love (19 / 30); similarly Abder, Driss A., Slaoui, Amidou, and several Mohammeds are more or less lightly woven into Barthes's text.[37] Prostitution is, of course, the ultimate point of intersection of Barthes's twin obsessions with economic need and desire. However, when the former belongs to Morocco and the latter to Barthes himself, it is clear that this can hardly be a utopian intersection in the Fourierist mode. It is here that the lines already quoted from Barthes's essay on Sade become fully resonant, with their reference to the easy recruitment of subjects, as well as to seclusion and impunity, all of which follow from economic and social division.[38] The apparent complicity of the Moroccan recruits—Barthes constantly includes anecdotes of being propositioned—merely stresses the extent of their alienation: 'Racinian opening: with a gentle willingness: "You see me? You want to touch me?" ' (21 / 34); 'Visit from an unknown boy, sent by his friend: "What do you want? Why are you here?—It's nature!" (Another boy, on another occasion: "It's fondness!")' (23 / 37). Of all these examples, the most provocative test case for the politics of Barthes's pleasure is one that he himself foregrounds. When 'voluptuous' Abdellatif maintains that the accused of 'the Bagdad hangings' must have been guilty because the court had made its decision so quickly, Barthes notes: 'Contradiction between the brutality of this stupidity and the fresh warmth of his body, the availability of his hands, which I continue,

---

[37] Whatever his intentions, Barthes's allusion to the quantity of Mohammeds—'Mohammed (of course), a policeman's son' (*I* 28 / 43)—is a standard racist joke. Joseph Boone comments on Joe Orton's frequent recourse to the same joke ('his name, inevitably, was Mohammed'), describing it as a reinforcement of the anonymity and interchangeability of Moroccan boys as objects of exchange in Orton's text. See Boone, 'Vacation Cruises', 102.

[38] *SFL* 131 / 135, discussed at the end of Ch. 4.

somewhat stupefied, to hold and caress while he pours out his vengeful catechism' (23 / 36).

Barthes's almost obsessive point about the language of Moroccan homosexuality is best illustrated in 'Incidents' by two examples. The first is the Marrakesh primary school teacher who, bubbling over with effusiveness, goodwill, and complicity, declares, 'I'll do anything you want.' To which Barthes adds: 'And that means *je vous niquerai*, and that's all it means' (36 / 53–4). The second is a certain 'H', whose friends describe him as 'very sensual', which also turns out to mean '*H. se fait niquer*' (27 / 42). Yet Barthes's way of writing about this seems, somewhat ironically, to have been contaminated by the phenomenon he describes, not least through his use of a relatively crude sexual vocabulary, both here and elsewhere. At one stage he represents himself combining an unintended lesson in French philology with a fully intended lesson on French vocabulary for the genitalia, whereby teacher and pupils ('three young *Chleus*, on a clifftop') discover to their scholarly amazement that *cul/con/queue* forms an 'occlusive paradigm' (38 / 57). A similar example of 'phonological pertinence' is recorded: 'a young market salesman (with a seductive manner): *tu/ti* (non-pertinent) want *tapis/taper* (pertinent)?' (19 / 31).[39] The sexually suggestive ambiguity of the example seems here to be blamed on the stallholder, whether on account of his imperfect French or his desire to proposition Barthes. In a much later text, however, Barthes will allude to a Moroccan stallholder who thinks that Barthes is interested in his goods, only to realize—Barthes's gaze having lingered for the prerequisite few seconds—that the latter is perhaps more interested in the stallholder himself.[40] A conflation of the two examples underscores all that is involved—

---

[39] *Tu* is the French (familiar form) for 'you', *ti* (*tu* as pronounced by the Moroccan) is meaningless in correctly pronounced French; *tapis* means a carpet, *taper* is a vulgar word for sexual intercourse.

[40] 'Thus, walking in a Moroccan *souk* and looking at someone selling handicrafts, I can see that this salesman reads nothing in my eyes but the possibility of a purchase: like the tick, he only perceives passers-by as a single species, customers of his goods. But if my gaze insists (for how many seconds? that would be a good semantic problem), his reading of the situation is suddenly unsettled: what if it were in him, and not in his goods, that I was interested? ... And nothing so excites a semanticist, even on a stroll through the *souk*, as a silent dawning of meaning observed in someone's eyes' ('Right in the Eyes' [1977], RF 241–2 / 282).

sexually, linguistically, and economically—in this most commercial of postcolonial exchanges.

Only once, in 'Incidents', are language and sexuality linked in a positive fashion, and perhaps appropriately this comes about because of the non-standard lexical choices of the gentle, poor, and good-natured Amidou, fifth-year pupil (*élève de seconde*), beautiful but shabbily dressed, whose homework for the next day is to 'reflect on Molière's notion of comedy': 'I like Amidou's vocabulary: to *dream* and to *burst forth* for to have an erection and orgasm. To *burst forth* is vegetal, spattering, dispersing, disseminating; to have an orgasm (*jouir*) is moralistic, narcissistic, replete, closed in on itself' (29 / 44–5).[41] If the Molière homework and the age of Amidou remind us of all that is problematic about the context, there follows, nevertheless, an example of the delayed, coded, and delicate love-making that Barthes mistakenly thought could not be understood in Morocco: 'Ramadan: the moon will soon be up. There's another half hour to wait before we can make love: "I'm starting to dream". "Is that allowed?". "I don't know." ' (29 / 45). Moreover it is 'young Mohir, who sells semi-precious stones', who turns an arrogant Western Orientalism back upon itself when, at Ito, 'before a vast and very noble landscape', one of Barthes's companions ironically offers Mohir a picture of a nude woman from *Playboy* or some such magazine: 'the boy smiles, but in a reserved, serious, and distant manner, he is the one who masters a scene originally intended to make him look stupid; the hysteria of the other is left stranded, deflated' (34 / 51).

On the whole, however, Barthes seems to be too caught up in the situation he describes to do other than reaffirm his negative perception through a choice of words which tends to link language and sexuality in a fairly crude way. The situation he perceives is also reflected in his choice of form, so that the *either/or* style of thought that he will later identify and criticize could well be illustrated by the schematized paradigm of Occident

---

[41] The French is '*rêver et éclater* pour *bander* et *jouir. Éclater* est végétal, éclaboussant, dispersant, disséminant; *jouir* est moral, narcissique, replet, fermé.' As ever, *jouir* is difficult to translate; here its first meaning is to have an orgasm, but the connotation is the alternative meaning of 'to enjoy', as in 'to enjoy one's rights'.

versus Orient that structures his own observations. Moreover, Barthes's decision to make the Morocco of 'Incidents' into the ideological reverse side of a utopian 'Japan' has consequences for his portrayal of the former. For it means that he has projected elsewhere, and hived off into a separate text, any overturning of Moroccan alienation that he might otherwise have undertaken on its behalf.

However, this was perhaps the retrospective aim of a section of *Roland Barthes by Roland Barthes*. In 'Letter from Jilali', Barthes reproduces a personal letter from a Moroccan friend, before describing it as a perfect example of his conception of utopian discourse. The letter begins with a celebration of the close and flawless friendship between Jilali and Barthes, and then continues:

On this occasion, my dear Roland, I shall speak to you of a tiresome subject (as I see it). It is as follows: I have a younger brother, a student in the Third AS, mad about music (the guitar) and in love. But poverty conceals him and keeps him hidden in his dreadful world (he suffers from the present, 'which is what your poet says'), and I am asking you, dear Roland, to find him a job in your kind country as soon as you can, since he's leading a life full of anxiety and worries. Now you know the situation of young Moroccans and this indeed astounds me and denies me all radiant smiles. And it astounds you, even though there is no xenophobia or misanthropy in your heart. Whilst looking forward impatiently to your reply, I ask my god to keep you in the best of health. (*RB* 111 / 115)

For Barthes the joy of this letter ('sumptuous, sparkling, literal and yet instantly literary, literary in an uncultured way') is that without censoring its sensual delight in language—as his grim French compatriots would apparently have done in the same situation—it speaks *at the same time* both 'truth' and 'desire': 'all of Jilali's desire (the guitar, love), all the political truth of Morocco.' Here then, despite the negative social situation (the poverty) of Jilali's brother, is a language which, in its interweaving of both need and desire, meets the criteria of Barthes's Fourierist ideal. However, reading this in the light of 'Incidents', it is impossible not to reflect on the unspecified nature of the relationship which permits Jilali's appeal to the superior economic status of the benevolent Barthes; similarly, the latter's delight in Jilali's lack of 'culture' and his less than perfect French seems condescending to say the least.⁴² This is the language in which Jilali is after all obliged to communicate a 'tiresome' and doubtless humiliating request. In short, the political truth that Barthes reads in Jilali's letter is a partial one, unless it includes the postcolonial context of their own relationship.

It is, of course, Barthes's commentary (rather than Jilali's 'utopian' letter) that creates the problem here, just as, in a later text (1979), he produces some surprisingly inappropriate comments on the autobiography of Abdelkebir Khatibi, the Moroccan friend who enters into Barthes's couscous debate in a footnote to his essay on Fourier.⁴³ *La Mémoire tatouée* (tatooed memory) was first published in 1971 with the subtitle *Autobiographie d'un décolonisé* (autobiography of a decolonized subject) and an afterword by Khatibi himself, in which he commented upon the hybrid form of his work—part narrative, part meditation, part dramatized play of voices—as an attempt to come to terms with the history of Morocco by playing off the old against the new.⁴⁴ For *La Mémoire tatouée* is basically a classic investigation of the profoundly ambiguous relationship to the French language of a Moroccan poet and intellectual, traced through his colonization by French culture at school, his experience of the 1950s struggle for independence (participation in acts of civil disobedience, an episode of interrogation by the French army), his encounter with French racism during his years as a student in Paris during the Algerian War, 'in short, all the ways in which history reduces you to the status of a humiliated eunuch'. It is within this historical context that the text sustains a meditation on the author's impossible relationship with a linguistic and cultural identity that has been sacrificed—and his book itself is presented as a votive offering—to a French

---

⁴² Indeed, this is a condescension reminiscent of that of Sade's libertines, in *La Philosophie dans le boudoir*, towards the engagingly rustic language of Augustin the gardener. In his second essay on Sade, Barthes describes Augustin's language as 'a style that the aristocratic gathering somewhat snobbishly enjoys as rural exoticism ("Ah! charming! . . . charming! . . .")', pointing out that Augustin is of course sent away when the conversation turns serious (notably for the famous speech, 'Français, encore un effort si vous voulez être républicains'). See *SFL* 159 / 162–3, and Sade, *La Philosophie dans le boudoir* [1795] (Paris, Gallimard, 1976), 147 and 186.
⁴³ See *SFL* 78–9 / 84.
⁴⁴ Abdelkebir Khatibi, *La Mémoire tatouée* (Paris, Denoël, 1971). For Khatibi's afterword see 191–2.

language that he loves, in a reversal of an Orientalist cliché, 'like a foreign woman both beautiful and maleficent'. These are the last words of a new preface to the 1979 re-edition of the text, which also included an appendix of afterthoughts on the possibility of a genuine palimpsest of languages and cultures.[45]

Barthes's short essay 'What I Owe to Khatibi' (first published in the journal *Pro-Culture*) is reprinted as an afterword to the 1979 edition of *La Mémoire tatouée*. It is somewhat unfortunately positioned so as to present the final comment on Khatibi's multilayered text; worse, it actually replaces the author's own afterword to the original edition. Barthes appears not to have recognized the importance of Khatibi's analysis of the Franco-Moroccan language war, or of his attempt to find a form of writing that would inscribe it yet move beyond it. Barthes begins, promisingly enough, with a recognition of the ethnocentrism of the French semiological enterprise, of the extent to which it has remained a prisoner of the universal categories which regulate post-Aristotelian Western thought: 'By investigating the structure of signs, I innocently claimed that this structure revealed a generality, confirmed an identity which was basically, because of the nature of the corpus on which I have always worked, simply that of cultural man of my own country.' But Barthes makes no attempt to situate this ethnocentrism—as he surely would have done in the 1950s and early 1960s—relative to the history of French colonialism, nor is Khatibi's investigation of 'the signs which will reveal to him the identity of his populace (*peuple*)' set in its historical context. Strangely, Barthes instead chooses to underline (with apparent envy) what he describes as the genuinely 'popular' focus of this investigation: 'an integrally "popular" man, who speaks only with his own special signs, who finds himself constantly betrayed by others, either because he is spoken (by folklore specialists) or quite simply forgotten (by intellectuals).' Khatibi's originality ('at the heart of his own ethnicity') is equated with his assumed stress on a singular identity which is so pure and

[45] Khatibi, *La Mémoire tatouée* (Paris, UGE 1979). For Khatibi's new preface ('Présentation'), see 9–13, for his appendix ('Repères'), see 205–12, and for Barthes's afterword ('Ce que je dois à Khatibi'), see 213–15 (*OC* iii. 1002–3). Quotations from the latter are easily locatable. Denoël republished the text in 1982 without any of the prefaces or afterwords.

incandescent that we are forced to read it as a 'difference'. Not only is it hard to see where this 'popular' reading of the evidently middle-class Khatibi comes from, but Barthes goes on to subsume the internal differences of Morocco into internal differences of a completely generalized Orient:

> It is in this respect that an Occidental (like myself) can learn something from Khatibi. We cannot do what he has done, for our language base is not the same, but we can learn from him a lesson of independence. For example: we are, of course, aware of our ideological imprisonment, and some of us are seeking a notion of difference by investigating the absolute Other of the Orient (Zen, Tao, Buddhism); but what we need to learn is not to imitate a formula (language absolutely separates us from this possibility), but to invent for our own use a 'heterological' language, a jumble of differences, the mixing together of which will shake up a little the terrible compactness (terrible because historically very old) of the Occidental *ego*. This is why we are trying to be 'Mixers', borrowing from here and there some fragments of 'elsewhere' (a little Zen, a little Tao, etc.), trying to confuse this Occidental identity which often weighs us down like a heavy cloak (not always: it has its value, its luxury). We cannot, in order to achieve this, turn towards our populace (we do not have one any more); but we can open ourselves up to other populaces, we can 'decentre' ourselves as they say nowadays.

In short, this late essay is as striking an instance of Orientalist discourse as one could fear to encounter in Barthes's work. Not only is the 'difference' of Khatibi's text—in which Islam is a constant point of reference—subsumed into a mish-mash of Eastern religions, but Barthes's whole afterword speaks over Khatibi's head to Western intellectuals. What 'I' or 'we' can learn from the complex and fascinating autobiography of a Moroccan writer is how to decentre the Western subject and the consistency of the Western self.

Fortunately, Barthes's creative and theoretical investment in a handful of foreign cultures was generally more thoughtful and subtle than these rather glib claims might imply. The problem remains, however, of whether Barthes's Orient is really so different from that which he himself attributed to Voltaire in 1964, whereby, in the passage already quoted in Chapter 4, 'these Oriental countries, which today have so heavy a weight, so pronounced an individual role in world politics, are for Voltaire simply so many empty squares, mobile signs without any content of their own, zero degrees of humanity, deftly appropriated in an act of self-signification (*CE* / 88 / 98–9). It is true that the underlying concern is no longer—as in Barthes's version of Voltaire—to reinforce the centrality, consistency, and universality of the self. Yet when, in *Roland Barthes by Roland Barthes*, Barthes lists 'the Orient' as one of those 'apparently special themes' which appear and reappear in his writing (*RB* 177 / 180), he should surely have realized that a desire to decentre the Western subject is simply the latest avatar of the Orientalist imaginary.

6
'A Reader not a Visitor': Barthes in 'Japan'

> A delicate tuck, by which a deft hand swiftly pleats the page of life, the silk of language.[1]

IN February 1980, Barthes had intended to introduce a conference paper on Stendhal with a personal (and perhaps invented) anecdote. On a recent trip to Italy ('A few weeks ago . . .'), one cold, foggy, and grimy evening at the station in Milan, his attention had been caught by the yellow stickers ('*Milano-Lecce*') on the carriages of a departing train, and he had imagined travelling all night to find himself the next day in 'the warmth, the light, the peace of a faraway town' (*une ville extrême*).[2] Barthes's Lecce is a fantasy, for he has no idea what it is really like. What matters is that it be part of Italy, but as far away as possible, 'for beautiful Italy is always further away, elsewhere'. The parallel between Barthes's two Italies and his two Orients is obvious: from the imperfect reality of Morocco the Oriental fantasy is projected into the Far East (*Extrême-Orient*) of Japan.

Stendhal can be seen as a writer whose passion for another culture mediates Barthes's own reflections, both on this theme in itself and on how to transpose it into writing. Barthes's

---

[1] Barthes, *ES* 78 / 101. French references are to the original Skira edition, reissued in paperback in 1993, since the Flammarion (Champs) edition of the text leaves out some of the visual material and its accompanying captions. Richard Howard's English translation, based on the Flammarion edition, has further omissions and is illustrated in black and white only.
[2] 'One Always Fails in Speaking of What One Loves' [1980], *RL* 296–305: 296 / 333–42: 333. The title of Barthes's paper, 'On échoue toujours à parler de ce qu'on aime', would be more accurately translated as 'we never manage to speak of what we love' (i.e. the problem is how to express one's love in the first place).

posthumously published paper addresses Stendhal's attempts to express his love for Italy across a range of written forms, from the euphoric but vaguely defined admiration of early travel notes (*Rome, Naples, Florence*) to its jubilant communication in the opening pages of the novel written twenty years later, *The Charterhouse of Parma*. The paper contains passing comparisons between Stendhal's 'transference love' for Italy (' "it's like love, and yet I'm not in love with anybody" ' (*RL* 298 / 335)) and Barthes's own for Japan, for example his unconditional promotion, through a sort of 'inverted racism', of such arbitrary features as the red-painted fire hydrants in the streets of Tokyo, with which he claims to have been in love (297 / 334). Beyond the explicit parallels lies Barthes's elaboration, via his favourite notion of *la drague*, of the *plural* quality of Stendhal's passion. In Italy it is not 'woman' or 'a woman' who is declared adorable, but *women*, and cruising (*la drague*) is elevated to a Stendhalian principle which is at once 'aesthetic, psychological, and metaphysical' (298 / 335), obliging its subject to flit, as free from complexes as Fourier's 'butterfly', from pleasure to pleasure.[3] Indeed, like Fourier's Harmony, Italy offers a polyphony of simultaneous and overdetermined pleasures, for which La Scala acts as a microcosm. The fact that Stendhal rushes to La Scala, the moment he arrives in Milan, leads Barthes to compare him with 'some obsessive arriving in a city favourable to his passion and dashing off that very evening to the haunts of pleasure which he has already located' (297 / 334). Thus, according to Barthes, it is this multiplicity of pleasures which brings Stendhal sexual pleasure. This is a reversal of Stendhal's own notion of the *fiasco*, which is used by Barthes to describe Stendhal's frequent bouts of writerly impotence: 'thus lyrical desire too is always threatened by failure (*le fiasco*)' (300 / 337).

This is a negative mirror image of Barthes's own successful merging of sexuality and writing in *Empire of Signs* where, in the well-known words from *Roland Barthes by Roland Barthes*, 'a happy sexuality found its naturally corresponding discourse in the continuous, effusive, jubilant happiness of the writing' (*RB* 156 / 159). In this sense, then, Barthes seems to be several

---

[3] See *SFL* 101 / 106.

steps ahead of Stendhal. But when Stendhal does finally unblock his inability to 'speak' his love of an eroticized Italy, he does so, according to Barthes, by adopting 'that great mediating form which is Narrative or, better still, Myth' (*RL* 304 / 341). This involves (along with the introduction of the figure of Bonaparte) the creation of a strong paradigm that opposes the sad, negative, and patriarchal qualities of Austria and Grianta to the festive and feminized Republican liberation of Milan. It is this triumphant 'writing' that 'takes apart the immobile sterility of the amorous imaginary and gives to its adventure a symbolic generality' (305 / 342). This stress on the positive creative function of a paradigm is an interesting comment on Barthes's own adherence to the opposition of Occident and Orient, despite his apparent desire to get outside of the binary oppositions that he attributes to Western thought. On the basis of Barthes's analysis of the function of the oppositions that structure the opening chapter of *The Charterhouse of Parma*, it is tempting to substitute 'the Orient' for 'utopia' in the section of *Roland Barthes by Roland Barthes* entitled 'The Purpose of Utopia': 'Confronting the present, my present, utopia [the Orient] is a second term that allows the sign to function: discourse about reality becomes possible, I emerge from the aphasia into which I am plunged by the turmoil of everything that upsets me, in this world which is mine' (*RB* 76 / 80).

Although Stendhal's successful espousal of *narrative* may form a parallel for Barthes's own late solution to the problem of how to write about photography, none of Barthes's earlier writing on other cultures takes this form. In general, the 'novelistic' (*le romanesque*) which Barthes explores as a utopian mode is conceptualized in opposition to a traditional narrative with plot, characters, and descriptions. However, here too we may detect a Stendhalian influence, for in 1957 Barthes had published another text on Stendhal, a little-known preface to an edition of *Promenades dans Rome* and *Les Cenci*.[4] Some of the points that Barthes makes about *Promenades dans Rome* throw light in a very interesting way upon his own project in *Empire of Signs*, not least because the preface contains an important first

---

[4] Stendhal, *Quelques promenades dans Rome* suivi de *Les Cenci* (Lausanne, Guilde du livre, 1957), OC i. 758–63, all quotations from 758–9.

version of his recurrent theme of the difference between tourism, residence, and citizenship. In the 1980 paper, Stendhal's irresponsibility *vis-à-vis* Italy—'neither entirely a traveller (a tourist) nor entirely a native' (*RL* 299 / 336)—is a point of comparison (as I mentioned in Chapter 5) for Barthes's own experience of how settling in Morocco to work was a different matter from spending long periods of time there as a tourist. Against this, as we shall see in the next chapter, a wavering beween temporary residence and the temptation of citizenship is at the heart of Barthes's reading of Pierre Loti's *Aziyadé*. In 1957, however, tourism *per se* is the apparent subject of *Promenades dans Rome*, a text that is often taken, according to Barthes, for 'a tourist guide compiled by a witty man for the benefit of intelligent travellers'. Written entirely in Paris, Stendhal's *Promenades* manage to give the impression of a spontaneous diary actually produced in Rome, and filled with 'everyday notations such as the light breeze which is just blowing up or the coffee that has just been consumed'. Not only does the title place the book firmly within a contemporary genre of travel writing (*Promenades*), but Stendhal offers the traveller all sorts of practical advice: 'suggestions for possible itineraries, length of stop-overs, cost of "tickets", hire of carriages, inspection of passports, timetables, and procedures for making incidental purchases.'

However, Barthes suggests that this touristic apparatus, offered in apparent good faith, is shadowed by a secret scorn for tourism, which enters the text with Stendhal's ironic distinctions between the English tourist and a superior variety of tourist best represented by himself. In fact the English are quintessential tourists in that their trips abroad are precisely 'tours' or mere *visits*, for they lack the necessary imagination to shed their Englishness and actually *live in* the countries to which they travel. Thus they will never share the effusion of the adaptable, open-minded traveller who might 'marvel at the sight of the Pope's towels drying at the Vatican windows, or the scent of orange trees on Mount Coelius or in the Costaguti gardens'. Whereas the Italy of the English tourist is at best an object of curiosity or liking, for the Stendhalian traveller it is a *world* that he wants to inhabit, 'of which he agrees to become a citizen without for all that losing his freedom of observation: have we not all dreamed of reconciling the privileges of a foreigner with those of a native?' The wager of Stendhalian travel is to immerse oneself in the foreign experience but without losing oneself in it: 'to maintain a slight distance the better to appreciate one's psychological investment.'[5]

Barthes's really important point follows from the somewhat ambiguous attitude to tourism that he attributes to Stendhal in this text. Tourism is not only presented by Barthes as one of those *masks* of which Stendhal was so fond, it is actually the mask of 'anti-tourism'. Thus *Promenades dans Rome* is much more than an intelligent travel guide, 'it is a science of reality, a body of knowledge about the world, a cosmogony even, whose haphazard, low-key, and almost off-hand dimension should not blind us to its overall coherence'. Stendhal's Italy is not just a pretext for the writer's curiosity or exoticism, nor is it simply a *pays d'élection*, for it is literally conceived as a *world*. Thus, Stendhalian travel is basically a coherent system of knowledge about reality, whereby Italy and 'the real' are one and the same thing. Barthes likens Stendhal's intensified representation of Italy to a bringing out of its photogenic qualities, a heightening of reality—rather than its distortion or embellishment—which through a singular combination of climate and history 'triggers a cognitive experience'. This, surely, is a formulation that prefigures Barthes's discussion, some ten years later, of Fourier's 'marvellous real', for the imagination of Stendhal's traveller is not some 'wild power which distorts and lies', but rather a 'mental capacity which succeeds in restoring to reality its multiple dimensions'.[6] Since it is only this fantasmatic dimension that can capture and convey the intensity of reality, it is necessary that Stendhal's travels should be not just accounts of real 'lived moments', but that they should *also* have an imaginary status.

This accounts not only for the deliberate conflation of a real and imaginary Japan in the opening paragraph of *Empire of*

---

[5] This phrase is quoted by Bernard Comment in *Roland Barthes: Vers le neutre* (Paris, Christian Bourgois, 1991), 66, as part of a discussion which first alerted me to the possible importance of this early preface (see 'Ailleurs: Le Japon, le Maroc', 64–73).
[6] See Ch. 3 for discussion of Barthes, Fourier, and the 'marvellous real'.

Signs (*ES* 3 / 9), but also, perhaps, for Barthes's willingness to discuss the real Japan when he is interviewed about this text.⁷ Barthes's fantasmatic construction of Japan as 'Là-bas' (over there/faraway) should not be confused with the watering down of the characteristics of any recognizable African country in the *Paris-Match* fairy-tale of 'Bichon and the Blacks'.⁸ What he wants to say remains the same whether he is talking about the real Japan or its 'imagined' double, so that published interviews contain relevant points about the unusual historical position of Japan, about Zen and haiku, or about Barthes's own night-time wanderings in far-flung districts of Tokyo. Moreover, Barthes's conference paper on 'Semiology and Urbanism', delivered in 1967, draws heavily upon the experience of his recent visit to Japan, and discusses many of the aspects of Tokyo that are built into the imaginary systematics which will constitute *Empire of Signs*.⁹ This is despite Barthes's claim, in the opening chapter of the latter, that cultural products such as 'Japanese urbanism' do not (or so he hopes) constitute the matter of his text (*ES* 4 / 11).

What is striking about the lecture on 'Semiology and Urbanism' is the degree to which Tokyo is already discussed as an eroticized urban space, a dimension which Barthes declares never to have explicitly encountered in academic investigations of the city. By this he claims to mean not specific functional sites of sexual commerce, but a generalized eroticism of social encounters, for the city is precisely the site of 'our encounter

---

⁷ He does, however, claim in an interview that he always knew that his Japanese readers would neither recognize themselves in his book nor really appreciate it ('from the outset I was totally lucid about this'), adding that he hopes this has been understood. He also points out that he had not known that he was going to write about Japan while he was there, that his 'Japan' had been entirely reconstructed from memory, and that he would need to go back if he wanted to write a different sort of book about the 'real' country. See 'Pour la libération d'une pensée pluraliste', *OC* ii. 1699–709: 1704, first published in *UNI*, a Japanese journal, in 1973.

⁸ On the deliberately vague location of the African country that is the subject of this mythology, see Ch. 4. Another interesting point of comparison is Barthes's introduction to Bernard Minoret and Danielle Vezolles, *La Fuite en Chine* (Paris, Christian Bourgois, 1970), a play 'freely adapted' from Victor Segalen's *René Leys* (*OC* ii. 964–6). Barthes discusses the way a real, political system (Beijing in 1911) is transformed into a fantasized system, and Beijing into an almost imaginary place ('every city is a system' (964)).

⁹ 'Semiology and Urbanism', *SC* 191–201 / 261–71. For an earlier discussion of this lecture see Ch. 2.

with the other'. Barthes justifies his lack of differentiation between 'sociality' and eroticism with reference to 'the metaphorical chain which substitutes for Eros':

> We must especially investigate, among the major categories, other great habits of humanity, for example food and shopping, which are actually erotic activities in a consumer society. I refer once again to the example of Tokyo: the great railway stations which are the points of reference for the main neighborhoods are also department stores. And it is certain that the Japanese railway station, the station-as-shop, has a unique meaning and that this meaning is erotic: purchase or encounter. (SC 200 / 270)

The frequenter of Barthes knows perfectly well, retrospectively at least, that *la rencontre* is for Barthes an encounter that is literally erotic. Indeed, the 'purchase or encounter' of the Japanese railway station is remarkably similar to the overdetermined appeal for Barthes of the Moroccan *souk*.[10] As spokesperson for semiology, however, Barthes inscribes this metaphorically erotic 'chain' under the sign of Lacan, carefully explaining to his audience that the latest discourse of symbolic meaning no longer operates in terms of a one-to-one correlation between signifiers and signifieds, whereby a signifier such as a site or a neighbourhood might have a stable semantic content. The naming of meanings is historically variable and above all extremely imprecise, so that signifieds constantly turn into the signifiers 'of *something else*' (197 / 267).

Barthes argues that this network of shifting urban meanings can never be grasped as a totality, and suggests that the best way of approaching it might be through the linguistic model of the sentence. It is in this context that Barthes makes another suggestive allusion to Victor Hugo's novel *Notre-Dame of Paris*. It will be remembered that Hugo's 'bird's-eye view of Paris' was an important point of reference both for the cognitive function of Michelet's *tableaux*, and for Barthes's own description of the view from the Eiffel Tower as at once 'concrete' and 'abstract', in that it derives from an implicit structuralist model (the panoramic view) which inserts a dimension of intelligibility into material reality.[11] However, if Hugo is recommended to this audience of urban specialists as one of the authors who has best

[10] See Ch. 5.   [11] See Ch. 2.

expressed the signifying nature of urban space, Barthes now draws a rather different lesson from *Notre-Dame of Paris*, and it is one that graphically illustrates the shift in focus of his own interest from 'structures' to 'structuration'. In the chapter of Hugo's novel entitled 'This Will Kill That', architecture (the monument) and the printing press are set up as two rival modes of *writing*. Both the monument and the city itself are conceptualized as the written inscription 'of man in space' (193 / 263), a notion that Barthes takes over as his own: 'The city is a discourse, and this discourse is actually a language: the city speaks to its inhabitants, we speak our city, the city where we are, simply by inhabiting it, by traversing it, by looking at it' (195 / 265).[12] Thus, whoever moves around the city 'is a sort of reader who, according to their obligations and their movements, samples fragments of this discourse in order to actualize them in secret' (199 / 268). The city may be a structure, but for Barthes it is a shifting and ever renewed structure like his favourite example of the mythical ship *Argo*, an infinitely variable *poem* which 'deploys the signifier' rather than centring itself on one subject: 'and it is this deployment which the semiology of the city must ultimately attempt to grasp and to turn into song' (201 / 271). Thus Barthes calls for more of those personal readings of the city of which literature has provided 'some examples' (201 / 270). The establishment of a personal project is clear enough, and the links with *Empire of Signs* both direct and obvious. Yet the problem remains of what sort of creative writing could best celebrate the city in this way, of what sort of 'poem' a semiologist could aspire to, and of who, in this

---

[12] These words are quoted by Michel de Certeau, who develops this basic idea (opposing it to what is cognitively at stake in the panoramic view from the World Trade Centre) in 'Marches dans la ville', Ch. 7 of *L'Invention du quotidien* [1980] (Gallimard, Paris, 1990), 164. Without framing his argument as explicitly utopian, de Certeau seems to have developed many of Barthes's quite early ideas on human reappropriations of alienated spaces. Barthes's lecture on semiology and urbanism obviously has its own context of writing on the city in the late 1960s and early 1970s, for example the collection of papers edited by Françoise Choay, *L'Urbanisme: Utopie et réalités* (Paris, Seuil, 1965), to which he refers (SC 193 / 262). See too, of course, as well as Marin, the work of Henri Lefebvre, e.g. *Le Droit à la ville* (Paris, Anthropos, 1968), and *La Révolution urbaine* (Paris, Gallimard, 1970). It is a context of which Barthes was aware, but which throws into relief the originality of the way he writes about the Japanese city in *Empire of Signs*.

conflation of readers, writers, and the city itself, would be the subject of such writing.

If semiology is something of a mask in the 1967 lecture, I wish to argue that both urbanism and tourism operate as masks in *Empire of Signs*. If the human face is one of the circulating signifiers (body, face, writing) that make up the system of Japan—see Barthes's caption to the wonderful 'face within a face' of a wooden statue in a museum at Kyoto—how much more is this true of the mask, which is actually figured in the third chapter ('Without Words') by a photograph of an ancient theatrical mask (19).[13] The chapters on the 'empty centre' of Tokyo, on its idiosyncratic system of addresses, and on the spatial signification of local stations, intermittently adopt the discourse of the urbanist—'according to certain urbanists' (38 / 52), and so on—at the same time as developing the notion of the city as writing. Thus the chapter 'City Centre, Empty Centre' contains a beautiful late eighteenth-century colour map of Tokyo, likened by Barthes to an ideogram through his caption: 'The City is an ideogram, Text goes on (*le Texte continue*)' (31 / 45). Not only is Barthes's Tokyo marked by the absence of any high building from which the metaphorical structuralist might mentally appropriate the city in its totality, but its centre is occupied by the supposedly functional 'emptiness' of the Emperor's palace. This is provocatively described by Barthes as a forbidden but entirely 'indifferent' site, an opaque ring of low-lying roofs and trees, around which the traffic, and with it the whole activity of the city, is obliged to circulate (32 / 46). Moreover, there are no street names in Tokyo, and since the grid used by the postal services is entirely inaccessible to the 'visitor', this enormous and modern city is virtually unclassified, 'the small-scale spaces of which it is made up are unnamed' (33 / 47). Given that where people live lacks the legal status elsewhere conferred by an official home address, their domicile becomes a contingent factual matter: identity and property are no longer merged. According to Barthes, the visitor to Tokyo is entirely without our more familiar printed support system of maps, guides, and telephone directories, and must discover the city by an 'ethnographic' type of activity involving

---

[13] Skira edition only.

walking, looking, and remembering: 'to visit a place for the first time is thereby to begin to write it: since the address is not written, it must establish its own writing' (36 / 51).

This is an activity in marked contrast with that of the colonists of Verne's *Mysterious Island* who, in mapping their newly discovered territory from its highest point, take literal possession through a naming of parts.[14] The reproduced map of 'Lincoln Island', to be found in illustrated editions of Verne's text, demonstrates this clearly enough.[15] If Barthes reproduces four maps in *Empire of Signs*, none of them acts as a two-dimensional representation of an appropriated space or static structure.[16] Three of them depict the printed or hand-drawn sketch maps which situate the home relative to a landmark like a railway station, and which are Barthes's favourite example of the 'system of expedients' that compensates for the anonymity of the detailed spaces of the city (34–6 / 48–50). Like the ideogram of Tokyo, these more ephemeral maps stand in for and promote Barthes's notion of writing the city, not only by sketching out a route to be taken, but by inscribing the history of their production:

> The inhabitants excel at these impromptu drawings, where we see a street, a block of flats, a canal, a railway line, a shop sign taking form right there on a piece of paper, and which turn the exchange of addresses into a delicate communication in which the life of the body and an art of the graphic gesture refind their place: it is always pleasurable to watch someone write, all the more so to watch someone draw: of all the occasions on which someone gave me an address in this way, I retain the gesture of my interlocutor turning his pencil upside down to gently erase, with the rubber at the other end, the excessive curve of an avenue, the intersection of a viaduct. (34 / 48–9)

Not surprisingly, we learn that the fabrication of the address was always more important to Barthes than the address itself:

---

[14] See my earlier discussion of Barthes and Verne in Ch. 4.

[15] See Jules Verne, *L'Île mystérieuse* (Paris, Librairie générale française, 1989), 287. This edition reproduces the fine illustrations of the original Hetzel edition of the text.

[16] For a reading of the ideology of modes of representation in three 17th-century maps, see Louis Marin, 'The City's Portrait in its Utopics', in *Utopics: The Semiological Play of Textual Spaces* [1973], 201–32. See, too, Michel de Certeau, 'Récits d'espaces', Ch. 9 of *L'Invention du quotidien*, where Barthes's sketch maps are referred to in a discussion of literal and metaphorical narrative mappings (178).

'fascinated, I could have hoped it would take hours to give me that address' (35 / 49). A delicate eroticism of the Japanese body has already been established by Barthes in the 'Without Words' chapter, where he dismisses as erroneous the assumption that his lack of knowledge of the language must have made it impossible for him to communicate with Japanese people. His response to this view—and it is a perception central to the project of the book—is that the Japanese 'empire of signifiers' is much more important than speech, that the exchange of signs remains rich, mobile, and above all subtle despite (or perhaps on account of) the opaqueness for him of the language. The underlying reason for this is that in 'Japan' 'the body exists, displays itself, gives itself without hysteria, without narcissism, but according to a purely—though subtly discontinuous—erotic project' (10 / 20). Therefore it is not the voice that communicates, but a body made up of 'eyes, smile, hair, gestures, clothing' that maintains a perfectly coded exchange: 'Fixing up a meeting (by gestures, drawings on paper, proper names) may take an hour, but during that hour, for a message which would be over within an instant if it were to be spoken (simultaneously essential and insignificant), it's the other's entire body which has been known, savoured, received, and which has displayed (to no real purpose) its own narrative, its own text.'

What is more, *la rencontre* is declared to be the main reason for travelling in the first place. 'Open a travel guide', suggests Barthes in a prominent handwritten caption, and 'usually you will find a brief lexicon which strangely enough concerns only boring and useless things: customs, post offices, hotels, barbers, doctors, prices. Yet, what is travelling? Meeting people (*la rencontre*). The only lexicon that counts is that of the *rendez-vous*' (13 / 23). Barthes therefore provides a series of specially designed lexicons of the *rendez-vous*. The first two are dispersed in his chapters on Japanese food (*where? when? both?* and so on (17 / 28)); the third, and most explicit (*maybe, tired, impossible, I want to sleep* (37 / 51)), is placed in the chapter about the exchange of addresses. If we consider these passages in the light of 'Incidents'—or of Barthes's preface to *Aziyadé*[17]—it is impossible to ignore their subtext of a literally erotic quest. In

---

[17] To be discussed in Ch. 7.

1975 he alludes to the unusual behaviour and energies that had been provoked in him by Japan, and to his happiness in distant *quartiers* of Tokyo at four in the morning: 'nocturnal wanderings in a huge city, the largest in the world, a city completely unfamiliar to me, and I don't speak a word of Japanese.'[18] In 1977, pressed by Bernard-Henri Lévy on the exact nature of his 'ethnologist's enthusiasm' for Tokyo, he replies ('frankly') that 'travelling is also an adventure for me, a series of possible adventures of great intensity. Travelling is obviously linked to a kind of amorous awareness, one is always on the alert...'[19]

These autobiographical 'revelations', which may or may not be considered interesting in themselves, raise the more important issue of the *status* of the traces that they leave within the text of *Empire of Signs*. I want to suggest that the whole of the text maintains an ambivalent relationship to a travel guide. On the one hand, Barthes provides an overview of the most important features of traditional Japanese culture, with an introduction to Bunraku, sumo wrestling, and Zen Buddhism (haiku, gardens, flower arranging, tea ceremony, and so on). Moreover, in the best tradition of the *Blue Guide* to Spain,[20] Japanese culture and religion are largely dehistoricized. On the other hand, Barthes offers practical advice on eating out, shopping, getting around the city, how to manage if you cannot speak the language, and even includes street maps and some useful Japanese vocabulary. However, the function of the vocabulary is so explicit that what we seem to have here is a parody of an Orientalist sexual

---

[18] 'Twenty Key Words for Roland Barthes' [1975], *GV* 205–32: 230 / 194–220: 217.

[19] 'Of What Use is an Intellectual?' [1977], *GV* 258–80: 264 / 244–62: 249. The apparently confessional mode of Barthes's comments on wandering around Tokyo at night could be usefully counteracted by remembering that, as ever, his representation of his behaviour has a literary ancestry, from the *flâneur* to the *dragueur*. An essay on Jean Cayrol, written some twenty years earlier ('Jean Cayrol et ses romans', *OC* i. 115–31, first published in *Esprit* in March 1952), contains the following account by Barthes of the Cayrolian hero as a nocturnal *promeneur aventureux*: 'There are three Cayrolian themes which testify to the completely new situation of modern man immersed in space: Walking, the City, the Night. The City is a modern myth which has introduced into the aesthetics of space a dimension quite unknown to its classical representations; movement derives not from the spectacle of the city itself, but from the human body.... space is linked here to the muscular timescale of the walker on the alert for adventure (*promeneur aventureux*)' (124).

[20] See Ch. 4.

tourism—sublimely uninterested in learning any Japanese, the author is nevertheless willing to master (and pass on) those few words necessary to the pursuit of sexual pleasure.[21] In short, if Barthes offers his vocabularies of the *rendez-vous* as an improvement upon those to be found in useless guidebooks, he nevertheless stays firmly within the genre. What Barthes seems to have produced here is a fragment of some parodic *Gay Guide to Tokyo*, whereby he himself is ironically inscribed in the text as a sexual tourist of the worst sort.

My argument is that Barthes has repeated Stendhal's strategy of using tourism as a mask for anti-tourism, but that he has extended its scope. Barthes's *Empire of Signs* is an engaging 'book on Japan' which allows for the potential sexual encounters of the tourist abroad. But all of these guidebook elements are subsumed into a serious and coherent cosmogony. Japan has the same status in this work as Italy in Stendhal's *Promenades dans Rome*; neither *pays d'élection* nor mere pretext for exoticism or eroticism, it has, rather, been conceived as a world. The circulating signifiers of body, city, and writing construct 'Japan' as a systematics, and in so doing they absorb sexuality as a dimension of reality.

Where Barthes differs from Stendhal is in presenting himself not as an *inhabitant* of this reality, but as its *reader*: 'I am, in that country, a reader, not a visitor' (79 / 107). These words occur in the middle of Barthes's discussion of Japanese haiku. This does not mean that what Barthes reads in Japan is literally a set of haiku poems, though he quotes a number of them and pursues throughout the four chapters devoted to them a powerful analysis of their relationship to language, meaning, and the world.[22] His attraction to haiku is underpinned by an enthusiasm for Zen Buddhism which needs to be placed in the context of his negative perception of a 'Western' war of languages, and his literally utopian search for a realm which lies beyond meaning rather than simply foreclosing it. Barthes

---

[21] Barthes seems to have done some retrospective research into the structures of Japanese in order to produce the vast generalizations of the second section of *Empire of Signs* (see 'The Unknown Language', 6–8 / 13–17). However, he represents himself as understanding nothing at the time.

[22] See 69–84 / 89–112.

presents the rigours of the Zen training—the long meditations on absurd riddles and anecdotes—as a dogged attempt to find a way beyond logic and connotation:

All of Zen, of which haiku is merely the literary branch, thus appears as a vast set of protocols destined to *halt language*, to jam that kind of internal radiotelephony constantly transmitting within us, even in our sleep (perhaps this is the reason the apprentices are kept from falling asleep), to empty out, to stupefy, to dry up the soul's incoercible babble; and perhaps what Zen calls *satori*, which Westerners can translate only by certain vaguely Christian words (*illumination, revelation, intuition*), is no more than a total suspension of language, the blank which erases within us the reign of the Codes, the breach of that internal recitation that constititutes our person; and if this state of *a-language* is a liberation, it is because, for the Buddhist experiment, the proliferation of secondary thoughts (the thought of thought), or what might be called the infinite supplement of supernumerary signifieds—a circle of which language itself is the depository and the model—appears as a jamming: it is on the contrary the abolition of secondary thought which breaks the vicious infinity of language. (74–5 / 99–100)

Barthes finds in haiku an ideal solution to the *literary* problem of how to write about the world. Whereas Western modern writing typically tries to get beyond ideological connotations by making its discourse incomprehensible, these poems achieve their 'exemption from meaning' within a simple, readable, and referential discourse, whose delicate designation of objects and events is captured by Barthes's adaptation of the Zen *tathata* into what he calls the *tel!* Like some young child pointing at a random object which has caught their attention (haiku has no particular subject matter)—'*It is that, it is thus*, says the haiku, *it is so*. Or, better still: *so!*' (83 / 113).[23]

The title of the chapter in which Barthes declares himself a reader rather than a visitor is 'L'Incident', and it becomes clear that he wants to use the minimal happenings of haiku as a model for conceptualizing and reading the reality of Japan:

---

[23] In *The Way of Zen* (Harmondsworth, Penguin, 1970), Alan Watts explains *tathata*, usually translated as 'suchness', as 'the world just as it is, unscreened and undivided by the symbols and definitions of thought' (87–8). Barthes refers to Watts in discussions of the *tel!* in *A Lover's Discourse* (262, omitted from the English translation) and *Camera Lucida* (5 / 15). A translation of Watts, *Le Bouddhisme Zen* (Paris, Payot, 1960), is included in the bibliographies of both texts.

What I am saying here about haiku could also be said about everything which *happens* (*advient*) when one travels in that country I am here calling Japan. For there, in the street, in a bar, in a shop, in a train, something always *happens*. This something—which is etymologically an adventure—is of an infinitesimal order: it is an incongruity of clothing, an anachronism of culture, an impropriety of behaviour, an illogicality of itinerary, etc. (79 / 107)

Une aventure has the second meaning in French of a love affair; appropriately, therefore, Barthes describes the accumulation of these trivial adventures in the course of a day as provoking in him a sort of 'erotic intoxication'. These incidents take effect at the very moment of 'reading' them, and whereas traditional haiku are likened to the deft insertion of a delicate tuck (*un pli*) in the 'page of life, the silk of language' (78 / 103), what is read in modern Japan is 'the lively writing of the street' (79 / 107). One sees, retrospectively, that the Barthes of the Moroccan 'Incidents' was trying to produce his own version of haiku out of everyday adventures of this sort; here he recognizes that a 'Westerner' like himself could only gather them together and record them by integrating some sense of his own distance from them. Barthes therefore maintains his external perspective as a Westerner, which allows him to focus on all that haiku enables—but from which he is excluded—at the same time as transposing this haiku-like perception of a very ordinary reality into the familiar high register (and very long sentences) of his own preferred discourse:

> '*When you walk*', says one Zen master, '*be content to walk. When you are seated, be content to be seated. But, above all, don't shilly shally!*': this is what, in their way, everyone seems to be telling me—the young cyclist carrying a tray of bowls on his raised arm; the young saleswoman who bows to the customers in a department store, as they pile on to an escalator, with an action so deep, so ritualized, that it loses all servility, the Pachinko player inserting, propelling, and scooping up his marbles, with three gestures whose very coordination is a work of art; the dandy in the café who, with a ritual gesture (abrupt and male), pops open the plastic wrapper of the hot napkin with which he will wipe his hands before drinking his Coca-Cola: all these incidents are the very substance of haiku. (80 / 108–9)

What is most striking about Barthes's choice of haiku—any discontinuous trait or event of Japanese life that seems to ask to be read (83 / 113)—is the contemporary and not obviously aesthetic nature of his Pachinko player, Coca-Cola drinker, and so on. Indeed Barthes states precisely that his haiku have eschewed the 'picturesque', detached as it is from what for him is distinctive about Japan, namely its 'modernity' (79 / 107). Barthes stresses in interviews the fragile and unusual historical position of Japan, a country which has modernized itself very rapidly, but which, until relatively recently, was a completely feudal society. It is the continued presence of aspects of this feudal culture that produces the 'semantic luxury' to which Barthes is attracted, for it has not yet been diluted or destroyed by the petty bourgeois mass culture that so haunts his perception of France. Yet what fascinates him above all is the conjunction of these feudal traces with the very modern aspects of a new Japanese society.[24] Thus, it is certainly a severe misreading of *Empire of Signs* to suggest (as negative critiques of the text's Orientalism tend to do) that it is nostalgically fixated upon Japan's cultural and historical past.[25] Just as I earlier argued that Barthes's Eiffel Tower mythology was written against the architectural nostalgia expressed by Hugo in his 'Bird's-Eye View of Paris', so Barthes's application of metaphors of writing to Tokyo contrasts with Hugo's anxiety that the 'this' of the printing press will kill the 'that' of Parisian architecture (those monuments with which the inhabitants of Paris had traditionally written their city). Basically, Barthes conceives of Japan as a contemporary and forward-looking reality that is written through highly codified forms and protocols. These, for Barthes, are the very opposite of the promotion of naturalness and spontaneity that he associates with the West. Hence, the infinitely variable poem to which he likens the city in his lecture on 'Semiology and Urbanism' finds its appropriate and perfect form in an infinite circulation of Japanese haiku.

---

[24] See GV 158 / 150.
[25] See, for example, Scott L. Malcomson, 'The Pure Land beyond the Seas: Barthes, Birch and the Uses of Japan', *Screen* 26 / 3–4 (1985), 23–33. For two sympathetic accounts of *Empire of Signs*, both of which see Barthes as challenging Orientalist ethnocentrism and narcissism, see Roger Laporte, 'L'Empire des signifiants', *Critique*, 302 (1972), 583–94, and Khatibi, 'Le Japon de Barthes', in *Figures de l'étranger dans la littérature française*, 57–85.

Barthes describes an individual haiku poem as 'a recollection without a subject' and its reader as a mere 'locus of reading' replacing our inevitably narcissistic Western self (78 / 103, 106). This reader, he claims, has no other 'self' than the totality of haiku that he or she infinitely *refracts*. Barthes himself adopts this position of refractor in his marvellous chapter on the stations of Tokyo, where what starts as a straightforward example of modern urban discourse is absorbed by the end of the chapter into a seventeenth-century haiku by Bashō. Barthes makes some of the same points about the overdetermined function of these stations (travel, shopping, eating, pleasure) that he had made in the urbanism lecture, and contends that each station acts as the sunken and entirely non-sacred focus of the district in which it is situated, while the constant coming and going of its trains lends an instability and constant movement to the commercial activities concentrated there. This, then, is a smaller-scale version of the empty space of the Emperor's palace which supposedly keeps all of Tokyo on the move. The station for Barthes seems to be the equivalent of La Scala for Stendhal—the microcosm of an Italy that is itself a world—and one imagines Barthes, newly arrived in Tokyo by plane, rushing off that very evening to immerse himself in the pleasures of the nearest railway station. Tokyo's stations are precisely microcosms of their respective districts, just as these districts are themselves microworlds within the 'veritable urban territory' (38 / 52) that is Tokyo. Barthes particularizes these districts to such an extent that he likens them to villages, each with a population as individual as a 'tribe', of which the vast city would be the 'bush'. These ethnographic metaphors echo Barthes's claims, in interviews, to have visited Japan as an ethnographer, 'but without the bad faith of the Western ethnographer who goes to examine foreign customs' (*GV* 230 /217). Despite being led by Bernard-Henri Lévy into agreeing that as ethnographer he was largely interested in communing with the natives, it is, I think, the cosmogonic aspect of ethnography that Barthes wishes to stress: 'Not the ethnology of primitive peoples, which has run out of territory and dried up, but the ethnology of modernity, of the big city, or the ethnology of France, introduced by Michelet.' Thus the fictional worlds of Proust, Sade, and Racine contain whole 'tribes' as well as whole societies (*GV* 230 / 218).

What is above all striking about the chapter on stations is the panache with which Barthes leads his reader through a series of distinct districts, each with its own people or tribe. The clue that this was to be a somewhat literary sequence is in fact clearly placed in the opening paragraph. Barthes comments that the names of Tokyo's districts conjure up their identity as distinct and self-contained areas of the city. Moreover, since there are no street names, the name of a district stands out on the map like a banner headline (*un gros flash*): 'it assumes that strongly signifying identity which Proust, in his own way, explored in his "Place Names" ' (*ES* 38 / 52).[26] Thus, when Barthes sets off to the station of Ueno, it is without any aim other than 'a sort of prolonged awareness (*perception*) of its name' (39 / 53). Here he knows that the upper level of the station will be filled with young skiers, but that its underground passages ('extensive as a city' (39 / 53)) will be lined with tramps, working-class bars, stalls with people selling things, travellers chatting, eating, and sleeping on the dirty corridor floors, in short the 'romantic essence of seediness'. 'On another day' he is drawn to the pedestrianized streets of Asakusa, decorated with artificial cherry blossom, where he will discover an entirely different 'people'. Here the shops sell modern, cheap, and comfortable clothing: leather caps and jackets, fur-edged gloves, long woollen scarves which are thrown over the shoulder in the manner of village children on their way home from school, 'all the gleaming and woolly paraphernalia of the good workman who must dress warmly, reinforced by the abundance of huge steaming bowls of simmering noodle soup' (39 / 56). On the other side of the city lies Ikebukuro with a population of workers and peasants which is different again, 'rough and friendly like a large mongrel dog'. In short, all these districts produce 'different races, other bodies, an ever-renewed familiarity' (39 / 56), so that to cross the city, or to penetrate its depths, is to travel from the top to the bottom of the whole country, to superimpose upon the topography of Japan 'the writing of its faces' (42 /56). It is this that each local name 'chimes' (*sonne*), and 'this chime (*son*) of the place is that of history; for the

[26] 'Place Names' occurs in the titles of two important sections of Proust's novel *Remembrance of Things Past*.

signifying name here is not a memory but an anamnesis, as if all of Ueno, all of Asakusa came to me from this old haiku (written by Bashō in the seventeenth century)':

> A cloud of blossoming cherry trees:
> The bell.—That of Ueno?
> That of Asakusa? (42 / 57)

The subdivision and infinite multiplication of social and physical types is a basic feature of 'Japan' that Barthes returns to in a later chapter, 'Millions of Bodies'. He begins by imagining a Frenchman who, as long as he stays in France, is unable to classify the faces and bodies of his compatriots, for they seem merely to repeat each other: 'the *déjà vu* of faces has no intellectual value for him' (95 / 127). However, should he see a Japanese man in Paris, he will instantly abstract him into the category 'Japanese race'. In fact, unable to see any difference between 'these rare Japanese bodies', the Frenchman is likely to perceive an isolated Japanese person through the lens of a cultural stereotype—some unimportant office worker, small, bespectacled, and ageless, and dressed in a nondescript suit. Barthes then proceeds to undo this stereotype by his somewhat delirious account of what happens when this same Frenchman goes to Japan and encounters a multiplicity of Japanese faces. To begin with, in the first of a series of linguistic metaphors that will run through the chapter, it becomes possible to establish a Saussurean dialectic between the *langue* of the race and the *parole* of the individual body. Next, Barthes mischievously suggests that 'quality is transformed by quantity' (96 / 130),[27] so that the rather pathetic stereotype of the office worker is transformed into 'exuberant diversity', and modern Japan unfolds the pages of a 'vast dictionary of faces':

The discovery is prodigious: streets, shops, bars, cinemas, trains unfold the huge dictionary of faces and physical shapes in which each body (each word) means only itself and yet refers to a class; hence one has both the voluptuousness of an encounter (with fragility, with singularity) and the illumination of a type (the feline, the peasant, the chubby cheeked, the recluse, the simpleton, the intellectual, the sleepyhead, the

---

[27] I assume that Barthes is quite deliberately confronting the racist myth of the 'yellow peril' (Far Eastern overpopulation as a threat to the West).

moonface, the beaming, the dreamer), source of an intellectual jubilation, since the unmasterable is mastered. Immersed in this nation of a hundred million bodies (a quantification preferable to that of 'souls'), we escape the double platitude of absolute diversity, which is finally no more than pure repetition (as in the case of the Frenchman surrounded by his compatriots), and of the single class, rid of all differences (the case of the Japanese petty official as we imagine we see him in Europe). (96 / 130–1)

Thus Barthes's teeming dictionary of bodies and faces—reminiscent of Michelet in its fascination with faces and its obvious pleasure in identifying or inventing physical types[28]—has both an erotic and a *cognitive* dimension, relentlessly pursued by Barthes through examples that act as the vanishing points of this 'semantic system', but always maintain the double pleasure of a physical surprise and an intellectual abstraction. Like the countless haiku which have been written in Japan, each drawing on familiar material and a shared syllabic form, yet each in its way an 'irreducible event', so with the country's bodies—all Japanese and forming a general body, and yet 'a vast tribe of different bodies', as individual as the response of the Zen master when he invents an absurd answer to his disciple's serious yet banal question. This is an individuality which Barthes claims is devoid of hysteria or a Western 'originality': it is simply difference that is refracted, like haiku, from body to body. Similarly beauty is simply repeated here and there, across these multiple differences, written into the 'great syntagm of bodies' (97–8 / 132–3).

In what may seem an ironic parallel, the catalogue of the infamous 1950s photography exhibition *The Family of Man* compared the millions of faces in the world to an 'alphabet' and a 'multiplication table' of faces.[29] As we saw in Chapter 4, this exhibition was also intended as a utopian cosmogony. However, its aim was to subsume difference into universality, to place 'Man' at the centre of creation, and to use its plethora of

---

[28] For a fine introduction to Barthes's early liking for this aspect of Michelet's writing, see the section of *Michelet* entitled 'Robespierre-Cat, Marat-Toad' (*Mi* 90–2 / 82–4).

[29] 'An alphabet here and a multiplication table of living breathing human faces' (Carl Sandburg, prologue to *The Family of Man*, 3).

photographs, with their gnomic and sentimentalizing legends, to convey this knowledge. Barthes's attempt to read the 'tribes' and 'peoples' of Japan as the inhabitants of a metaphorical world is a radical alternative to this American myth of a united and idealized 'family'. If *Empire of Signs* shares with *The Family of Man* a mask of ethnography, it overturns the ideology of the photography exhibition by choosing the ultimate Western 'other' as the physical basis of a *centrifugal* cosmogony, the elements of which (the different bodies) each refer to a class 'which vanishes, without disorder, into an infinite order; in short: ever open, like a logical system' (97 / 132–3).

Barthes's application of a literal 'writing of the body' to the crucial issue of how to conceptualize 'ethnic difference' is a curious but courageous fantasy which runs more or less explicitly through the text and illustrations of *Empire of Signs*. In a rare reference to the points at which the utopian semantic system of Japan is beginning to break down, Barthes captions the photographs of two Westernized pop singers as follows: 'Japan is entering into the Western moult: it is losing its signs, just as one loses one's hair, teeth, and fur; it is in the process of passing from (empty) meaning to (mass) communication. Here are two charming Tigers, popular singers (tigers of the postcard, the calendar, or the juke-box).'[30] Similarly, the juxtaposition of Barthes's picture in a Japanese newspaper with the photo of a Westernized Japanese actor appears to suggest that racial characteristics are simply cultural: 'What, then, is our face, if not a quotation?' While 'this Western lecturer, the moment he is quoted by the *Kobe Shinbun*, finds himself Japanified, his eyes elongated, his pupils blackened by the Nipponese typography', Teturo Tanba, who is 'quoting' Anthony Perkins, 'loses his Asiatic eyes' (90 / 120–1).

However, at the same time as focusing upon these cultural masks, Barthes pursues a long meditation on the 'writing' of the theatrical face—rather than its painting or its making up— which is implicitly based on the two beautiful photographs of a traditional Japanese actor which frame Barthes's text (2, 109 / 8, 151). Barthes maintains a delicate balance between an artificially whitened 'face to be written', and the metaphorically

---

[30] Skira edition only.

'already written' morphology of the Japanese face: 'The face is simply *the thing to be written*; but this future has itself already been written by the hand which has whitened out the eyelashes, the tip of the nose, the flat cheeks, and given to the page of flesh its black border of a head of hair which is as compact as stone' (88–9 / 120–1). Moreover, much of what is said about the 'incision' of the eyes and the mouth passes directly—via Barthes's likening of the eye to Mallarmé's 'night of the inkwell' (89 / 121)—from the actor's theatrical face to the close-up photograph of the faces of real children watching a street puppet show (100–1 / 136–7). In the chapter entitled 'The Eyelid', the 'written face' has now been narrowed down to the ultimate Western stereotype, the Japanese slit eye. Again, Barthes confronts the stereotype head on, arguing that our 'Western' frames of reference are inappropriate for a morphology which is 'not sculptural but scriptural'—'it is quite erroneously (by an obvious ethnocentrism) that we call the eye slit (*bridé*); nothing holds it back ... the Japanese face has no moral hierarchy; it is completely alive, even lively (contrary to the myth of Oriental impassivity)' (102 / 135).[31] If we accept Barthes's metaphor of the 'anatomical calligrapher', we can accept, too, that the Japanese eye has been literally written with the order, control, and expertise that go into the writing of an ideogram:

> You can imagine the anatomical calligrapher placing his brush down flat on the inner corner of the eye and, turning it slightly, with a single line, as required by *alla prima* painting, opening the face with a slit in the shape of an ellipse which, with a rapid twist of his hand, he closes up in the vicinity of the temple; ... The eye is thus contained between the parallel lines of its lids and the double (inverted) curve of its end points: it looks like the cut-out imprint of a leaf, or a wide comma lying on its side. (99 / 134)

Further on in the text Barthes includes an even closer close-up of a pair of eyes, with a caption (set out as a poem) which sums up the contrast he wishes to establish with the Western association of the concepts of depth and interiority:

---

[31] The French word *bridé* means held back or constrained. On Barthes's deliberate foregrounding of Japanese 'slit eyes', see 'Japanese Eyes', in D. A. Miller, *Bringing out Roland Barthes* (Berkeley and Los Angeles, University of California Press, 1992), 33–42.

> The eyes,
> and not the look,
> the slit,
> and not the soul. (146–7)[32]

However, the 'Eyelid' chapter ends with a distancing device which returns us to the more everyday world of 'Japan'. This is Barthes's description of the lightness with which the eye slips into sleep, an operation 'which we can observe on so many faces, in trains and on the subway in the evening' (102 / 138), and we imagine Barthes in the Tokyo subway, reading not the newspaper or even a book of haiku, but another delicately erotic incident from the 'page of life'.

In his brief foreword to *Empire of Signs*, Barthes describes the 'interlacing' of written text and pictures as ensuring the circulation and exchange of three signifiers: the body, the face, and writing (p.xi / 7). In fact, the connections established between the three terms become so dense that any one seems able to stand for the others. Barthes uses writing metaphors for every aspect of Japanese culture, from cooking and Pachinko, to Bunraku, flower arranging, bowing, and Zengakuren riots, as well as for his dizzying series of faces and bodies. Moreover, the concept of *alla prima* writing is already linked to the body. The most developed example of this is Barthes's chapter on the slot-machine game of Pachinko, the skill of which depends upon the player applying the correct degree of force to a single (and irreversible) movement of the flipper. Inevitably, Barthes compares the player's hand to that of an *alla prima* artist who must make their brush stroke once and for all, for the quality of paper and ink mean that correction is impossible.

Reading Barthes's gloss on the game in conjunction with his colour illustration of a Pachinko hall, it is impossible not to interpret it as a sustained allusion to male masturbation. Despite his claim that the halls are full of a varied public of both sexes, the players in Barthes's photo are all men, elbow to elbow in two long rows, each facing his machine (40).[33] The 'latrines' of Barthes's caption, 'Mangers and latrines', are not referred to in

---

[32] Skira edition only.
[33] Photograph omitted from the English translation.

his commentary, but an implicit allusion to men's lavatories obviously underpins it:

> What is the point of this art? to regulate a nutritive circuit.... The machines are mangers, lined up in rows; the player, with an abrupt gesture renewed so rapidly that it seems uninterrupted, feeds the machine with marbles; he stuffs them in, the way you would stuff a goose; from time to time the machine, gratified beyond measure, releases its diarrhea of marbles; for a few yen, the player is symbolically spattered with silver. We can understand then the seriousness of a game which counters the constriction of capitalist wealth, the constipated parsimony of salaries, with the voluptuous flood of silver marbles, which, all of a sudden, fill the player's hand. (28–9 / 43)

The *hand* is a crucial link between writing and sexuality, in that it is already both part of the body and the instrument of writing. Here, it is clearly connoted as the instrument of masturbation, a connotation passed on in its turn to the gesture of the graphic artist. Indeed, this sexualization of the primal gesture of Japanese writing is unambiguously developed in a chapter entitled 'At the Stationer's':

> As for the brush (passed across a faintly moistened block of ink), it has its movements, as if it were the finger; but whereas the pens we used to use could only produce thick or thin strokes and, what is more, could only scratch the paper in one direction, the brush can slide, twist, raise itself off the paper, the stroke being made, so to speak, in the volume of the air; it has the carnal, lubrified flexibility of the hand. (86 / 118)

It is the physical hand passing through the 'volume of the air' which now acts as a metaphor for the paintbrush of ideographic writing. This writing is precisely ideographic—and therefore three-dimensional—in many of Barthes's metaphorical examples, but most clearly in Japanese flower arranging, where what is 'written' is the circulation of air within a volume, so that 'you can move your body into the interstices of the branches', not in order to read their symbolism, 'but to follow the trajectory of the hand which has written them: a true writing, since it produces a volume' (45 / 60). This notion of an airy volume, here interwoven with references to a Japanese room (with its delicate sliding partitions and easily movable furniture), is finally applied to the Japanese habitat as a whole—be it the literal habitat of the 'ideal Japanese house', or the metaphorical 'cabinet of Signs' (*cabinet des Signes*) into which the whole world of Japan has been absorbed by the end of the text (108 / 148, 150). Alluding to the Western obsession with projecting a space of which one is both subject and master, Barthes describes the decentring of Japanese space as a 'painful frustration for Western man, everywhere "furnished" with his armchair and his bed, owner of a designated domestic *site*' (110 / 150). In Chapter 1, I discussed the single-mindedness with which the early Barthes unmasked the mythical forms of this obsession. In *Empire of Signs*, he has adopted an alternative strategy of abandoning the 'Occidental enclosure' to its *pantouflard* values, meanwhile projecting an alternative conceptualization of space, sexuality, and subjectivity on to an imaginary Japan.[34]

At the beginning of this chapter, I quoted Barthes's description of the 'inverted racism' which motivates Stendhal's unconditional admiration for random features of Italian culture. The example he gave of his own partiality for all things Japanese was a passion for the red fire hydrants to be seen in the streets of Tokyo. Searching for an example that Barthes had actually used in *Empire of Signs*, I alighted upon his arguably absurd promotion of the merits of the Japanese typewriter over its pathetic Western counterpart:

Our typewriter is quick to transform writing into a commercial product: it pre-edits the text even as you write it; theirs, with its countless characters, no longer aligned in letters on one sided keys but wrapped around cylindrical drums, calls for drawing and ideographic marquetry which will be scattered across the sheet of paper—in a word, across space; hence the typewriter continues, at least potentially, a truly graphic art which would no longer involve the artistic crafting of a solitary letter, but rather the abolition of signs, these being flung aslant, with full force, all over the page. (87 / 119)

In that this fantasy turns out to be the literal climax of Barthes's interweaving of sexuality and *alla prima* writing, it is a fine *modern* equivalent of the twelfth-century manuscript that is reproduced earlier in the text. Moreover, in the Flammarion re-edition of *Empire of Signs*, the caption to this manuscript is

---

[34] 'We must get out of the Occidental enclosure, as I postulated in my text on Japan' ('The Semiological Adventure' [1974], *SC* 3–8: 8 / 9–14: 14).

transposed into handwriting and is repositioned above the illustration: 'Rain, Seed, Dissemination, Weave, Fabric, Text, Writing' (*Pluie, Semence, Dissémination, Trame, Tissu, Texte, Ecriture*) (14).[35] Thus the beautiful ideographic writing rains down from Barthes's own hand.

---

[35] Not included in the English edition. *La semence* means both 'seed' (literary register) and 'semen'.

7
Turkey and China: 'But Where is the Orient?'

> When Loti finds himself forced to *opt*, . . . meaning ceases, the book stops, for there is no longer any signifier, and the signified resumes its tyranny.[1]

IN the early and mid-1970s Barthes often draws a distinction between 'the political' (*le politique*) and 'politics' (*la politique*). The political, he claims, is a fundamental order of history, of thought, of all that is done and spoken; it is the very dimension of the real. Politics, on the other hand, emerges when the political is converted into a repetitive, fixed discourse. This, clearly, is the general realm of politics evaluated through the familiar distinction between positive signifier (the political) and negative signified (politics). As we know, Barthes is irritated by the discourse of politics, and finds it oppressive even when it comes from the left. Yet it is not, he insists, a case of turning his back on politics. What he wants is to find an acceptable way of speaking the basic category of reality to which he is profoundly attached—the category that he calls the political.[2]

In his comments on the theme of 'Utopia Today' Barthes equates utopia—the political form of fantasy—with another favourite concept. This is the novelistic (*le romanesque*), one of the keys to Barthes's conception of utopian discourse throughout the 1970s.[3] Derived from his analysis of Fourier, and developed in all sorts of registers and contexts, it is certainly Barthes's

---
[1] Barthes, 'Pierre Loti: *Aziyadé*' [1971] in *NCE* 105–21: 116–17 / *DZN* 170–87: 182.
[2] See 'Twenty Key Words' [1975], in *GV* 203–32: 218.
[3] See *OC* iii. 44.

preferred mode for inscribing the everyday reality of the so-called political. Thus *Empire of Signs* represents 'something of an entry, not into the novel, but into the novelistic', in that 'a system which is almost totally immersed in the signifier works in conjunction with a perpetual withdrawal of the signified: this is what I tried to show at the essential level of everyday life (as much for food as for housing, make-up and the system of addresses)' (*GV* 84 / 83). As we have seen, the novelistic underpins Barthes's strategy of conflating the real Japan with a fantasized one at the beginning of this text, just as he will later refuse to choose between the real and the fictional when he invokes his own teaching seminar as a utopian space: 'Is it a case of a real place or a fictional place? Neither one nor the other. An institution is handled in the utopian mood: I trace a space and I call it *seminar*.'[4] In an interview the novelistic is somewhat differently described as 'a mode of discourse that is not structured as a narrative; it's a mode of notation, of investment, of interest in everyday reality, in people, in everything that happens in life' (*GV* 222 / 210). The novelistic is a mode to which he himself increasingly aspires, even though he cannot imagine himself writing a traditional novel with a plot and named characters: 'In daily life, I feel a sort of curiosity about everything that I see and hear, an almost intellectual affectivity which belongs to the order of the novelistic. A hundred years ago, I would probably have walked through life with a realist novelist's notebook in my hand' (*GV* 203 / 192).

The novelistic can be differentiated from the novel in that it is not a genre but a fragmentary form which Barthes will trace from Japanese haiku to German Romantic song and the figures of the lover's discourse. While it may traverse narrative forms it will never coincide with '*a story or a destiny*', largely because it corresponds to the 'fundamental discontinuity of our mental life'—a tissue of minor outbursts and wavering moods—to which coded language alone gives an illusion of fixity.[5] As such, one of Barthes's most interesting elaborations of the novelistic is to be found in a radio talk on Romantic song where it can be

---

[4] 'To the Seminar' [1974], *RL* 332–42: 332 / 369–79: 369.
[5] See 'Texte à deux (parties)' [1977], *OC* iii. 761–7: 763, first published in *Wunderblock*.

seen to cut across (and to link) both inner and outer reality. Even the song cycles of Schumann or Schubert do not recount a love story, but simply a journey: they are devoid of any sense of general significance, personal destiny, or spiritual transcendence. Instead of this, they are made up of a multitude of little *tableaux*, 'each of which consists, in turn, of a memory, a landscape, a walk, a mood, of anything at all which motivates a moment of distress, nostalgia, or happiness'.[6] To imagine, to improvize, to fantasize in this way is precisely to elaborate the discontinuity of the novelistic without turning it into a novel. Yet the physical world caught up in such fantasizing is not at all unreal. In Schumann, for example (in piano pieces as well as songs), 'reality is not discounted. His music, through its titles, sometimes through discreet descriptive sketches, refers endlessly to concrete things: seasons, times of day, landscapes, festivals, occupations (*métiers*).'[7]

Barthes's conception of the novelistic is a useful framework for reading his preface to Pierre Loti's *Aziyadé* (1879), an inspired piece of literary criticism first published in 1971. What Barthes claims to find important in *Aziyadé* is the novelistic status of a discourse that is mediated by the hero's neurotic psychology, and by the insignificant 'incidents' that convey the quality of his everyday experience. In short, the text inscribes the particular relationship between signifier and signified, between the political and politics, that has become central to Barthes's notion of utopia and its distinctive modal relationship to reality. But, at the same time, his reading of *Aziyadé* exemplifies a sexualization of this utopian discourse, and a second important context of Barthes's preface is therefore, once more, Orientalism.[8] If Barthes is interested in Loti's attempt to

---

[6] 'The Romantic Song' [1976], *RF* 286–92: 290 / 253–8: 257.
[7] 'Loving Schumann' [1979], *RF* 293–8: 295 / 259–64: 261.
[8] Rana Kabbani is fiercely critical of Loti's Orientalism: 'The Western male could possess the native woman by force of his domination over her native land; she was subjugated by his wealth, his military might. . . . She was his colonial acquisition, but one that he pretended enjoyed his domination and would mourn his departure' (*Europe's Myths of Orient: Devise and Rule*, 81). See, too, Alec Hargreaves, 'Literary Imperialism', Ch. 5 of *The Colonial Experience in French Fiction: A Study of Pierre Loti, Ernest Psichari and Pierre Mille* (London, Macmillan, 1981), 68–85. Hargreaves accuses Loti of failing to distinguish one nation from another, of

give creative form to the difference and appeal of a foreign culture, this is because that difference and appeal are explicitly eroticized. By a happy coincidence of Orientalist determinations, *Aziyadé* is set in Constantinople, chosen by Fourier as the capital city of Harmony. Loti's Turkey is certainly an Amorous World, but hardly a new one, in that its social and sexual structures are reminiscent less of Fourier than of Sade and of the Morocco of 'Incidents'.[9] Does Barthes's preface mark a retreat from *Empire of Signs* into a negatively Oriental *pays d'élection*, focusing as it does upon Loti's portrayal of a fantasmatic immersion in a Turkish culture which is prized for its regressiveness?

Although *Aziyadé* is a sexual idyll, Loti provides it with a very specific historical and political context. The novel opens in May 1876 as its hero—an English naval officer also called Loti—impassively witnesses the hanging of six Turks on the quayside of Salonica, a revenge demanded by the governments of France and Germany for the murder of their respective consuls. It continues against the background of the 'Eastern Crisis' of the Ottoman Empire, with its uprising in the Balkans, its rapidly deposed sultans, its government of 'Young Turks', its new constitution, and finally the super-power politics which lead to the outbreak of war between Turkey and Russia in 1877. The novel closes with the death of the fictional Loti, who has taken up arms for Turkey, at the Battle of Kars in the autumn of 1877.[10]

However, Barthes's interest in the specific politics of the situation is limited to this final political commitment to Turkey, for it is a commitment that will kill off the novel as well as its hero: 'When Loti finds himself forced to *opt* (as it is put in administrative language) he must shift from the imaginary level

---

refusing a subject position to any culture but his own, and of endless plots of passionate devotion until the ship leaves. For a more sympathetic discussion, though one equally aware of these problems, see the discussion of *Aziyadé* in Tzvetan Todorov, *Nous et les autres: La Réflexion française sur la diversité humaine* (Paris, Seuil, 1989), especially the section 'Exotisme et érotisme', 347–51.

[9] See Chs. 3 and 5.

[10] For details of the historical context see the preface and very useful editorial material of the Folio edition of the text: Pierre Loti, *Aziyadé* [1879] suivi de *Fantôme de l'Orient*, ed. and annotated by Claude Martin (Paris, Gallimard, 1991). References to the text of *Aziyadé* are to this edition.

to the real level, from an ethos to a status, from a way of life to political responsibility, he must yield to the constraints of a *praxis*: meaning ceases, the book stops, for there is no longer any signifier, and the signified resumes its tyranny' (NCE 116–17 / DZN 182). This is very much the Barthes of the *Promesse* interview discussed in Chapter 5, a Barthes who wishes to replace the paradigm of *imperialism/socialism* with *imperialism/something else*. In fact, the section from which this quotation is drawn, significantly entitled 'But Where Is the Orient?', is helpful for understanding how Barthes's own use of the *Occident/Orient* paradigm maps on to these concerns. The issue of the competing locations of the Orient is addressed— Turkey rather than 'Egypt or Morocco'—but is rapidly dismissed as a question the answer to which is historically contingent. This is not really what Barthes means by 'where is the Orient?', for 'the Orient is merely a square of a board game, the marked term of an alternative: the Occident or *something else*. As long as the opposition is unresolved, merely subjected to forces of *temptation*, meaning functions positively, the book is possible, *it develops*' (116 / 182). The element that turns out to be crucial to a utopian Orient is *fantasy*, which is not necessarily apolitical or ahistorical, as was seen in the discussion of Fourier in Chapter 3. Indeed, in Loti's case, it involves the violent temptation to plunge into the major political and ethical step of a change of national loyalties from England to Turkey, and it is a step which, when Loti is first called away to England, he cannot quite bring himself to take. Barthes works hard, I think, to keep Loti's Orientalism—and indirectly his own—in the realm of 'the political' as he has defined it, of material reality conceptualized through the fantasmatic dimension that he equates with the signifier. It is this that collapses once the claims of the political signified take over with Loti's decision to fight for Turkey.

This fragile conceptualization of the world is precarious, and Barthes proceeds to the interesting (if somewhat slippery) argument that it is best maintained by a neurotic investment in the past:

What should be noted is that the fantasmatic cathexis, the *possibility* of meaning (and not its cessation), what *precedes* the decision and remains exterior to it, always occurs, it seems, with the help of a political regression: when it concerns a lifestyle, desire is always feudal: in a Turkey which is already out of date, it is a still older Turkey that an anguished Loti seeks out: desire always proceeds toward an extreme archaism, there where the greatest historical distance assures the greatest unreality, there where desire finds its pure form: that of an impossible return, that of the Impossible. (117 / 182)

This theme of the impossible status of the Orient is continued into the next section of the preface, 'Travel, Residence'. Here Barthes explores once more the difference between the possible degrees of immersion in a foreign country: the tourist's visit, the extended stay of the temporary resident, and the naturalization of a change of citizenship. Loti passes through all three, from initial touristic explorations of Salonica, to a lengthy period of residence in a suburb of Constantinople (when he sets up house in Eyoub), to his final signing on as an officer in the Turkish army. It is the *transitional* status of residence that interests Barthes here, ambiguously situated between an 'ethical intoxication' with a lifestyle and a permanent commitment:

As resident the subject no longer has the ethical irresponsibility of the tourist (who is simply a national on holiday), nor does he yet have the citizen's responsibility (civilian, political, military); he is placed between two strong statuses, and yet this intermediary position *lasts*— it is defined by the very slowness of its development (whence, a mixture of eternity and precariousness in Loti's stay in Eyoub, which both 'keeps returning' and is 'always about to end'): the resident is, in short, a tourist who *repeats* his desire to remain (*'I am living in one of the loveliest countries of the world'*—words of a tourist, lover of pictures and photographs—*'and my freedom is limitless'*—intoxication of the resident, whom a good knowledge of localities, customs, and the language allows to satisfy every desire without fear (this is what Loti calls freedom). (117–18 / 183)

If this last notion of the resident's freedom to pursue his desires with impunity is again reminiscent of 'Incidents', the stress on residence is in fact very different from Barthes's negative comparison of the actuality of living in Morocco with the mere fantasy of doing so that had descended upon the tourist.[11] In Loti's tripartite scheme residence subsumes and goes beyond the

---

[11] See Ch. 5.

original fantasy, so that what is really desired is a *permanent state of temporary residence*. It is the self-evidently untenable status of this contradictory ideal that fascinates Barthes, and which causes him to describe Loti's veritable submersion in the fantasmatic materiality of Constantinople as leading him to the brink of madness. If Loti no longer suffers, no longer has a memory, and would pass by with indifference those whom he once adored, this is because he has literally lost himself in the depths of the city, 'dying to everything but his desire' (118 / 183).

The seriousness of Loti's immersion in Turkey is figured by his crash course in the language and his use of a Turkish name, but it is above all his adoption of traditional Turkish dress that encapsulates what Barthes aptly describes as a conversion: 'A philosopher one day exclaimed: I would gladly undergo a conversion for the right to wear the caftan, the djellaba, the selham! In other words: all the lies in the world for the truth of my costume!' (114 / 179). Although Loti does not intend literally to convert to Islam if he takes up Turkish nationality, he is otherwise ethically and psychologically committed to the total construction of his desired identity. Yet there are several moments in the novel where he is self-consciously ironic about this artificial persona, capable as he still is of seeing his costume as the fancy dress of a tenor in some Orientalizing operetta.[12] This ability to step back from his chosen image—like his decision to maintain a religion the precepts of which, after all, he hardly follows—may have the function that Barthes attributes to Stendhal's self-conscious cathexis of Italy: a slight stepping back in order to be all the more aware of one's psychological investment.[13] However, Barthes also analyses an interesting quotation from the novel whereby Loti refers to the desire 'to be oneself a part of this picture which is so full of movement and of light' (115 / 180). Thus, according to Barthes, it is a 'pictorial being' that Loti the author lends to Loti the character by dressing him up in beautiful and old-fashioned Turkish clothing in which to carry out his daily circuit of the mosques, bars, baths, and squares that make up the *tableaux* of Turkish life:

---

[12] Loti, *Aziyadé*, 118.   [13] See opening of Ch. 6.

The goal of transvestism (once the illusion of identity is exhausted) is *finally* to transform oneself into a describable object—and not into an introspectable subject. The consecration of the disguise (belied by its very success) is pictorial integration, the passage of the body into an overall writing, in a word (if it is taken literally), *transcription*: dressed *accurately* (that is to say in clothes from which any excessive accuracy has been banished), the subject is dissolved, not through intoxication but though Apollinism, through participation in an harmonious combination. (115–16 / 180–1)

One of the values which most attracts Loti, and which makes him want to take up position in the general picture, is subsumed in his predilection for the Turkish word *eski*: ' "I examined the old men who surrounded me: their costumes betrayed a scrupulous concern with the fashions of the good old days; everything that they wore was *eski*, down to their huge silver spectacles and the shape that these gave to their old faces. *Eski*, a word uttered with veneration, which means *ancient* and which is used in Turkey as much for old customs as for traditional forms of clothing or materials" ' (120 / 185–6).[14] The picturesque *eski* is also an ethical value. In quoting this passage Barthes does not mention, but is obviously aware, that these are the old men whom the novel also portrays as resenting and resisting the new Turkish constitution. The *eski* is an emblem of Loti's anti-egalitarian fantasy of fusing with a hierarchical Ottoman society. As such, it is the focus in Barthes's reading of *Aziyadé* of his general claim that, 'when it concerns a lifestyle, desire is always feudal' (117 / 182).

The *eski* is in itself a neurotic value, in that it is trying to deny the movement of history. If it survives at all, it is because Turkey finds itself at a strange moment of historical dislocation whereby a more modern society is *about* to take over, but has not yet done so, and where it is already apparent that the *eski* is an artificial cult of the past: 'Such is Loti's Constantinople: a living and lively scene, colourful and odorous, but no longer owned by anyone: Turkey in its death throes (as a politically powerful nation), modernism at the gates, minimal defences, and here and there the cult of the old-fashioned, of past refinement—of the past as refinement' (120 / 185). This historically specific state of political disconnection is equated by

---

[14] Loti, *Aziyadé*, 112.

Barthes with an important concept for him, the *déshérence*, or lack of inheritors by default, of which the equivalent legal term in English is *escheat*: 'Everything subsists and yet nothing belongs to anyone any more; each thing, present in its complete form, is drained of that combative tension attached to property, there is a loss, not of possessions but of inheritances and inheritors' (120 / 185). Significantly, to explain what he means, and also to convey the appeal of this strangely suspended state of affairs, Barthes elaborates a Moroccan parallel: 'Even a few years ago, during the summer, the European district of the city of Marrakesh was completely dead (tourism has now brought it back to life, excessively so); in the heat, along the wide avenues with their open but useless shops, their virtually empty café terraces, their parks with here and there a man asleep on a rare patch of grass, one could savour a penetrating feeling: that of *déshérence*' (120 / 185). If Marrakesh is the city of *déshérence*, it is Tangiers that exemplifies Constantinople's closely related quality of *drift* (*la dérive*): 'There exist cities of drift: neither too large nor too new, they must have a past (like Tangiers, a former international city) and yet they must still be alive; cities inside of which several cities mingle, cities without social ambition, cities which are lazy and idle and yet not at all luxurious, cities full of a debauchery which does not take itself seriously' (119 / 184). There are, of course, a number of points that could be made on the basis of these quotations. For example, the Moroccan atmosphere that Barthes evokes in a positive way clearly depends upon a recent colonial past, and economic stagnation is implicitly preferred to the revival of local commerce that will follow from the development of tourism. Although *déshérence* is a legal and economic metaphor, the claims of 'need' seem once more to have been absorbed into those of Barthes's pleasure. However, it is apparent that it is partly the momentary suspension of social struggle that appeals to Barthes, rather than some upholding of the past for its own sake. This illusory truce in the war of languages has its utopian dimension, just as the detachment from any struggle for ownership is in marked contrast to the appropriative ideology that an earlier Barthes associated with Voltaire, Verne, or *Paris-Match*.

Orientalism itself, in these formulations, is reduced to a lazy form of contestation which is precisely that of *drift* : its manner of 'rejecting the Occident or of absconding from it is neither violent, nor ascetic, nor political' (119 / 184). If Loti is an emblematic hero of drift, so too, it seems, is the hippie: 'Loti is basically a hippie dandy: like him, hippies have a taste for expatriation and transvestism' (118–19 / 184). In Barthes's essay on hippies—the hippie movement as an ambiguous form of cultural contestation—as well as in 'Incidents', Barthes seems to be ironic about the adoption by American and European hippies of versions of Oriental dress.[15] Yet Barthes also describes himself in 'Incidents' as searching unsuccessfully for a blue djellaba, and my favourite fragment of this text portrays him precisely ensconced in a djellaba, albeit of unknown colour: 'Happiness at Mehiula: night-time in the huge kitchen, a storm outside, the simmering *harrira*, big butane lamps, an endless round of minor comings and goings, warmth, a djellaba, and reading Lacan! (Lacan invaded (*gagné*) by these trivial comforts.)' (*I* 39 / 58). The scene is remarkably reminiscent of descriptions of Loti at home on chilly evenings at Eyoub. But above all, in the movement between Lacan and the djellaba, it portrays Barthes drifting between Occident and Orient in the prerequisite non-violent manner. On this basis we will hardly expect Barthes to take up arms for Morocco. When Barthes, seeking a contemporary parallel for the 'Oriental fantasy of lieutenant Loti', chooses a young French teacher in Egypt or Morocco who decides to side with the Arab cause against Israel, we know that this never was, nor could be, himself (*NCE* 116 / *DZN* 181). Nevertheless, he has chosen as his example two countries in which he has lived and worked. There is an interesting reference, in the 'Archives du XXe siècle' interviews filmed in 1970 and 1971, to the veritable turning point in Barthes's life when he made the difficult decision to return from Alexandria to a job in France, rather than adopting an expatriate lifestyle on a permanent basis.[16] What is more, according to Calvet's biography, one city that he did not wish to leave was Bucharest, where, it will be remembered—against the background of another transitional period both politically and

---

[15] See 'Un cas de critique culturelle', *OC* ii. 544–6: 544, and 'Incidents', *I* 18 / 30.
[16] *Océaniques* (FR3, 1988), not included in the extracts published in *Tel Quel* in 1971.

culturally—he had channelled his 'talent' into leading a hedonistic life. There is something strikingly like the postponed departures of Lieutenant Loti in Calvet's account of a Barthes who stays on in Romania until the last possible moment, presiding over the death throes of the French Institute in Bucharest even after his colleagues have been expelled from the country.[17]

Barthes's own cathexis of other countries and cultures seems to resemble that of Loti the author, who, having created a hero more neurotic than himself, and having, as Barthes puts it, disposed of him in a suitably noble manner, 'will go on describing cities of Japan, Persia, and Morocco, that is to say he will indicate and stake out (by emblematic discourses) the space of his desire' (114 / 179). For a major feature of Barthes's definitions of drift and *déshérence* is precisely sexual desire: 'the drift of Lieutenant Loti (on the waters of Salonica, in the suburb of Eyoub, carried along by winter evenings with Aziyadé, or debauched meanderings through the underground passages and the cemeteries of Stamboul) is, therefore, the exact figure of his desire' (119 / 185). And just as Barthes finds an emblem of drift in the 'floating bed' (the boat) in which Loti and Aziyadé spend their first nights off the shores of Salonica, so cemeteries in particular are central to the thematics of *déshérence*: 'grass sprouting between the paving stones of the street, black cypress trees standing out against white marble, cemeteries (so numerous in Loti's Turkey), which are not so much places of death as spaces of debauchery, of drift' (120 / 186).

Barthes describes Loti's wish to be become part of the picture as that dissolution of active subject and passive object which is the goal of a very modern writing, and seems surprised to find this sort of logic at work in a 'minor and old-fashioned' author (116 / 181). In fact the analysis is typical of Barthes's general attempt to uphold *Aziyadé* as a paradoxical novel which is at once insipidly outdated and very modern. The introductory section of the preface exaggerates the paradox in a somewhat artificial manner, by opposing the 'sumptuous' signifier of the title ('Aziyadé') to a derisory signified: 'the preconception of dealing with a quaint, insipid (*fade*), and conventionally

[17] See Calvet, *Roland Barthes*, 87–9.

sentimental novel' (105 / 170). Given that what Barthes means by the signifier is not just the material sound and appearance of language, but the fantasmatic perception and upholding of a reality that is itself outdated, it is somewhat perverse of him to conclude his essay with the statement that 'the signifier is never old-fashioned' (121 / 187). What is more, it becomes clear that Barthes has fostered the sad image of a sickly sweet novel the better to offset what he actually (and very rapidly) discovers in *Aziyadé*—a transgressive and morally dubious *text*: 'having slipped from the precious name to the sad image of an outdated novel, we might make our way back towards the idea of a *text*: a fragment of infinite language which does not recount anything but which is crossed by "something unprecedented and murky" ' (106 / 170–1). Barthes is quoting here from a scene early in the novel, where Samuel, the ragamuffin boat boy, first betrays his physical desire for Loti: 'Something unprecedented and murky had flashed through poor Samuel's mind—in the old Orient anything is possible!' (111 / 176).[18] Thus, Barthes knows from the outset that the novel has not only been written to recount the unhappy love story of Loti and Aziyadé, for this 'odyssey of an expatriate soul' is above all 'the muted and allusive tale of an Oriental-style debauchery' (121 / 186–7).

If there has been a critical debate, passing through Edmond de Goncourt, Gide, and Jean Cocteau, over whether the biographical source for Aziyadé was 'really' a woman or a man, the question is irrelevant to the reading of the novel into which Barthes soon settles.[19] For Barthes, Aziyadé has a largely functional role, whereby transgression is displaced to an unhappy passion for a forbidden woman. The harem is a substititute for the prohibition on homosexuality, and it is not so much the forbidden Aziyadé, as Constantinople and its 'pale debauchery' that Loti will finally choose against his country, his family, and his career. This pale debauchery is 'that of daybreak, as a whole night of erotic meandering draws to a close' (112 / 177). Along with such phrases as 'a strange prostitution' and 'the vices of Sodom', 'pale debauchery' is a direct quotation from Loti's text.[20] Barthes uses it as the title of a section of his

---

[18] Loti, *Aziyadé*, 44.
[19] See Claude Martin, preface to Loti, *Aziyadé*, 20–1.
[20] Loti, *Aziyadé*, 66.

essay, in order to conjure up the mood of this decentred tale of homosexual desire drifting free though a night-time city: 'Stamboul and Salonica (their poetic descriptions) take the place of encounters which are hypocritically declared irksome, of the stubborn pursuit (*la drague*) of young Asian boys' (113 / 178). Moreover, desire drifts through the city with a Sadeian impunity: Loti is 'a little too late' in condemning the orgies that are organized for him, 'as in the case of the cemetery keeper, whose advances he accepts before pitching him over a precipice; as in the case of old Kairoullah, whom he provokes into offering his twelve-year-old son, "beautiful as an angel", but whom he then ignominiously dismisses at dawn' (113 / 178). As a result, it is not the innocence and fidelity of Aziyadé's heterosexual love that is set up as the binary opposite of homosexual debauchery. It is constraint that forms a paradigm with 'Asiatic debauchery' (113 / 179): a constraint not only in the form of the British moral institutions represented in the text by Loti's mother, his sister, and his dull friends Plumkett and Brown, but above all in the form of the Turkish police whom Loti must twice placate. Barthes argues that 'the forbidden' is an abstract category for Loti the author, so that the sanctity of the mosque or the harem is instantly and interchangeably transgressed in the *imagination*: 'the Forbidden is an idea: it matters little, in short, that it be violated in reality; what matters, and what is endlessly stated, is that it be posited, and that one should posit oneself in relation to it' (112 / 177). Thus the *invraisemblance* of the ease with which Loti infiltrates the most closely guarded corners of Turkish life is irrelevant. What matters is to emphasize the enormous difficulty of penetrating the mosque or the harem, or of learning to pass for a Turk within a few weeks, not to discover *how* such feats were accomplished. Indeed, as Barthes also points out, the author hardly bothers to tell us.

Thus even the role and significance of Samuel are left entirely undeveloped. In the section entitled 'The Two Friends', Barthes draws attention to the contrast between Loti's two loyal servants: the 'masculine', strongly built, comradely Achmet, loyal defender of the interests of both Loti and Aziyadé, and the feline and feminized Samuel, Aziyadé's rival for Loti's affections. Yet, as Barthes argues, what is apparently formulated as a distinct paradigm (*friend/lover*) is in fact of no consequence at all. In that it is not transformed into any action, plot, or drama, its meaning remains somehow indifferent: 'This novel is an almost motionless discourse, which posits meanings but does not resolve them' (111/176). The title of the third section of the preface asks the question 'What Happens?', only to answer it in the title of the fourth—'Nothing'. It is in unpacking the space between this question and answer that Barthes links Pierre Loti's novel to a now familiar dimension of utopian discourse:

> What is recounted is not an adventure, it is *incidents*: we must take the word in as slight, as modest a sense as possible. The incident, already less strong than the accident (but perhaps more disturbing) is simply *that which falls* gently, like a leaf, on to the carpet of life; it is that light, fleeting crease which ruffles the fabric of the days, it is what is *just about* worth noting: a sort of zero degree of notation, the minimum necessary to be able to write *something*. (108 / 172–3)

Barthes gives as examples of Loti's insignificant incidents a walk, an excursion, a conversation, a puppet show, a winter's evening, the unexpected visit of a cat to Samuel's bed. Although Barthes does not use the term here, these minor happenings constitute themselves as the material of recollections, the *anamneses* that he identifies as the basic material of haiku, and that he will try to produce himself in *Roland Barthes by Roland Barthes*.[21] But his best example of 'this external (externalized) emptiness which constitutes happiness' (108 / 173), an example that again overlaps with his comments on haiku, is Loti's endless recourse to noting the *weather*. For to make 'nothing' happen one has nevertheless to write something, and Loti's way of upholding the insignificance of his discourse is to approach the desired lack of meaning indirectly: 'a thousand delicate notations whose object is neither an idea, feeling, or fact but simply, in the broadest sense of the term: the weather (*le temps qu'il fait*)' (108 / 173).

Barthes suggests that the weather is the envelope of the human body, and operates as its point of contact with the physical world: 'the weather refers to a kind of complex existence of the world (of what is) in which place, setting, light, temperature, and synaesthesia all merge; it is that fundamental

[21] *RB* 107–10 / 111–14.

mode according to which my body is in the world, and feels itself existing' (109 / 174). This is an unmediated relationship between human beings and the world, especially precious because it bypasses the language war—'where meaning begins, so too does interpretation, that is to say a battle' (109 / 174). A counter-example of the latter is provided by Barthes's anecdote, recorded in *Roland Barthes by Roland Barthes*, of *talking about the weather* with the local baker. Her lack of response to his comment about the beautiful light makes him realize the degree to which perceptions of the weather are class-bound: 'nothing could be more cultural than the atmosphere, nothing more ideological than the weather' (*RB* 176 / 178). Barthes's point about Pierre Loti is that—like the great haiku poets, or like Amiel in his diary—he has inscribed the weather in language, but in such a way as to cut it off from connotation, just as he exploits the very insignificance of the weather to 'disappoint meaning' (*NCE* 109 / *DZN* 174). More than this, Barthes even finds a passage in *Aziyadé* where the weather fulfils the rhetorical function of an anacoluthon, so that it manages to interrupt the construction of meaning, the narrative, and the world all at once. Loti (on board his ship) is in the middle of an enigmatically erotic dream about Aziyadé and Samuel, when he is woken up to go on watch—we hear no more about the dream, but are told: 'It poured with rain that night, and I got soaked' (110 / 175). Thus, Barthes declares, 'the dream discreetly sheds all meaning, even the meaning of meaninglessness; the rain (the notation of the rain) stifles that lightning flash, that flash of meaning that Shakespeare speaks of: meaning, broken off, is not destroyed, rather—that rare, difficult thing—it is *exempted*' (110 / 175).

If the novelistic discourse that Barthes tried to use in his own

---

[22] Barthes may have confused Shakespeare and Wordsworth, but his point remains that haiku is like a flash photograph taken with an empty camera—it does not in fact *reveal* anything at all. In *Empire of Signs*, Barthes actually quotes 'When the light of sense goes out, but with a flash that has revealed the invisible world' (*ES* 83 / 111), and one could well imagine him, in order to make his point about *Aziyadé*, setting out Loti's 'incident' in the approximate form of a haiku: 'It poured with rain | that night | and I got soaked'. Michael Moriarty has generously saved Barthes scholars present and future from repeating the master's blunder: the lines attributed to Shakespeare are from *The Prelude* (Moriarty, *Roland Barthes*, 4).

'Incidents' failed to achieve an entirely utopian effect, this was partly because he was unable to resist introducing significance into his fragments of Moroccan reality—unsurprisingly, given the postcolonial context, he remained entirely caught up in a world structured around paradigmatic (conflictual) divisions of meaning.[23] A more Loti-like side-stepping of significance was attempted in the short essay on China that Barthes was to publish in 1974; ironically, it was the cause of the text's notoriously negative reception. 'So How Was China?' (*Alors, la Chine?*) is an important contribution to the development of Barthes's thinking on utopia as both concept and mode of discourse; it is also important as the last of the series of travel texts that involve representations of the so-called Orient.

The essay is something of an overturning of the thoroughly political and theoretical context from which it emerged. Barthes, who often described himself as a sort of fellow traveller of his friends at *Tel Quel*, enacted this role literally when, in April 1974, along with François Wahl, he joined Philippe Sollers, Julia Kristeva, and Marcelin Pleynet on a three-week visit to China. The visit spawned a whole spate of publications, of which the best known is probably Kristeva's book on Chinese women. There were also two special issues of *Tel Quel*, four articles by Wahl in *Le Monde*, and, some years later, Pleynet's *Le Voyage en Chine*.[24] Barthes's own 'So How Was China?' appeared in *Le Monde* in May 1974; it was republished by Christian Bourgois in 1975, with an important afterword in which, in the light of the text's initial reception, Barthes comments upon what he had been trying to achieve. In a brief preface, Bourgois alludes ironically to the scandal, for 'militants' of all persuasions, of a

---

[23] See Ch. 5.
[24] See *Tel Quel*, 59 and 60 (Autumn 1974); Julia Kristeva, *Des Chinoises* (Paris, des femmes, 1974); François Wahl, 'La Chine sans utopie', *Le Monde* (15–19 June 1974); Marcelin Pleynet, *Le Voyage en Chine: Chroniques d'un journal ordinaire (11 avril–3 mai 1974)* (Paris, Hachette, 1980). The immediate political context in France was not so much post-1968 Maoism as the presidential election following the death in office of Georges Pompidou, an election in which François Mitterrand was very narrowly defeated in the second round by Valéry Giscard d'Estaing. The *Tel Quel* party returned from China on the Sunday of the first round of voting; Pleynet's diary contains several references to the campaign (such as news of opinion polls filtering through to China), and the editorial of *Tel Quel*'s first special issue on China opens with a reference to this electoral defeat for the French Left.

Barthes who not only had nothing to say on China, the Chinese, and their 'Great Revolution', but who had the cheek to say so on the front page of *Le Monde*.[25] Claude Roy, for example, had commented that the sarcastic demystifier of *Paris-Match*, the Tour de France, fashion, Balzac, Sade, and Réquichot had come strangely unstuck on the China of the Cultural Revolution ('no unconscious to bring to consciousness, no secrets to decipher, no depths to penetrate'), and had summed up Barthes's quest and its findings in a single word: '*nothing*'.[26]

From such an account, it might be tempting to compare Barthes's record of the *Tel Quel* expedition to China with that of the two journalists from *Le Figaro* who, in 1955, set off to explore a Soviet Union newly opened to Western eyes. It was Barthes himself who, in 'The *Batory* Cruise', uncovered their bad faith, a demystification that earlier served to introduce my own discussion of Barthes's travel mythologies.[27] The two right-wing journalists, who regularly denounced the evils of Soviet communism in the pages of their newspaper, suffered a bizarre crisis of agnosticism once they reached Soviet shores, declaring themselves unable to judge the true facts of the situation on the basis of such a short visit. Instead they took hypocritical refuge in what Barthes then called the 'neutral' territory of the street, the everyday life deemed the appropriate domain of the tourist. As a result they could simply 'note' things without claiming to draw conclusions, their touristic alibi allowing them 'to look without understanding, to travel without taking any interest in political realities' (*ET* 95 / *My* 131). It is easy to see how the terms of Barthes's sarcastic and convincing critique might be turned back against his public response to China, for example by focusing upon his preference for the everyday over overt political comment, or his elaboration of the *neutre* as an ethically positive category.

---

[25] Bourgois sees in Barthes's essay a discretion and modesty at odds with the habits of 'our loquacious mandarins'. See Barthes, *Alors, la Chine?* (Paris, Christian Bourgois, 1975), 5. All other page references for 'Alors, la Chine?' are to OC iii. 32–5.
[26] This was part of an assessment of Barthes on the occasion of the publication of *Roland Barthes by Roland Barthes*, 'Barthes par lui-même/Barthes par les autres', *Le Monde* (14 Feb. 1975), 16–17: 17.
[27] Barthes, 'The *Batory* Cruise', *ET* 95–8 / *My* 130–3 (see Ch. 4).

However, in picking up phrases from the second paragraph of 'So How Was China?', Roy does not acknowledge Barthes's almost ironic stress on the very phrases he quotes. Barthes portrays the group setting off for China armed with pressing and seemingly obvious questions about the status of sexuality, women, the family, and morality, or about the role of linguistics and psychiatry: 'We shake the tree of knowledge so that it will shed the reply to our questions, so that we can return bearing our standard intellectual nourishment: a secret fathomed. But the tree sheds nothing. In a sense (apart from the political reply) it is precisely with *nothing* that we return' (OC iii. 32). Roy does not mention the conclusions that Barthes will draw from this disappointment of received habits of intellectual curiosity, nor does he address what might actually be meant by Barthes's 'nothing'.

In the light of Barthes's distinction between politics and the political discussed at the beginning of this chapter, and in the light of his reading of *Aziyadé*, one can easily imagine the sort of essay on China that he might have intended to write. Given his strong dislike of stereotypical political discourse, and given the certainty of exposure to it on a visit of this nature, he would surely have looked forward to replacing the received discourse on China with a novelistic account of the daily details of Chinese life, upon which he would have bestowed the elevated status of signifiers of material reality. What Barthes ends up writing about China is rather different, and in trying to understand why, I have found Marcelin Pleynet's *Le Voyage en Chine* (based on a diary kept throughout the visit) both interesting and illuminating.[28] To begin with, it is clear that the

---

[28] Pleynet comments in his preface on how different this text is from the essays he had published in *Tel Quel* on his return, not least because the latter were influenced by the perceived obligation to address his reflections on China to the French Communist Party. *Le Voyage en Chine*, on the other hand, betrays a striking overlap of response with that of Barthes, both as it can be read in 'So How Was China?' and in the references to Barthes's reactions which are scattered through Pleynet's diary. One of the few significant mistakes in Calvet's biography of Barthes is his original substitution of Severo Sarduy for Pleynet when he lists Barthes's travelling companions in China. Although this is rectified in the English translation, it means that Calvet missed out on the possibility of using Pleynet as a source. Pleynet's picture of Barthes's behaviour and reactions is quite different from that projected by

group was endlessly exposed to political discourse as wooden as anything Barthes could have foreseen: 'After the meal we return briefly to our discussion with those in charge of political and union affairs within the factory: slogans from the current campaign (*pi-Lin pi-Kong*), benefits of the Cultural Revolution, organization of political and ideological work. From schools to People's Communes to factories, the same unchanging protocol.'[29] Pleynet also quotes Barthes's description of an earlier exposé on 'the Stalin question' as an *ex cathedra* lecture—'history linked to an ossified truth rather than its living, evolving reality'—and makes it clear that he agrees.[30] Their last day in Beijing is taken up by seven hours of so-called discussion at the University during which they never once escape from 'stereotypes': 'we have learned nothing and seen nothing', writes Pleynet, convinced that they are being deliberately, if courteously, kept away 'from what is going on here'.[31]

However, the group was also completely cut off from any contact with ordinary Chinese life. If they crossed Shanghai it was in official chauffeured cars, if they travelled by train it was in private compartments, if they ate in restaurants it was always in private dining rooms separating them from the other customers.[32] Pleynet soon draws two conclusions: first, that their hosts wish to prove to them that politics now controls all aspects of Chinese culture; second, that there is therefore not the slightest possibility of any unplanned event bringing them accidentally face to face with the 'habits, prejudices, and customs' of ordinary Chinese people, since all access to the latter

---

Julia Kristeva, through the character of Armand Bréhel, in *Les Samouraïs* (Paris, Fayard, 1990). Kristeva has invented an apolitical Barthes obsessed only with eating and sex, whereas Pleynet's essay on China could almost have been written on the basis of Barthes's distinction between *le* and *la politique*.

[29] Pleynet, *Le Voyage*, 81.
[30] Ibid. 42. Not that Barthes seems any keener on political discussion with his companions. During a hotel-room discussion of the 'revolutionary potential of the petty bourgeoisie' Pleynet describes him as staring at the others 'like a fish at an apple' (43), and in one of many amusing insights into the internal dynamics of this bizarre group we learn that Barthes put up stoically with their political discussions, despite finding quite intolerable one such discussion with 'M., his wife, and a friend of theirs, whom Ph. S. had invited to share our table at the *Hôtel des Nationalités* in Beijing' (31).
[31] Ibid. 118–19.
[32] See ibid. 35, 68, and 110.

is mediated (via their guides) by official political discourse.[33] Pleynet also commends Barthes's 'most fortunate insistence' on eating and on the purchase of sundry objects, such as the Mao jacket that 'he will drag the whole group off to buy'.[34] Was Barthes hoping, like Lieutenant Loti in his ancient Turkish costume, to merge with China by putting himself in the picture? Did he, as seems more likely, enjoy being a naïve sort of tourist, for whom eating and shopping are a way of establishing oneself in unfamiliar surroundings?[35] Whatever the attitude of Barthes and the *Tel Quel* delegation to the political actuality of China, there was certainly no possibility of touristic, psychic, or aesthetic escape into the everyday life of the street.[36]

If Pleynet's text betrays his frustration over this situation, Barthes's does not. He does, however, allude to it elsewhere, confessing to Bernard-Henri Lévy that he was unable to find in China any possibility at all of 'erotic, sensual, or amorous investment' (*GV* 265 / 250). It would be foolish to interpret this as regret on Barthes's part that he was not allowed out on the streets in pursuit of sexual pleasure (despite Kristeva's fictional caricature of a Barthes ill at ease in China for this reason).[37] We know that an erotic cathexis of everyday reality has a more fundamental meaning for Barthes, and that in many ways it is the motor of his writing. He tells Lévy that despite writing little in China he had looked at and listened to everything with the greatest intensity. However, he adds that 'something else' is

---

[33] See Pleynet, *Le Voyage*, 38–9 and 68. He includes an interesting account of how the group compensates for this by drawing comparisons with memories of past travels. Two examples given for Barthes are 'Switzerland during the 1950s' (32), and 'an Italian station' (66).

[34] Whereas Sollers, apparently, merely 'humours' what he calls Barthes's 'epicureanism' (31).

[35] See 31 and 103. Barthes is also reported as claiming that one needs to go to a department store in order to get to know a city (50), and as having very much liked the fact that on Japanese trains people would come round with trivial items for sale (53).

[36] If *Les Samouraïs* contains an accurate account of Kristeva's experience in China, it seems that she was also unable to make herself understood in the street, and remained dependent upon the group's two interpreters (215).

[37] Pleynet does, however, record one wistful allusion on Barthes's part to his normal social life in Paris: 'R.B.: only half past eight: in Paris that's when I usually have a shave and get ready to go out' (*Le Voyage*, 91).

needed in order to write, 'a sort of spice to what is seen and heard, something that I didn't find'.

Barthes therefore devotes an unusually small proportion of his essay to the signifiers of China—'signifiers (which go beyond meaning, which make it overflow and spill into the distance, into desire), signifiers are scarce' (OC iii. 33)—referring, in a single paragraph, to cookery, children, and writing. But the fact that Barthes is excluded from his favourite terrain does not prevent him from aiming at a utopian reading of China, and it is one of considerable subtlety and generosity. Instead of denouncing the ascendancy of the strictly political text (although 'nothing escapes it' (33)), he looks for utopia under its repetitive and clichéd rhetoric: 'What, no freedom? Why, yes. Under the veneer of rhetoric Text bursts forth (desire, intelligence, struggle, work, everything which divides and overflows)' (34). First, Barthes suggests that the elements of the clichéd code will be combined in different ways ('what a difference between the rigid discourse of this official of a People's Commune and the lively, clear, and focused analysis of this shipyard worker at Shanghai!'); second, that the discourse is vigilant rather than complacently triumphalist (a warning to the revolution not to become rigid and stultified); finally, that there is a ludic dimension in the current campaign against Confucius and Lin-Piao: ('a caricature, a poem, a sketch performed by children, in the course of which a little girl with a made-up face will assail, between two ballets, the ghost of Lin-Piao: the political Text (but it alone) engenders these minor "happenings" ') (34).

Meaning, then, is relatively active and alert in politics, but what has happened to it in all those domains in which the Western visitors had expected to find it? Pleynet's book is again a useful point of reference for the infamous 'nothing' that Barthes chose to foreground in his essay: 'As R.B. says, if you hope to find something in China by casting a net or using a rake you stand a good chance of returning with nothing at all.'[38] According to Barthes, it is from hermeneutic habit that we want objects to decipher and problems to solve, but what if the objects which we insist on turning into questions—sexuality, subjectivity, language, knowledge—should turn out to be

[38] Ibid. 54.

'historically and geographically determined, mere cultural idioms' (OC iii. 32)? If China appears to refuse to share its meanings this is not from secretiveness, but because, more subversively, 'concepts, topics, and names are dissolved, China does not divide up the objects of knowledge in the same way that we do.' Not only is it 'our' notion of knowledge which is shown up as a phantasmagoria, but preconceptions about how meaning functions and about the questions that matter will block an appropriate reading of China.

Once Barthes has abandoned the received 'turbulence of symbols' he can evaluate China differently. In the afterword he describes the effect he had tried to create as a 'negative hallucination' (35), a phrase which conjures up an interesting reversal of the 'photogenic', heightened, erotic reality of Stendhal's Italy or his own 'Japan'. The paucity of the erotic signifier—'discreet to the point of scarcity' (32)—has been turned into a virtue, since such discretion makes way for a new field, that of a delicate *fadeur*.³⁹ China is 'gently hallucinated' as 'an object placed beyond the realm of bright colours, strong flavours, and blunt meanings (none of which is unconnected with the sempiternal flaunting of the Phallus)' (35). What exactly is the nature of the link that Barthes tries to establish here between the *fadeur* of China and its exemption of 'phallic meaning'?

Barthes gives three examples of what he means by *fadeur*. The first is the flat landscape, devoid of bright colours and uninterrupted by historical objects ('no churchtowers, no manor houses'): 'in the distance, just two grey oxen, a tractor, regular but asymmetrical fields, a group of workers dressed in blue. Everything else, as far as the eye can see, is beige (tinged with pink), or pale green (wheat and rice)' (32–3). The second is the omnipresent green tea, upon which Barthes bestows moral qualities ('tea is courteous, even friendly, and yet reserved at the same time'), so that the hysterical behaviour that he so dislikes

---

³⁹ The usual translation of *fadeur* is the negatively connoted 'insipidity'. Pleynet reports that Kristeva dislikes Chinese *fadeur*, whereas he finds it crucial to the subtlety of Chinese painting (ibid. 53). *Fadeur*, it will be remembered, was part of Barthes's introductory caricature of the received view of *Aziyadé* as an old-fashioned, insipid, and cloying novel (*NCE* 105 / *DZN* 171, see above).

('chumminess, exuberance, the whole histrionics of social exchange') is rendered impossible—it would seem completely out of place. Thus *fadeur* is crucially linked (through tea-drinking) with the qualities of language: 'it is as if tea only existed in order to punctuate meetings, discussions, and journeys with a delicate and agreeable ritual: now and then a few sips of tea, a mild cigarette, speech is somehow silenced and pacified' (33). *Le fade* in its turn gives way to peacefulness (*le paisible*): 'Isn't peace (*la paix*) that region, which for us is a utopia, where the war of meanings has been abolished?' Barthes suggests that even labour, in the workshops they visited, seemed to have absorbed these peaceable qualities. But the most significant site of Chinese *fadeur* is the body. The apparent lack of *coquetterie*, the standardized clothing, the prosaic gestures, endlessly multiplied throughout the very dense crowds of people, lead Barthes to the controversial insight that in China the body 'is no longer something to be understood, that it refuses to signify anything, or to lend itself to an erotic or dramatic reading (except on the stage)' (33).

This is Barthes's best example of how, in China, 'meaning is nullified, dispensed with, in all those places where we Westerners seek it out'. The idea is developed (though in a somewhat less courteous register) in the fragment of *Roland Barthes by Roland Barthes* entitled 'Happy Demise of Sexuality?' (*Fin heureuse de la sexualité?*): 'The Chinese: everyone asks (not least me): wherever is their sexuality?' (*RB* 165 / 167).[40] The answer is mediated by Barthes's description of a scene from Antonioni's 'film about China'. Visitors to a museum are looking at a model representing a barbarous scene from Ancient China, in which soldiers are pillaging a poor peasant family: 'the expressions are brutal or sorrowful; the model is a large one, very brightly lit, the bodies are at once quite immobile (with the strange gloss of waxworks) and contorted, wrought to a kind of paroxysm which is both carnal and semantic' (*RB* 165 / 167–8). It is this sense of a relationship between bodily and semantic exaggeration that leads Barthes to an illumination—the scene, like a Sadeian tableau, is '*over-sexualized*', and sexuality, '*in the manner in which we speak it, and insofar as we speak it*, is a product of

---

[40] Richard Howard's translation is 'Sexuality's Happy Ending?'

social oppression, of the wretched history of humanity: in short, a result of civilization'. If this is true, 'then perhaps sexuality, *our* sexuality, could be exempted, invalidated, nullified, *without repression*, through social liberation: an end to the Phallus! ... Might not materialism pass through a certain sexual *distancing* whereby sexuality would simply drop out of discourse and knowledge?' (165 / 168).[41]

While this may be an important comment on Sade, the key phrase, as far as the Cultural Revolution is concerned, is undoubtedly 'without repression'. Pleynet records an amusing dialogue in which Barthes (wearing his intellectual hermeneut's hat) poses earnest questions about psychological theories to a group of Chinese doctors:

> R.B.: Can it be possible that there is no sexual tension, above all if marriage is delayed? Is this taken into account in some way in cases of illness?
>
> Reply: Young people concentrate their efforts on their studies and on a healthy life. They don't think about sexual matters.[42]

If Chinese sexuality is simply repressed, the situation is no more utopian than its alienated Western counterpart. François Wahl, whose own articles in *Le Monde* were precisely entitled 'La Chine sans utopie' (no utopia in China), considers the foreclosure of the past and its traditions both socially and psychically dangerous, while Pleynet muses anxiously on whether Chinese traditions have really disappeared or whether they are being hidden from the *Tel Quel* visitors.[43] Barthes, for whom the past was an important dimension of the erotic, novelistic signifier of Loti's Turkey and his own 'Japan', might well have written negatively of the repression of China's past as well as of Chinese sexuality, and might well have claimed that these repressions were linked. What is interesting is that he does not do this, preferring to lend to China his vision of a sexuality which is not repressed but exempted, of a utopia where material liberation

---

[41] There are interesting parallels between this notion and the argument developed by Stephen Heath in *The Sexual Fix* (London, Macmillan, 1982).

[42] Pleynet, *Le Voyage*, 47.

[43] See François Wahl, 'Révolution culturelle ou accidentalisation?', *Le Monde* (19 June 1974), 8, and Pleynet, *Le Voyage*, 65.

has led in its turn to the joint liberation of language and sexuality.

Even more interesting is the link that Barthes establishes between this reading of China and the way he had tried to write the essay, for utopian discourse can be seen, yet again, to absorb the value system of its subject matter. In the opening paragraph of 'So How Was China?', Barthes had introduced the idea that the Chinese interlocutors of the *Tel Quel* delegation were attentive not to their 'identity' but to the fact of their interest, as if it mattered to them to be recognized and understood, not in a spirit of 'militant agreement' but in that of a courteous 'approval' (*assentiment*) (OC iii. 32). It was this subtlety of response to China that had been misinterpreted by Barthes's 'intellectual' readers who, as he comments in *Roland Barthes by Roland Barthes*, could understand no other concept than that of 'choice': 'you were supposed to come out of China like a bull bursting out of his pen into the crowded arena: furious or triumphant' (*RB* 48 / 52). By 'approval' Barthes had meant that he was not 'opting for China' but that 'he was acquiescing in silence (he called it *fadeur*), . . . to what was being developed there'.⁴⁴ In the afterword to the original essay Barthes links its reception to what he describes as a 'question of principle': not what is it permissible to say, 'but what is it possible to say or not to say?' (OC iii. 34).⁴⁵ Not only are speakers of French, in his familiar example, forced to filter all concepts through the masculine and feminine genders, but even discourse, which ought in theory to be free of constraints, imposes the ideological strait-jacket of a limited choice of grammatical moods: to affirm, to deny, to doubt, or to question. Yet Barthes had wished to write about China ('a vast, and for many people, a

---

⁴⁴ Barthes refers to an early essay in which he had developed the idea of a 'gradual approval' (*assentiment progressif*) rather than a political commitment. This is his preface to Michel Vinaver's play about a French soldier, captured during the Korean War, who decides to stay in Korea rather than to return to France ('A propos d'*Aujourd'hui ou les Coréens* de Michel Vinaver', OC i. 556–7, first published in *France-Observateur* (Nov. 1956)).

⁴⁵ This, of course, is the problem that Barthes was so to focus upon in his inaugural lecture, with his infamous formulation that 'language is quite simply fascist' (*BR* 461 / *L* 14). Fourier's linguistic *impossibilia*, discussed in Ch. 3, would be one utopian counterpart to this conception of 'fascist' language (*SFL* 120 / 124).

passionate subject') in a technically impossible mood that would 'suspend, but not abolish, the object of its discourse': 'I tried to produce—this was the truth of my project—a discourse which would neither assert, nor negate, nor adopt a neutral position . . . an approval (a linguistic mode deriving from an ethic and perhaps from an aesthetic) and not necessarily an indication of support or refusal (modes which, for their part, derive from specific reasons or beliefs)' (35). Barthes saw this bringing together of the subject matter and vehicle of his discourse as a *political* gesture—a comment on the standard Western way of 'hallucinating' contemporary China 'in a dogmatic mode, either violently for or against, or insincerely liberal'. This 'Western' mode can only imagine politics entering language through 'directly' political forms, whereas the intellectual (or the writer) has to speak from the non-place of the 'Indirect': 'this is the utopia for which I tried to find a (musically) *true* discourse.' One could perhaps suggest that the musical equivalent of the positive but muted discourse of *fadeur* would be that of a minor key.

Barthes himself produces a final metaphor for the 'single movement' of a discourse that would convey China's unprecedented manner, both 'peaceful and powerful', of outflanking meaning—'that of a gentle drift' (35)'. The metaphor is striking in that it recalls his description of the novelistic in *Aziyadé* as the appropriate motor (both narrative and descriptive) of 'the *nothing* of Drift' (*NCE* 121 / *DZN* 186).[46] In that *Aziyadé* was presented as a 'novel of Drift', this was for its withdrawal from the Occident in a manner 'neither violent, nor ascetic, nor political' (119 / 184). In Barthes's essay on China, this gentle movement is reversed in the drift-like assent of his friendly but suspended empathy. If drift is a figure that takes Barthes in and out of the Orient, it is also the figure that best captures the desired utopian status of the Orient in Barthes's writing—the Orient is that imaginary locus of the Indirect via which 'the West' as alienated meaning is itself exempted. Yet, in the preface to *Aziyadé*, Drift was also linked to the idea of a

---

[46] For a detailed and sustained discussion of Barthes's exploitation of the figure of 'Drift', see Chs. 1 and 2 of Andrew Brown, *Roland Barthes: The Figures of Writing* (Oxford, Clarendon Press, 1992), 13–109. See 47–9 for specific discussion of 'So How Was China?'.

debauchery that does not take itself seriously. Does this return of a repressed sexual element in Barthes's metaphor undermine his attempted exemption of sexuality—the dissolution of an erotic cathexis of Oriental reality—in the interests of a utopian vision? It is time, perhaps, to trace more precisely the place of sexuality in the metaphors for utopia that Barthes develops in the 1970s.

8
Tricks of the Text

> Text, for example, is a utopia.[1]

IN the early 1970s Barthes published a series of essays on the politics of utopia, all of which addressed, at least in passing, the question that had first appeared in his work more than twenty years earlier: could language be liberated ahead of history? The dilemma is clearly posed in a section of 'Writers, Intellectuals, Teachers' (1971) where Barthes argues from the helpful analogy of two sorts of typing error.[2] The first produces a non-existent nonsense word, the second an unintended but recognizable word which creates strange reverberations in the sentence that contains it. On this basis, Barthes distinguishes between two types of criticism, reflecting upon the differing 'historical stake' of each in a way that extends the significance of his discussion to all forms of utopian writing.

The first sort of discourse (emblematized by the nonsense word) would be justified by the right of the signifier to spread itself where and as it will, for once monological meaning has given way to plural meanings, why not escape meaning altogether? 'Like any radical right', says Barthes, 'this one supposes a utopian version of freedom', and it is clear that he is here using 'utopian' in Engels's negative sense: 'the law is lifted *immediately*, outside of any history, in defiance of any dialectic' (*RL* 324 / 361). Attempts to bypass political motivations from a position within an alienated society are therefore dismissed as petty bourgeois subjectivism:

By liberating reading from all meaning, it is ultimately *my* reading that I impose, for in *this* moment of History the economy of the subject is not yet transformed and the refusal of meaning (of meanings) falls back

---

[1] *Roland Barthes by Roland Barthes*, 76 / 80.
[2] 'Writers, Intellectuals, Teachers', *RL* 309–33 / 345–68.

into subjectivity; at best, we could perhaps say that this radical criticism, defined by a foreclosure of the signified (and not by its escape), *anticipates* History, anticipates a new and unprecedented state in which the efflorescence of the signifier would not be at the cost of any idealist counterpart, of any closure of the person. (324–5 / 361)

Despite this concessionary 'at best', Barthes identifies his second type of criticism as the ideologically correct strategy in the context of a divided society, for this is a criticism that takes up position within the war of meanings that in turn determines the sorts of communication currently possible: 'the liquidation of the old criticism can only make progress *within* meaning (in the volume of meanings) and not outside it. In other words, we need to practise a certain semantic infiltration. Ideological criticism is today precisely condemned to operations of theft: the signified, exemption of which is the materialist task *par excellence*, is more easily spirited away in the *illusion* of meaning than in its destruction' (325 / 362).

These operations of theft correspond to the semantic 'breaking and entering' (*l'effraction du sens*) that Barthes attributes to Japanese haiku in *Empire of Signs*.[3] Indeed, it is clear that Barthes's own quest for utopian forms and strategies *always* operates within the terms of his *second* form of criticism. The point is an important one because Barthes's use of slippery concepts like *text* and *jouissance* has often quite wrongly been associated with the unanchored, runaway, and ultimately subjective wordplay which belongs with his first sort of nonsensical typing error. Barthes's questioning of subjective wordplay should doubtless be read in the context of *S/Z*, where he had precisely applied himself to loosening as far as possible the monological signifieds of Balzac's 'modestly plural' text. Although Barthes opens *S/Z* with the postulation of a radically asymbolic writerly text (*texte scriptible*), it is soon clear that this is simply a utopian concept (which is why a writerly text cannot be found on the shelves of a bookshop)[4] and that it has been

---

[3] 'L'Effraction du sens', rather misleadingly translated by Richard Howard as 'the breach of meaning', is the title of the first of Barthes's four chapters on haiku (*ES* 69 / 89).
[4] 'The writerly text is not a thing, it would be hard to find it in a bookshop' (*SZ* 5 / 11).

floated to highlight its ideological opposite: the plenitude of Balzac's realism. Although Barthes is attracted to *Sarrasine* as a story that represents, paradoxically, a catastrophic disturbance to the plenitude upon which it is founded, Balzac's text is conceptualized as a vast network of 'readerly' connotations. Barthes's analysis stays within the parameters of the cultural codes that structure that network, and if he is always keen to identify their vanishing points, he also (and more often) magnifies their ideological effect. Thus Barthes's favourite image of an *egg*-like fullness for the values of the *pantouflard*—variously associated, as we have seen, with the Dutch canal boat, Verne's *Mysterious Island*, and petty bourgeois France of the 1950s[5]—now recurs for the 'Full Literature' of which *Sarrasine* is an example, however ambivalent: 'the text is replete with multiple, discontinuous, accumulated meanings, and yet burnished, smoothed by the "natural" movement of its sentences: it is an egg-text' (*SZ* 200 / 206). This symbolic plenitude is mimicked by the string of metaphors that Barthes produces for it: 'like a linen cupboard where meanings are tidied away, stacked up, checked over (in this text nothing is ever wasted: meaning recuperates everything); like a pregnant female, full of signifieds which criticism will not fail to deliver; like the sea, full of depths and movements which give it its appearance of infinity, its vast drapery of thoughtfulness.'

This is the dense volume of ideological signifieds that Barthes aspires to break into and to undermine through his own utopian stress on the signifier: 'The signifier: we must resign ourselves to excessive use of this word for a long time yet (but let us note once and for all that it is not a question of defining the signifier but of using it metaphorically—mainly in opposition to the signified, which was believed in the early days of semiology to be its correlate, but which can now be better understood as its adversary)' (*GV* 125 / 119). Thus, unlike the haiku poets whom he so admires, Barthes himself will stay within the realm of metaphors in order to try to conceive, for example, the paradoxical lightness of the volume that constitutes the signifier:

the signifier is not 'deep', it does not unfold in terms of inwardness and secrecy; on the other hand, what are we to actually do with this famous

---

[5] See especially Ch. 1.

signifier unless we somehow immerse ourselves in it, unless we leave the signified far behind by diving into matter, into text? How can one escape into lightness? ... To what substance can the signifier be compared? Certainly not to water, not even to the oceans, for oceans have a bed; to the sky rather, to what is precisely *unthinkable* about cosmic space. (GV 125–6 / 119).

In *S/Z*, Barthes likens himself to an auspex tracing the flight of birds (the migrating signifieds) across the imaginary rectangles (the lexias) that he has drawn in the sky.[6] In the light of the foregoing quotations, it can be seen that this image is born of a desire to oppose the signifier of Fourier's well-ventilated cosmos to the signifieds of the heavy depths of a Balzacian ocean.

By far the most important of Barthes's metaphors for the signifier is 'Text'—'Text, for example, is a utopia' (RB 76 / 80)—the scope of which extends far beyond the written texts of literature. Text is staked out very clearly as a utopian and socially liberated *space*, in that the *jouissance* with which Barthes links it implies 'pleasure without separation': 'Text belongs to the realm of the signifier, and thereby participates in its own way in a social utopia; before History (supposing the latter does not opt for barbarism), Text achieves, if not the transparency of social relations, that at least of language relations: Text is that space where no language has a hold over any other.'[7] Although, as Barthes consistently argues, we must always commit ourselves by assuming 'one of the individual languages into which our world and our history force us', yet 'we cannot give up the *jouissance*, no matter how utopian, of a displaced, liberated language'. It is this utopian space that Barthes calls Text: 'Writing is atopical; relative to the war of languages, which it does not wipe out but which it displaces, it anticipates a particular state of the practice of reading and writing, where it is desire that circulates, and no longer domination.'[8] Thus the concept of Text, which first emerged in opposition to the literary work (*œuvre*), gradually subsumes all social and sexual relationships into its sphere. But what does it mean to say that 'desire' has displaced 'domination' in this

---

[6] SZ 14 / 20–1.
[7] 'From Work to Text' [1971], RL 56–64: 64 / 69–77: 77.
[8] 'The War of Languages' [1973], RL 106–10: 109–10 / 127–31: 130–1.

extended sphere of human relations? As we shall see, Barthes's erotic metaphors (oral pleasure, *la drague, le trick*) come to saturate not just the creative writing of 'Incidents' or *Empire of Signs*, but even theoretical discussions of utopian discourse. In my discussion, in Chapter 5, of the Orientalism of 'Incidents', I suggested that Barthes had taken a subjective leap ahead of history, and that he had done so by wishing to liberate homosexuality in advance of (in isolation from) the liberation of the alienated social relations that determine the very forms of its oppression. Does Barthes's recourse to sexual metaphors to explain his utopian notion of Text mean that this has remained a blind spot?

In his quest for appropriate images for Text, Barthes will constantly trawl everyday reality, including that remembered from his visits to Japan and Morocco.[9] These metaphors are not necessarily (or not explicitly) sexualized. For example, Barthes's idea of the café as a complex stereophonic space (fragments of conversation, various comings and goings) makes it the site of a 'textual' experience,[10] just as a walk by a Moroccan *wadi* is at once synaesthetic, familiar, and yet uniquely 'novelistic':

> the reader of Text might be compared to someone at a loose end (someone who has relaxed their imaginary): this somewhat empty subject is going for a walk (this is what happened to the author of these lines, then it was that he conceived a vivid notion of Text) along the side of a valley at the bottom of which flows a wadi (I use the word wadi to attest to a certain feeling of strangeness); what he perceives is multiple, irreducible, coming from heterogeneous, disconnected substances and perspectives: lights, colours, vegetation, heat, air, subtle explosions of sound, delicate birds'-cries, children's voices from the other side of the valley, movements, gestures, and clothing of inhabitants close by or far off; all these incidents are half identifiable: they issue from known codes, but their combination is unique and grounds the walk in a difference which cannot be repeated except *as difference*. (RL 60 / 73)

---

[9] 'Text is only ever approached metaphorically: it is the field of the auspex, a seat in a bar, a polyhedron, an excipient, a Japanese stew, a clash of styles, a braid, a piece of Valenciennes lace, a Moroccan wadi, poor reception on a television screen, a flaky pastry, an onion, etc.' (*RB* 74 / 78).

[10] See GV 222 / 209–10.

Three years later, what was presumably the same walk by the same *wadi* provides retrospective insight into a new dimension of this textual experience, whereby what is now described as a stereophony of 'Virgilian' sounds is intermittently interrupted by a specifically man-made and modern noise: 'birds, the distant cries of children, rustlings of orange trees, but also, throughout the day, the even sound of a pump engine. This is what the countryside is, what Text is: an idyll disturbed by some machine: colours, silence, a breeze, a whole tissue of ancient cultural and romantic values, interrupted by the persistent noise of a moped.'[11] A walk by a *wadi* represents a minor and pleasurable disorientation of subjectivity which is merely intensified—rather than radically disturbed—by the occasional sound of an engine.

The imagery of the rustling orange trees and the *even* sound of the pump engine serves as an appropriate transition to Barthes's 1975 essay 'Le Bruissement de la langue', translated by Richard Howard as 'The Rustle of Language'.[12] In this short but important text we find a crucial statement on the utopia of language framed between metaphors which are both sexual and Oriental. Barthes's starting point is the irreversibility of spoken language whereby, in order to take back something that has been said, one is paradoxically obliged to *add* verbal corrections or retractions. This unhappy 'stammering' is compared with the sputtering of an engine which is running badly and in danger of stopping; however, Barthes summons up the contrasting notion of *bruissement* for a machine that is running well, for the humming or purring of an engine which is literally well *tuned*. This 'musical' sound becomes the sign of an absence of noise in the sense of disturbance or malfunction, and it is therefore 'happy machines which hum (*bruissent*)' (*RL* 77 / 94).

This specific image is then developed via two further metaphors. The first is the erotic machine—'a "thought-out"

---

[11] 'Situation' [1974], in *Sollers Writer*, trans. Philip Thody (London, Athlone, 1987), 93–5: 95 / 81–4: 83–4. The context is Barthes's discussion of his fascination with the 'discontinuous continuity' of the writing of Philippe Sollers.

[12] *RL* 76–9 / 93–6. The French noun *bruissement* covers the two rather different sounds that Barthes metaphorically exploits in this essay: the 'purring' of a well-running engine and the sound of rustling leaves. There does not seem to be an English equivalent with the same semantic range.

cluster of bodies whose amorous sites are carefully matched up with each other'—which was endlessly imagined and described by Sade: 'when this machine starts up, by the convulsive movements of its participants, it trembles and lightly hums: in short, it *works*, and it works well' (77 / 94). Barthes's second metaphor is the Japanese slot-machine game of Pachinko, discussed in Chapter 6, where it was already clear from the commentary in *Empire of Signs* that Barthes had construed its rewards as sexual. In this second account of Pachinko, Barthes perceives the general movement and rustle of silver marbles as a vast *bruissement* which conveys the smoothly running pleasure of a body which is both individually and collectively controlled. Indeed both examples (the Sadeian and the Japanese) imply a *community* of bodies: 'in the sounds of a pleasure which is "working", no voice is raised, gives orders, or stands out from the others, no voice is constituted at all: the hum is the very sound of a plural *jouissance*—but in no way of a mass *jouissance* (for the masses, in contrast, have only a single voice, and it is terribly loud)' (77 / 94). The central section of the essay returns to language in the light of these metaphors, to claim that language contains 'too many meanings' for it to rustle or hum in this happy fashion (to achieve an equivalent *jouissance*). However, as a good utopianist Barthes knows that 'what is impossible is not inconceivable' (77 / 94) and, in a detailed and important formulation, *le bruissement de la langue* is precisely put forward as a utopia:

> Which utopia? That of a music of meaning; by this I mean that in its utopian state language (*la langue*) would be stretched out or even *denatured* to the extent of forming a vast sonorous fabric whose semantic dimension would be derealized; the phonic, metric, or vocal signifier would spread itself in all its sumptuosity, without a sign ever becoming detached from it (thereby *naturalizing* this veritable sheet of *jouissance*), but also—and this is the difficult bit—without meaning being brutally dismissed, dogmatically foreclosed, in short, without its being castrated. Language (*la langue*) would rustle, it would be entrusted to the signifier by an unprecedented movement unknown to our rational discourses, but it would not for all that abandon a horizon of meaning: meaning, undivided, impenetrable, unnamable, would in this same movement be positioned in the distance like a mirage, . . . meaning would be the vanishing point of *jouissance*. (77–8 / 94–5)

Thus, like the humming of an engine that implies an absence of the wrong sort of noise, this happy sound of language would signal the desired exemption of meaning. Itself a 'non-meaning', it would call up the distant sound of a 'new meaning' henceforth freed from all the aggressions of which the sign, determined by a history of social oppression, represents for Barthes the veritable 'Pandora's box' (78 / 95).

Although Barthes refers somewhat half-heartedly to some avant-garde experiments with *bruissement* in post-serial music (on account of the extreme importance attributed to the voice), not to mention the 'latest texts by Pierre Guyotat or Philippe Sollers' (78 / 95), he fortunately turns instead to a fine example drawn, as ever, from the unexpected adventures of his daily life. This is Barthes's sudden encounter with an instance of the rustle of language whilst watching ('the other evening') the Antonioni film about China already referred to in the last chapter. In a village street some children are leaning against a wall, and each child is reading aloud from a different book. Although Barthes is cut off from literal meaning by his incomprehension of the language, as well as by the confusion of the simultaneous readings, his impression is that this is a language machine that is working well: 'I could hear, in a kind of hallucinatory perception (so intensely did it receive all the subtlety of the scene), the music, the breath, the tension, the application, in short something like an *aim*' (78–9 / 95–6). Not that the fact of everyone speaking at once, in however special a way, could be all that is required for a utopian rustle of language: 'the sonorous scene needs an erotics (in the broadest sense of the term), the impetus, or the discovery, or the simple accompaniment of an emotion: this was precisely what was added by the faces of the Chinese children' (79–96). As in *Empire of Signs*, the erotic aspect of a given reality (however vaguely defined) seems to have a cognitive dimension, and Barthes compares himself to Hegel, seeking to discover an intelligent design behind the sounds of the leaves, springs, and breezes that constitute the rustle (*bruissement*) of Nature: 'For my part, it is the stirring (*frisson*) of meaning that I question as I listen to the rustling (*bruissement*) of language, that language which for me, modern man, is my equivalent of Nature' (79 / 96).

The cinematographic example of the Chinese children all

reading aloud is an interesting variant on the apparently individual 'writing aloud' (*écriture à haute voix*) upon which Barthes reflects in the very last paragraph of *The Pleasure of the Text*.[13] Here he proposes as a contemporary example of the 'grain' of writing the sound-track of a film which would convey the effect of an aural close-up:

> In fact, it is enough for cinema to capture the sound of speech *close up* . . . to make us hear in their materiality, in their sensuality, the breath, the guttural sounds, the fleshiness of the lips, a whole presence of the human mouth (for the voice, the writing, to be as fresh, supple, and lubricated, as delicately granular and vibrant as an animal's muzzle), to succeed in relegating the signified to a great distance and to throw, so to speak, the anonymous body of the actor into my ear: it granulates, it crackles, it caresses, it grates, it stings, it comes. (*PT* 67 / 105)

But Barthes also proposes in passing a very different example of this stereophonic Text in which can be heard 'the grain of the throat, the caress of the consonants, the voluptuousness of the vowels' (*PT* 66 / 105). This is the outdated 'art of song' that he will go on to discuss in a second crucial text on the utopia of language. 'Music, Voice, Language (*Langue*)' is the title of a 1977 lecture about Charles Panzéra, the French singer who before the war had actually given Barthes singing lessons, and with whose voice Barthes claims to have maintained an 'amorous relationship': 'not with the natural, physical voice, but with his voice in so far as it passes over language, our French language, like a desire: no voice has a natural quality; every voice is steeped in what it says' (*RL* 280 / 247).[14] Just as in 1975 what rustled or hummed in a utopian way was *la langue*—and not the more obvious *le langage*—here again the language juxtaposed with music and the voice in Barthes's title is in fact *la langue*. In 'The Rustle of Language' Barthes's choice of vocabulary may relate to the references to *langue* and *parole* that run through the essay, as well perhaps as to the children reading aloud in Chinese. In the Panzéra lecture Barthes's use of *langue* self-consciously embraces the two senses of 'tongue'—

---

[13] Barthes, *The Pleasure of the Text* [1973], trans. Richard Miller (New York, Hill and Wang, 1975).

[14] 'Music, Voice, Language', *RF* 278–85 / 246–52.

French as a specific language and the physical organ of speech and song.

Barthes's lecture pursues several interrelated arguments, the first of which is reminiscent of his analysis of Loti's attachment to the *eski* of feudal Turkey.[15] For Barthes equates French song in the age of Panzéra with the last throes of a cultured and highly refined French language: 'A certain French language is about to die, this is what we hear in Panzéra's singing: the perishable shines through this singing in a heartbreaking fashion; for the whole art of speaking the French language has taken refuge there' (281 / 249). Although French song has a specific class origin in the bourgeois drawing room, Barthes attributes an ethical and utopian function to the purely physical 'pronunciation' that characterizes Panzéra's vocal style: 'in a musical text, a consonant is never the same: each syllable—far from issuing from some Olympian code of phonemes, given in itself and once and for all—must be set (like a precious stone) into the general meaning of the sentence' (282 / 250). The negative counterpart of pronunciation is 'articulation', whereby the meaning of each word is overemphasized in an expressive or dramatic manner. But pronunciation, as practised by Panzéra and theorized in his teaching, maintains an ideal balance between the words and music of French song, so that 'it is music which enters the language and rediscovers there all that is musical, all that is "amorous" ' (283 / 250).

The necessary condition of this rare and precious eruption of music into language is the 'physicality' of the voice, by which Barthes means the way in which the voice is marked by the body. Hence his description of the fragility of Panzéra's pure vowels, the grain of his nasals, the caress of his consonants, and the almost abstract brevity of a rolled 'r' that aims to 'make gentleness virile but not to abandon it' (282 / 250). This intriguing mixture of delicate subtlety and 'virilization' is captured in Barthes's sexual metaphor for Panzéra's voice:

Through a perfect mastery of all the nuances imposed by a correct reading of the musical text—nuances which require knowing how to produce extremely delicate *pianissimi* and *détimbrages*—this voice was always *taut*, impelled by a quasi-metallic strength of desire: it was an

---

[15] See Ch. 7.

erect voice—*aufgeregt* (a Schumannian word)—or better still: an erectile voice—a voice in a state of erection. (283 / 251)

Juxtaposed with this explicitly erotic account of the physical qualities of Panzéra's voice—which foregrounds the throat and the tongue as its literal source—is a set of values which will assume considerable importance in Barthes's late writing: '*jouissance*, tenderness, delicacy, fulfillment, all the values of the most delicate imaginary' (284 / 251–2). In the opening section of his lecture Barthes had referred to the difficulty of speaking about music on account of its inherent resistance to commentary. In his concluding paragraph, music is described as a discourse of value and eulogy, crucially free of metalanguage, comparable to an amorous discourse which manages to 'speak' what is implicit rather than 'articulating' it. Moreover, a 'successful' relationship is deemed to be one which avoids falling into either the 'censorship of desire or the sublimation of the unsayable' (284–5 / 252). Declaring that a relationship of this kind 'can rightly be called *musical*', Barthes concludes his reflection on the utopian interrelationship of language, meaning, music, love, and desire with the following observation: 'Perhaps the value of something is relative to its metaphoric power; perhaps that is the value of music: to be a good metaphor' (285 / 252).

The register, values, and metaphors of the concluding paragraph will recur when Barthes seeks a way of writing about both photography and his mother in *Camera Lucida*.[16] What is interesting at this stage is that this particular formulation should occur in a *spoken* text, an appropriate form indeed in which to address his amorous relationship with Panzéra's voice. Similarly, Barthes's undelivered lecture on the difficulty that Stendhal experienced in trying to express his love for Italy is a delicate intertwining of metaphors of language, sexuality, and music. Quoting Stendhal who refers to 'the passion for music which inspires within the soul a movement so similar to that of love', Barthes compares Stendhal's two great passions—music and Italy—to 'spaces outside of language', marked by an 'exquisite suspension' of traditionally coded communication.[17] If it is

---

[16] See Ch. 10.
[17] 'One Always Fails in Speaking of What One Loves' [1980], *RL* 302–3 / 339–40.

often difficult to unravel the layers of metaphors in these texts, this is surely because Barthes is creating a new version of the circulating signifiers of *Empire of Signs*. If the metonymic, bodily exchange set up for 'Japan' moved between face, hand, and writing,[18] in later texts it is often the metonymic tongue (*la langue*) that mediates the sexuality of both language and the body.

This is exactly the writing strategy that Barthes attributes to the gastronomist Brillat-Savarin in his 1975 commentary on the latter's *Physiology of Taste*.[19] 'The Tongue'—Barthes's title for the most relevant section of this essay—is the organ of both taste and speech, an archetypal Fourierist *transition* enabling an overdetermination of pleasures.[20] In the first instance the tongue is the mediating term whereby the pleasures of eating are conflated with a verbal *gourmandise*, the latter expressed through Brillat-Savarin's slightly archaic lexis and his string of gastronomic neologisms. If 'B.-S.' desires words, just as he desires truffles or a tuna-fish omelette, this is because language and gastronomy share not only the same organ (the tongue) but also 'the same apparatus of production or appreciation: cheeks, palate, and nasal fossae, of which B.-S recalls the gustatory role and which produce fine singing' (*RL* 257 / 293). As usual, Barthes is closely (and convincingly) glossing an original text, at the same time as giving it his own particular slant: 'To eat, to speak, to sing (need we add: to kiss) are operations originating in the same site of the body' (257–8 / 293). Barthes produces a pseudo-scientific back-up for his crucial parenthetical addition: 'We know how insistently modernity has sought to uncover the sexuality concealed in the exercise of language: to speak, despite denials and justifications (including that of simple "communication") is an erotic act; a new concept has facilitated this extension of the sexual to the verbal: the concept of *orality*' (259 / 294). If Brillat-Savarin's physiology conflates the pleasures of food, language, and sexuality it is because 'taste' is at

---

[18] See Ch. 6.
[19] 'Reading Brillat-Savarin', *RL* 250–70 / 285–306, first published as a preface to Brillat-Savarin, *Physiologie du goût* (Paris, Hermann, 1975).
[20] Richard Howard has translated this section title (*La langue*) as 'Language'. Although Barthes's argument depends upon the ambiguity of the French *langue*, 'tongue' is surely its primary meaning in this section.

once 'oral like language' and 'libidinal like Eros' (259 / 294): 'it is obviously B.-S.'s intention to suggest a kind of metonymic exchange between the highest form of voluptuousness (even if it is censored) and the sense whose defence and illustration he has undertaken, namely taste' (266 / 302).[21]

Charles Fourier's more discreet displacements of sensuality from sexuality to ironic neologisms or bergamot pears are timid indeed relative to the following transition elaborated by Barthes on Brillat-Savarin's behalf: 'He comes up with the astonishing idea of classifying the movements of the tongue as it participates in manducation: there are, among other oddly learned words, *spication* (when the tongue forms a spike and moves sideways), and *verrition* (when it adopts a sweeping movement). A double *jouissance*?' (258 / 294). If we place this quotation alongside Barthes's reference, in *Roland Barthes by Roland Barthes*, to the insistent kiss of a male prostitute described in a medieval Arabic text ('he thrusts his tongue into your mouth and twists it obstinately') (*RB* 170 / 172), or a crudely expressed gloss on the *fruition* of love in *A Lover's Discourse*, we may begin to suspect that Barthes's set of metaphors for the utopia of language is underpinned by a personal erotic preference.[22] This would be true to the spirit of his reading of Fourier ('pull the end of the tablecloth' etc.) and it is perhaps no coincidence that the

---

[21] A similar exchange is proposed by Barthes in a 1974 reading of his own pastiche, written as a schoolboy in 1933, of Plato's *Crito*. Barthes had made Socrates' reason and virtue collapse when he was tempted by his friends with a plate of juicy figs (Socrates agreed to escape from prison, leaving Plato to arrange matters with history). Whatever, asks Barthes, made him make of the fig (which he did not even like at that age) a beguiling, immoral, and philosophical fruit, 'unless, perhaps, lurking behind the fig, lies *le Sexe* (sex/genitalia), *Fica*?' See Barthes, 'Premier texte', *OC* iii. 17–20: 17–18, first published in *L'Arc*. For further discussion, in particular on the role of Alcibiades in Barthes's pastiche, see Knight, 'Roland Barthes: An Intertextual Figure', 92–5.

[22] 'I dream that we delight in each other according to an absolute appropriation; this is a *fruitive* union, the *fruition* of love. (This word seems pedantic? With its initial fricative and its cascade of sharp vowel sounds, the word increases the ecstasy of which it speaks by an oral voluptuousness; by the very act of saying it, I savour this union *in my mouth*.)' (*LD* 226 / 267). Barthes includes a marginal reference to the *Littré* dictionary (omitted from the English translation) with legitimizing quotes from Montaigne and Corneille at the bottom of the page: 'Montaigne speaks of the *fruition* of life. And Corneille writes: "And without daily sacrifices | One will never preserve the *fruitive* union | Born of a perfect love" '.

'autobiographical' example that he actually used as the starting point of that essay concerned a taste in food (his preference for fresh rather than rancid couscous).[23]

In that Barthes's manner of putting together a utopian argument involves weaving between several overlapping metaphors, this very overlapping can easily lead to misreadings of that argument if one element is stressed at the expense of another. For example, the hedonistic dimension that Barthes builds into the concept of Text has often led to undue stress on pleasure without sufficient reference to what he means by Text.[24] It could seem that in following a particular chain of images for oral pleasure (which began from the aural perception of a 'writing aloud'), Barthes has moved a long way from his starting point of a language utopia, and that *jouissance* has become a subjective pleasure rather than the mediator of a socially liberated and metaphorically textual space. However, a self-consciously absurd fantasy elaborated in a fragment of *Roland Barthes by Roland Barthes* is a reminder of his determination to maintain the interdependence of linguistic, sexual, and social liberations. Barthes refers to the hypothesis that human speech came about when men no longer needed all four limbs in order to walk and no longer needed their mouths for hunting. He adds to this hypothesis a refinement, namely the suggestion that since the phonatory system also serves as the osculatory system, the ability to kiss must have come into being at the same time:

> In moving to an upright posture, man found himself free to invent language and love: this was perhaps the anthropological birth of a concomitant, twofold perversion: speech and kissing. In which case, the more men have become free (the more their mouths have been freed), the more they have spoken and kissed; and logically, once

---

[23] See *SFL* 77–80 / 83–6.
[24] The problem of how to translate the title *Le Plaisir du texte* underlines this: The Pleasure of Text? Pleasure of Text? Of the possible variations of interpretation of the value of the French articles, Richard Howard's *The Pleasure of the Text* surely distorts Barthes's own stress on Text as a concept. For a discussion of the meaning of this title, see Philippe Roger, *Roland Barthes, roman* (Paris, Grasset, 1986), 121–2. Roger devotes a chapter to an interesting attempt to debunk the mythical status of *le texte* as a key concept of Barthes's work (105–30).

progress has rid men of every manual task, they will do nothing but converse and kiss each other! (*RB* 141 / 144).[25]

Moreover, Barthes is keen to stress that gastronomy for Brillat-Savarin is a veritable social system, the underpinning of a cosmogony.[26] Even the physical link between speech and taste that is mediated by the tongue is generalized to the communicative space of the dinner table—the anticipated pleasures of eating merge with the pleasures of conversation and thereby introduce *jouissance* into the very act of communication.[27] The crucial point, I think, is this. One can say that Barthes uses sexual metaphors for his notion of Text or to elaborate what he means by a language utopia. But one must also say that in order for pleasure, sexual or otherwise, to become a utopian *jouissance*—in Barthes's sense of pleasure without social separation—*jouissance* must first pass through language, and that language must itself have been freed from social alienations. It is because this has not happened that Text remains a utopia, but this does not make it any less important as a social vision.

This seems to be the sense of the section entitled 'Community' in *The Pleasure of the Text* in which, in a specific allusion to Sade, the latter's *Society of the Friends of Crime* is transformed into a Fourierist *Society of the Friends of Text*. Yet this utopian community cannot exist within language and society as we know it: 'Such a society would have no place, could function only in total atopia; yet it would be a kind of phalanstery, for in it contradictions would be acknowledged (and the risks of ideological imposture thereby restricted), difference would be

---

[25] This is, of course, a somewhat different solution to the interrelationship of alienations from the vision of an exemption of sexuality discussed in the last chapter.

[26] See the section entitled 'Cosmogonies' (*RL* 254–6 / 290–1). There are, in fact, many parallels between Barthes's reading of Brillat-Savarin and his reading of Fourier ('to produce a utopia you have only to socialize the *unknown* quality of pleasure (here again we encounter Fourier)', 263 / 298). In many ways, Brillat-Savarin would have been a logical companion for Fourier and Sade in *Sade, Fourier, Loyola* (albeit a less provocative choice than Loyola). Annette Lavers, alluding to Barthes's 'affectionate presentation' of Brillat-Savarin, draws attention to the parallel: 'though he had written before in the same vein on Sade, Fourier or Loyola, a gourmet is more congenial than an eccentric utopian, an ascetic, or a coprophagist' (*Roland Barthes: Structuralism and After*, 208).

[27] See the section 'Sociality' (267–8 / 303).

respected, and conflict rendered insignificant (being unproductive of pleasure)' (*PT* 15 / 27). This is because Barthes conceives of difference not as something that masks or attenuates conflict, but rather as something existing 'beyond' and 'to one side' of conflict, just as he conceives of Text as 'that rare linguistic space which is devoid of all "scenes" (in the domestic, conjugal sense of the term), of all logomachy' (*PT* 15–16 / 28). Text is never a 'dialogue': 'no risk of dissimulation, aggression, or blackmail, no rivalry of ideolects; Text establishes a sort of island within (current) human relations, demonstrates the asocial nature of pleasure (only leisure is social), grants a glimpse of the scandalous truth about *jouissance*: that once the imaginary of speech has been abolished, *jouissance* might well be neutral (*neutre*)' (16 / 28).

Whereas conflict is always coded in our current language system ('aggression is merely the most hackneyed of languages' (*PT* 15 / 28), Sade, who as logothete invented his own code, filled his text with 'triumphs' but banished conflict. It is this intimation of a different relationship to meaning that lies behind the enigmatic principle of tact (*délicatesse*) elaborated in the final fragment of Barthes's second essay on Sade. The phrase is a quotation from Sade himself who, writing to his wife from prison, chose to read in her request for his dirty underwear a quirk of her desire: 'Do you know, that is exquisite tact (*délicatesse*)? You see how I recognize the value of things. . . . you know the respect I have for tastes and fantasies: however eccentric they may be, I find them all respectable, both because one is not the master of them, and because the most singular and bizarre of fantasies, if correctly analysed, always derives from a principle of tact' (*SFL* 170 / 174). In the preceding fragment Barthes had distinguished 'sadism' as the crude content of Sade's works from the 'Sadeian text', and it is clear that the principle of tact is intended to open up a utopian reading of Sade's writing as 'Text'. In struggling to formulate this currently incomprehensible concept Barthes opposes it to the project of violence that might also be read in Sade. Since violence follows a code 'worn out by milleniums of human history' (171 / 174), attempts simply to overturn it will come to nothing—they will remain trapped within the same code. Sadeian *délicatesse*, on the other hand (which Barthes specifically says is not a product of class, culture, or civilization), will combine analysis and *jouissance* to produce unprecedented exaltation and 'the most formidable of utopias': '*The principle of tact* postulated by Sade might alone constitute, once the bases of History have changed, an absolutely new language, that unprecedented mutation destined to subvert (not to overturn, but rather to fragment, pluralize, pulverize) the very meaning of *jouissance*' (171 / 174). And when asked, in an interview, to expand upon this 'principle of tact', Barthes simply requotes the long analysis of 'Western sexuality' that I have already discussed in my chapter on Barthes and Morocco.[28] Here, it will be remembered, the alienation of sexuality was entirely attributed to its mediation by an already alienated system of meaning. As long as sexuality remained trapped in conceptualization through binaries, homosexuality (Barthes's chosen example) would be recuperated as mere transgression and would reproduce its own alienating binary distinctions. However, 'sexual "tact" contrasts with the crude character of these practices, not on the level of transgression, but on the level of meaning; this *délicatesse* can be defined as a *confusion of meaning*, expressed in the following ways: either through protocols of "politeness", or through sensual techniques, or through a new conception of erotic "time"' (*GV* 123–4 / 118 and 161–2).[29]

In *The Pleasure of the Text*, a metaphorical sequence passes from a sleepy Barthes in a Tangiers night club, to Severo Sarduy's 'square in Tangiers', to a transformation of Barthes himself into a *souk*, all to suggest the loosening of the constraints of language within a stereophonic Text (*PT* 49 / 79). Reglossing the image of the Moroccan night club in *Roland Barthes*, Barthes completes the eroticization of this textual space—'in the nightclub the body of the other is never transformed into a "person" (either civil, psychological, or social): it offers me its company (*il me propose sa promenade*), not its interlocution' (*RB* 141 / 144)—and makes it clear that

---

[28] See Ch. 5.
[29] For the original passage from 'Digressions' see *GV* 123–4 / 118. For Barthes's quotation of this passage in the context of this specific discussion of Sade, see the interview 'Plaisir/Ecriture/Lecture', *GV* 149–64: 161–2. The Engish translation of the interview has omitted both question and answer.

the different sort of relationship to language and ideas that ensues is a creative one for him: 'the link between the production of my language, and the floating desire on which it feeds, is one of alertness, not of communication' (142 / 145). Similarly, Barthes tells us that he 'has ideas' when travelling by train (as opposed to by plane, which has quite the opposite effect): 'people are moving all around me, and the passing bodies act as facilitators'.[30] On the reproduced filing card which we are to assume was the starting point for this fragment (labelled 'out of doors', it is presumably the sort of thing he might have written on a train), Barthes equates the positive effect of these 'passing bodies' with a 'good system of circulation' (*RB* 75 / 79), a more lightly expressed version of his earlier description of Text as a space where it is desire that circulates, rather than domination, but which is presumably intended to convey the same idea. The filing card is juxtaposed with another, the better-known introduction to 'the Goddess Homo': 'Homosexuality: all that it allows us to say, do, understand, know, etc.' In the printed fragment the cognitive function that Barthes attributes to homosexuality is described as adding a dimension to reality: 'I am more sensitive, more perceptive, more loquacious, enjoy myself more, etc.—and it is in this *more* that difference takes root (as does, consequently, the Text of life, life as Text)' (*RB* 64 / 68). If this is very much the heightened, photogenic quality of reality given creative form in Barthes's 'Japan', we could not hope for a clearer statement of what has remained implicit in my argument so far—in Barthes's writing on the everyday world it is often homosexuality that crystallizes the transformation of 'life' into 'Text'.

Read together, the two filing cards lay out the intimate connection between the utopia of Text and two terms to which Barthes frequently refers in the 1970s—it is *la drague* and *le trick* ('il me propose sa promenade') that actually operate the 'good system' of textual circulation. The metaphor of Text subsumes these explicitly sexual terms which, though sometimes used metaphorically in their turn, depend for their value on their

---

[30] Barthes is implicitly comparing himself with Gide here, whom he used to imagine 'writing his notebooks in the dining car between courses' whilst travelling abroad (*RB* 77 / 81).

literal meaning. This can be seen in an important late text by Barthes, his 1979 preface to Renaud Camus's very novelistic *Tricks*.[31] Despite the graphic detail in which forty-five brief encounters between the narrator and previously unknown partners are recounted, the text has a paradoxical quality of innocence which Barthes convincingly locates in its tone and in its 'ethics of dialogue': 'This ethic is that of kindliness [*bienveillance*], which is surely the virtue most contrary to the amorous pursuit, and hence the most rare. Whereas ordinarily the erotic contract is presided over by harpy-like figures, who leave each party in a state of chilly solitude, here it is the goddess Eunoia, the Eumenid, the Kindly One, who accompanies the two partners; . . . Moreover, this goddess has her retinue: Courtesy, Obligingness, Humour, Generous Impulse' (*RL* 294–5 / 330–1). This elaboration of the qualities of Goddess Homosexuality is an acute reading of an author who elsewhere declares himself 'on the side of those who desire' because 'nothing is more kindly than desire, nothing is more gentle or less aggressive'.[32] Barthes is clearly attracted to the contractual aspect of Camus's *trick*, which he describes as 'a *potential* love, cut short by the express decision of both parties, in contractual deference to the cultural code which identifies cruising with Don Juanism' (*RL* 294 / 330). Yet the Don Juan to whom Barthes invariably likens the *dragueur* loses his aggressive power once infidelity is both kindly and contractually two-sided:

> Trick—the encounter that takes place only once: more than a *drague*, less than a love affair: an intensity, which passes without regret. Consequently, for me, *Trick* becomes the metaphor for many a non-sexual adventure, the encounter of a glance, an idea, an image, an intense but ephemeral association, which accepts its own easy dissolution, an unfaithful kindliness: a way of not getting bogged down in desire, though without evading it; all in all, a kind of wisdom. (295 / 331)

Barthes appears to argue that it is *because* this 'methodical conquest of happiness' refuses to sublimate desire that it is

---

[31] *RL* 291–5 / 327–31, originally in Renaud Camus, *Tricks* (Paris, Persona, 1979).
[32] Renaud Camus, *Chroniques achriennes* (Paris, POL, 1984), 241.

socially liberated ('neither alienation nor sublimation') (294 / 330).

Indeed it is clear from a number of references in Barthes's 1970s writings that he wants to resist the 'Socratic myth' that homosexual love should be sublimated in aesthetic creation. His reasons are helpfully set out in his own paper at the 1977 Cerisy colloquium on his work.[33] Discussing the power struggles whereby people impose images upon each other, Barthes makes specific reference to the sublimation of desire that necessitated Socrates' rejection of Alcibiades, famously recounted by the latter in *The Symposium*.[34] This rejection is adroitly linked to Barthes's familiar theme of the aggression of language. Socrates' method of developing an argument was erotic in that each careful step required 'the assent of a beloved whose replies marked the progression of reasoning'. However, this amorous method also involved manipulating language so as to force the other into logical contradictions. By scoring points in this way Socrates maintained 'the arrogance of truth' so that 'it is no surprise that he ultimately "sublimated"—rejected Alcibiades'. Barthes approves of the idea of speech depending on 'inspired love', but it is intrinsic to his textual ideal that no one should gain or maintain the upper hand.[35] It is this lack of linguistic aggression that he associates with *not* sublimating desire for Alcibiades.

This specific association of non-aggression with a refusal of sublimation recurs in an interview given the same year, where the specific ethics of *la drague* are linked to another favourite notion, the *non-vouloir saisir* (no-will-to-grasp) of 'Eastern philosophy': ' "Not to grasp" the object of love, and to let desire circulate freely. At the same time not to sublimate: to master desire in order not to master the other.'[36] In *Roland Barthes by Roland Barthes* non-aggression is explicitly linked with the

---

[33] 'The Image', *RL* 389–97 / 350–8, quotations from 358 / 397.
[34] Plato, *The Symposium*, trans. by W. Hamilton (Harmondsworth, Penguin, 1951), 96–113.
[35] 'Text is that space where no language has a hold over any other ... that *social* space which leaves no language safe, outside, nor any subject of enunciation in position as judge, master, analyst, confessor, decoder.' (*RL* 64 / 77)
[36] 'The Greatest Cryptographer of Contemporary Myths Talks about Love', interview with Philippe Roger (*Playboy*, 1977), *GV* 290–305: 297 / 271–90: 277.

prostitution that Barthes promotes as the model of a positive contract. This is because prostitution—'declared immoral by all societies and all political regimes (except the most ancient)'—is a contract that suspends anxiety over the assumption or imposition of self-image relative to the other's desire: 'it is in fact the only position that the subject can take up without falling into one of two contrasting but equally abhorred images: that of the "egoist" (who demands without caring that he has nothing to give), and that of the "saint" (who gives but forbids himself ever to demand anything at all).' What is more, Barthes creates an illuminating link between the refusal of these 'two plenitudes' and the subtext of homosexual encounters running through *Empire of Signs*—the section ends with a direct allusion to the 'golden rule' that he had discerned in the Shikidai Gallery of a seventeenth-century palace in Kyoto: 'No-will-to-grasp and yet no oblation' (*RB* 59 / 63–4).

All this, clearly, is the circulating desire that replaces domination within the utopia of Text. But it is not only the content and value system of Renaud Camus's *Tricks* that appeals to Barthes; if 'the flesh is not sad', it nevertheless requires 'a whole art to say so' (*RL* 294 / 330). Crucially, Barthes describes *Tricks* as 'speaking homosexuality' openly and simply, but never speaking *of* it: 'simplicity would amount to this: never to invoke Names, to keep them out of language—Names, the source of arguments, arrogance, and moralizing' (292 / 328). Barthes pays Camus the ultimate compliment of likening his tricks to haiku, not only for their combination of an ascetic form and a calm hedonism, but above all for their avoidance of interpretation: 'they are like smooth surfaces (*des à-plats*), without shadows, and as if *without second thoughts*' (292 / 328). Moreover, if Barthes finds the '*passage* from sex to discourse' especially successful, it is not only because the sexual acts are described in such a way as to free them from all connotation (from 'atmospherics' and 'adventitious thoughts' (293 / 329)), but also because the reader's interest (and the text's realism) is displaced from the acts themselves to 'the deambulation, the first signals, the manœuvres, the approach, the conversation, the setting off for the room, the domestic tidiness (or untidiness) encountered there' (293 / 329). These novelistic details, and especially the minimal but strikingly courteous conversations, form part of a discourse that maintains an extreme *pudeur*, for in *Tricks*—in Barthes's subtle and convincing reading—it is not sex but the 'person' who is the object of desire. Indeed, it is the distinctness of the person which provokes desire:

> Bodies can be classified into a finite number of types ('That's just my type'), but the person is absolutely individual. Renaud Camus's *Tricks* always begin with an encounter with the sought-after type (totally coded, he could figure in a catalogue or the small ads of a personal column); but once language enters the scene, the type is transformed into a person, and the relationship becomes inimitable, whatever the banality of the first words exchanged. The person is gradually revealed, yet lightly and without any psychological analysis, in what they wear and say, in their accent, in the decor of their room, in what might be called the individual's 'domesticity'—all that transcends his anatomy, yet over which he has control. (294 / 330)

This dialectic between a coded physical type and the uniqueness of an individual person (the way they look and speak, and the way in which they generally insert themselves into everyday reality) recalls Barthes's analysis of the 'millions of bodies' that constitute 'Japan'.[37] Moreover, the reference to small ads in the preceding quotation provides a link with the fantasmatic reading experience that Barthes associates, in an important interview given to *Libération* in 1979, with this newspaper's weekly personal column.[38]

It would be hard to imagine three pieces of writing more different in form and tone than Barthes's *Empire of Signs*, Renaud Camus's *Tricks*, and the personal small ads page of the Saturday edition of *Libération*. Yet Barthes analyses the latter as a successful form of utopian discourse which subsumes aspects of both *Empire of Signs* and *Tricks*. To begin with, the wider context of the personal columns is the completely heterogeneous and unpredictable range of objects and services on offer or requested, so that the whole section of classified advertisements forms a novelistic cosmogony: 'It covers absolutely every aspect

---

[37] See Ch. 6.
[38] Barthes, 'Mes petites annonces' (my small ads), interview with Michel Cressole, *Sandwiche* (supplement to *Libération*), 15 Dec. 1979, 5–6, quotations easily locatable. (Partial publication only in OC iii. 1092–3.)

of our daily lives and in that too it is a marvellous novel. . . . all these pages of ads are a representation of the world. It's what Thibetans called a *Mandala*, that's to say an enclosed space containing drawings which represent the whole world.' The second utopian feature of this discourse is that—with the ironic exception of Barthes's own commentary—it brings no 'meta-literature' in its wake: 'Normally, as someone who simply reads these ads, I really like this literal world which comes absolutely unaccompanied by any surrounding discourse; it's there to be taken just as it is, shielded from any intermediary interpretation.' Moreover, the small ads exemplify Barthes's ideal of the novelistic, in that they constitute a sort of 'splintered novel', a 'novel going off in all directions', whereby the formal genre is dispersed into light touches of this and that, into 'the beginnings of incidents, the beginnings of adventures'.

The small ads in Barthes's account undoubtedly represent one of his more successful examples of a textual space of desire. Their calm and understated hedonism, like that which Barthes reads in *Tricks*, is arguably more engaging than the theoretical promotion of pleasure and *jouissance*—or of the need to 'cruise' the reader—that we encounter in the self-conscious and sometimes pretentious formulations of *The Pleasure of the Text*. It is precisely the novelistic quality of the small ads which provokes an erotic reading experience, and one which is essentially performative since it is the fact of consulting them, of imagining that one really expects something from them, which makes of them a sort of 'verbal cruising', a 'mysterious exhortation to physical pleasure through the very distinctive mediation constituted by the small ad'. Although Barthes insists that, because of his age, he is 'targeted by very few, if any' of the advertisements, he adds: 'nevertheless sometimes I come across an expression, a turn of phrase, which isn't erotic in itself, but which suddenly and unexpectedly touches a sort of fantasmatic nerve, and quite transports me'.[39]

From *Text* to *trick*, Barthes's constant recourse to sexual metaphors is his way of eroticizing the world so as to introduce

---

[39] Barthes claims that this novelistic experience represents for him a profound pleasure of a completely different order from that of pornographic literature, 'which does not interest me in general'.

into it a particular utopian value system. What is more, his own relationship to language and theory is described through a similar set of metaphors. Clichés, for example, 'loiter' in language, and he claims that he can only speak at all by 'picking them up' (*BR* 461 / *L* 15). He identifies 'sexy sentences' which are 'disturbing by the very fact of their standing apart, as if they contained the promise which is made to us, their readers, of a special linguistic practice, as if we went looking for them in accordance with a physical pleasure *which knows what it wants*' (*RB* 164 / 167). Initially, Barthes stresses the fidelity of his desire for language: 'my work seems to be made up of a succession of "disinvestments": there is only one object from which I have never withdrawn the investment of my desire, ... it is language that I have chosen to love—and of course to hate at the same time.' This metaphorical relationship remains explicitly physical: 'as for the methods of approach, dependent on ideas developed around me and which drew them to me in distinctive ways, they may well have changed, that is to say: been tried out, given pleasure, transformed themselves, or been left behind: it is as if you always loved the same person but you tried out new erotic practices with them.'[40] Yet fidelity of desire is nowhere set up as an ideal. The notion of intellectual 'influences' on Barthes is transformed into a series of *promiscuous* relationships with the discourses of his day, so that the theoretical intertext emerges as a vast terrain through which he wanders, precisely in search of someone to love. Thus, he has *crushes* on concepts ('successive flushes, short-lived crazes') and 'discourse advances by minor twists of fate, by amorous crises' (*RB* 110 / 114). If key terms like 'History' and 'Nature' are woolly and malleable, others, like 'imaginary', are *dragueurs* in that they 'follow whoever they meet', be it Bachelard or Lacan (*RB* 126 / 129). Ideas become partners in 'a sort of cohabitation which is both risky and intensely pleasurable (*jouissive*), yet responsible at the same time. It's a sort of love affair (*aventure*).'[41]

In an interview given shortly before his inaugural lecture,

---

[40] 'Réponses' [1971], OC ii. 1307–24: 1317.
[41] 'Radioscopie', radio interview with Jacques Chancel (17 Feb. 1975), OC iii. 344–59: 351.

Barthes likens the *cours magistral* to a lover's soliloquy (*GV* 280 / 262). In the lecture itself, he suggests that it is a privilege of a professor at the Collège de France to be able to 'rêver tout haut sa recherche' (*BR* 458 / *L* 9). Readers of 'Incidents', recalling Amidou's idiosyncratic use of the verb 'to dream', may suspect an eroticization of Barthes's professorial fantasy.[42] In the course of the same institutionally prestigious lecture, Barthes compares the writer (and hence certainly himself) to the prostitute who waits at the crossroads of all discourses, 'in a position which is *trivial* in relation to the purity of doctrines (*trivialis* is the etymological attribute of the prostitute who waits at the intersection of three roads). In short, to persist means to maintain, over and against everything, the force of a drift and an expectation' (467 / 26). Moreover, through a further reference to the crossroads, the prostitute still loiters in the final words of the lecture. Here Barthes recommends to himself the experience of *unlearning* and *forgetting*, so that wisdom becomes a sort of kindly infidelity, and its engagement with knowledge a series of gentle and hedonistic *tricks*: 'This experience has, I believe, an illustrious and outdated name, which I shall venture to appropriate here at the very crossroads of its etymology: *Sapientia*, no power, a little knowledge (*savoir*), a little wisdom, and as much flavour (*saveur*) as possible' (478 / 46). If *Sapientia* is a suitably scholarly goal for a new professor at the Collège de France, etymology, as ever, is a fine excuse for a transition worthy of Brillat-Savarin. 'What is the principal theme here?' asks Barthes, as he outlines the insistent and overdetermined kiss of the prostitute Al Tifâchi (*RB* 170 / 172). The answer could well be applied to his own body of work: 'The subject is not complicated (as current opinion would claim with irritation) but *composite* (as Fourier would have put it)'.

[42] See *I* 29 / 44–5.

9
Return Journey: The South-West

> Whenever I superimpose the memory of childhood upon my adult life, something is set in motion within me, and that something is the specifically human meaning of utopia.[1]

IN the first part of *Camera Lucida*, Barthes reproduces a beautiful nineteenth-century photograph of the Alhambra in Granada: 'An old house, a shadowy porch, tiles, a faded Arab decoration, a man sitting against the wall, a deserted street, a Mediterranean tree (Charles Clifford's "Alhambra").' In the first instance the photograph moves him (*me touche*), and what it supposedly moves him to is a recognition: 'it's quite simple—I want to live *there*.' The words are echoed by the caption to the photograph that is enclosed in quotation marks: ' "That's where I should like to live ..." ' (*CL* 38 / 66). Barthes does not comment on the possible motivations that he lists ('warmth of the climate? Mediterranean myth? Apollinism? *Déshérence*? Retreat? Anonymity? Noblesse?'), though the details of the photograph certainly echo the thematics of *déshérence* (a lack of ownership in the absence of inheritors) that Barthes had read in Loti's historically dislocated Constantinople: a cypress tree, distant gravestones, grass sprouting up through broken stones, a solitary male figure in the empty street, a setting for relaxed debauchery sliding into the figure of 'drift'.[2] Yet Barthes himself gives no special emphasis to this theme. Claiming that the roots of his fantasy lie too deep for conscious understanding, he turns

---

[1] Barthes, 'Préface à *Le Refuge et la source* de Jean Daniel', OC iii. 701–2: 702, first published in 1977 in *Le Nouvel Observateur* as 'Le Grain d'une enfance'.
[2] See Ch. 7.

to Pascal for a vocabulary of purely intuitive knowledge: 'Whatever the case (with regard to myself, my motives, my fantasy), I want to live there, *en finesse*—and that *esprit de finesse* is never satisfied by the touristic photo' (38 / 66).[3]

Ironically, although the Alhambra did indeed fall into a long period of neglect in the nineteenth century, photographs of this very gatehouse (the now restored *Puerta del Vino*) do in fact feature in many a tourist guide to the Alhambra. Barthes appears to be unaware of this, and avoids passing through any mask of tourism as he distinguishes once more between modes of travel, including those which are imaginary: 'For me, photographs of landscapes (town or country) must be *habitable*, not visitable' (38 / 66). Focusing more closely on his insistent desire to inhabit, Barthes decides that it is neither oneiric (no spectacular settings) nor empirical (no practical plans for buying a house), but simply fantasmatic: 'deriving from a kind of second sight that seems to bear me forward to a utopian time, or to carry me back to somewhere in myself: a double movement which Baudelaire celebrated in "L'Invitation au voyage" and "La Vie antérieure" ' (40 / 68).[4] By the end of Barthes's commentary it is clear that his initial lack of understanding was a mere structuring device, for the 'old photo' that had moved him has been unambiguously constituted as a landscape of desire. The Freudian unconscious is a cultural reference on a par with the others that weave through this passage, as Barthes offers himself up to Freud's analysis (in *The Interpretation of Dreams* and 'The Uncanny') of the psychic phenomenon of false recognition of landscapes:

Looking at these landscapes of predilection, it is as if *I were certain* that I had been there or would go there. Now Freud says of the maternal body that 'there is no other place of which one can say with so much certainty that one has already been there'. Such then would be the

---

[3] The French is less specific: 'j'ai envie de vivre là-bas, *en finesse*—et cette finesse, la photo de tourisme ne la satisfait jamais.' However, the translator (Richard Howard) is undoubtedly right to see this as the *esprit de finesse* outlined in Pascal's *Pensées*. For further comments on Barthes's allusions to Pascal, see Ch. 10.

[4] Literally 'Invitation to Travel' and 'Former Life'. See Charles Baudelaire, *Les Fleurs du mal* [1857], ed. Antoine Adam (Paris, Garnier, 1961), 58–9 and 20. It is interesting to note that the two Baudelaire poems, set to music by Henri Duparc, were part of Charles Panzéra's repertoire.

essence of the landscape (chosen by desire): *heimlich*, awakening in me the Mother (in no way disturbing). (40 / 68)

Barthes has obviously reversed cause and effect here, proclaiming a sense of familiarity with the landscapes he wants to inhabit so as to allude to Freud's description of the mother's genitals as 'the entrance to the former *Heim* of all human beings, to the place where each of us lived once upon a time and in the beginning'.[5]

Barthes's commentary on the Alhambra photograph is relatively self-contained (there is no obvious connection with the chapters that precede and follow it), and the reference to Baudelaire is as suggestive as that to Freud. 'La Vie antérieure' and 'L'Invitation au voyage' were first published in 1855, which makes them exactly contemporaneous with Clifford's photograph, dated as 1854 in the text, and as '1854–1856' beneath the reproduction. Barthes's three variations on the phrase 'it's there that I want to live', with special stress on a vocabulary of *là* and *là-bas*, anticipate the specific naming of Baudelaire.[6] Certainly, both Baudelaire poems are fantasies of habitation rather than of mere exotic travel, the one nostalgic ('J'ai longtemps habité sous de vastes portiques' / 'For a long time I dwelt beneath vast porticos'), the other projective ('Songe à la douceur | D'aller là-bas vivre ensemble' / 'Imagine the pleasure | Of going to live there together'). Both characterize *là-bas* as a space of ordered and serene sensuality, either retrospectively

---

[5] 'Whenever a man dreams of a place or a country and says to himself, while he is still dreaming: "this place is familiar to me, I've been here before", we may interpret the place as being his mother's genitals or her body. ... the *unheimlich* is what was once *heimisch*, familiar; the prefix "un" is the token of repression' (Freud, 'The Uncanny' [1919], trans. James Strachey, in *The Pelican Freud Library*, ed. Angela Richards and Albert Dickson, 15 vols. (Harmondsworth, Penguin, 1973–86), xiv. 335–76: 367–8); 'In some dreams of landscapes or other localities emphasis is laid in the dream itself on a convinced feeling of having been there before.... These places are invariably the genitals of the dreamer's mother; there is indeed no other place about which one can assert with such conviction that one has been there before' (Freud, *The Interpretation of Dreams* [1900], trans. James Strachey, *The Pelican Freud Library*, iv. 524 [1909 addition]). The genuine neurotic *dreams* of the familiar landscape, or might have found the photo *unheimlich* in symptomatic acknowledgement of a repression; Barthes's allusions to Freud, obviously, are simply part of his standard cultural baggage.

[6] Just as, of course, they recall the *là-bas* by which Barthes conjures up an 'imaginary' Japan in *Empire of Signs* (see Ch. 7).

('C'est là que j'ai vécu dans les voluptés calmes' / 'That's where I lived amidst calm sensual delights'), or through the imaginary present of the famous refrain: 'Là, tout n'est qu'ordre et beauté | Luxe, calme et volupté' / 'There, all is order and beauty | Sumptuousness, tranquillity, and voluptuousness.' And both, of course, have an Oriental connotation, so that the hybrid setting of 'La Vie antérieure' (seashore colonnades and naked slaves with palm leaves) is echoed in 'L'Invitation au voyage': though conjuring up what is generally thought to be a Dutch townscape, the poet and his companion would inhabit a room filled with an 'Oriental splendour' culled from the ends of the earth. Despite the basic difference of form, the thematic and lexical similarities between these poems is so striking that it is tempting, as Barthes suggests, to conflate them into a single movement between past and future. Indeed, one of the most significant aspects of Barthes's investment in these poetic utopias is precisely his stress on their intersection of space with past and future time.

In the case of Baudelaire, it is obvious that the utopias in question are a poetic construct, whereas Barthes's commentary on the Alhambra photograph, inspired by its subject matter, contains no reference to the role of Charles Clifford. However, in an important text on a series of rural scenes by the photographer Daniel Boudinet, Barthes attributes the utopian qualities of these 'French Georgics' to a conscious (and highly intelligent) photographic effect. Boudinet's twelve photographs, which had been taken in Alsace in 1973, were published in 1977 in the journal *Créatis*, with a brief commentary on each photo by Barthes. The latter describes Boudinet as treading successfully ('with precision, power, and subtlety') the narrow line between aestheticism and naturalism, as producing a photographic signifier that has avoided both 'art' and an illusory referential 'naturalness'.[7]

Barthes speaks once more of a desire for habitation provoked by these scenes: 'I desire the subject matter of all of D. B.'s

---

[7] OC iii. 705–18: 706. For a brief discussion, see Jacques Leenhardt, 'Arrêts sur images: Une évolution de Barthes', in Catherine Coquio and Régis Salado (eds.), *Barthes après Barthes: Une actualité en questions* (Pau, Publications de l'Université de Pau, 1993), 159–65: 162–4.

photos; his work is for ever establishing the space in which I want to live' (OC iii. 712). It is true that he qualifies this desire with an 'or at least, so I believe', and it is true that he characterizes his longing for the meadows and sloping roofs as the naïve desire of a city dweller—doubtless this is but one small part of his total capital of desire. Yet this in no way undermines its force: 'one could say that a desire does not have to be absolute in order to be wholehearted.' If longing for a dwelling is associated in the Alhambra commentary with nostalgia for the mother's body, that body is specifically fantasized as a locus of comfort and security.[8] Barthes reads in Boudinet's photographs a familiar and reassuring world which is mediated by a tissue of cultural references, from Virgil's *Georgics* to an almost stereotypical construction of 'rurality'. 'The commonplace of the orchard', for example, 'grants me vague but exquisite access to a whole culture: myths, poems, stories, songs, paintings, and tapestries' (714). Barthes claims that 'culture', in this sense of a stock of vague memories, is not necessarily repressive ('it delights me, makes me feel expansive'); indeed, his reaction to a distant village scene is euphoric: 'What a lot of different cultures are bound up in this view!... all of the cultures (in the metaphorical sense) that determine what I see: geography (distinctive vegetation and roofs, a distinctive church spire), history (every village emanates as it were the odour of ancestral time), rurality (how I like this path linking the dwelling places to the labour of the earth)' (708).

If Barthes reads this scene positively, when one might have expected him to discuss a more stifling ideological effect, it is because it is 'compact, coherent, and intelligible and yet, as ever, D. B. opens it out and liberates it through his masterly representation of foliage'. The function of the leafy trees that fill Boudinet's photographs is to introduce air into this rural utopia, to give it a 'textual' dimension. Thus even a dense, leafy thicket has a paradoxically liberating effect on Barthes's body: 'it is a leafy substance, a delicate fabric, dense and yet flimsy, spreading

---

[8] This too, of course, is mediated by Freud: 'the dwelling house was a substitute for the mother's womb, the first lodging, for which in all likelihood man still longs, and in which he was safe and felt at ease' (*Civilization and its Discontents* [1930], trans. James Strachey, *The Pelican Freud Library*, xii. 243–340: 279).

everywhere and yet centred: these upright masses of foliage, without air or light, inexplicably help me to breathe, have an uplifting effect on my "soul" (as we would have put it a hundred years ago: but in fact the soul is always the body)' (707). The resulting 'shimmer of intensities' (*une moire*, literally a watered fabric like shot silk) is 'light, compact, and luminous', a substance (rather than a form) which Barthes perceives as 'stretched out upright on the carpet of meadows and roofs'.[9] The notion that the uplifted 'soul' is really the body is a major theme of Barthes's essays on Romantic music,[10] so it is appropriate that Boudinet's photographs should be described as 'very musical', and their effect as cathartic and appeasing (never violent): 'the body breathes more easily, it *drinks* what Baudelaire called *vegetal ambrosia*' (716).[11]

Barthes stresses 'peacefulness' as the ultimate connotation of a bucolic scene (grazing cattle), whereby quotation of other peaceful scenes is Boudinet's strategy for avoiding the imposition of meaning (and thereby disturbing the peaceful effect):

> The trees that stand on each side are like inverted commas surrounding some vast pictorial quotation, as if all the *peaceful* pictures that there have ever been had been superimposed upon each other. The author speaks this peacefulness indirectly, in order that we may rest; for were he to speak it directly, there would be either no effect, or an effect contrary to that intended. (709)

Both method and effect are reminiscent of Barthes's essay on China, which might well have emerged as a Georgic had he thought of it at the time.[12] The peaceable power of Boudinet's landscapes is intimately connected with *la culture* in its literal French sense of agriculture. In a photograph of a distant figure hoeing the land, peacefulness is associated with both labour and its liberation: 'nature, in the sense of a vegetal mass, retreats before the hoe of a timeless human being (the action of hoeing, the head-dress) who clears the land for cultivation. However, there is no sense of a battle (with the land), rather a sense of

---

[9] Similarly, Barthes comments that photographer Lucien Clergue represents sand as a substance. See 'Note sur un album de photographies de Lucien Clergue' [1980], OC iii. 1203–5, first published in *Sud*. [10] See Ch. 10.
[11] The reference is to Baudelaire's poem 'L'Âme du vin' ('The Soul of Wine'). See *Les Fleurs du mal*, 119–20: 120. [12] See Ch. 7.

something austere and impartial (*neutre*)' (711). If Boudinet's meadows and roofs merge into a single substance, this is because rurality is precisely that space where human and natural products become indistinguishable. The solitary figures who work the soil sign these landscapes with the mark of their activity, but do not invade it with their presence. The history that Barthes reads in these pictures is a very 'primitive' one: 'how man gradually frees himself from his original condition of a *homochromic* insect' (710). Boudinet underlines the mythical value of labour—'a power of liberation and pacification' (711)—by distancing it in space (the figures are viewed from afar) and in time ('a timeless human being', 'an ancestral action'). Better still, in a picture that contains no human figure, he liberates labour by Barthes's preferred method—he *suspends* it in a moment of repose and of positive alliance between animate and inanimate: 'The trees, the animals, the instruments for ploughing return to a sort of insistent repose. By gathering together these provisionally inactive (but not idle) agents, the photograph speaks time: we have just been working, producing (milk and hay), we shall start again before long' (713). There is something very different at stake here from the leisurely laziness of Baudelaire's idylls, or from the historical dislocation of moments of Oriental (and Orientalist) *déshérence*.[13] According to Barthes, Boudinet's suspension of labour inscribes a conscious representation of time. Whereas photography is so often considered an instrument for capturing the passing moment (*l'actuel*), 'here, more philosophically, it speaks that difficult temporal concept: the present (*le présent*)' (713).

Perhaps strangely, but in keeping with this more philosophical register, the last of Boudinet's photographs is a close-up of a decaying cabbage and the corpse of a duck. Barthes maintains his positive reading, and describes this image of the earth as an inevitable overturning of the 'beautiful tree-filled Nature from which we are parting'. It is the shimmering trees that will linger on in the memory as 'a sort of vegetal expanse, both sumptuous and austere, a sort of silent invitation to . . . "philosophize" ' (718).

---

[13] It is also different, of course, from the mystifying consecration of labour denounced in Barthes's mythologies 'The Great Family of Man' and '*Lost Continent*' (see Ch. 4).

In Boudinet's photographs, labour mediates the relationship of human beings to nature, while cosmic themes of time and death inflect the everyday rural scenes. Though Barthes does not mention it in his several references to the *Georgics*, he is obviously aware that Virgil's bucolic utopia is no mere treatise on agriculture, and that the final book on bee-keeping is the context for Virgil's version of the story of Orpheus and Eurydice.[14]

Although Barthes uses the phrase 'Georgics *à la française*', he never alludes to the specifically regional setting of these photographs of Alsace—the significant opposition that structures his desire is that of city and country rather than that of Paris and the provinces.[15] However, in 'The Light of the South-West' (also published in 1977), Barthes's fantasmatic desire to inhabit focuses unequivocally upon provincial France.[16] It is not until some way through the essay that Barthes reminds the reader that he had spent his childhood and adolescent holidays in Bayonne, and that he now spends time each year in the unnamed village described on the opening page. 'His' village is described as typical of all French villages in that it is a 'contradictory space', both 'centred' and centrifugal, relatively small with a central square, church, and handful of shops, yet with scattered and distant pockets of habitation—indeed the road that passes his house 'meanders off to irrigate a whole outlying district of the village' (*I* 3 / 13). The road itself, compared with a peaceful river, picks up themes reminiscent of the Virgilian and very textual *wadi* which was discussed in Chapter 8. However, what were there described as vaguely disruptive mechanical noises are here assimilated as elements of a rural code in keeping with one of Boudinet's photographic Georgics: 'a moped or a tractor occasionally make their way

---

[14] Virgil, *The Georgics*, trans. L. P. Wilkinson (Harmondsworth, Penguin, 1982), see especially 139–42.

[15] Given Barthes's tendency to mention his mixed (Gidean) family origins in two distant corners of France ('a diagonal cross-breed of Alsace and Gascony', *RB* 99 / 103), one might have expected him to draw a connection between his desire for these settings and the roots of his mother's family in Alsace. If he does not do this, it is perhaps because, as will be seen, he has transposed maternal space to his own childhood province of the South-West.

[16] Translated by Richard Howard as 'The Light of the Sud-Ouest', *I* 3–9 / 13–20, first published in *L'Humanité* (10 Sept. 1977).

along it (these are the real sounds of the countryside now, no less poetic, after all, than birdsong: by their infrequency they emphasize the silence of nature and stamp upon it a discreet sign of human activity)' (3 / 13). Similarly, Barthes's favourite road from his village to Bayonne—a former towpath staked out with habitations—is no merely functional route between two places. This road incarnates 'that balance of nobility and familiarity which is particular to the South-West', and becomes the focus of a complex experience whereby vision (the sight of the beautiful River Adour) is juxtaposed with 'memories of an ancestral practice: that of walking, of the slow and rhythmic penetration of the landscape, which accordingly assumes different proportions' (6 / 17). As with the slow-motion reading undertaken in *S/Z*, a change in rhythm entails a change in level of perception; moreover, the resulting alteration to spatial relations interferes with a stable representation. Barthes speaks of the power of the South-West to outplay the 'frozen immobility' of postcards, and suggests that the taking of photographs is not the way to get to know and love this region: 'you must come and you must stay, so that you can explore every detail of the shimmer (*la moire*) of places, seasons, weather, and light' (6 / 17). That this textile image of watered silk is also applied to Boudinet's leafy landscapes emphasizes all the difference for Barthes between a postcard or holiday snapshot and one of Boudinet's constructed photographic Georgics.

In order to transform the South-West into a utopian Text (to create his own verbal *moire*), Barthes plays throughout with the notion of 'complex proportions': 'my South-West is extensible, like those pictures that change their meaning according to the chosen level of perception' (4 / 14). He sets his structural imagination to work and conceptualizes the South-West as three possible spaces, the last of these subdivided into the four different routes from his village to Bayonne. Although the South-West is established as a microcosm of the complex proportions of France as a whole, its utopian status is initially established through a series of comparisons with another region of France—the 'other' south of the Mediterranean *Midi*. This theme is introduced through a reference to the accent of Gascony ('the models of intonation that marked my earliest childhood' (4 / 14)) as mediator of Barthes's loyalty to the

South-West and of his subjective investment in all things associated with it. Its Mediterranean counterpart is accused of having a triumphant quality to it, one that is upheld by 'a whole folklore of the cinema (Raimu, Fernandel), of advertising (olive oil, lemon juice), and of tourism' (4 / 14). Barthes has returned to one of his favourite utopian themes: the *Midi* is a region for touristic visits and for the colourful holiday photographs to which its light lends itself, the South-West is somewhere to inhabit. It is a vocation incarnated in its magnificent light ('both noble and subtle'), what Barthes calls its 'light-space, defined less by the colours it imparts to things (as in the other Midi) than by the eminently *habitable* quality it bestows on the earth. . . . it safeguards this region from all vulgarity, from "gregarity" too, rendering it unsuitable for facile tourism' (5 / 15). Like Boudinet's cathartically peaceful landscapes this *lumière-espace* has synaesthetic qualities which affect the body rather than 'the soul'—'this light should be seen in the autumn (it is so musical that I would almost say it should be heard)' (5 / 15–16).[17]

Even when the atmosphere is oppressive there is no Baudelairian mental 'spleen', for even tiredness becomes 'somehow exquisite, as ever when it is my body that is affected' (5 / 16). In a curious fragment of *Roland Barthes*, Barthes wonders why, despite the rest and the fresh air, he has more headaches than usual 'in the country (in the South-West)'. In fact, unlike full-scale migraines, his headaches are both dull (*mates*) and quite mild, and seem to be directly related to synaesthesia (an 'absence of migraine', for example, is equated with the 'zero degree of synaesthesia' (*RB* 124–5 / 128–9)). Headaches, claims Barthes, deprive the body of any complacently healthy transparency—the body becomes opaque and stubbornly 'there' in what constitutes a passing rejection of meaning and symbolization. If headaches represent a refusal of hysteria in Barthes's sense of combative and theatrical scenes of language, they are a mild form of hysteria in the clinical sense of the physical symptom of an affect. Thus

---

[17] For interesting discussions of synaesthesia in Barthes's work, see Claire Oboussier, 'Barthes and Femininity: A Synaesthetic Writing', *Nottingham French Studies*, 33/2 (Autumn 1995), 78–93, and 'Synaesthesia in Cixous and Barthes', in Diana Knight and Judith Still (eds.), *Women and Representation* (Nottingham, WIF Publications, 1995), 115–31.

Barthes asks what his headaches might be repressing or to what they might be reacting, and suggests that 'the country' is a point of contact with his 'Bayonne past'. In 'The Light of the South-West', Barthes's reaction to both the weather and the light conflates physical sensation and affect—both pass through his body, and it is his body which links the South-West of the present to the South-West of his past.

The car journey from Paris into the habitable light of the South-West is effectively a journey into childhood. Around Angoulême—'my second South-West is not a region; it is simply a line, a journey completed'—some geographical feature will send the crucial signal: 'that I have crossed the threshold of my home and am entering the land of my childhood' (I 4 / 15).[18] The metaphorically homely space of the South-West contains the literal home, both the adopted village of Barthes's adulthood and the Bayonne in which he spent eight years of his childhood: 'My third South-West is even smaller: it is the city where I spent my childhood and then my school holidays as a teenager (Bayonne), it is the village to which I return every year, it is the road linking them together which I have taken so many times' (5 / 16). For the adult Barthes this local journey into town (on which he dwells by describing the four possible roads) is another metaphorical route into childhood: it precisely links the present place and time of writing—Barthes's village home, 17 July 1977—with his Bayonne past (3 / 13).

By the end of the essay, roads, routes, regions, and countries have developed a metaphorical dimension that conflates geographical space with time, and the South-West itself has become indistinguishable from childhood: 'In fact, there is no Country but that of childhood' (9 / 20). These words are the culmination of a general inflation of Proustian rhetoric that marks the final section of Barthes's essay, and that is structured as a defence against an imagined accusation of impressionistic and vaguely aesthetic subjectivism: 'But people, social structures, industry, commerce, problems . . .? You may be a mere resident, but don't you see any of that?' (7 / 18). Barthes's answer is that he does

---

[18] The signal is triggered by, for example, 'a pine grove to one side of the road, a palm tree in a courtyard, a distinctive height of the clouds that makes the ground as mobile as a human face' (I 4 / 15).

enter into these 'regions of reality', but in his own way. That way is with his body, and his body is his childhood, 'just as history made it'. History gave him a childhood which was provincial, southern, and bourgeois, three elements which have become indistinguishable for him so that the bourgeoisie has merged with the provinces, the provinces with Bayonne, and even 'the countryside' with the hinterland of Bayonne, a network of childhood excursions, visits, and narratives. Social realities have been refracted into memories that operate at the level of sensations:

> Thus, at the age when memory is formed, all I acquired of those important 'realities' was the *sensation* they afforded me: smells, moments of tiredness, sounds of voices, shopping errands, the changing light, all those aspects of reality which are somehow irresponsible and whose only meaning is that they will constitute, at a later stage, the memory of lost time. (7 / 18)[19]

Barthes gives two examples of the way in which these subjective residues of reality operate as gateways to the 'vast region' with which sociological and political analysis would be concerned. The first is his insistent memory of the smells of Little Bayonne, an old area of the city where 'all the objects of petty commerce mingled to form an inimitable smell: the rope for the *sandales* (we do not say "espadrilles" here) which were woven by elderly Basques, chocolate, Spanish olive oil, the stale air of the dark shops and narrow streets' (7–8 / 19). Since all this has now disappeared (the *sandales* have rubber soles, people buy their oil and chocolate in out-of-town supermarkets), smell becomes the key to a historical change in patterns of consumption.[20]

Barthes's second example is his personal access to a historically precise provincial bourgeois discourse, associated with the many

---

[19] Apart from this explicitly Proustian allusion, Barthes also refers to his belief in the words of Joubert: 'Do not express yourself as you feel, but as you remember' (I 7 / 18).

[20] There is a similar passage in *Roland Barthes by Roland Barthes*. Although Barthes begins by distancing himself from the privileged vehicles of Proust's involuntary memory, his stress on smell seems Proustian enough: 'Of what will never return, it is smells which come back to me. Thus it is with the odour of my Bayonne childhood: like the world encircled by the *mandala*, all of Bayonne is condensed into a composite odour: that of Petit-Bayonne' (136 / 139).

local families that he remembers from his childhood: 'I experienced their traditions, their rituals, their conversations, their way of life' (8 / 19). He describes this class as a professional bourgeoisie stuffed with prejudices but devoid of capital, so that there was a strange distortion between its reactionary ideology and its 'sometimes tragic' economic status (8 / 20). According to Barthes, such subtleties of social dialectics pass through the holes in the analytical sieve of sociology and politics, but are rescued by his corporeal memory: 'I experienced these subtleties—or these paradoxes of History—even if I could not formulate them: I was already "reading" the South-West, exploring the text that proceeds from the light of a landscape, from an oppressive day when the wind blowing from Spain made everything listless, to a specific social and provincial discourse' (8 / 20). This, then, is the way to read a region (*un pays*): to be aware of it through body and memory, 'through the memory of the body' (8 / 20). And this is why Barthes not only describes childhood as 'the royal road by which we know a region best', but also declares that this 'vestibule of knowledge and of analysis' is the assigned place of the writer: 'more conscious than competent, conscious of the very interstices of competence' (8–9 / 20).[21]

In a bracketed digression, Barthes claims that he has not retained any parallel physical 'impressions' of his Parisian childhood, marked as it was by material hardship and the 'severe abstraction of poverty' (7 / 18). In an illuminating radio broadcast about Proust and some of the key sites of the latter's life and novel, Barthes describes the mythical childhood village of Combray as an 'anti-Paris'.[22] The two poles of Proust's *A la*

---

[21] One could, of course, comment on Barthes's apparent lack of interest in the Basque language and in the region's separatist politics. One would not think, from his account of what is historically and discursively important in this region (a region that he tends to portray, moreover, as an archetypal French province), that its inhabitants are, at least indirectly, caught up in a literal language war.

[22] Three programmes were broadcast in 1978 under the general title *Un homme, une ville: Marcel Proust à Paris*, France-Culture (20 and 27 Oct., 3 Nov.), issued on three tapes by Cassettes Radio France. In the company of Jean Montalbetti, Barthes undertakes a journey around some of the key sites of Proust's life. The programmes are like outside broadcasts, whereby the discussions of Proust take place literally *sur place*, with authentic sound effects ranging from the cries of children at play to roaring traffic. The focus is supposed to be on settings and locations rather than

recherche du temps perdu (Parisian and provincial) take on significance in opposition to each other, so that Combray becomes a microcosm of *la province* (the entirety of provincial France in so far as it is not Paris) which is incarnated in 'its atmosphere, its daily rhythms, its language, its social and behavioural codes'. Barthes claims that it is French history itself which speaks through this fundamental opposition, common to all the great nineteenth-century novels written in the wake of Napoleonic centralization. Three days before writing his essay on the South-West, Barthes observed in his 'diary' that he seemed to learn more about France on a single circuit of his village than during weeks of life in Paris: 'An illusion perhaps? The *realist* illusion? The provincial world of countryside and village has traditionally provided the raw material of realism. In the nineteenth-century, to be a writer meant to write about the provinces from Paris. The distance makes *everything meaningful*' (RL 363 / 403).[23] Did the post-1975 Barthes start writing about the South-West so as to project himself as a writer in this tradition?[24]

When 'The Light of the South-West' was first published in *L'Humanité*, the communist daily newspaper, it was illustrated

biography. Despite the stress on Paris in the title of the series, the second programme is devoted to a pilgrimage to the anti-Paris of Illiers, the small village near Chartres whose name was officially changed to Illiers-Combray in homage to its mythical literary incarnation.

[23] The diary reproduced two years later in 'Deliberation' (first published in *Tel Quel* in 1979, RL 359–73 / 399–413) covers the period 13 July to 13 Aug. 1977. 'The Light of the South-West' opens with a reference to the day on which Barthes is writing (17 July). His diary entry for 17 July refers to the beautiful weather and the fact that it is Sunday, but there is no other useful overlap as such. Since the second diary extract concerns an evening in Paris (367–8 / 408–9), the two extracts could be seen as establishing contrasting provincial and Parisian poles, just as 'Paris Evenings', of which the setting is basically Paris, builds in a provincial contrast by recording a brief visit to Urt. For further comments on the relationship between the two texts, see Ch. 10.

[24] See Jean-Marie Planès, 'Il n'est pays que de l'enfance', *Magazine littéraire*, 314 (1993), 33–8, on the literary nature of Barthes's late assumption of nostalgia for childhood and his stress on a provincial home. The theme of Barthes as a provincial writer is also discussed by Alain Buisine in 'Barthes et les noms', in Pierre Bonnefis and Alain Buisine (eds.), *La Scène capitale* (Lille, Presses universitaires de Lille, 1981), 71–103. Buisine alludes to what he ironically calls Barthes's *provinsèmes* (94) and to Barthes's 'portrait of the literary critic *en provincial*' (96). This code of the provincial writer is one to which Barthes himself alludes with conscious irony.

by several photographs from *Roland Barthes by Roland Barthes*. No doubt it was Barthes's picture gallery of a provincial childhood that had provoked the invitation to contribute to a series of essays by 'regional' writers, and Barthes's generally Proustian approach was entirely predictable. Yet Barthes's eloquent defence of this approach—his insistence on its indirect inscription of history—takes on extra significance in the context of the specifically politicized readership of *L'Humanité*. Barthes, who always thought of *A la recherche* as a cosmogony, would doubtless describe Proust's *Combray* as a vestibule in itself of socio-historical knowledge, not least because he also describes the opposition between Combray and Paris in class terms—the former petty bourgeois, the latter worldly, upper middle class, or aristocratic.

Barthes seems keen to draw attention to the bourgeois status of his paternal grandparents, and to defend his right, as a would-be utopian writer, to a bourgeois class sensibility.[25] Two passages of *Roland Barthes* are especially relevant to Barthes's foregrounding of this sensibility. The first is the discussion (already referred to) of what Barthes chooses to call migraines. Despite admitting that the term is technically inaccurate for what are simply headaches, he claims that it is 'socially accurate'. This is because migraines (the mythical attribute of both 'bourgeois women' and 'men of letters') are a product of *class*: 'whoever heard of a member of the proletariat or a shopkeeper having migraines? Social division passes through my body: my body itself is social' (*RB* 124 / 128).[26] The second passage contains Barthes's account (already referred to in

---

[25] Perhaps to the extent of slightly misrepresenting his social class by projecting himself into this tradition? If Barthes's family status was distinctly marginal, this was not only because his father was killed in the First World War. Unlike Proust's father, who left behind his petty bourgeois background in order to study medicine in Paris (the first of his family to leave the provinces), Barthes's father left Bayonne to become an ordinary sailor in the merchant navy (see Calvet, *Roland Barthes*: 'Louis Barthes had the minimum schooling and began a career at sea at a very young age' (8)). If Michael Moriarty, for example, describes a Barthes who occupies the normal class position of the writer ('bourgeois: the armed forces, the professions'), this is certainly because the photographs in *Roland Barthes by Roland Barthes* 'tell a story of a childhood in a respectable bourgeois family' (Moriarty, *Roland Barthes*, 209 and 173).

[26] Of course the member of the proletariat and the shopkeeper, unlike the socially self-conscious Barthes, are perfectly likely to suffer from genuine migraines.

Chapter 7) of a conversation with the village baker about the weather. To her comment on the warm weather he adds his own on the beauty of the light. From her lack of response he concludes that to 'see' the light in this way is to betray a particular class origin, and that there is 'nothing so cultural as the atmosphere, nothing so ideological as the weather' (*RB* 176 / 178). Yet Barthes's physical and aesthetic sensitivity to the light is the veritable key to his utopian reading of the South-West, which would not be the same reading without it. In short, the light which utopia throws upon this world (which has its own language, history, economy, etc.) is an avowedly partial one—the baker's memories of the South-West, and her 'reading' of the region, might well be somewhat different. Indeed, if Barthes proceeds as he does, taking as his point of departure an engagement with reality that is culturally and ideologically marked as 'bourgeois', this is perhaps, paradoxically, *because* he is writing for *L'Humanité*. This might explain his single *clin d'œil* in the direction of his readership—it so happens that the only *méridionalisme* that still marks his speech is a distinctive pronunciation of the word socialism: 'I say "socializme" rather than "socialissme" (who knows, perhaps that makes for two different socialisms?)' (*I* 4 / 15).

In May 1977 Barthes published a review of Jean Daniel's autobiographical *Le Refuge et la source*. The positions worked out in this review undoubtedly feed into Barthes's essay on the South-West, written just two months later, though they also throw retrospective light on his conception both of the photo section and of the section of *anamneses* in *Roland Barthes by Roland Barthes*. Daniel, who is perhaps best known as editor of *Le Nouvel Observateur* (in which Barthes's review appeared), records in his book memories of his childhood in French Algeria. In the first part of his review, Barthes describes his own almost passionate identification—'to hell with objective reviews'—with this 'book of inflections', inflections which he differentiates from the methodical recall at the origins of the Proustian stream.[27] Like Daniel, he claims, he too is occasionally

---

[27] Barthes, 'Préface à *Le Refuge et la source* de Jean Daniel', OC iii. 701–2, quotations easily locatable. For a very interesting discussion of the role of memory in autobiographical writing see Michael Sheringham, 'The Otherness of Memory', Ch.

seized by a sudden desire 'to remember', whereby the deliberate recall of 'scenes, smells, tastes, lights, faces' has a voluptuous, fantasmatic, and enigmatic dimension, in that its subject matter is reality and its temporal referent the past. Barthes stresses that there is no objective similarity between his own childhood and Daniel's upbringing in a large family, at a different point in time, in an entirely different country: 'it is not the same history'.[28] It is, however, the same 'grain of memory', indeed memory reduced to its grain, to the 'subtle sensations of which the narrative is simply the vehicle, . . . for to remember passionately is not to recollect a succession of events but to summon up inflections'.[29] As examples of these inflections Barthes lists 'the heat, food, the burning-hot balcony, the lay-out of the family apartment, the mother's delicacy, the father's face, the comings and goings of the brothers and sisters, the recollection of a teacher, or that of an emotion or fear'. What he has identified here, though he does not use the word, is clearly the same novelistic utopian discourse best exemplified in the undeveloped 'incidents' of Loti's *Aziyadé*.[30]

Barthes identifies two other ways in which Daniel's memories of childhood are utopian, and it is these that are especially relevant here. One is the very fact that someone whose normal discourse is political commentary should have chosen to write a book which is, apparently, not political at all. Barthes, of

---

9 of *French Autobiography: Devices and Desires* (Oxford, Clarendon Press, 1994), 288–326. Sheringham writes, for instance, of the commonplace manœuvre of setting one's own particular sort of memory against an inferior counterpart (289).

[28] Barthes does not mention the specifically Algerian context of Daniel's childhood (he uses the vague word *contrée* when alluding to this), so that one might suspect him of choosing to read it as a traditional (French) provincial childhood despite this acknowledgement of many differences. Nor does he specifically mention Daniel's Jewish background, despite the pages which Daniel devotes to his childhood discovery of his specific 'difference'. See Jean Daniel, *Le Refuge et la source* (Paris, Grasset & Fasquelle, 1977).

[29] The metaphor of the grain of memory attributes a substance to recollections, which is arguably unlike Platonic *anamnesis* ('properly speaking the recollection of eternal forms'). See Sheringham, *French Autobiography*, 289.

[30] See Ch. 7. Barthes describes *anamnesis* in a similar way in *A Lover's Discourse* as recollecting 'insignificant features which are not in any way dramatic, as if I remembered time itself and only time: it is a smell without a material basis, a grain of memory, a simple fragrance; something like pure expenditure which only Japanese haiku has been capable of articulating without recuperating it into any destiny' (*LD* 216 / 257).

course, wants to argue that this atypical text, in its enigmatic entirety, is *indirectly* political. Like Bologna stone, giving out at night the light rays absorbed during the day, it radiates something 'which has to do with that utopian supplement which occasionally nourishes political reflexion, once it no longer takes the arrogant analysis of reality as its sole aim'. Barthes assembles a series of qualities in an attempt to explain the ethical dimension of Daniel's writing (nobility, simplicity, precision, tenderness, humour), equating it finally with 'an outbreak of goodness' (*une crise de bonté*) that suspends 'fear': 'the fear of finding ourselves suffocated and crushed by thinking machines, of which, precisely, political discourse is so often an example.' To underline his point Barthes ends with a curious challenge: 'does one think of Saint-Just or Lenin as having had childhoods?' The anticipated negative answer highlights the indirectly political value of Jean Daniel's 'supplement-book' which inflects with its values his other (more familiar) political discourse: 'it is his particular way of making that work and that struggle fraternal.'

Barthes's other general point places Daniel's attachment to his childhood in a rather different utopian context. He suggests that he has written about it in such a way as to place childhood 'outside of time'. Though anchored in a specific society that he has reconstituted in some detail, on another level it appears *free* ('freed from all determinations'): 'it is a temporal utopia, a "uchronia" ', which means that it is an 'age' in the mythical sense of the word. Barthes circles somewhat enigmatically around his perception that a utopia is at stake here, expressing it in different ways, and clearly wishing to generalize Daniel's case. He alights finally upon the idea that the very memory of childhood is integral to what it means to be human, that, however childhood may actually have been lived (however bored we may have been), memory will inject a utopian dimension: 'childhood (by what mysterious inversion?) offers us the fragmented image of a sovereign good, because in childhood I am still close to the mother and because my life stretches infinitely ahead—in other words, I am immortal. Thus, whenever I superimpose the memory of childhood upon my adult life, something is set in motion within me, and that something is the specifically human meaning of utopia.'

'Does one think of Roland Barthes as having had a childhood?' It is perhaps obvious that I have been spiralling my way backwards in order to arrive at the photo section of *Roland Barthes by Roland Barthes*. This is because the occasional texts written in the wake of *Roland Barthes* provide an interpretative framework (for Barthes as well as his readers) for what might have been at stake, for an adult writer and intellectual, in the projection of a provincial childhood. The South-West of the photo section, like Proust's Combray, quite simply *is* Barthes's childhood. At the same time, the particularity of this Bayonne childhood is the vehicle for more general meanings relating to time and space. As such, it is precisely the utopian supplement (the gateway or lobby) to the more political and theoretical preoccupations around which the later fragments of *Roland Barthes by Roland Barthes* are insistently woven.

To conclude this chapter, therefore, I shall look at the captions or brief commentaries which accompany four of Barthes's chosen photographs, each of which elaborates a specifically utopian space. The first is Bayonne itself: 'Bayonne, Bayonne, the perfect city: built on a river, ventilated with sonorous suburbs (Mouserolles, Marrac, Lachepaillet, Beyris), and yet a city closed in on itself, a novelistic city: Proust, Balzac, Plassans' (*RB* 6 / 8). Like so many of Barthes's utopian cosmogonies Bayonne is self-contained but not claustrophobic, in that it is made airy by the sonorous signifiers of its outlying districts. Despite rubbing shoulders with Balzac and Zola, it is Proust whose presence dominates here, as the already Proustian theme of place names give way to an overview of the significance for Barthes of Bayonne: 'Primordial imaginary of childhood: the Provinces as spectacle, History as odour, the bourgeoisie as discourse.'[31]

Barthes's second utopian space is contained within the first: the house and garden of his paternal grandparents on the Allées Paulmy in Bayonne. The reader must consult the table of

---

[31] See, too, Barthes's allusion to his grandmother's obsession with worldly gossip, which he doubtless includes so as to be able to comment: 'for the next episode, see Proust' (13 / 16). Similarly, his grandmother supposedly spends much time dwelling on the names of the local bourgeoisie, and thereby takes her place in 'Proper nouns', another Proustian fragment (*RB* 50 / 55).

illustrations at the end of the book to realize that this is not Barthes's actual childhood home, and to establish that he and his mother lived, in a manner certainly less bourgeois, in the above-mentioned suburb of Marrac. Nevertheless, Barthes presumably visited his grandparents often and, after moving to Paris in 1924, would return to Bayonne and stay at their house there for most of his school holidays. Did these visits as an older child absorb the earlier memories of Marrac, or was Barthes drawn to the parallel of Combray as the site of ritual school-holiday visits to the paternal grandparents (for both Proust and his fictional narrator)? Did Barthes exaggerate the bourgeois lifestyle of his Bayonne childhood in order to mislead his readers, or was this very exaggeration in itself a Proustian gesture? In the radio broadcast from Illiers-Combray to which I have already referred, Barthes dwells on the paucity of the setting, so much smaller and duller than its mythical literary avatar. For example, the epic and elaborately prepared meals lead readers of *Combray* to imagine a dining room of vast and noble proportions, whereas the dining room and kitchen that inspired them are actually tiny and cramped, like the house in general, which resembles a small suburban *pavillon*. Barthes claims not to be disappointed by the contrast between Combray, one of the great mythical sites of world literature, and Illiers, a very ordinary French village of limited suggestive potential. The contrast confirms for him the 'quite extraordinary power of literature, of writing', in that the fictitious Combray remains 'an absolutely fabulous place from the point of view of its fantasmatically precise descriptions'.[32]

No such pilgrimage can be made to the house of Barthes's paternal grandparents since it no longer exists—swept away, as Barthes himself comments, by 'Bayonne real estate'. It is therefore impossible to explore the degree of literary enhancement in his description: ' "This house was a real ecological marvel: not very big, standing on one side of an extensive garden, with mellow, faded grey shutters that made it look like a wooden toy. On the one hand it was like a simple chalet, on the other it was full of doors, ground-level windows, extra staircases, like a *château* in a novel" ' (*RB* 8 / 10). The close-up

---

[32] *Un homme, une ville: Marcel Proust à Paris*, tape 2.

photograph of one side of the house is indeed a mass of doors, shutters, and low windows (9 / 11), while the entire description of the house and garden is contained within quotation marks.[33] In yet another example of the 'complex proportions' that emerge from Barthes's shifting perceptions of the South-West, the garden itself is subdivided into three adjacent but symbolically differentiated spaces—'to cross the boundary of each space was a significant action' (8 / 10)—each of which is endowed with its own function and qualities. The 'worldly garden' was the social antechamber to the house itself and was typically traversed, with lengthy pauses, when visiting local 'ladies' were accompanied to the gate. The second garden ('in front of the house itself') was more like an extension of living space with its lawns, paths, flowers, shrubs, and culinary herbs: 'it was here, in the summer, that the ladies of the B. family, undaunted by the mosquitoes, would install themselves in garden chairs with their elaborate knitting.' The third and most distant garden was vaguely defined and only intermittently cultivated with vegetables which required no attention: 'you rarely went there, and then only down the centre path.' With this conceptualization of three contrasting human spaces, the grandparents' garden becomes the springboard of Barthes's all-embracing utopian imagination: 'The worldly, the domestic, the wild: is this not the very tripartition of social desire? From this Bayonne garden I pass on without surprise to the novelistic and utopian spaces of Jules Verne and Fourier' (8 / 10).

On the next page we are also informed that the third, unfrequented garden was the site, for Barthes, of early episodes of sexual experimentation (10 / 12). Sexuality then migrates to Barthes's description of the riverside gardens bordering the Adour, though the sexuality involved here, to judge by the lexical echoes, is a projection of the adult Barthes's elaborations

---

[33] This, presumably, is one of Barthes's allusions to the discourse of dictation, for he claims to have placed implicit inverted commas around some of his attempts at the genre: 'The natural discourse of memory is school discourse, the discourse of dictation. Instead of completely foreclosing this mode of expression, I decided to assume it from time to time, to give myself a dictation or the subject of a composition. As if I myself were providing some future selected extract for a schools' anthology' ('Twenty Key Words for Roland Barthes' [1975], GV 205–32: 210 / 194–220: 199).

of Text as a space of *déshérence*, drift, and erotic encounters: 'Coming home in the evening, a frequent detour through the *Allées marines* alongside the River Adour; tall trees, boats lying idle (*en déshérence*), people strolling around in seemingly haphazard fashion, the drift (*la dérive*) of boredom: it was the sexuality of public gardens that lurked here' (17 / 21). This third example of a utopian space is clearly intended to be read alongside the fourth—a photograph of Barthes's village house at Urt, the caption to which contains a specific allusion to a suspension of sexuality (with an implied coupling of sexuality and aggression): 'The sheer delight of these mornings in U.: the sun, the house, the roses, silence, music, coffee, work, a quietism undisturbed by sexuality, an absence of all conflict' (26 / 30). Once again the caption is enclosed in quotation marks to be explained, perhaps, by its similarity with part of the final fragment of the whole text: 'today, 6 August, in the country, it's the morning of a splendid day: sun, warmth, flowers, silence, calm, radiance. Nothing lurks here, neither desire nor aggression' (180 / 182). Here, too, the prowling sexuality of the riverside gardens of Barthes's adolescence has been dissolved or suspended.

The final lines of Barthes's text were apparently the first to be written, since they are immediately followed by the dates between which the whole book was composed: '6 August 1973–3 September 1974'. Logically, the peace of the countryside gives way to the calm pleasures of anticipated work ('only work awaits'), and it is the photograph of Barthes's provincial home, placed early on in the text, which illustrates this privileged moment.[34] At the same time the photo inscribes the initial scene of writing, paradoxically also its endpoint, of this most self-conscious of texts. But why has a photograph of the adult Barthes's house at Urt—referred to in both text and table of illustrations as 'U'—been placed in the middle of the scenes and spaces of his Bayonne childhood? Chronologically, this picture is slipped into a sequence of photographs running from

---

[34] 'The country is solitude', says Barthes, opposing it to the atmosphere and bustle of a Parisian café: 'The ideal is to arrive in the country with a clear month or two ahead, but with some intellectual work already well in hand, so that one could work on it methodically like a civil servant or a roadmender' (*GV* 221–2 / 209).

Barthes's earliest childhood to his adolescence; topographically, it is inserted between a photo of Barthes in Marrac in 1923, and a radiant family photo of mother and two sons in 1932 on the beach at Bicarosse in the Landes. It is no wonder that the odd hasty reader seems to have thought that Urt was Barthes's childhood home.[35]

Barthes appears to have short-circuited the 18 kilometres and several decades that separate his regular but occasional periods of residence in Urt from his childhood in Bayonne, a childhood which was itself divided between infancy in Marrac and the later years of school-holiday visits to the Allées Paulmy. For a reader not already familiar with his biography, the varieties of habitation (visits, temporary residence, permanent abode), which Barthes tends to emphasize and to find interesting in other texts, are not clearly differentiated. All, of course, are subsumed into the habitable light of the South-West, the key to a desire for habitation which is invariably conflated, in Barthes's writing, with nostalgia for the familiarity, comfort, and security of the maternal body. Perhaps the most interesting of these conflations—fostered by Barthes for whatever reason—is that which confuses the status of the bourgeois grandparental house on the Allées Paulmy with the completely unspecified accommodation that sheltered Barthes and his mother in Marrac. Only once, in the *anamnesis* that recalls their Sunday evening return by tram from visits to the grandparents, are the two childhood homes clearly differentiated in the text: 'We would eat our supper of broth and toast in the bedroom, by the fire' (*RB* 107 / 111). *Roland Barthes by Roland Barthes* contains, in fact, just three photographs of Marrac. Two of these are taken out of doors on visibly rough ground, and are surely linked in the text by Barthes's anecdote 'A Childhood Memory'. Marrac, Barthes recalls, was full of building sites in which the local children used to play; one day he was unable to follow the other children who had all managed to climb out of a deep hole in the

---

[35] An article by James Williams is the only example that I have to hand, though I feel that I have encountered others. Williams refers to the photo of Barthes in his mother's arms at Marrac as an 'emblem of U.(rt) and its diffuse, U.(raninan) "sexualité enfantine" ' ('The Moment of Truth: Roland Barthes, "Soirées de Paris" and the Real', *Neophilologus*, 79 (1995), 33–51: 43).

ground: 'Then I saw my mother running towards me; she pulled me out of there and carried me far away from the children—joined in with me against them' (122 / 125). One photograph shows Barthes, aged 7 or 8, sitting alone on rough ground with a half-built house in the background (24 / 28); one positioned earlier in the text ('The Demand for Love'), shows Barthes at the same age and in identical clothing, clasped cheek-to-cheek in his mother's arms (5 / 7).

Is this the mythical period of childhood that Barthes will later project into Jean Daniel's autobiography, a childhood that is utopian because, in the words already quoted, 'I am still close to the mother, and because my life stretches infinitely ahead—in other words, I am immortal'? If Marrac is in any sense a utopian space it does not seem to be an especially happy one. In the third photograph of Marrac (the only interior), a 3- or 4-year-old Barthes stands by a child's tiny chair with an unfathomable expression of distress on his face: 'in the child, I see the dark underside of myself openly displayed on the body: boredom, vulnerability, a tendency to fits of despair (fortunately plural), inner emotions, cut off, unfortunately for me, from all hope of expression' (26). Yet Barthes makes a curiously positive comment on what he reads in this photo: 'Of the past, it is my childhood which most fascinates me; it alone, when I contemplate it, does not make me regret the passage of time. For it is not the irreversible that I discover in my childhood, it is the irreducible: everything which is still in me, by fits and starts' (22–3 / 26–7).[36] Barthes has represented here, in the isolated maternal space of Marrac, the irreducible affective kernel of his personality. This is not a lost childhood paradise, but the utopian childhood that he still carries within him. And utopia, for Barthes, was never consistently a place of pleasure and happiness.

In Chapter 1, in my discussion of essays written in the 1950s, I suggested that Barthes could be seen to hesitate over the best way to inject a utopian element into the alienated spaces of the French theatre and of everyday French life. I argued that his

---

[36] The English translation has laid out the captions and photos on 22–3 in a rather confusing way. Contrary to appearances, it is obviously the case that the caption on 22 belongs with the photograph on 23.

commitment to a Marxist analysis of social division and liberation was accompanied by a positive investment in the stark existential universe of Greek tragedy. Barthes's belief in the utopian potential of the tragic stage underpinned a nostalgia for ethical and metaphysical complexity occasionally detected in *Mythologies*. Thus a darker side of utopia was already adumbrated in some of Barthes's earliest writing, in particular where the largely metaphorical space of the stage intersected with time. In the mid- and late 1970s, Barthes conflates the real space of south-western France with the metaphorical space of his childhood. It is perhaps this return to the past which accounts for the resurfacing of a metaphysical dimension whereby Barthes reads in Boudinet's Georgic rural scenes an invitation to 'philosophize', or gives a Pascalian inflection to his commentary on a nineteenth-century photograph of the Alhambra. If a fantasmatic desire to inhabit the latter arouses in Barthes an acute sense of his past and his future, it is not, of course, only his own relationship to mortality that is represented in the sequence of photographs of Marrac. According to Barthes in 1953, tragic time, once consumed, will leave a bare place 'where something has happened for ever' (*OC* i. 204). The 1970s texts explored in this chapter bear the trace of the knowledge that something irremediable is indeed about to happen. No utopian writer can entirely set aside the problem of death, and my last chapter will explore Barthes's own attempts to surmount through writing what Ernst Bloch has memorably called 'the harshest' and 'the strongest non-utopia'.[37] It is a non-utopia figured, both metaphorically and literally, by the death of the mother.

[37] Bloch, *The Principle of Hope*, iii. 1101 and 1103.

10
Maternal Space

Schubert lost his mother at fifteen; two years later his first great lied, *Gretchen at the Spinning Wheel*, spoke of tumultuous absence, of hallucinatory return.[1]

IN *Beyond the Pleasure Principle*, the to-and-fro movement that marks Freud's speculations on life and death is initiated by the now mythical anecdote of the *fort/da*—a young child teaches himself mental control over his mother's absences in what turns out to have been a literal rehearsal for her early death.[2] Towards the end of his writing career, Barthes was to take a similar step beyond the pleasure principle. Is what has come to be known as 'late Barthes' a period, the inception of which can be dated from the death of Barthes's mother in October 1977?[3] Is it rather a mode, where personal sorrow takes its place within a general preoccupation with emotion—abandonment, love, and pity—which crystallizes around Barthes's formulation of the photographic *punctum* and his escalating identification with Proust, but which had already underwritten his interest in the figures of the lover's discourse, and in the Romantic music of Schubert and Schumann? This is utopia in a different register from that of the hedonistic textual spaces explored in some earlier chapters, with their positive and unproblematic inscriptions of homosexual desire. Chronologically, however, the two modes overlap, so that the melancholic *Camera Lucida* was actually written in 1979, the year in which Barthes published his relaxed preface to *Tricks* and gave an interview on *Libération*'s personal column.[4]

---

[1] Barthes, 'The Romantic Song', *RF* 286–98: 289 / 253–8: 255, first broadcast on French radio (France-Culture, 12 Mar. 1976).

[2] Freud, *Beyond the Pleasure Principle* [1920], trans. James Strachey, *The Pelican Freud Library*, xi. 269–338, especially 283–6.

[3] The expression 'late Barthes' probably derives from an article by Tzvetan Todorov, 'Le Dernier Barthes', *Poétique*, 47 (Sept. 1981), 323–7.

[4] These two texts are discussed in Ch. 8.

In September 1979 Barthes also published 'Deliberation', an essay which purported to reflect on the worth of the private diary as a publishable literary form.[5] At the same time, this text tested the potential of a particular *content*, in that the sample diary entries prefigure those—dated August and September 1979—posthumously published by François Wahl as 'Paris Evenings'. In the latter, allusions to Barthes's continued despair at the loss of his mother intermingle with representations of a lifestyle in which casual encounters with homosexual prostitutes, as well as relationships with male friends, form a significant element. The conventional form of the literary diary is thus the final vehicle of Barthes's attempt to embody the affective space which underlies all of his late work—a single space into which homosexual desire and mourning for the mother are subsumed.

The first of the diaries included in 'Deliberation' records a month at Urt (13 July to 13 August), the summer before the death of Barthes's mother in October 1977. From the first entry, Barthes's panic in the face of this approaching separation is a recurrent theme. The second diary is a single entry dated 25 April 1979, some eighteen months after his mother's death, and appears to be a prototype for the staged nightly wanderings of Barthes's 'Paris Evenings'.[6] Indeed this first 'Futile Evening' of 25 April 1979 (reproduced in 'Deliberation') is suspiciously similar to that of 14 September 1979 (recorded in 'Paris Evenings'), not least because both actually begin with the words 'Futile Evening' (*Vaine Soirée*, literally either a futile or a fruitless evening).[7] Both portray Barthes setting out on a cold and wet evening to a bleak area of Paris, in both he escapes from

---

[5] *RL* 359–73 / 399–413, first published in *Tel Quel*.
[6] Although it records an evening in Paris, it also includes a brief reference to Urt through Barthes's ambivalent fantasy of making it his permanent home. Wandering along the Quai de la Messagerie, Barthes notices plants for sale and garden herbs in pots: 'I saw myself (with a mixture of longing and horror) buying up a stock before returning to U., where I would settle for good, only ever coming to Paris for "business" and shopping' (*RL* 368 / 409).
[7] *RL* 367 / 408; *I* 70 / 111. It is for this reason that I assume 'Vaines Soirées' to be Barthes's intended title for this text, and 'Soirées de Paris' an editorial intervention. The status of the title is unclear in Wahl's preface to *Incidents* (7–10), which does however quote Barthes's own apparent use of it in a note at the end of his manuscript: 'Arrêté ici (22 sept. 79) les Vaines Soirées' (9, n. 3). (Wahl's preface has not been included in the English translation.)

the social chore of a private view of an exhibition only to launch himself into a depressing quest for a decent film, this simply to fill in the time before he can return, tired and cold, unwell or afraid that he soon will be, to his home territory, the Café de Flore. If the entry in 'Paris Evenings' records his lack of response to the propositions of 'Lucien Naise' and, later, due to tiredness and lethargy, to two possible homosexual encounters, the entry in 'Deliberation' (only slightly more discreet) sums up his bad day by its failure to provide him with a single face over which to fantasize. The similarity in the detail and structure of these two entries suggests, therefore, that neither is a close factual recording of an evening in Barthes's life. Rather, both strike me as literary exercises within Barthes's general project of linking his life and his writing in some new way.

If Wahl's editorial juxtaposition of 'Paris Evenings' with the Moroccan 'Incidents' foregrounds their homosexual content, his inclusion in *Incidents* of 'The Light of the South-West' highlights the parallel theme of maternal space. In fact, Barthes wrote his essay for *L'Humanité* on Sunday, 17 July 1977, during the period covered by the first set of diary entries reproduced in 'Deliberation'. This means that the unstated context of Barthes's celebration of the 'habitable' South-Western light—a repository of childhood memories and comfort—is actually his mother's approaching death.[8] Moments of panic ('Sombre thoughts, waves of anxiety and anguish: I foresee the death of the one I dearly love, I lose my head, etc.' (*RL* 362 / 402)) are interwoven in Barthes's diary with bursts of euphoria which are precisely attributed to the synaesthetic qualities of the light: 'The window is wide open, the grey day has lifted now. I experience a euphoric sensation of floating: everything is melting, airy, *drinkable* (I drink the air, the weather, the garden)' (365 / 406).[9] The fine Sunday morning

---

[8] See my analysis of this essay in Ch. 9.
[9] On the previous day Barthes had written: '*Moods*, in the strong, Schumannian sense: an incoherent succession of contradictory outbursts: waves of anxiety, imaginings of the worst, and untimely moments of euphoria. This morning, in the midst of Worry, a moment of pure happiness: the weather (very fine, not at all heavy), the music (Haydn), coffee, a cigar, a good pen, household noises (the capriciousness of the human subject: its inconsequential behaviour is terrifying, exhausting)' (*RL* 365 / 405).

weather that introduces the *Humanité* essay had in fact set in on the previous day: 'After several overcast days, another fine morning: radiance and fragility of the atmosphere: like fresh, shimmering silk. This blank moment (devoid of meaning) induces a feeling of well-being: clearly, life is worth living' (363–4 / 404). This moment of realization, at once profound and naïve, enters into dialogue with Barthes's description of the beautiful but desolate evening at Urt (on a two- or three-day visit at the end of August 1979) which briefly interrupts the insistent rhythm of his more worldly 'Paris Evenings'. Indeed it is the light that leads Barthes's brother and sister-in-law to force him into an after-dinner walk, determined as they are that he should not miss such a lovely evening: 'The late twilight was extraordinarily beautiful, so perfect that the effect was almost strange: a fleecy, airy grey, not at all melancholy' (*I* 60 / 89). Elements of a pastoral utopia—banks of mist on the far side of the River Adour, a golden half-moon, a peaceful yet inhabited rural scene—build up in this case to a climax of self-conscious, and would-be literary, sorrow:

Crickets chirping, *as in the old days*: nobility, peace. My heart swelled with sadness, with something like despair: I thought about mother, about the cemetery where she was lying not far away, about 'Life'. I experienced this romantic swelling as a value and felt sad that I could never express it, 'my worth always greater than what I write' (theme of my lecture course). (60 / 89–90)

The 'life' that Barthes thinks about here is no longer a life that is self-evidently worth living, while the light, for all its beauty, is no longer the mediator of a longing to inhabit. Confronting all the pain of Urt without his mother (an absence all the more sharply reinforced by the proximity of her grave in the local cemetery), Barthes describes himself as homeless and ill at ease in the world: 'in despair too at never feeling comfortable either in Paris, or here, or when I'm away: no real refuge' (60 / 90).

In a sort of reversal of the comfort and security called up by Barthes's reading of Charles Clifford's photograph of the Alhambra, the world has lost the *heimlich* qualities associated with the mother.[10] It has acquired instead the vaguely sinister qualities exemplified by the unfamiliar *quartiers* of Paris into

[10] See the opening of Ch. 9.

which Barthes constantly strays—'struck by the depressing atmosphere of this area' (52 / 75); 'at the Museum of Modern Art (a bleak district)' (70 / 111)—and by the frequently unpleasant weather ('a chilly wind' (52 / 74), 'a wet, unpleasant wind' (70 / 111)). It is the latter that causes Barthes, on the quintessential 'futile evening' of 14 September, to sally forth in a new and badly fitting blouson, the comic epitome of *unheimlichkeit*: 'I can't move properly in it, the sleeves are too long and there's no inside pocket, I feel as if I'm bulging with objects, in danger of losing them at any moment—like the time I lost my cigar case because of this same blouson; from the outset, I am ill at ease with this Evening' (70 / 111). In contrast to the comfortable bodily envelope of the light of Urt, Barthes's blouson acts as a leitmotif punctuating his dismal evening ('The mere thought of having to go to the opening of Pinter's *No Man's Land* makes me miserable in advance—perhaps it's because of my blouson'; 'disconcerted at the idea of waiting in a first-night audience, with my blouson' (71 / 112)). That the Paris of 'Paris Evenings' is Paris without the mother is made explicit in the most painful moment of the text. Returning by car from an evening out with 'FW and Severo', Barthes notes that the streets are full of young men. He would like to be dropped off to wander around on his own, but is held back by the superego of habit, since his normal practice in this particular company is to be dropped at home: 'Returning alone, through a bizarre oversight which distressed me, I climbed the stairs and inadvertently went past my own floor, as if I had been coming home to our apartment on the fifth floor, as in the old days when mother would be waiting up for me' (65 / 97).

Yet it would be a mistake (a retrospective illusion) to imagine that all of the text of 'Paris Evenings' is marked by a mood of failure and depression. In the opening sequence of entries Barthes records moments of physical and mental well-being ('I felt relaxed in the company of friends' (53 / 75); 'I'm in a good mood, glad that all that I have to do is take myself home and climb into bed' (57 / 83)), of friendship and intellectual exchange ('a moment of pleasure that made the evening' (55 / 80); 'euphoria, ideas, self-confidence, and enthusiasm' (58 / 86)), while bedtime comfort is provided, in four consecutive entries, by Chateaubriand's *Mémoires d'outre-tombe*, 'the real book' (55 / 80). Even the bizarre episode of being stood up by a prostitute whom he had paid in advance is taken stoically, and turned to good account ('since mere eye contact and an exchange of words arouses me, this was the pleasure for which I had paid' (59 / 87)).

Structurally, it would seem to be the brief visit to Urt (one-third of the way through the text) which introduces a mood of unease, with the sad *lapsus* of walking past his own landing occurring three days later. The evening of Barthes's return from Urt is typical of the more 'futile' pattern that sets in from this point. Leaving what he snobbishly implies was a rather cheap and nasty dinner party ('supermarket bread in a Cellophane wrapper, wine from a carafe' (61 / 91)), Barthes responds to the earlier verbal overtures of a fellow guest. The response to his own physical advances is very half-hearted, when he gets home ('tired and edgy') the music on the radio is unbearable, and the personal columns in '*Libé*' and the '*Nouvel Obs*' (which he reads in bed) contain 'nothing for anyone "old" ' (61 / 92). The final diary entry of the text (17 September), in which Barthes is politely but unambiguously rejected by Olivier G. (with whom he fancies himself to be in love), leads to a moment of despair similar to that occasioned by his sense of loss at Urt: 'I was overcome by something like despair, I felt like crying' (73 / 115). It is a despair which underpins Barthes's decision to renounce all hope of a successful relationship not only with Olivier G., but also with all other young men of his age. It is suddenly apparent to Barthes that his life is a sad one, that he is basically bored, and that he must rid himself of the distraction of wanting to be in love with all these young men. But what, he asks, will he put in its place: 'What would I do when I go out? . . . What will the spectacle of the world mean to me?' (73 / 116).

Barthes includes in his diary entry for 2 September an account of the plane journey from the South-West back to Paris. Amidst the irritating chaos of a packed and noisy plane, he sits motionless without unfastening his seatbelt: 'I read a bit of Pascal's *Pensées*, recognizing in the "wretchedness of man" all of my sadness, my "heavy heart" (*cœur gros*) at U. without Mother. (All this truly impossible to write: when I think of Pascal's austere and taut style)' (61 / 91). This is the first of four references to reading Pascal; in the three that follow, Barthes portrays himself reading the *Pensées* at the worldly centre of his home *quartier* of Saint-Germain-des-Prés—the Café de Flore. On one of these occasions (the day after his sad return from Urt) Barthes looks up from the *Pensées* to notice 'Renaud C.' (Camus) passing by and remarks that he cannot think of a 'less metaphysical being' (62 / 93). The implied negative judgement suggests that the value system of 'late Barthes' is no longer in line with the unproblematic world-view celebrated in Barthes's preface to *Tricks*—what is valuable, and what needs somehow to be written, is the misery of 'U. without Mother', a world as wretched and empty as Pascal's without God. The Barthes who at Urt reflects sadly on 'Life' uses the ironic quotation marks to foreground his naïvety. Yet it is just such basic questioning of the world that leads Barthes, in *Camera Lucida*, to a moment of identification with the simplicity of Bouvard and Pécuchet reflecting on 'the sky, the stars, time, life, infinity, etc.', an identification which makes him wonder whether Flaubert was 'really' making fun of them: 'It is questions like these that Photography makes me ask: questions which derive from a "stupid" or simple metaphysics (it is the answers which are complicated): this, no doubt, is true metaphysics' (*CL* 84–5 / 131–3).

A curious passage of *A Lover's Discourse* blames the lover's complicity with worldly values—'I sit down on my own in a café; people come up to say hello; I feel surrounded, sought after, flattered'—on the 'absent other' who is mediated, as ever, by the symbolic figure of the mother: 'I *invoke* the other's protection, their return: let the other appear and, like a mother seeking her child, take me away from worldly brilliance and social infatuation, let the other restore to me "the religious intimacy and the gravity" of an amorous world' (*LD* 17 / 23).[11] Once the absent mother and Pascal have been brought together in the text of the futile 'Paris Evenings', Barthes begins to peel away the layers of *divertissement*, from worldly private views

---

[11] The only hint of worldly vanity included in 'Paris Evenings' is Barthes's comment on being known at the Bofinger restaurant: 'The majordomo addresses me by name, which I find flattering and embarrassing' (*I* 56 / 82). In *Camera Lucida* he describes how, in the period of his mother's final decline, 'all social life appalled me' (*CL* 72 / 112).

and dinner parties, to attempts to fill his evenings with films, outings, sexual encounters, or fantasies of being in love with young men known and unknown. The two references to reading Pascal on 3 September frame the failure of Barthes's relationship with J.-L.P., yet appear to mark a change in his attitude: 'I'd decided to give him up ... I wanted to clear all these messy leftovers out of my life' (*I* 62 / 94). In the final diary entry of the text, a sad but resolute Barthes sends Olivier G. away with the claim that he wants to get on with his work, an ending which is perhaps intrinsic to his conception of the text as a whole. For the blueprint *Vaine Soirée* of 'Deliberation' concludes with a hint that this work might be linked to the lifestyle which it claims to replace: 'The pathetic failure of the evening persuaded me to try to adopt the changed lifestyle that I have had in mind for a long time. This first note being the trace of such a will to reform.' (*RL* 368 / 409). Like Proust's time which is wasted as well as lost, the manner in which Barthes's *vaines soirées* are idled away could nevertheless form the subject matter of literature—as long, that is, as their very futility is redeemed by a fruitful literary project.

At the same time as reading Pascal at the Flore, Barthes's bedtime reading appears to have switched to Dante, not least at the end of the literally 'Futile Evening' of 14 September (the penultimate diary entry): 'I struggle home, dazed by a migraine, and go on with Dante, after taking an Optalidon' (*I* 72 / 113). It was therefore no real surprise to discover, from Éric Marty's brief revelations on French radio in 1992,[12] that the *Vaines Soirées* were to form the first section of Barthes's projected but never written work, *Vita nova*. Marty read out an extract from the fifth of Barthes's eight outline plans, dated 26 August 1979, just two or three days into the period covered by 'Paris Evenings'. In what is surely an explicit allusion to *The Divine Comedy*, the 'Prologue' states simply 'Mother as guide' (*Mam. comme guide*). This is followed by an overview of the *Vaines Soirées* ('+ politics (the *Monde* at the Flore)'; ' "This is how I spent my evenings" '), a list of words with Proustian and

---

[12] A series of programmes about Barthes (*Roland Barthes: Les Saveurs du savoir*) was broadcast on France-Culture, 9 Aug. 1992 (Cassettes Radio France, Collection 'Grands Entretiens', 1993).

Dantean connotations ('Quests' (*Recherches*), 'Journeys', 'Circles', 'Guides'), a further list of four characters ('the prostitute' (*le gigolo*), 'The unknown young man', 'The Friend', 'The writer'), and, after a space on the page, the affirmation: 'Mother is still the guide.' Finally, the 'Decision of 15 April 1978' is followed by 'VN' (obviously 'Vita nova') and a statement contained within quotation marks: ' "I withdraw from the world to embark upon a major work in which ... it is Love that would be expressed" ' (*où serait dit ... l'Amour*).[13]

From this sample alone, and from the *Vaines Soirées* published by François Wahl as 'Paris Evenings', it is possible to sense the scope and intent of Barthes's project, a general announcement of which was also contained in the lecture delivered in October 1978 at the Collège de France, ' "Longtemps je me suis couché de bonne heure" '.[14] It is retrospectively obvious that Dante is as important to this lecture as Proust; indeed, the alternative title under which the same lecture was given in December in New York—'Proust and Myself'[15]—might well have been 'Proust, Dante, and Myself'. The lecture is divided into two sections, respectively introduced by the famous opening lines of *A la recherche du temps perdu* and *The Divine Comedy*: 'Longtemps je me suis couché de bonne heure' (for a long time I used to go to bed early) and 'Nel mezzo del camin di nostra vita' (half-way along the road of our life) (*RL* 277; 284 / 313; 320). In the second section Barthes

---

[13] For the full plan of Barthes's *Vita nova* see *OC* iii. 1287–94 (facsimile) and 1299–307 (transcription). The third volume of the *Œuvres complètes* was published as this book was about to go to press. My argument here was therefore established in ignorance of the detail of this extremely important material: had this not been the case, specific discussion of Barthes's projected *Vita nova* would have been more fully developed. However, the plan of 26 August contains most of the key details for my purposes, while others, such as reference to Pascal in the seventh plan, support the interconnection of threads that I had anyway sensed. Barthes appears to abandon the whole project as a piece of childishness on 3 September, but returns to it once more on 12 December. In this last plan Barthes's reference to the 'Decision of 15 April 1978' shows that he had originally written '15 April 1979' before changing the nine to an eight. Eric Marty refers to this in a footnote as a 'correction' (*OC* iii. 1307); it is worth noting, however, that 15 April 1979 is the very day on which (according to the dates at the end of the text) Barthes claims to have begun writing *Camera Lucida*. See *La Chambre claire*, 184 (dates omitted from the translation).

[14] See *RL* 277–90 / 313–25.

[15] See Calvet, *Roland Barthes*, 233.

plays insistently on Dante's reference to the mid-point of life in order to develop his own sense of a symbolic break inaugurated by his 'cruel and irreducible' bereavement. It is this 'radical transformation of the landscape' (285 / 321) which motivates Barthes's desire for a decisive personal and literary mutation: 'to change my life, to break off and inaugurate something, to submit myself to an initiation, like Dante making his way into the *selva oscura* under the guidance of a great instructor (*initiateur*), Virgil (and for me, for this lecture at least, the instructor is Proust)' (*RL* 284 / 320). Barthes uses the expression 'this utopian Novel' (289 / 325) for this unspecified new writing practice in which Dante's Virgil and Beatrice, as well as Proust and Barthes's mother, compete for the role of guide, and which would speak the love, emotion, and unalloyed grief that Barthes finds perfectly embodied in his recent rereading of two literary death scenes: the first the harrowing separation of father and daughter in *War and Peace* (the death of Prince Bolkonsky), the second the death of the narrator's grandmother in *A la recherche* (286–7 / 322–3).

Barthes clearly identifies with Proust's quest for 'a form which will both record his suffering (he has just experienced it in an absolute form through the death of his mother) and transcend it' (279 / 315). At the same time, he is intrigued by Proust's long hesitation over the nature of this 'form', in that his mother had died in 1905, yet it was not until 1909 that he resolved the unknown problem which had been holding him back, and launched himself headlong into *A la recherche*. In Proust's case, then, it is not the mother's death alone which accounts for the writer's new sense of direction, and Barthes adduces possible reasons, notably the resolution of basic formal problems (his finding of a 'third form' between essay and novel that would combine affect and intelligence, and the assumption of a narrative 'I').[16] However, according to recent Proust scholarship, it was his interest in the Eulenberg Affair, a German homosexual scandal which broke out in 1907, that crystallized Proust's final conception of his novel, whereby homosexuality in general, and the Baron de Charlus in particular, would play a prominent

---

[16] Barthes had long been intrigued by this mysterious mutation. See also 'Ça prend' [1977], *OC* iii. 993–4, first published in *Magazine littéraire*.

thematic and structural role.[17] Ironically, Barthes seems unaware that it was this projected inclusion of homosexuality as content that unblocked Proust's creative sterility. Yet, surely, this homosexual content is an element of Barthes's identification with Proust, and has fed into the *Vita nova*, his own final project.

The second half of *La Chambre claire* is one superb outcome of Barthes's literary mutation—a new writing practice that would speak love and pity—and perhaps relates to the redemptive final work referred to in the plan for the *Vita nova* ('a major work in which ... it is love that would be expressed'). Moreover, it too plays with the idea of 'Mother as guide'. 'Who could guide me?' asks Barthes, as he sets out on his quest for the essence of photography (*CL* 4 / 14). After the false start in which a subjective, hedonistic approach is eventually rejected,[18] Barthes decides to adopt as his 'Ariadne' the Winter Garden Photo of his mother as a little girl, 'to take it, so to speak, as a guide for my final quest (*recherche*)' (73 / 114). In a radio broadcast Barthes describes *A la recherche* as a modern myth that one could imagine attempting to rewrite.[19] In a similar way, he must also have imagined rewriting Dante, both the *Vita nova*—which recounts the love and loss of Beatrice, with whom he had fallen in love when they were both children—and *The Divine Comedy*, in which Beatrice, with whom Dante is reunited at the summit of Mount Purgatory, chides him for his worldly behaviour after her death, replaces Virgil as guide, and introduces him to Paradise.

Barthes described the central project of his utopian Novel as the desire to develop its 'loving or amorous power', adding that

---

[17] See Maurice Bardèche, *Marcel Proust romancier*, 2 vols. (Paris, Les Sept Couleurs, 1971), i. 160–3, and Antoine Compagnon's preface to Proust, *Sodome et Gomorrhe* [1921–2] (Paris, Gallimard (Folio), 1989), pp. xiv–xvi.

[18] 'I decided to adopt as guide for my new analysis the attraction I felt for certain photos' (*CL* 18 / 37); 'I had to concede that my pleasure was an inadequate mediator, and that a subjectivity reduced to its hedonist project could not recognize the universal' (60 / 95–6).

[19] When asked if this is what he intends to do, he says 'No! it's a dream', but then arguably contradicts himself by adding that the function of the dream is to nourish a sort of creative energy, even if the project is quite likely to end in failure (Barthes, *Un homme, une ville: Marcel Proust à Paris*, France-Culture, 3 Nov. 1978).

'certain mystics did not dissociate *Agape* from *Eros*' (*RL* 288 / 324). Could this be one reason for Barthes's interest in the mystic tradition, which seems to have resurfaced with particular force at around this time?[20] Philippe Roger notes that one of the most cited authors in the margins of *A Lover's Discourse* is the medieval Flemish mystic J. von Ruysbroek. There are indeed a dozen or so quotations from Ruysbroek, rubbing shoulders with references to Plato, to a plethora of German Romantic writers and musicians, and to Proust, Freud, and Lacan.[21] The key to Barthes's own conflation of Agape and Eros is his sexualization of key terms of the Romantic or religious lexicon, most notably the heart and soul: ' "Soul", "feeling", and "heart" are the Romantic names for the body. Everything becomes clearer in the Romantic text if we translate the effusive, moral word by one connected to the body, to the drives' (*RF* 308 / 273).[22] Quotations from Ruysbroek are placed in such a way that they mediate between the mystic's and the lover's discourse, as in the example of Barthes's figure of 'Fulfilment' (*comblement*): ' "Now, take all the delights of the earth, melt them into one single delight, and cast it entire into one single man—all this will be as nothing to the delight of which I speak" ... "my soul is not only filled, it runs over" ' (*LD* 54 / 65). Such fulfilment could indeed be spiritual, emotional, or physical. In the case of the figure of 'Absence', it is Barthes's gloss on Ruysbroek's quoted words which achieves the desired effect. According to Ruysbroek, 'Desire is present, ardent, eternal: but God is higher still, and the raised arms of Desire never attain the adored plenitude'. In Barthes's hands this becomes: 'The discourse of Absence is a text with two ideograms: there are *the raised arms*

---

[20] In particular in Barthes's lecture course on the *Neutre*. On Barthes and mysticism, see Philippe Roger, *Roland Barthes, roman*, 318–26, and ' "Une fidélité particulière à l'infini" (de Barthes et des mystiques)', in Coquio and Salado (eds.), *Barthes après Barthes*, 37–41.

[21] This is a very selective list. See the *Tabula gratulatoria* (279–81), omitted from the English translation, for the full intertextual network of some eighty references to writers, theorists, musicians, and personal friends.

[22] Barthes argues that the original meanings have been distorted: 'By restoring the body to the Romantic text, we correct the ideological reading of this text, for this reading, that of our current opinion, never does anything but *invert* (in the manœuvre common to all ideology) the motions of the body into movements of the soul' (*RF* 308 / 273).

of Desire, and there are *the stretched-out arms of Need*. I oscillate, I vacillate between the phallic image of the raised arms, and the babyish image of the stretched-out arms' (16–17 / 23).

But the ultimate phallic organ is the heart, which emerges as a Fourierist transition of far broader scope than the tongue discussed in Chapter 8. In Barthes's imaginary anatomy, the Romantic heart subsumes the phallus to become the bodily signifier of both emotion and physical desire: 'The heart is the organ of desire (the heart swells, fails, etc, like the sexual organs) just as it is captured, transfixed, within the field of the Imaginary' (*LD* 52 / 63). Despite Barthes's claims for the ungendered nature of the Romantic lover's discourse, this is a resolutely male version of such a discourse, drawing unambiguously on the male body for its images of erection and tumescence. The 'heart' of Romantic song is described as 'a powerful organ, pinnacle of the inner body where, simultaneously and as though in a contradictory way, desire and tenderness, the demand for love and the claims of physical pleasure (*jouissance*) violently merge: something lifts up my body, swells it, stretches it, carries it to the point of explosion, then immediately, mysteriously, makes it depressed and languid' (*RF* 289 / 255).[23] A 'heavy heart' (*cœur gros*) is the exclusive prerogative of the lover and the child (*LD* 53 / 64) who are linked by their tears: 'Where does the lover get his right to cry, if not in a reversal of values, of which the body is the first target? He willingly reverts to his child's body' (180 / 213).[24] Barthes's conflation of adult sexuality and childish affects turns the figure of the Romantic lover into a curious chiasmus—on one side an adult who cries, on the other a child with an erection ('the lover

---

[23] Barthes's comments on the 'unisex' nature of Romantic discourse only really make sense if we assume that they refer to its object, so that homosexual lovers will indeed draw upon the same language and discourse as heterosexual ones. See, for example, 'The Greatest Cryptographer of Contemporary Myths Talks about Love' [1977], in *GV* 290–305: 293 / 271–84: 273–4.

[24] I have already quoted the final entry of 'Paris Evenings' in which Barthes 'felt like crying' because Olivier G.'s lack of desire for him had become obvious ('no hint of a response; what is more, he soon disappeared into the other room' (*I* 73 / 115)). Given the connections established in *A Lover's Discourse*, this seems an emotion not unrelated to Barthes's 'Romantic swelling' and 'heavy heart' at U. (60–1 / 90–1).

could be defined as a child having an erection: just like the young Eros' (105 / 122)).

In that Barthes so readily merges the discourse of the lover with that of the child (both solitary, lost, or abandoned subjects) he might appear to be *conflating* the claims of genital desire with need for the mother. But this should not be understood as genital desire *for* the mother, since the imaginary of the lover's discourse is one that accepts the non-unitary subject of 'the demand for love' and 'the claims of physical pleasure': 'I am then two subjects at the same time: I want the maternal and the genital' (*la maternité et la génitalité*) (104–5 / 122). These are explicitly figured as two contradictory embraces, whereby the adult is superimposed upon the child. The maternal embrace is a metaphor for an illusory moment of total and eternal union with the loved person, a regression to a moment (that of the real mother) when desires are abolished because they seem definitively fulfilled. However, in the middle of this childish embrace, 'the genital never fails to break through; it breaks up the diffuse sensuality of the incestuous embrace; the logic of desire is set in motion, the will-to-grasp (*le vouloir-saisir*) returns, the adult is superimposed upon the child' (104 / 121–2).

The twin claims of the maternal and the genital are wonderfully figured in the first and second of the photographs of Barthes that are included in *Roland Barthes by Roland Barthes*. The maternal embrace, in which Barthes's mother holds an overgrown infant in her arms, is specifically captioned 'The Demand for Love' (*RB* 5 / 7). The Barthes who clings solemnly to his mother, cheek to cheek, is 7 or 8 years old. In the second photo an older Barthes, with all the awkwardness and indefinable age of the Proustian narrator, stands alone and smiling in his grandparents' garden at Bayonne. This, according to the caption, was the site of 'a few episodes of childhood sexuality' (10 / 12). These two photos of Barthes stand apart from the others, in that it is only after portraits of great-grandparents, grandparents, father, and aunt that a new sequence begins, which runs in roughly chronological fashion from Barthes as a baby to Barthes as a young adult. I commented at the end of the last chapter that the photographs taken at Marrac (the original maternal space) represent the affective core of the adult Barthes's personality. The two photos in which Barthes displays his inner distress (23–4 / 27–8) are directly preceded by one of him as a toddler ('around 1918') tottering across a local beach. This photograph has a provocative caption: 'Contemporaries? I was beginning to walk, Proust was still alive, and was finishing *A la recherche*' (22–3 / 26–7). Unsurprisingly, the ten references to Proust in *A Lover's Discourse* are shared between the Baron de Charlus, Albertine, the mother, and the grandmother.[25] Barthes's Proust, as he himself implies, is not the Proust of the largely French tradition of paranoid jealousy (a tradition which dates back to Racine, and which could well be exemplified by the jealous love of Swann for Odette). Rather, Barthes associates Proust with the German Romantic tradition of amorous discourse, of which the song cycles of Schubert and Schumann are his favourite incarnation. This is a tradition which does not exclude jealousy, but is not based upon it: 'an amorous sentiment which is much more effusive and aspires to fulfilment. The essential figure here is that of the Mother' (*GV* 287 / 268).[26]

The radio broadcast in which Barthes describes *A la recherche* as a myth waiting to be rewritten was part of three programmes on 'Marcel Proust in Paris', made in collaboration with Jean Montalbetti in 1978. At one stage, their perambulations around some of the key sites of Proust's life take them to a nineteenth-century *pavillon* in the gardens of the Champs-Élysées. This is the still existing public lavatory in which Proust chose to locate the episode of the grandmother's stroke, on what was to be the narrator's last outing with her. Barthes's comments associate this setting with the parallel themes of the development of the narrator's adolescent sexuality, his love for his grandmother, and the grandmother's illness and death. He alludes too to the episode of the narrator's first orgasm whilst pretending to wrestle with Gilberte. Barthes does not specifically mention what is clear in Proust's text: that it is the narrator's attraction

---

[25] Barthes includes a self-conscious allusion to the Baron de Charlus in the very first entry of 'Paris Evenings': 'I noticed the Rue d'Aboukir and thought of Charlus, who mentions it' (*I* 52 / 74).

[26] Schubert's music is described as having the effusiveness, unity, and demand for love and tenderness associated with a 'maternal climate' (contribution to a radio broadcast, 'Pourquoi Schubert aujourd'hui?', France-Culture, 30 Jan. 1978, see *OC* iii. 906–7: 906).

to the indefinable smell of the *pavillon*, combined with the attentions of the louche attendant (her offer of a free cubicle as he waits for Françoise), that interrupts the narrator's game with Gilberte and seems specifically to precipitate this first orgasm.[27] Yet Barthes is clearly intrigued by Proust's choice of a public lavatory as the setting for the grandmother's stroke. With a disingenuous 'it's best to be honest about these things', he refers to Proust's odd ritual, when calling on his friends, of disappearing to spend up to fifteen minutes in the lavatory: 'it was a place he liked.'[28] In that the grandmother seems to mediate the needs, emotions, and sexuality of both Proust and his narrator, and in that she recurs in Barthes's discussions of Proust, she is a useful focus for the intersection of the maternal and the genital in Barthes's late writing. For example, there could be no better example of Barthes's enchanted and immobile embrace than that between Proust's narrator and his grandmother on his first wretched day in Balbec: 'And when I felt my mouth glued to her cheeks, to her brow, I drew from them something so beneficial, so nourishing, that I remained as motionless, as solemn, as calmly gluttonous as a baby at the breast.'[29] When the grandmother dies, Proust chooses to locate the narrator's delayed mourning in the volume that also brings him face to face with homosexuality. For *Sodom and Gomorrah* opens with the narrator spying on a primal scene of male homosexuality (the fortuitous 'mating' of Charlus and Jupien) and closes with his memory of the lesbian scene at Montjouvain on which he had spied in *Combray*. Clearly, Proust has chosen to delay the narrator's mourning so that the two themes can be juxtaposed in this way.

My argument is that Barthes uses the Proustian grandmother as a symbolic mediator of his own creative explorations of maternal space. By associating his mourning for his mother with that of Proust's narrator for his grandmother, he gains access to the representations of homosexuality which surround the latter in *A la recherche*. In *Camera Lucida*, the involuntary memory in

---

[27] See Marcel Proust, *Remembrance of Things Past*, 3 vols., trans. C. K. Scott-Moncrief and Terence Kilmartin (Harmondsworth, Penguin, 1983), i. 530–3.
[28] *Un homme, une ville: Marcel Proust à Paris*, tape 3.
[29] Proust, *Remembrance*, i. 718.

which the narrator, stooping to remove his boots, rediscovers the face and the goodness of his 'real grandmother' is an explicit point of reference for Barthes's own narrative of rediscovering his 'real mother' in the Winter Garden Photograph (*CL* 70 / 109).[30] At first sight, the allusion serves to mediate Barthes's specific argument about the ghostly status of the photographic referent, as well as his determination to respect the specificity of his suffering.[31] However, I want to suggest that the implicit references to *Sodom and Gomorrah* extend beyond this famous scene. When the narrator paradoxically understands, for the first time, that he has lost his grandmother for ever,[32] sexual desire and all interest in worldly pleasures desert him, and he shuts himself up in his hotel room to wallow in his grief. If desire slowly returns, it is the suggestion and then certainty of Albertine's lesbianism that produces his desperate need for her presence, to such an extent that she is declared a necessary part of himself.[33] This quasi-internalization of homosexuality takes the form of a horrible hallucination whereby the scene at Montjouvain, with Albertine in the place of Mlle Vinteuil's friend, looms up from behind the view from the hotel window at Balbec. In his anguish, the narrator wonders if this is a punishment for having allowed his grandmother to die. Yet it is precisely this melodramatic tussle with homosexuality which motivates the grandmother's second resurrection. The setting is still the hotel room in which she had once bent down to untie his boots, in which he had stood transfixed in her life-giving embrace, in which she had returned to him in an involuntary

---

[30] See Proust, ii. 783: 'I had just perceived, in my memory, stooping over my fatigue, the tender, preoccupied, disappointed face of my grandmother, as she had been on that first evening of our arrival, the face not of that grandmother whom I had been astonished and remorseful at having so little missed, and who had nothing in common with her save her name, but of my real grandmother, of whom, for the first time since the afternoon of her stroke in the Champs-Élysées, I now recaptured the living reality in a complete and involuntary recollection.'

[31] 'I could say, like the Proustian Narrator on the death of his grandmother: "I was determined not merely to suffer, but to respect the original form of my suffering" ' (*CL* 75 / 117–18). See Proust, *Remembrance*, ii. 786.

[32] 'I had only just, on feeling her for the first time alive, real, making my heart swell to breaking-point, on finding her at last, learned that I had lost her for ever' (Proust, *Remembrance*, ii. 785).

[33] For the discovery of Albertine's lesbianism and the narrator's 'Désolation au lever du soleil' (distress at sunrise), see ibid. ii. 1150–69.

memory, in which he had shut himself away to mourn, and in which he had earlier that night drawn momentary relief from the knowledge of Albertine's lesbianism through a long and chaste kiss on her neck. As the narrator's long night of misery reaches its climax, dawn breaks over the sea at Balbec. Never, he says, has he seen the dawn 'of so beautiful or so sorrowful a morning'. As the sun bursts through the curtains he hears himself crying, 'but at that moment, to my astonishment, the door opened and, with a throbbing heart, I seemed to see my grandmother standing before me, as in one of those apparitions that had already visited me, but only in my sleep'.[34]

We cannot know whether this particular conflation of homosexuality, the reincarnated grandmother, and the beautiful but desolate dawn is a conscious intertext for the recognition scene at the centre of *Camera Lucida*. But the symmetry of the two scenes—the involuntary memory of the grandmother's face, her illusory dawn resurrection—is surely obvious to a reader as well acquainted as Barthes with the text of *Sodom and Gomorrah*. Moreover, from his plans, it is clear that Proust had intended to signal the parallel through his use of a common title, 'The Intermittencies of the Heart'. In 1912 Proust had even thought of giving this wonderfully Barthesian title—which metaphorically links 'the world of the mind' to 'an illness of the body'—to the novel as a whole.[35] Well might the heart of the weeping narrator throb at the sight of his resurrected grandmother!

In fact, the mystery of this second miraculous resurrection is immediately explained, for Proust's narrator has mistaken his *mother* for his dead grandmother. The grandmother has borrowed the body of her more than willing daughter, for it is the latter, separated from the narrator by the same thin partition that had once kept him in touch with his grandmother, who has

---

[34] Ibid. ii. 1166.
[35] See Antoine Compagnon's editorial notes in *Sodome et Gomorrhe*, 569 and 628. The first episode was published as 'Les Intermittences du cœur' in the *Nouvelle Revue française* (Oct. 1921), hence the survival of the title (as a subheading) in editions of *A la recherche*. 'Les Intermittences du cœur II' was Proust's title in a 1918 plan for the chapter containing the climactic scene at dawn. The phrase is used by Proust early in the first episode: 'For with the perturbations of memory are linked the intermittencies of the heart' (ii. 784).

heard his sobs and repeated the grandmother's earlier action of coming in to comfort him: 'Her dishevelled hair, the grey tresses of which were not hidden and strayed about her troubled eyes, her ageing cheeks, my grandmother's own dressing-gown which she was wearing, all these had for a moment prevented me from recognizing her and had made me uncertain whether I was asleep or whether my grandmother had come back to life.'[36] In fact, the earlier involuntary memory had been prolonged, to some extent, by the arrival at Balbec of the narrator's mother: 'as soon as I saw her enter in her crape coat, I realised—something that had escaped me in Paris—that it was no longer my mother that I had before my eyes, but my grandmother.' This process of the reincarnation of a mother in her daughter is explained by the image of a male genealogical line of descent in aristocratic families. Just as, on the death of the head of the household, the son takes the father's title, 'so, by an accession of a different order and more profound origin, the dead often annex the living who become their replicas and successors, the continuators of their interrupted life'.[37] By splitting the mother figure into mother and grandmother, and by splitting the grieving child into daughter and grandson, Proust thus interweaves the theme of the succession and merging of generations into his fictional fantasies of resurrection.

If the actual photo of Barthes's mother is withheld from the chapter which recounts its discovery, its place is taken by what he calls one of the most beautiful photos in the world, Nadar's photo of his mother, 'or of his wife, no one actually knows' (*CL* 70 / 109).[38] The grey tresses of Nadar's mother or wife, as well as Barthes's stress on this confusion of generations, form a wonderful link with the Proustian hallucination of the grandmother's resurrection at sunrise. Moreover, the genealogical

---

[36] Proust, *Remembrance*, ii. 1166–7. The mother acts out the grandmother's role and the narrator takes her in his arms. However, this is not to repeat the entranced, static, and appeasing embrace of his grandmother on their first day at Balbec. Rather, in an excellent illustration of Barthes's juxtaposition of the 'two embraces' of maternity and genitality (*LD* 104–5 / 122), it is to tell his mother of his absolute need for Albertine (ii. 1169).

[37] Proust, *Remembrance*, ii. 796.

[38] On Barthes's 'exploitation' of the confusion over the subject of Nadar's portrait, and on its official sources, see Daniel Grojnowski, 'Le Mystère de *La Chambre claire*', *Textuel* 34/44, 15 (1984), 91–6: 93 and 96 n. 2.

theme is a suggestive link between the Nadar photo and the photo of Barthes's mother as a small child—grouped with her brother and grandfather—which *is* included later in the text (104 / 163). For Barthes captions this photograph 'La Souche' (The Stock), which in French means both the ancestral founder of the line and the lineage itself. Though the section ends with an assertion of the mysterious differences between members of the same family, not least the child-mother and her monumental grandfather, what precedes it is a meditation on the cross-generational genetic links sometimes foregrounded in photographs. Thus, looking at a photo of his maternal grandmother holding his mother's brother as a child, Barthes thinks at first that the grandmother is his mother and the child himself. Looking more closely, he sees that the structure of his mother's face has been marked by her father, just as his own face has been marked by his father. Yet this link to his father is more visible in photos of his father as a child than as an adult: 'certain details, certain features connect his face to my grandmother's and to mine—in a sense over his head' (105 / 161).

More indirect still is the genetic link between Barthes and his unmarried aunt: 'in one photo, I have the "face" of my father's sister' (103 / 161). If photographic evidence of the continuity of the family line is reassuring ('for the thought of our origins reassures us'), the aunt herself may also conjure up the future which 'perturbs us, fills us with anguish' (105 / 162). Barthes had earlier reproduced her photo as a child in *Roland Barthes by Roland Barthes*, where he added the caption: 'The father's sister: she was alone all her life' (*RB* 14 / 18). The preceding page showed her as a young woman with her parents, in a family group reminiscent of that of the black family in Van der Zee's photo in *Camera Lucida* (*RB* 13 / 17; *CL* 44 / 75). The young black woman whom Barthes, in another confusion of generations, identifies as the sister or daughter (*CL* 43 / 73) stands in the same position as his aunt relative to her parents, and is linked to the aunt by the supposed retrospective *punctum* of her necklace: 'this sister of my father had never married, had lived as an old maid with her mother, and it had always saddened me to think of the dreariness of her provincial life' (53 / 87–8). Of Barthes's various delvings into past generations of his family, I am struck by his sympathetic identifications with his unmarried and childless aunt. For Barthes and his aunt between them incarnate the termination of the paternal line. His own role in this is stressed in the caption in *Roland Barthes by Roland Barthes* to a posed family portrait of his grandfather as a young man, surrounded by his parents (Barthes's great-grandparents) and his brother and sister (Barthes's great-uncle and -aunt): 'Final stasis of this descent: my body. The last product of the family line is a purposeless being (*un être pour rien*)' (*RB* 19 / 22–3). Similarly, in *Camera Lucida* he refers to his lineage as a disturbing entity of which he represents the term (*CL* 98 / 152).

Barthes's concern with this theme is embedded in the Winter Garden Photograph through his discussion of the photographic *air*, variously glossed as 'that exorbitant thing by which we infer the soul from the body' (109 / 167), as 'the irreducible supplement of an identity' (109 / 168), and as 'something moral, which mysteriously reflects onto the face the quality of a life' (110 / 169). Barthes's attempts to convey the meaning of the *air* come to rest in the metaphor of the 'luminous shadow which accompanies the body', and without which the body remains as sterile as that of the mythical Woman without a Shadow: 'It is by this flimsy umbilical cord that the photographer gives life to the subject; if he fails, either through lack of talent or bad luck, to give the transparent soul its bright shadow, that subject dies for ever' (110 / 169).[39] In a parallel image in an earlier chapter, the umbilical cord is made up of the light rays which Barthes imagines as linking the photographic referent to his gaze: 'a flesh-and-blood medium, a skin I share with the person whose photo has been taken' (81 / 127). If the point seems to apply to the light emanating from any photographic referent, by the end of the chapter it is clear that the image of the umbilical cord has

---

[39] The libretto of Richard Strauss's opera *The Woman without a Shadow* was written by Hofmannsthal, who later turned it into a prose text. The Emperor's daughter loses her shadow (her fertility) as punishment for her choice of non-procreative sexual pleasure. Barthes also refers to the Woman without a Shadow in *The Pleasure of the Text* (32 / 53), where she is an image for the sterility of a text that is cut off from all representation and ideology. For further discussion see Knight, 'Barthes or the Woman without a Shadow', in Jean-Michel Rabaté (ed.), *Writing the Image after Roland Barthes* (Philadelphia, University of Pennsylvania Press, forthcoming).

a special status relative to the light rays linking Barthes himself to the child-mother of the Winter Garden Photo. Barthes represents himself, as he looks through photos of his mother, working his way backwards through her life, from her last summer to her childhood. In her final illness this movement has been repeated in reality, his mother becoming his little girl as he cares for her and feeds her. In a strange moment of his handling of the narrative chronology, Barthes suggests that she has merged with the child of her first photo, even though she has not yet died and he has not yet discovered that photo, the setting of which—a Winter Garden at Chennevières-sur-Marne (69 / 106)—returns her to her literal place of birth. And this, declares Barthes, is his personal solution to death (his mother's and his own) as the supposed 'harsh victory' of the species: 'if the individual dies having reproduced themselves through another person, and having thereby negated and transcended themself, I who had not procreated had engendered my mother in her very illness. Now that she was dead, I no longer had any reason to attune myself to the progress of the superior Life Force (the species)' (72, 113). The passage continues with what sounds like a splendid line for the ending of Barthes's *Vita nova* (where he was to retire, Proust-like, to write his major work): 'My particularity could never again universalize itself (unless, utopically, by writing, a project which, henceforth, would become the unique goal of my life)' (*CL* 72 / 113).

If Barthes declines to reproduce the Winter Garden Photo, it cannot be for the reasons given in the bracketed apology that has so often been taken at face value.[40] If *Camera Lucida* recounts a 'true story' of Barthes rediscovering his mother in a photo of her as a child, then that photo must surely be 'The Stock' (104 / 163). Although the mother as child is younger than 5, and although she and her brother stand with their grandfather (rather than alone in a conservatory), her pose, her expression, and the position of her hands exactly match Barthes's description

---

[40] 'I cannot show you the Winter Garden Photo. It exists only for me. For you it would be nothing but an indifferent photo, one of a thousand manifestations of the "banal" (*le "quelconque"*); it cannot in any way constitute the visible object of a science; it cannot establish an objectivity, in the positive sense of the term; at most it might appeal to your studium: a period, clothes, photogenic subject matter; but in the photo, for you, there would be no wound' (*CL* 73 / 115).

of the Winter Garden Photograph. Barthes describes the child as neither 'flaunting herself nor hiding herself' (69 / 107)—and this seems to me to describe the way Barthes has positioned the original photo ('The Stock'). Like the famous purloined letter in Edgar Allan Poe's story, it is so obvious that it is overlooked. It is therefore my belief that the Winter Garden Photo is simply an invention, a transposition of the 'real' photo to a setting that provides Barthes with the symbolism of light and revelation appropriate to a recognition scene and to his inversion of the *camera obscura* of photography into a *chambre claire*.[41]

Just before he relates the discovery of the Winter Garden Photo, Barthes refers to the brightness (*clarté*) of his mother's eyes as something that stands out in all of her photographs: 'For the moment it was simply a physical luminosity, the photographic trace of a colour, the blue-green of her pupils' (66 / 104). This, he says, is the mediating light that will guide him at last to the essence of her face. Their blue-green luminosity is shared by the only colour photograph included in the book (9), the polaroid by Daniel Boudinet that Barthes positions as frontispiece and identifies simply as '*Polaroid, 1979*'.[42] Although Barthes himself gives no details, Boudinet's photograph is one of a sequence that he entitled *Fragments of a Labyrinth*, taken at night in his own apartment, between dusk and dawn, using only light entering through the windows from outside.[43] Barthes has chosen for *Camera Lucida* the photograph that corresponds to the light of dawn, a light which bestows upon the curtains their blue-green luminosity, but is not yet strong enough to illuminate the foreground of the room. However, through an opening low down where the curtains

---

[41] This striking similarity has been noted by Ralph Sarkonak in 'Roland Barthes and the Spectre of Photography', *L'Esprit créateur* (Spring 1982), 48–68: 56–7, and by Antoine Compagnon in 'L'Objectif déconcerté', *La Recherche photographique* (June 1992), 72–7: 77. Yet neither appears to suggest that the Winter Garden Photo could be fictional. Sarkonak comments on the sense of *déjà lu* when we encounter 'The Stock', only to wonder 'Why did this photo not affect Barthes the same way as the one he does describe but does not allow us to see?' (57).

[42] Not included in the translation.

[43] See *Fragments d'un labyrinthe* in *Daniel Boudinet*, ed. Christian Caujolle, Emmanuelle Decroux, and Claude Vittiglio (Besançon, Éditions de la manufacture, 1993), 108–15, and Gianni Burattoni, 'La Mort de Daniel Boudinet', *Lettres françaises* (Oct. 1990), 21.

meet, a brighter chink of light falls on to a corner of the bed and the empty pillow. Boudinet's labyrinthine dawn polaroid is surely an integral part of Barthes's symbolic narrative of rediscovering his mother in the *chambre claire* of a glass conservatory, and of his adoption of the Winter Garden Photo as a metaphorical Ariadne to guide him to the essence of photography. Moreover, Barthes must have viewed the Boudinet photograph for the first time in the middle of writing *Camera Lucida*, when he attended the private view described in 'Deliberation' (*RL* 368 / 409). That this photo should emerge from the context of his founding *Vaine Soirée*—the one juxtaposed with his mother's last summer at the luminous Urt— gives Barthes's frontispiece an extraordinary resonance.

One final intertextual reference harmonizes all the others that weave in and out of chapter 28 of *Camera Lucida*. Barthes likens the Winter Garden Photograph to Schumann's first *Dawn Song* (from the *Gesänge der Frühe*), 'which is in such perfect harmony both with my mother's being and with my sorrow at her death' (*CL* 70 / 110). In a radio discussion with Claude Maupomé, Barthes says that he cannot listen to this enigmatic piece of music without a sort of anguish. Moreover, he declares himself especially moved by the fact that this very late composition, written on the threshold of Schumann's final descent into madness, should have conveyed such a sombre entry into the night with a title referring to daybreak. Indeed, night and daybreak are inextricably entwined, and Barthes suggests that the night is a fundamental but ambivalent *substance*, a theme mediating the diffuse moods (part carnavalesque, part lyrical and effusive) of Schumann's piano pieces: 'discordant nights, adventurous nights, funereal nights.'[44] Elsewhere, Barthes describes Schumann as 'the musician of solitary intimacy, of the amorous and imprisoned soul that *speaks to itself*... in short, of the child who has no other tie than their tie to the Mother' (*RF* 293–4 / 259);[45] finally, he describes his

---

[44] See 'Le Désir de musique', *Les Nouvelles littéraires* (10–17 Apr. 1980), 28 (extracts from 'Comment l'entendez-vous?', France-Musique, 21 Oct. 1979).

[45] This corresponds to Barthes's descriptions of his isolated childhood and early adolescence: he stresses that he was enveloped in maternal affection but cut off from wider social relationships. See, for example, 'Radioscopie' [1975], *OC* iii. 344–59: 353, and 'Réponses' [1971], *OC* ii. 1307–24: 1308–9.

music as 'sheltering always in the luminous shadow of the mother' (298 / 263). In *Camera Lucida* Barthes portrays himself shut up in his apartment, presumably at night since he is looking through photographs of his mother by the light of a lamp (*CL* 67 / 105–6). Just as the beautiful sunrise at Balbec incarnates the suffering of Proust's narrator—even as it illuminates the hallucinatory resurrection of his grandmother—so Barthes finds in Schumann's *Dawn Song* the musical equivalent of the Winter Garden Photograph. According to Ernst Bloch, 'death-space borders mediately on music'.[46] In *Camera Lucida* Barthes has turned to the music of Schumann in order to weave that death-space into an intertextual, metaphorical, and utopian staging of the mother's luminous return.

Barthes's mother or *the* mother? When Barthes first assembled his figures of the lover's discourse, maternal space, with its twin poles of distress and fulfilment, was an imaginary space in both senses of the word, whatever the autobiographical dimension. Even the *fort/da*, the archetypal rehearsal for maternal absence, was simply the founding paradigm of Romantic discourse, with its inconsequential series of figures, 'a fiction with numerous roles (doubts, reproaches, desires, melancholies)' (*LD* 16 / 22). Indeed, Barthes was partly drawn to the Romantic song cycles as examples of the narrative and psychological discontinuity of the novelistic (*le romanesque*), with its exemption from teleology and 'spiritual transcendence' (*RF* 291 / 257). Yet the literal death of Barthes's mother—in the very year of the publication of *A Lover's Discourse*—casts over this text the same retrospective shadow that affected readings of *Camera Lucida* in the wake of Barthes's own death. Once absence is both real and permanent, it is clear that Barthes needs to find a form of writing that will communicate his mother's irreducible moral value, a form that will precisely transcend his loss by subsuming her individual value into a general law.[47] Seeking one character trait by which to define his mother as he rediscovers her in the Winter Garden

---

[46] Bloch, *The Principle of Hope*, iii. 1097. Bloch attributes to music the capacity to deny death ('the harshest non-utopia') on its own ground. Beethoven's *Fidelio* and Brahms's *German Requiem*, for example, are described as 'musical initiations into the truth of Utopia', in that they are 'tied to a death-consciousness and to a wishful consciousness of anti-death' (iii. 1100).

[47] In the penultimate plan for the *Vita nova* (dated 3 Sept. 1979), Barthes writes: 'Which law? Mother's absolute law [*celle, absolue, de mam.*].' See OC iii. 1306.

Photo, Barthes chooses the indirect example of something she never did: 'that she never once, in all our life together, uttered a single "reproach" ' (*CL* 69 / 109). I have always taken these words as an allusion to his mother's acceptance of his homosexuality, and believe that this was one of his reasons for wishing to subsume homosexuality into a symbolic projection of an all-embracing maternal space.[48]

Like Stendhal who wanted to express the *Sovereign Good* of Milan—'literally a Paradise, a place without Evil' (*RL* 299 / 337)—Barthes wants to convey the goodness, kindness, gentleness, and sovereign *innocence* of his mother (*CL* 69 / 107), 'the Sovereign Good of childhood, of the mother, of the mother-as-child' (71 / 111).[49] Stendhal, who had been locked into the 'sterile immobility of the imaginary', finally manages (triumphantly) to communicate his passion for Italy by seeking 'symbolic generality' in the mediating forms of narrative and myth (*RL* 305 / 342). The solution attributed to Stendhal is of course Barthes's own, as he turns to a narrative of quest and discovery in *Camera Lucida*, and plans a reworking of the mythical narratives of Proust and Dante in his own *Vita nova*. It is ironic that Barthes's shimmering paper on Stendhal should be his literal—and never delivered—last word.[50] It is also ironic that his final utopian project should have remained precisely a project. Yet, like every good novel of the artist, Barthes's *Vita nova* is a dilatory text in the best Fourierist tradition, for what never gets written is already there to be read in all of 'late Barthes'.

---

[48] 'Given the importance to 'Paris Evenings' of the Flore and other cafés, it is very interesting to note that the café itself is described by Barthes as yet another affective, maternal space, whereby to wait for someone in a café (which then, moreover, takes on an 'infernal' dimension) is always to place oneself in the position of the child waiting for its mother: 'the café is a place both of distress and of fulfilment' (*Les Saveurs du savoir*, tape 2, side A, no reference provided).

[49] In another interesting parallel, Bloch links Brahms's *German Requiem* to the utopia of the sovereign good: 'In the darkness of this music gleam the treasures which will not be corrupted by moth and rust, the lasting treasures in which will and goal, hope and its content, virtue and happiness could be united as in a world without frustration, as in the highest good:—*the requiem circles the secret landscape of the highest good*' (*The Principle of Hope*, iii. 1101). As far as I am aware, Barthes never referred to Bloch's work.

[50] According to an editorial note (omitted from the English translation), Barthes had just started to type up his paper on Stendhal on the day of his accident. The second page was found in his typewriter. See *RL* 342.

Afterword

> The intellectual (or writer) has no place—or that place is precisely Indirectness: this is the utopia for which I tried to find a (musically) *true* discourse.

As early as 1963, Barthes wrote of works 'which are, by a fundamental ruse, nothing but their own project' (*EC*, p. xiii / 11), and referred, for the first time, to the peculiar status of Proust's *A la recherche*, caught between the narrator's initial impulse to write and his decision to do so. Rarely can an author have written so prophetically of the forms, themes, and values of his future work as Barthes in his preface to *Critical Essays*. Mindful of Barthes's own warning, that 'the retrospective is never anything but a category of bad faith' (p. xi / 9), I have taken, as a pretext for my brief concluding remarks, two passages from this densely projective preface.

The first contains Barthes's musical metaphor for the work of the writer who, 'at once stubborn and unfaithful', knows only an art of 'theme and variations': 'The variations on the theme have to do with struggle, values, ideologies, time, the yearning to live, to find out, to talk, to take part, in short, the contents; but the theme itself embraces the stubbornness of forms, the great signifying function of the imaginary, which is to say, the very process of understanding the world' (p. xii / 10). Barthes claims that the writer's ideological content would normally be seen as the founding theme, and the writer's form as mere expression of that content in a series of contingent variations. However, for Barthes, something like the opposite is true. The writer's work has an ambiguous relationship to the 'evolutive timescale of ideas' (p. xiii / 10), and to write is necessarily to abandon the stable meanings that the world may confer on the work once written. Whereas 'social ethics' tends to expect

---

[1] Barthes, 'So How Was China?', OC iii. 35.

'fidelity to content', the writer's deepest commitment is 'fidelity to form' (ibid.).

I hope to have shown that Barthes's own theme and variations on utopia—and the relationship between them—take us to the heart of his imaginative processes. Utopia mediates the various 'phases' of Barthes's intellectual and writerly career, just as it mediates two dimensions of his work that are often erroneously separated: his desire to write social values for the world, and his desire for self-definition as a creative writer. At the centre of Barthes's understanding of utopia is the writer's permanent commitment to *writing* the world, by which he means an act of conceptualization, understanding, complicity, and projection. This recreation of the world as a meaningful whole is the impulse behind the novelistic cosmogonies that Barthes so admired, from those of his logothetes, Sade and Fourier, to the mythical fictional worlds of Balzac, Zola, and Proust. Barthes's fascination with cosmogonies suggests why, with the exception of the idiosyncratic Fourier, his utopian points of reference tend to be literary rather than theoretical. But this is not at all to say that Barthes was 'merely' a writer, or to deny the significance of his engagement with contemporary reality.[2] Barthes believed that present-day language is the intractable site of social division, so that the liberation of the one could not be thought without that of the other. For this reason too, his reflection on utopian values could not proceed without a parallel reflection on the appropriate form of a utopian writer's discourse: the figure of utopia necessarily embraces both content and form.

The second passage from Barthes's preface is his sustained and convoluted apology for the writer's strategic recourse to indirectness. In the first instance this follows from the vision of a

---

[2] In *Michelet*, Barthes quotes a letter to Taine in which Michelet points out that he is often praised as a 'writer' in order to devalue the seriousness of his contribution as a historian: 'New as you are to criticism, you are as yet unaware that this name of *poet* which you apply to me is precisely the accusation by which the historian is always damned.... I have made every effort to give history a serious and positive basis on numerous points. Examples: the history of the bank (in my book on the Reformation), the budget of King Philip (in the wars of religion, etc.). The election of Charles V, discussed from the political perspective by Mignet, has been discussed from a *financial* one by me, that is, in terms of its truth. Yet everywhere people have described me as a historian *with a felicitous imagination*' (Mi 99 / 89).

socially divided language to which I have just referred. Barthes claims that language is too saturated with already existing connotations for it to be possible to state in sincere fashion the simple affects which he puts forward, even in this early essay, as the basic subject matter of literature: love, suffering, compassion, the fear of death. From his hypothetical example of a doomed attempt to express genuine sympathy in a letter to a bereaved friend, Barthes concludes that in literature, as in private communication, 'to be least "false" I must be most "original", or, if you prefer, most "indirect" ' (pp. xiv–xv / 12).

Indirectness, of course, is the basic strategy of the utopian writer: to take detours via hypothetical utopias was Barthes's way of writing about the world. In the words already quoted from his essay on China: 'The intellectual or writer has no place—or that place is precisely Indirectness: this is the utopia for which I tried to find a (musically) true discourse' (OC iii. 35). Many of Barthes's detours were literally or metaphorically geographical, in that his quest for a world to inhabit, for liberated and well-aired living space, involved many expeditions to the so-called Orient, before the return home that characterizes his late work. Other circuits were intertextual. In a 1974 interview, Barthes claimed that he had maintained the same interests and values first discussed in *Writing Degree Zero*: language, literature, and the interrelated utopias of an exemption from meaning, an undivided language, and a transparency of social relations. However, 'what has changed in me, fortunately, has been other people, for I am also that other who speaks to me, to whom I listen, and by whom I am carried away' (GV 195 / 185).[3] It is not surprising that Barthes was at pains, in the preface to *Critical Essays*, to collapse the distinction between critics and writers. For discussion of other writers, painters, musicians, and photographers was, as has been evident in this study, crucial to Barthes's elaboration of his own ideas. As he himself wrote in *Roland Barthes by Roland Barthes*, in answer to the question 'what is influence?': 'he evolves progressively, according to the authors he discusses. The inductor, however, is not the author I am talking about, but rather *what he leads me*

---

[3] He goes on to quote Brecht: 'He thought in the heads of others; and in his own, others than he were thinking. That is true thought' (GV 195 / 185).

to say about him: I influence myself *with his permission*' (*RB* 106 / 110).

What is more, Barthes's equation of originality with an ideal indirectness offers an interesting utopian perspective upon a striking aspect of Barthes's collected works: the extraordinary inventiveness of the basic formal conception of each new book that appeared. Barthes never repeated a successful form. Each text was a new link in a chain of self-conscious engagements with utopia, yet no single one of the links could really be said to resemble another. In order to escape from the banality of such affects as love and suffering, on the one hand, and from a language encumbered with secondary meanings, on the other, the writer who aspires to speak the world simply must institute an indirect and original language, 'at once stubborn (provided with a goal) and circuitous (accepting infinitely varied stations)' (p. xviii / 15). And this, declares Barthes, is not only an epic situation (one reinforcing the curiously defective timescale—without present or past—of works which are simply their own project). Above all, the writer's situation is that of Orpheus: 'not because Orpheus "sings", but because the writer and Orpheus are both under the same prohibition, which constitutes their "song": the prohibition from turning back toward what they love' (ibid.).

Orpheus appears to have lost his chance of bringing Eurydice back from the dead because, by turning back to look at her, he failed to respect Barthes's law of indirectness. In Virgil's version of the story, Orpheus, on losing Eurydice for ever, enters into a great lament, and his mourning takes the form of stubborn fidelity to her memory in a refusal of remarriage or other loves.[4] In Ovid's *Metamorphoses*, Orpheus also refuses to remarry, but goes on 'to centre his affections on boys of tender years, and to enjoy the brief spring and early flowering of their youth: he was the first to introduce this custom among the people of Thrace'.[5] If only through this mythical juxtaposition of mourning and homosexuality, Orpheus would take his place alongside the many guides to Barthes's utopia whom I have followed in this

---

[4] Virgil, *The Georgics*, 141–2.
[5] Ovid, *Metamorphoses*, trans. Mary Innes (Harmondsworth, Penguin, 1955), 227.

book. The writerly, homosexual spaces that characterize Barthes's late work will restore to him what he loves—be it reality or the mother—through the indirect circuits of other quests and other loves: 'only epic man, the man of the house and of travels, of love and of love affairs, can represent for us so faithful an infidelity' (*EC*, p. xiv). This claim, appropriately oblique in its context of Barthes's preface to *Critical Essays*, stakes out the utopian themes and forms of Barthes's future writing.

Bibliography

1. BOOKS BY BARTHES

Listed chronologically by date of first publication in French. Essays collected in book form have not been separately listed. Page extents for essays in collected volumes can be found in the notes, as can details of the original publication (dates, journals, interviewers, etc.) where considered significant.

Le Degré zéro de l'écriture (Paris, Seuil, 1953) / *Writing Degree Zero*, trans. Annette Lavers and Colin Smith (London, Jonathan Cape, 1970).
Michelet (Paris, Seuil, 1954) / *Michelet*, trans. Richard Howard (Oxford, Blackwell, 1987).
Mythologies [1957] (Paris, Seuil (Points) 1970) / partial translations in *Mythologies*, trans. Annette Lavers (London, Granada, 1973), and *The Eiffel Tower and Other Mythologies*, trans. Richard Howard (New York, Hill and Wang, 1979).
Sur Racine (Paris, Seuil, 1963) / *On Racine*, trans. Richard Howard (New York, Performing Arts Journal Publications, 1983).
Essais critiques (Paris, Seuil, 1964) / *Critical Essays*, trans. Richard Howard (Evanston, Ill., Northwestern University Press, 1972).
Éléments de sémiologie [1964], in *Le Degré zéro de l'écriture*, suivi de *Éléments de sémiologie* (Paris, Seuil, 1965) / *Elements of Semiology*, trans. Annette Lavers and Colin Smith (London, Jonathan Cape, 1967).
La Tour Eiffel, text by Roland Barthes, photographs by André Martin (Paris, Delpire, 1964) / partial translation in *The Eiffel Tower and Other Mythologies*, trans. Richard Howard (New York, Hill and Wang, 1979), 3–17.
Système de la mode (Paris, Seuil, 1967) / *The Fashion System*, trans. Matthew Ward and Richard Howard (London, Jonathan Cape, 1985).
L'Empire des signes (Geneva, Skira, 1970) / *Empire of Signs*, trans. Richard Howard (London, Jonathan Cape, 1983).
S/Z (Paris, Seuil, 1970) / *S/Z*, trans. Richard Miller (New York, Hill and Wang, 1974).
Sade, Fourier, Loyola (Paris, Seuil, 1971) / *Sade, Fourier, Loyola*, trans. Richard Miller (New York, Hill and Wang, 1976).

Nouveaux Essais critiques, published with *Le Degré zéro de l'écriture* (Paris, Seuil, 1972) / *New Critical Essays*, trans. Richard Howard (Berkeley and Los Angeles, University of California Press, 1990).

Le Plaisir du texte (Paris, Seuil, 1973) / *The Pleasure of the Text*, trans. Richard Miller (New York, Hill and Wang, 1975).

Alors, la Chine? (Paris, Christian Bourgois, 1975).

Roland Barthes par Roland Barthes (Paris, Seuil, 1975) / *Roland Barthes by Roland Barthes*, trans. Richard Howard (New York, Hill and Wang, 1977).

Fragments d'un discours amoureux (Paris, Seuil, 1977) / *A Lover's Discourse: Fragments*, trans. Richard Howard (New York, Hill and Wang, 1978).

Leçon (Paris, Seuil, 1978) / 'Inaugural Lecture, Collège de France', trans. Richard Howard, in *A Barthes Reader*, ed. Susan Sontag (London, Jonathan Cape, 1982), 457–78.

Sollers écrivain (Paris, Seuil, 1979) / *Sollers Writer*, trans. Philip Thody (London, Athlone, 1987).

La Chambre claire: Note sur la photographie (Paris, Gallimard/Seuil, 1980) / *Camera Lucida: Reflections on Photography*, trans. Richard Howard (London, Fontana, 1984).

Le Grain de la voix: Entretiens 1962–1980, ed. François Wahl (Paris, Seuil, 1981) / *The Grain of the Voice: Interviews 1962–1980*, trans. Linda Coverdale (London, Jonathan Cape, 1985).

L'Obvie et l'obtus: Essais critiques III, ed. François Wahl (Paris, Seuil, 1982) / *The Responsibility of Forms: Critical Essays on Music, Art, and Representation*, trans. Richard Howard (Oxford, Basil Blackwell, 1986).

Le Bruissement de la langue: Essais critiques IV, ed. François Wahl (Paris, Seuil, 1984) / *The Rustle of Language*, trans. Richard Howard (Oxford, Basil Blackwell, 1986).

L'Aventure sémiologique, ed. François Wahl (Paris, Seuil, 1985) / *The Semiotic Challenge*, trans. Richard Howard (Oxford, Basil Blackwell, 1988).

Incidents, ed. François Wahl (Paris, Seuil, 1987) / *Incidents*, trans. Richard Howard (Berkeley and Los Angeles, University of California Press, 1992).

Œuvres complètes, ed. Eric Marty, 3 vols. (Paris, Seuil, 1993–5).

2. UNCOLLECTED MATERIAL BY BARTHES

Listed chronologically by date of first publication in French.

'Le Degré zéro de l'écriture', *Combat* (1 Aug. 1947), 2.

'Phénomène ou mythe', *Lettres nouvelles* (Dec. 1954), 951–3.
Un homme, une ville: Marcel Proust à Paris, with Jean Montalbetti, France-Culture (20 and 27 Oct., 3 Nov. 1978), Cassettes Radio France, 3 tapes.
'Mes petites annonces', interview with Michel Cressole, *Sandwiche* (supplement to *Libération*), 15 Dec. 1979, 5–6.
'Le Désir de musique' [1979], *Les Nouvelles littéraires* (10–17 Apr. 1980), 28.
'Le Désir de neutre' [1978], *La Règle du jeu*, 5 (1991), 36–60.

3. OTHER REFERENCES

BAMMER, ANGELIKA, *Partial Visions: Feminism and Utopianism in the 1970s* (New York, Routledge, 1991).
BARDÈCHE, MAURICE, *Marcel Proust romancier*, 2 vols. (Paris, Les Sept Couleurs, 1971).
BAUDELAIRE, CHARLES, *Les Fleurs du mal* [1857], ed. Antoine Adam (Paris, Garnier, 1961).
BEECHER, JONATHAN, *Charles Fourier: The Visionary and his World* (Berkeley and Los Angeles, University of California Press, 1986).
—— and BIENVENU, RICHARD (eds.), *The Utopian Vision of Charles Fourier: Selected Texts on Work, Love, and Passionate Attraction* (Boston, Beacon Press, 1971).
BENTAHILA, ABDELÂLI, *Language Attitudes among Arabic-French Bilinguals in Morocco* (Clevedon, Multilingual Matters Ltd., 1983).
BINGER, LOUIS-GUSTAVE, *Esclavage, islamisme et christianisme* (Paris, Société d'éditions scientifiques, 1891).
BLOCH, ERNST, *The Principle of Hope* [1959], trans. Neville Plaice, Stephen Plaice, and Paul Knight, 3 vols. (Oxford, Basil Blackwell, 1986).
BOONE, JOSEPH, 'Vacation Cruises; or, The Homoerotics of Orientalism', *PMLA* 110 (Jan. 1995), 89–107.
BOUDINET, DANIEL, *Fragments d'un labyrinthe*, in *Daniel Boudinet*, ed. Christian Caujolle, Emmanuelle Decroux, and Claude Vittiglio (Besançon, Éditions de la manufacture, 1993), 108–15.
BOWMAN, FRANK PAUL, '*Roland Barthes par Roland Barthes* et Charles Fourier', *Romanic Review*, 3 (1978), 236–41.
BROWN, ANDREW, *Roland Barthes: The Figures of Writing* (Oxford, Clarendon Press, 1992).
BUISINE, ALAIN, 'Barthes et les noms', in Pierre Bonnefis and Alain Buisine (eds.), *La Scène capitale* (Lille, Presses universitaires de Lille, 1981), 71–103.

BURATTONI, GIANNI, 'La Mort de Daniel Boudinet', *Lettres françaises* (Oct. 1990), 21.
CALVET, LOUIS-JEAN, *Roland Barthes: A Biography* [1990], trans. Sarah Wykes (Cambridge, Polity, 1994).
CAMUS, RENAUD, *Chroniques achriennes* (Paris, POL, 1984).
CERTEAU, MICHEL DE, *L'Invention du quotidien* [1980] (Gallimard, Paris, 1990).
CHAMBERS, ROSS, 'Pointless Stories, Storyless Points: Roland Barthes between "Soirées de Paris" and "Incidents" ', *L'Esprit créateur* (Summer 1994), 12–30.
CHOAY, FRANÇOISE (ed.), *L'Urbanisme: Utopie et réalités* (Paris, Seuil, 1965).
CLERGUE, LUCIEN, *Langage des sables* (Paris, AGEP, 1981).
COMMENT, BERNARD, *Roland Barthes: Vers le neutre* (Paris, Christian Bourgois, 1991).
COMPAGNON, ANTOINE (ed.), *Prétexte: Roland Barthes*, colloque de Cerisy (Paris, UGE, 1978).
—— 'L'Objectif déconcerté', *La Recherche photographique* (June 1992), 72–7.
DANIEL, JEAN, *Le Refuge et la source* (Paris, Grasset & Fasquelle, 1977).
DOLLIMORE, JONATHAN, *Sexual Dissidence: Augustine to Wilde, Freud to Foucault* (Oxford, Clarendon Press, 1991).
DOUBROVSKY, SERGE, 'Une écriture tragique', *Poétique*, 47 (1981), 329–54.
DUCHEN, CLAIRE, *Women's Rights and Women's Lives in France 1944–1968* (London, Routledge, 1994).
FLAUBERT, GUSTAVE, *Dictionary of Received Ideas*, trans. Robert Baldick, in *Bouvard and Pécuchet*, trans. A. J. Krailsheimer (Penguin, Harmondsworth, 1976).
FOUCAULT, MICHEL, 'Des espaces autres' [1967], *Architecture, Mouvement, Continuïté* (1984), 46–9.
—— *Discipline and Punish: The Birth of the Prison* [1975], trans. Alan Sheridan (Harmondsworth, Penguin, 1982).
FOURIER, CHARLES, *Œuvres complètes*, 12 vols. (Paris, Anthropos, 1966–8).
FREUD, SIGMUND, *The Pelican Freud Library*, ed. Angela Richards and Albert Dickson, 15 vols. (Harmondsworth, Penguin, 1973–86).
GEOGHEGAN, VINCENT, *Utopianism and Marxism* (London, Methuen, 1987).
GIDE, ANDRÉ, *Voyage au Congo: Carnets de route* (Paris, Gallimard, 1927).
—— *Si le grain ne meurt* [1920] (Paris, Gallimard, 1928).

GOODWIN, BARBARA, and TAYLOR, KEITH, *The Politics of Utopia: A Study in Theory and Practice* (London, Hutchinson, 1982).
GROJNOWSKI, DANIEL, 'Le Mystère de *La Chambre claire*', *Textuel 34/44*, 15 (1984), 91–6.
HARGREAVES, ALEC, *The Colonial Experience in French Fiction: A Study of Pierre Loti, Ernest Psichari and Pierre Mille* (London, Macmillan, 1981).
HARVEY, DAVID, *The Condition of Postmodernity: An Enquiry into the Conditions of Cultural Change* (Oxford, Blackwell, 1980).
HEATH, STEPHEN, *Vertige du déplacement* (Paris, Fayard, 1974).
—— *The Sexual Fix* (London, Macmillan, 1982).
HUSS, ROGER, 'Nature, Final Causality and Anthropocentrism in Flaubert', *French Studies*, 33 (1979), 288–304.
JACKSON, LEONARD, *The Poverty of Structuralism: Literature and Structuralist Theory* (London, Longman, 1991).
JAMESON, FREDRIC, *The Prison-House of Language: A Critical Account of Structuralism and Russian Formalism* (Princeton, Princeton University Press, 1972).
—— *The Political Unconscious: Narrative as a Socially Symbolic Act* (London, Methuen, 1981).
—— *Postmodernism; or, The Cultural Logic of Late Capitalism* (London, Verso, 1991).
KABBANI, RANA, *Europe's Myths of Orient: Devise and Rule* (London, Macmillan, 1986).
KATZ, BARRY, *Herbert Marcuse and the Art of Liberation: An Intellectual Biography* (London, Verso, 1992).
KHATIBI, ABDELKEBIR, *La Mémoire tatouée* (Paris, Denoël, 1971/UGE, 1979).
—— *Figures de l'étranger dans la littérature française* (Paris, Denoël, 1987).
KLOSSOWSKI, PIERRE, 'Sade et Fourier' [1970], in *Derniers Travaux de Gulliver, suivi de Sade et Fourier* (Montpellier, Fata Morgana, 1974), 33–70.
KNIGHT, DIANA, 'Roland Barthes: An Intertextual Figure', in Michael Worton and Judith Still (eds.), *Intertextuality: Theories and Practices* (Manchester, Manchester University Press, 1990), 92–107.
—— 'Vie de Barthes', *Modern and Contemporary France*, NS 3: 4 (1995), 463–8.
—— 'Barthes or the Woman without a Shadow', in Jean-Michel Rabaté (ed.) *Writing the Image after Roland Barthes* (Philadelphia, University of Pennsylvania Press, forthcoming).
KRISTEVA, JULIA, *Des Chinoises* (Paris, des femmes, 1974).
—— *Les Samouraïs* (Paris, Fayard, 1990).

KUMAR, KRISHAN, *Utopia and Anti-Utopia in Modern Times* (Oxford, Blackwell, 1987).

LAGET, SERGE, *La Saga du Tour de France* (Paris, Gallimard, 1990).

LAPORTE, ROGER, 'L'Empire des signifiants', *Critique*, 302 (1972), 583–94.

LAPOUGE, GILLES, *Utopie et civilisations* (Geneva, Weber, 1973).

LAVERS, ANNETTE, *Roland Barthes: Structuralism and After* (London, Macmillan, 1982).

LEENHARDT, JACQUES, 'Arrêts sur images: Une évolution de Barthes', in Catherine Coquio and Régis Salado (eds.), *Barthes après Barthes: Une actualité en questions* (Pau, Publications de l'Université de Pau, 1993), 159–65.

LEFEBVRE, HENRI, *Le Droit à la ville* (Paris, Anthropos, 1968).

—— *La Révolution urbaine* (Paris, Gallimard, 1970).

LEJEUNE, PHILIPPE, 'Le Roland Barthes sans peine', *Textuel 34/44*, 15 (1984), 11–19.

LEVITAS, RUTH, *The Concept of Utopia* (Hemel Hempstead, Philip Allan, 1990).

—— 'Utopian Literature and Literality: Nowhere and the Wanderground', *News from Nowhere*, 9, special issue on 'Utopias and Utopianism' (1991), 66–79.

LOTI, PIERRE, *Aziyadé* [1879] suivi de *Fantôme de l'Orient*, ed. and annotated by Claude Martin (Paris, Gallimard, 1991).

MACHEREY, PIERRE, *The Object of Literature* [1990], trans. David Macey (Cambridge, Cambridge University Press, 1995).

MALCOMSON, SCOTT L., 'The Pure Land beyond the Seas: Barthes, Birch and the Uses of Japan', *Screen*, 26, 3–4 (1985), 23–33.

MANNHEIM, KARL, *Ideology and Utopia: An Introduction to the Sociology of Knowledge* [1936], trans. Louis Wirth and Edward Shils (New York, Harcourt Brace Jovanovich, 1985).

MANUEL, FRANK E., 'Toward a Psychological History of Utopias', in Frank E. Manuel (ed.), *Utopias and Utopian Thought* (London, Souvenir Press, 1973), 69–98.

MARCUSE, HERBERT, *Eros and Civilisation: A Philosophical Inquiry into Freud* [1955] (London, RKP, Ark Paperbacks, 1987).

—— 'The End of Utopia' [1967], in *Five Lectures: Psychoanalysis, Politics and Utopia* (Boston, Beacon Press, 1970), 62–82.

—— *An Essay in Liberation* (London, Allen Lane, 1969).

—— *One Dimensional Man: Studies in the Ideology of Advanced Industrial Society* (London, RKP, 1964).

MARIN, LOUIS, *Utopics: The Semiological Play of Textual Spaces* [1973], trans. Robert A. Vollrath (Atlantic Highlands, NJ, Humanities Press International, Inc., 1990).

MARX, KARL, and ENGELS, FREDERICK, *Collected Works* (London, Lawrence and Wishart, 1975–).
MILLER, D. A., *Bringing out Roland Barthes* (Berkeley and Los Angeles, University of California Press, 1992).
MORIARTY, MICHAEL, *Roland Barthes* (Cambridge, Polity, 1991).
OBOUSSIER, CLAIRE, 'Barthes and Femininity: A Synaesthetic Writing', *Nottingham French Studies*, 33/2 (Autumn 1995), 78–93.
—— 'Synaesthesia in Cixous and Barthes', in Diana Knight and Judith Still (eds.), *Women and Representation* (Nottingham, WIF Publications, 1995), 115-31.
OVID, *Metamorphoses*, trans. Mary Innes (Harmondsworth, Penguin, 1955).
PALMIER, JEAN-MICHEL, *Herbert Marcuse et la nouvelle gauche* (Paris, Minuit, 1973).
PEYROT, MAURICE, 'L'Écriture "contrefaçon" de la parole', *Le Monde* (22 Nov. 1991), 46.
PINKNEY, TONY, 'Space: The Final Frontier', *News from Nowhere*, 8 (1990), 10–27.
PLANÈS, JEAN-MARIE, 'Il n'est pays que de l'enfance', *Magazine littéraire*, 314 (1993), 33–8.
PLATO, *The Symposium*, trans. W. Hamilton (Harmondsworth, Penguin, 1951).
PLEYNET, MARCELIN, *Le Voyage en Chine: Chroniques d'un journal ordinaire (11 avril–3 mai 1974)* (Paris, Hachette, 1980).
PRENDERGAST, CHRISTOPHER, *Paris and the Nineteenth Century* (Oxford, Blackwell, 1992).
PROUST, MARCEL, *Remembrance of Things Past*, 3 vols., trans. C. K. Scott-Moncrief and Terence Kilmartin (Harmondsworth, Penguin, 1983).
—— *Sodome et Gomorrhe* [1921–2] (Paris, Gallimard (Folio), 1989).
RICŒUR, PAUL, *Lectures on Ideology and Utopia*, ed. George H. Yaylor (New York, Columbia University Press, 1986).
ROGER, PHILIPPE, *Roland Barthes, roman* (Paris, Grasset, 1986).
—— ' "Une fidélité particulière à l'infini" (de Barthes et des mystiques)', in Catherine Coquio and Régis Salado (eds.), *Barthes après Barthes: Une actualité en questions* (Pau, Publications de l'Université de Pau, 1993), 37–41.
ROSS, KRISTIN, *Fast Cars, Clean Bodies: Decolonization and the Reordering of French Culture* (Cambridge, Mass., MIT Press, 1995).
SADE, D.-A.-F. DE, *La Philosophie dans le boudoir* [1795] (Paris, Gallimard, 1976).
SAID, EDWARD, *Orientalism* [1978] (Harmondsworth, Penguin, 1985).
—— *Culture and Imperialism* (London, Chatto and Windus, 1993).

SARKONAK, RALPH, 'Roland Barthes and the Spectre of Photography', *L'Esprit créateur* (Spring 1982), 48–68.

SHERINGHAM, MICHAEL, *French Autobiography: Devices and Desires* (Oxford, Clarendon Press, 1994).

SOJA, EDWARD W., *Postmodern Geographies: The Reassertion of Space in Critical Social Theory* (London, Verso, 1989).

SOYINKA, WOLE, 'The Critic and Society: Barthes, Leftocracy and Other Mythologies', in Henry Louis Gates, Jr. (ed.), *Black Literature and Literary Theory* (New York, Methuen, 1984), 27–57.

STARKIE, ENID, *Rimbaud in Abyssinia* (Oxford, Clarendon Press, 1937).

STEICHEN, EDWARD (ed.), *The Family of Man* (New York, Maco Magazine Corporation for the New York Museum of Modern Art, 1955).

TODOROV, TZVETAN, 'Le Dernier Barthes', *Poétique*, 47 (Sept. 1981), 323–7.

—— *Nous et les autres: La Réflexion française sur la diversité humaine* (Paris, Seuil, 1989).

TROUSSON, RAYMOND, *Voyage au pays de nulle part: Histoire littéraire de la pensée utopique* (Brussels, Éditions de l'Université de Bruxelles, 1975).

VERNE, JULES, *L'Île mystérieuse* [1874] (Paris, Librairie générale française, 1989).

VIRGIL, *The Georgics*, trans. L. P. Wilkinson (Harmondsworth, Penguin, 1982).

WAHL, FRANÇOIS, 'La Chine sans utopie', *Le Monde* (15–19 June 1974).

WATTS, ALAN, *The Way of Zen* (Harmondsworth, Penguin, 1970).

WILLIAMS, JAMES, 'The Moment of Truth: Roland Barthes, "Soirées de Paris" and the Real', *Neophilologus*, 79 (1995), 33–51.

WILLIAMS, PATRICK, and CHRISMAN, LAURA (eds.), *Colonial Discourse and Post-Colonial Theory: A Reader* (Hemel Hempstead, Harvester Wheatsheaf, 1993).

YOUNG, ROBERT, *White Mythologies: Writing History and the West* (London, Routledge, 1990).

—— *Colonial Desire: Hybridity in Theory, Culture and Race* (London, Routledge, 1995).

Index

Aeschylus 92
Alembert, Jean le Rond d' 53
Allégret, Marc 131
Amiel, Henri Frédéric 181
Antonioni, Michelangelo 189, 201

Balzac, Honoré de 41, 59, 90, 183, 195–7, 237, 271
Bammer, Angelika 11 n.
Bardèche, Maurice 254 n.

Barthes, Roland:
'Alors, la Chine?' 182–93, 224, 270, 272
'A propos d'*Aujourd'hui ou les Coréens* de Michel Vinaver' 191 n.
Archives du 20e siècle 27–8, 51–2, 121, 176
'Avignon, l'hiver' 26–7, 28, 39
'Buffet Finishes Off New York' 48–9
Camera Lucida: Reflections on Photography 8, 29, 118–19, 154 n., 219–22, 244, 247, 250, 252 n., 254, 259–69
'Un Cas de critique culturelle' 129, 176
'La Cathédrale des romans' 42–3, 57
'Ce que je dois à Khatibi' 137–9
'Le Choix d'un métier' 108
'Comment vivre ensemble' 17
'Cottage Industry' 106–8
Critical Essays: 'The Last Happy Writer' 97–8; 'The Last Word on Robbe-Grillet?' 7 n.; 'Literature Today' 6; 'Mother Courage Blind' 28; 'Preface' 270–4; 'The Structuralist Activity' 52, 55, 64; 'Taking Sides' 98 n.; 'The World as Object' 21, 39–40
'Critique et autocritique' 18 n.
'D'eux à nous' 4–5
'Le Degré zéro de l'écriture' 123
'Le Désir de musique' 267
'Le Désir de neutre' 18, 79, 255 n.

'Éditorial', *Théâtre populaire* 23–4, 28, 30
'Entretien avec Roland Barthes' 4 n.
The Eiffel Tower 53–61, 62, 71, 75, 147
Elements of Semiology 70–1
Empire of Signs 1, 7, 8 n., 16, 62, 64, 71, 75, 109, 122, 124, 128, 141, 142, 143, 145–6, 148, 149–66, 168, 170, 190, 195, 198, 200, 201, 205, 211, 214, 215, 221 n.
The Fashion System 47 n.
'Fin de *Richard II*' 24
'Folies-Bergère' 22–3, 24, 25, 30
The Grain of the Voice: Interviews 1962–1980 2, 9 n., 63, 67, 84, 85, 124–5, 126–7, 128, 152, 157, 167, 168, 196, 210, 213, 218, 239 n., 240 n., 256 n., 258, 272
Un homme, une ville: Marcel Proust à Paris 231–2, 238, 254, 258–9
'Inaugural Lecture, Collège de France' 5, 8–9, 12, 18 n., 191 n., 217, 218
Incidents: 'Incidents' 14, 16–17, 91, 122, 124, 129–36, 155, 170, 176, 181–2, 198, 218; 'The Light of the South-West' 226–34, 246; 'Paris Evenings' ('Soirées de Paris') 16–17, 131 n., 245–52, 256 n., 258 n., 269 n.
A Lover's Discourse: Fragments 60, 154 n., 206, 235 n., 250, 255–7, 258, 268
'Matisse ou le bonheur de vivre' 30–1, 33
'Mes petites annonces' 215–16, 244
'Michelet, l'Histoire et la Mort' 55–6, 109 n.
Michelet 55–7, 160 n., 271 n.
Mythologies: 5, 8, 15, 75, 243; 'African Grammar' 102 n., 125 n; 'Agony Columns' 33; 'Astrology' 34–5; 'At the Music

BARTHES, ROLAND (cont.):
'Hall' 113–14; 'The *Batory* Cruise' 93–5, 117, 183; 'Bichon and the Blacks' 103–5, 108, 146; 'The *Blue Guide*' 100–1, 117, 152; 'The Brain of Einstein' 42, 63; 'Conjugations' 31–3; 'A Few Words from Monsieur Poujade' 96; 'The Great Family of Man' 98–100, 112, 160–1, 225 n.; 'The Iconography of the Abbé Pierre' 131; '*The Lady of the Camellias*' 35 n.; 'The Lost Continent' 105–6, 113, 225 n., 'Martians' 105 n.; 'Myth Today' 2–3, 31, 44–7, 52, 55 n., 57, 61, 75, 81 n., 83; 'The *Nautilus* and the Drunken Boat' 40–2, 108–9; 'The New Citroën' 50; 'Novels and Children' 34; 'Ornamental Cookery' 34; 'Paris Not Flooded' 37–9, 80; 'Poujade and the Intellectuals' 96 n.; 'Steak and Chips' 95–6 n.; 'The Tour de France as Epic' 35–7, 80; 'Toys' 34; 'The Writer on Holiday' 131 n.
New Critical Essays: 'Pierre Loti: *Aziyadé*' 144, 151, 167, 169–81, 184, 186, 190, 192–3, 203, 219, 235; 'The Plates of the *Encyclopedia*' 40, 53; 'Where to Begin?' 109–14
'Notes sur un album de Lucien Clergue' 224 n.
On Racine 29, 91
'Phénomène ou mythe' 45 n.
The Pleasure of the Text 202, 207 n., 208–9, 210, 216
'Pour la libération d'une pensée pluraliste' 146 n.
'Préface à *Le Refuge et la source de Jean Daniel*' 219, 234–6, 242
'Preface à Stendhal, *Quelques promenades dans Rome*' 143–5, 153
'Premier texte' 206 n.
'*Le Prince de Hombourg* au TNP' 20, 24–6, 29, 243
'Radioscopie' 217, 267 n.
'Réponses' 28 n., 51, 65, 121 n., 124 n., 217, 267 n.
The Responsibility of Forms: Critical Essays on Music, Art, and Representation: 'Loving Schumann' 169, 267; 'Music, Voice, Language' 18–19 n., 202–4; 'Rasch' 255; 'Right in the Eyes' 115, 134; 'The Romantic Song' 19 n., 169, 244, 256, 268
Roland Barthes by Roland Barthes 1, 3, 4, 5, 7, 15, 16, 57, 60, 61, 62, 63–6, 69–70, 73, 80, 82, 87 n., 92, 118–19 n., 122, 127–8, 136–7, 140, 142, 143, 180, 181, 189–90, 191, 194, 197, 206, 207–8, 210–11, 213–14, 217, 218, 226 n., 228–9, 230 n., 233–4, 237–42, 257–8, 263–4, 272–3
The Rustle of Language: 'The Death of the Author' 18; 'Deliberation' 98 n., 232, 245–7, 251, 267; 'From Work to Text' 197, 198, 213 n.; 'The Image' 213; ' "Longtemps, je me suis couché de bonne heure" ' 19 n., 252–4; 'One Always Fails in Speaking of What One Loves' 19 n., 122, 141–3, 144, 165, 204, 269; 'Preface to Renaud Camus's *Tricks*' 212–13, 214–15, 216, 244, 250; 'Reading Brillat-Savarin' 66 n., 205–8; 'The Rustle of Language' 199–201, 202; 'To the Seminar' 168; 'The War of Languages' 197; 'Writers, Intellectuals, Teachers' 194–5
Sade, Fourier, Loyola 19, 64, 84–5, 87–8, 117; 'Fourier' 14, 67–85, 88–9, 109, 115–17, 142, 145, 167, 191 n., 206–7; 'Sade I' 89–90, 91 n.; 'Sade II' 16, 89, 90–1, 133, 137 n., 209–10
The Semiotic Challenge: 'Introduction to the Structural Analysis of Narratives' 6, 71; 'The Semiological Adventure' 55 n., 62 n., 165 n.; 'Semiology and Urbanism' 62–3, 146–9
Sollers Writer 199
'Structuralisme et sémiologie' 85 n.
'Sur l'astrologie' 1
'Sur un emploi du verbe "être" ' 101–2, 125 n.
'Sur des photographies de Daniel Boudinet' 222–7, 243

INDEX

S/Z 7 n., 18 n., 64, 71, 79, 109, 195–7, 227
'Texte à deux (parties)' 168
'The Two Salons' 44, 50–1, 71
'Utopia Today' 9 n., 86–7, 167
Vita nova 251–4, 265, 268 n., 269
Writing Degree Zero 4, 80, 272
Bashō 157, 159
Baudelaire, Charles 220–2, 224, 225
Baudouin I 103
Beecher, Jonathan 67 n.
Beethoven, Ludwig van 268 n.
Bellamy, Edward 13
Bentahila, Abdelâli 125–6 n.
Bentham, Jeremy 57 n.
Bernardin de Saint-Pierre, Jacques-Henri 72 n.
Bienvenu, Richard 67 n.
Binger, Louis-Gustave 118–19 n.
Bloch, Ernst 12 n., 67 n., 243, 268, 269 n.
Bobet, Louis 36–7
Bobet, Jean 36
Bonaparte, Napoleon 85, 143
Boone, Joseph 121 n., 133 n.
Bossuet, Jacques Bénigne 131 n.
Boudinet, Daniel 222–7, 243, 266–7
Bourgois, Christian 182–3
Bowman, Frank Paul 76, 82
Brahms, Johannes 268 n., 269 n.
Brando, Marlon 32, 45 n.
Brazza, Pierre Savorgan de 118–9
Brecht, Bertolt 28, 29, 31, 35 n., 44, 272 n.
Brillat-Savarin, Anthelme 66 n., 205–6, 208, 218
Brown, Andrew 192 n.
Buffet, Bernard 48–9
Buisine, Alain 232 n.
Burattoni, Gianni 266 n.

Cabet, Étienne 81
Calvet, Louis-Jean 17, 84, 92 n., 119 n., 125, 126 n., 176–7, 184 n., 233 n., 252 n.
Camus, Renaud 212–13, 214–15, 250
Canetti, Elias 132 n.
Carpentier, Sylviane 33
Castries, Général de 95–6 n.
Caunes, Georges de 103 n.
Certeau, Michel de 148 n., 150 n.
Césaire, Aimé 96 n.
Chambers, Ross 131 n.
Chateaubriand 248

Choay, Françoise 148 n.
Chrisman, Laura 93 n.
Clergue, Lucien 224 n.
Clifford, Charles 219, 222, 247
Cocteau, Jean 178
Comment, Bernard 145 n.
Compagnon, Antoine 254 n., 261 n., 266 n.
Corneille, Pierre 206 n.
Courbet, Gustave 21, 22

Daniel, Jean 234–6, 242
Dante 251–3, 254, 269
Debout-Oleszkiewicz, Simone 67 n., 88
Defoe, Daniel 111–112, 113
Diderot, Denis 53
Dollimore, Jonathan 119–21
Doubrovsky, Serge 79 n., 122 n.
Duchen, Claire 33 n.
Duparc, Henri 220 n.

Einstein, Albert 42
Engels, Friedrich 68, 69, 74–5 n., 76, 81, 82, 83, 100 n.

Fanon, Frantz 96 n.
Flaubert, Gustave 7, 15 n., 72 n., 93, 250
Foucault, Michel 57 n., 65, 98 n., 114
Fourier, Charles 1, 3, 9, 14, 15, 47, 64, 66, 67–91, 109, 115–18, 123, 137, 142, 170, 171, 197, 205, 206–7, 208, 239, 256, 269, 271
Freud, Sigmund 85 n., 86 n., 220–1, 223 n., 244, 255

Gaulle, Charles de 107 n.
Geoghegan, Vincent 11 n., 68 n., 74 n.
Gide, André 120, 121, 130–1, 178, 211 n., 226 n.
Giscard d'Estaing, Valéry 182 n.
Goncourt, Edmond de 178
Goodwin, Barbara 11 n.
Grojnowski, Daniel 262 n.
Guyotat, Pierre 201

Hargreaves, Alec 169–70 n.
Harvey, David 13
Hassan II 125
Heath, Stephen 65 n., 190 n.
Hegel, Friedrich 81 n., 201
Hofmannsthal, Hugo von 264 n.

Hugo, Victor 42–3, 54, 57–8, 59, 147–8, 156
Huss, Roger 72 n.

Jackson, Leonard 47 n.
Jameson, Fredric 11 n., 12 n., 13, 20 n.
Joubert, Joseph 230 n.

Kabbani, Rana 131–2 n., 169 n.
Katz, Barry 86 n.
Khatibi, Abdelkebir 92, 137–9, 156 n.
Kleist, Heinrich von 24
Klossowski, Pierre 88 n.
Knight, Diana 17 n., 120 n., 206 n., 264 n.
Kristeva, Julia 182, 184–5 n., 186, 188 n.
Kumar, Krishan 11 n.

Lacan, Jacques 9, 63, 65, 69, 129, 147, 176, 255
Laget, Serge 36 n.
Laporte, Roger 156 n.
Lapouge, Gilles 88 n.
Lavers, Annette 65 n., 208 n.
Leenhardt, Jacques 222 n.
Lefebvre, Henri 148 n.
Le Guin, Ursula 13
Le Pen, Jean-Marie 96
Lejeune, Philippe 1
Lévy, Bernard-Henri 152, 157, 186
Lévi-Strauss, Claude 65
Levitas, Ruth 11 n., 12 n., 74 n.
Lincoln, Abraham 111
Loti, Pierre 14, 169–81, 182
Loyola, Ignatius de 87, 88, 208 n.

Macherey, Pierre 90 n.
Malcomson, Scott L. 156 n.
Mallarmé, Stéphane 162
Mannheim, Karl 12 n., 74
Manuel, Frank E. 67 n., 116 n.
Mapplethorpe, Robert 119
Marcuse, Herbert 15, 85–6 n.
Marin, Louis 13 n., 64 n., 150 n.
Martin, Claude 178 n.
Marty, Éric 251, 252 n.
Marx, Karl 2, 8, 9, 11, 12, 37 n., 67, 68, 69, 76, 81, 82, 84, 85, 87, 90, 92, 100 n., 125, 243
Massu, Général 106
Massu, Madame 106
Matisse, Henri 30–1, 33

Maupassant, Guy de 59
Maupomé, Claude 267
Michelet, Jules 41 n., 54, 55–7, 109 n., 147, 157, 160, 271 n.
Miller, D. A. 162 n.
Minoret, Bernard 146 n.
Mitterrand, François 182 n.
Molière 54, 135
Montaigne, Michel de 206 n.
Montalbetti, Jean 231 n., 258
Montesquieu 105
More, Thomas 10, 13 n.
Moriarty, Michael 102 n., 181 n., 233 n.
Morris, William 13

Nadar 118–19, 262–3
Newton, Isaac 85
Nietzsche, Friedrich 85 n.

Oboussier, Claire 228 n.
Orton, Joe 133 n.
Owen, Robert 74 n., 81
Ovid 273

Palmier, Jean-Michel 86 n.
Panzéra, Charles 202–4, 220 n.
Pascal, Blaise 220, 243, 249–51, 252 n.
Perkins, Anthony 161
Perkins Gilman, Charlotte 13
Peyrot, Maurice 18 n.
Pinkney, Tony 13 n.
Planès, Jean-Marie 232 n.
Plato 13, 206 n., 213
Pleynet, Marcelin 182, 184–6, 187, 188 n., 190
Poe, Edgar Allan 266
Pompidou, Georges 182 n.
Poujade, Pierre 85 n., 95–6
Prendergast, Christopher 57 n.
Proust, Marcel 41, 70, 126, 129, 157, 158, 229, 230 n., 231–2, 233, 237, 238, 244, 251, 252–4, 255, 257–62, 265, 268, 269, 270, 271

Racine, Jean 29, 41 n., 91, 157, 258
Réquichot, Bernard 183
Ricoeur, Paul 12 n., 67 n., 72 n., 74 n.
Rimbaud, Arthur 40, 42, 45 n., 108–9
Rivière, Jean-Loup 28–9 n.
Robbe-Grillet, Alain 7
Roger, Philippe 207 n., 255
Ross, Kristin 20 n., 33 n., 47 n., 95 n.
Rousseau, Jean-Jacques 5 n., 55

INDEX 287

Roy, Claude 183–4
Roy, Jean 94
Ruysbroek, Jan van 255

Sade, D.-A.-F. de 15, 41 n., 87–91, 109, 137 n., 157, 170, 183, 190, 200, 208–10, 271
Saenredam, Pieter 39
Said, Edward 14–15, 92–3
Saint-Simon, Claude Henri de 81, 116 n.
Sandburg, Carl 98–9, 160 n.
Sarduy, Severo 184 n., 210
Sarkonak, Ralph 266 n.
Saussure, Ferdinand de 5, 8, 44, 51, 55, 110, 159
Scarpetta, Guy 124, 128
Schubert, Franz 169, 244, 258
Schumann, Robert 169, 204, 244, 246 n., 258, 267–8
Schweizer, Albert 103
Segalen, Victor 146 n.
Shakespeare, William 181 n.
Sheringham, Michael 234–5 n., 235 n.
Simon, Michel 94
Soja, Edward W. 13
Sollers, Philippe 182, 185 n., 186 n., 199 n., 201
Solynka, Wole 100 n.
Stalin 185
Starkie, Enid 109 n.
Steichen, Edward 99

Stendhal 14, 122, 141–5, 153, 157, 173, 188, 204, 269
Strauss, Richard 264 n.

Taylor, Keith 11 n.
Till, Emmet 100
Todorov, Tzvetan 170 n., 244 n.
Tolstoy, Leo 253
Trousson, Raymond 76 n.

Van der Zee, James 263
Verne, Jules 40–3, 108–14, 126, 150, 175, 196, 239
Vezolles, Danielle 146 n.
Vilar, Jean 24, 26, 27, 28, 29, 31
Vinaver, Michel 191 n.
Virgil 226, 253, 254, 273
Voltaire 5 n., 97–8, 105, 124 n., 139–40, 175

Wahl, François 16, 17, 182, 190, 245, 246
Watts, Alan 154 n.
Wilde, Oscar 120, 121
Williams, James 241 n.
Williams, Patrick 93 n.
Wilson, Bob 119
Winnicott, D. W. 29 n.
Wordsworth, William 181 n.

Young, Robert 93 n., 96 n., 100 n.

Zola, Émile 26, 41, 64, 90, 237, 271